# MUSIC PHILOSOPHY IN CHRISTIAN PERSPECTIVE
*A Philosophy of Music Education and Church Music*

by
GAREN L. WOLF I
Chairman Emeritus, Division of Music,
God's Bible School and College,
Cincinnati, Ohio

Author of
*Music of the Bible in Christian Perspective*
*Church Music Matters*

SCHMUL PUBLISHING COMPANY
NICHOLASVILLE, KENTUCKY

Copyright © 2018 by Garen L. Wolf I
All rights reserved. No part of this book may be used or reproduced in any manner whatsoever without written permission except in the case of brief quotations embodied in critical articles and reviews.
For more information contact
Garen L. Wolf I
8394 Pippin Road
Cincinnati, Ohio 45239

Unless otherwise indicated, all Scripture quotations are from the Cambridge Edition of the Authorized Version (KJV, AV)
Quotations from the HOLY BIBLE, NEW INTERNATIONAL VERSION (NIV), Copyright © 1973, 1978, 1984 by International Bible Society. Used by permission of Zondervan Publishing House. All rights reserved.
Quotations marked NKJV are from the Holy Bible, New King James Version, copyright © 1982 Thomas Nelson, Inc. Printed in the USA Used by permission. All rights reserved.
Quotations marked ESV are from THE HOLY BIBLE, ENGLISH STANDARD VERSION (ESV), copyright © 2001 by Crossway, a publishing ministry of Good News Publishers. Used by permission. All rights reserved.

Published by Schmul Publishing Co.
PO Box 776
Nicholasville, KY 40340
USA

Printed in the United States of America

ISBN 10: 0-88019-608-4
ISBN 13: 978-0-88019-608-6

Visit us on the Internet at www.wesleyanbooks.com, or order direct from the publisher by calling 800-772-6657, or by writing to the above address.

# Contents

**Acknowledgments** .................................................................. **12**

**Introduction** ........................................................................... **15**
    *The Musician Taken from the Sheepcote* ........................................ *15*
    *How I Began this Philosophical Journey* ........................................ *16*
    *Why I Include Transliterations and Strong's Numbers* ................ *17*
    *Why I Use Lexical Forms of Words* ............................................... *19*
    *About the Bibliography* .................................................................. *20*
    *About the Two Indices* .................................................................... *20*
    *Symbols and Abbreviations* ........................................................... *21*

## PART ONE
## Getting Started with a Music Philosophy

**1  Music Philosophy In and Beyond the Genesis Record ... 24**
    *How did Music Begin?* .................................................................... *24*
    *Did God Create the Building Blocks of Music?* ........................... *25*
    *Knowing Based on the Genesis Record* ......................................... *28*
    *God Intended for Music to be Under Man's Supervision* ........... *31*
    *Is All Music Created Equal?* .......................................................... *32*
    *God Created Sound* ........................................................................ *38*

## 2 Why Develop a Philosophy of Music? ............ 41

*A Christian's Worldview of Music ................................. 41*
*The Christian Musician Thinks Differently ..................... 42*
*Direction Determines Destiny Philosophically ................ 43*
*Defending Philosophy Biblically ................................... 44*
*What is a Music Philosophy? ........................................ 46*
*A Music Philosophy Is a Belief System ......................... 47*
*Is There Philosophical Truth Concerning Music? ............ 49*
*Thinking Before we Act ................................................ 51*
*Why Musicians do What They Do ................................. 52*
*"True Truth" Not Exhaustive Truth ................................. 53*
*We Know that We Know Only in Part ............................ 55*
*Music Study is Essential .............................................. 57*
*Is All Scripture Inspired and Accurate? ......................... 58*
*Is a Written Music Philosophy Important? ..................... 60*
*Music Philosophy Must Please God .............................. 63*
*Wise Choices of Secular and Sacred Music ................... 64*

## 3 The Underpinnings of a Music Philosophy ............ 68

*Building on the Presupposition that God Created Music .......... 68*
*The Significance of Music's History .............................. 69*
*Retaining God in Our Musical Knowledge ..................... 70*
*Evidence that Demands Our Attention .......................... 71*
*Does Satan Have the Power to Pervert Music? .............. 72*
*No Musical Absolutes— A Flawed View ........................ 73*
*Humanism and Christian Music Philosophy ................... 74*

## 4 Building a Christocentric Music Philosophy ............ 78

*Is Your Musical Ship Driven by the Wind? ..................... 78*
*Are They Biblical Principles or Personal Preferences? ... 79*
*God Owns Music .......................................................... 79*
*Good and Perfect Musical Gifts .................................... 81*
*"True Truth" Comes from God ...................................... 83*
*Developing a Unified Music Philosophy ........................ 84*
*What is a Christocentric Music philosophy? .................. 85*
*The Essence of a Musical Praxis is "Doing" ................... 86*
*Testing One's Music Philosophy ................................... 87*
*All Musical Actions Exude from a Philosophy ................ 88*
*Proving Music's Acceptability to God ............................ 89*
*All Musicing Should be Discussable ............................. 91*
*Recognizing that All Music Has Purpose ....................... 92*

### PART TWO
### Understanding Music Philosophy

## 5 Developing a Philosophy of Music Education ............ 97

*A Music Education Credo ............................................. 97*
*Music's Historic Place in Education .............................. 98*
*Music's Place in an Academic Curriculum .................... 99*

Why Christian Music Education? ... 101
Defending Christian Music Education ... 102
What is the Essence of Music Education? ... 106
Critical Thinking vs. Being Critical ... 108
Music Education Philosophy must be Positive ... 110
There is No Substitute for Musical Skill ... 112
Submitting Music Education to Christ ... 114
Training Our Own ... 115
Music as a Part of the Larger Educational Picture ... 118
"Write this Song and Teach It" ... 119
A Philosophy that Covers the Whole of Music ... 120
Defining "Secular Music" ... 121
Philosophies of Utilizing the National Standards ... 122
Utilizing the National Standards in a CMEP ... 124
The Performance Emphasis Debate in Music Education ... 126
Christian Musicians Who Know Teach More Effectively ... 128

## 6 Congruency in Music Education and Musicing ... 134

Definitions of Terms Used in Music Education ... 134
Keeping Music Education Christian ... 136
Keeping Christian Music Education Academic ... 138
Can Music Transform the Musician? ... 140
The Precursor of Instrumental Music Education ... 142
Instrumental Music in Christian Music Education ... 144
Aesthetic Experiences in Education and Worship ... 145
In the Kosmos but Not of the Aion ... 149
Congruency in a Christian's Music and Musicing ... 150
Musical Truth Found in the Bible ... 151
Moral Implications of Music ... 154
The World may Consider You to be a Fool ... 155
Be Ready to Fall Down ... 156
Does God call Music Teachers? ... 156
Conclusions about Congruency in Our Musicing ... 158

## 7 Musicing Without a Congruent Music Philosophy ... 167

What may Happen if We do not
Develop a Music Philosophy? ... 167
What may Happen if We Resist all Change in Music? ... 168
What may Happen if We do not Resist Destructive Change? ... 169
What may Happen when we Become
Trendy with our Musicing? ... 171
What may Happen if We do not Sing at all in Worship? ... 172
What may Happen if We do not Distinguish
Between Sacred and Profane Music? ... 173
What may Happen if We try to Cater to
Everyone's Musical Tastes? ... 174
What may Happen if We try to "Retask" Music Styles? ... 176
What may Happen if We Remove the Ancient Landmarks? ... 177

## Part Three
# Meaning in Music

## 8  Does Musical Sound Communicate Meaning? ............ 182

*Is Music Communicative?* .......................................................... *182*
*What does "Joyful Sound" Mean Philosophically?* ............... *184*
*Does Music Affect the Whole-life of a Person?* ..................... *186*
*Moses and Joshua Heard before They Saw* ........................... *187*
*Is Musical Meaning Inside or Outside of Music?* ................... *188*
*Denying Transmittable Meaning* ............................................ *191*
*Is Music a Closed System?* ...................................................... *193*
*The Visible and Invisible Parts of Music* ................................ *195*
*Those who Understand Receive the Most Meaning* ............... *196*
*Does a Formalist Believe in Music's meaning?* ...................... *198*
*Is Musical Style Involved in the*
*Communication of Meaning?* .................................................. *199*

## 9  Can We Understand Music's Meaning? ....................... 204

*Reading (Singing) Distinctly Gave the "Sense"* ..................... *204*
*Is Music's Meaning Related to Real Life?* .............................. *205*
*Musicing with the Musician's Intellect* .................................... *207*
*Bible Music Increased the Performer's And Listener's Understanding 208*
*Do Those Who Understand the Music Receive More Understanding? 210*
*What about Music that Has a Dual Intentionality?* ................ *210*
*Does All Musicing Have Moral Implications?* ....................... *211*
*Does Emotion, Communicated Through Music, Have Meaning? 212*

## 10  Is Music a Language? .................................................. 218

*What Can Music Say?* .............................................................. *218*
*Does a Musician Bring Anything to the Experience of Musicing? 220*
*Does It Matter Whether Music is a Language or Not?* .......... *221*
*Does Music Communicate in an Effective Way?* .................... *223*
*Do the Formal Properties of Music Communicate Meaning? 224*

## 11  Creativity and the Christian Musician ......................... 228

*Real Creation Took Place When God Created* ....................... *228*
*The Composer is Somewhat like a Carpenter* ......................... *229*
*"Music Alone" Expresses Meaning when Performed* ............. *231*
*Christian Musicians Should Fear "Rutual"* ........................... *232*
*Creativity and Conservatism* .................................................... *234*

## 12 Aesthetics and the Christian Musician ............ 236

Aesthetics in A Christian's Music Paradigm ............ 236
What is Music in Aesthetic Terms? ............ 237
Aesthetics and the Beautiful ............ 239
An Anti-music Music Aesthetic ............ 240
Aesthetics and Distortion ............ 241
Aesthetics after Impressionism ............ 243
Aesthetics and the Destruction of Musical Absolutes ............ 244
Developing a Music Aesthetic ............ 245
Developing a Christian Approach to Aesthetics ............ 246
A Music Aesthetic Based on Beauty ............ 247
Aesthetics and Embellishment ............ 248
Aesthetics and "Joyful Noise" ............ 251
A Music Aesthetic must Retain God in its Basis ............ 253
A Christocentric Music Aesthetic ............ 254
Aesthetics and Bible Principles ............ 255
A Distorted Music Aesthetic ............ 256
Aesthetic Meaning vs. Aesthetic Ends ............ 257
Music and the Allied Arts ............ 258
Visual Art ............ 258
Photography and Videography ............ 259
Drama ............ 260
Decorative Arts ............ 261
Dance ............ 263
Cinema ............ 265

# PART FOUR
# How We Should Music

## 13 Sacred Music Should Be Worthwhile Music ............ 270

Finding what is Worthwhile in Music ............ 270
Profound Music Lends Itself to Being Worthwhile Music ............ 271
Formal Properties Should Support Profoundness ............ 272
Formal Properties Should not be Banal ............ 273
Sacred Music Should Be Powerful Music ............ 273
Sacred Music Should be Dynamic Music ............ 274
Sacred Music Should be Intense Music ............ 275
Sacred Music Should be Interesting Music ............ 277
Sacred Music Should not be Obvious Music ............ 278
Sacred Music Should Expound the Message of the Bible ............ 279

## 14 Styles in Conflict with Historical Church Music ............ 282

Styles that Came in by Default ............ 282
Styles that did not Start like Historical Church Music ............ 283
Keeping our Statements Accurate ............ 284
Intentional Distortion ............ 286
All Music Represents Some Philosophical Presupposition ............ 286
Styles that Negate the Elements of Music ............ 288
A Healthy Psyche Demands Release from Tension ............ 290
Connecting Righteousness with Unrighteousness ............ 290

Religious Music is not the Bellwether of Christianity ............... 292
The Influence of Music Style ....................................................... 293
Is Rock a Better Vehicle? ............................................................. 296
Is the Music Part of a Style Neutral? ........................................... 297
Ancient Landmarks of Sacred Musicing ..................................... 298
Styles not Intended to be Worship Music .................................... 300

## 15 What Do We Do Now that Some Styles Are Here to Stay? ............... 303

From Rejection to Toleration ....................................................... 303
What Do We Do if Musical Tastes Change? ................................ 304
"Doing" Exercises One's Philosophy .......................................... 306
Musical Meaning in Musical Sounds ........................................... 307
Performance Style Makes a Philosophical Statement .............. 310
Style can say What the Musician did not Intend to Say .......... 311
Christian Musicing Should Not Be an Autonomous Act ......... 312
Squeezed into the World's Mold with our Musicing ................. 314
An Irresistible Connection to Rock Music ................................. 315
Addicted to the Elements and Themes of Rock ........................ 316
What Do We Do Now that Rock Won't Go Away? .................... 317
What is the Answer to the Worship Music Dilemma? .............. 318
What do We do About the Worship Wars? ................................ 319
Is it Possible to Keep Worshipers United? ................................ 320
Understanding Imagery and Art Forms ..................................... 321
Understanding the Music Genres We Perform ......................... 323

## 16 How Should We Then Music? ........................................ 326

What Should the Music Leader Do? ........................................... 326
Philosophical Justifications for "Doing" ................................... 328
Why Should we Use a Song Book with Written Musical Notation? 328
Why Should we Sing Praise Choruses? ...................................... 330
Why Should we Sing Hymns? ..................................................... 332
Why Should we Sing Gospel Songs? ........................................... 334
Why Should we Sing Psalms? ..................................................... 336
Why Should we Sing Songs that "Sting"? ................................... 337
Utilizing Great Music in Worship ............................................... 338
Why Should we Sing with Musical Instruments? ...................... 341
The Song of Fools ........................................................................ 343
Soli Deo Gloria ............................................................................ 344

## 17 To the Chief Musician ........................................................ 347

How Should the Chief Musician use his Tongue? ..................... 347
Will God Protect His Chief Musicians? ..................................... 348
Nothing Matters to the Chief Musician as Much as God ........ 349
Chief Musicians with Broken Cisterns ....................................... 350
Weary Chief Musicians ................................................................ 351
God Never gets Tired ................................................................... 353
Some Chief Musicians Feed on Ashes ....................................... 354
The Chief Musician's Inheritance ............................................... 355
Deliverance for Chief Musicians ................................................. 355
Why God Created Music ............................................................. 356
If Chief Musicians Save, They Lose ........................................... 357
Good and Faithful Chief Musicians ............................................ 358

**Appendix A** ............................................................. **363**
 *Annotated List of Some Well Known Philosophers
 (Including Several with Flawed Philosophies)* ........................ *363*

**Appendix B** ............................................................. **367**
 *Selected List of Terms Often
 Used by Music Philosopers* ........................................... *367*

**Bibliography** ........................................................... **371**

**Index** .................................................................. **379**

**Index of Hebrew, Aramaic, and Greek Words** ............... **391**

This book is
DEDICATED

to the memory of
Rev. Bence C. Miller
1929—2016

President of
God's Bible School & College, 1975-1995

who first gave me the opportunity to
serve Jesus Christ at this historic
Bible college.

# Acknowledgments

I want to thank Rachelle Wolf, who was the content editor for this work, and Deanna Mander, who gave me enduring support and patience as I prepared this work.

"And the Lord answered me, and said, Write the vision, And make it plain upon tables, that he may run that readeth it."—*Habakkuk 2:2*

"For precept must be upon precept, precept upon precept; line upon line, line upon line; here a little, and there a little."—*Isaiah 28:10*

"All these were under the hands of their father for song in the house of the Lord, with cymbals, psalteries, and harps, for the service of the house of God according to the King's order to Asaph, Jeduthun, and Heman."
—*I Chronicles 25:6*

# Introduction

"Now therefore so shalt thou say unto thy servant David, I took thee from the sheepcote, from following the sheep, to be ruler over my people, over Israel" (2 Samuel 7:8).

## The Musician Taken from the Sheepcote

EVERY TIME I READ THIS Scripture about King David's beginnings, I think of myself. I was raised on an eighty-acre farm five miles east of Fort Scott, Kansas, about a mile and a half west of the Missouri state line. No one in my family background was an important person. As they say in Kansas, I was born a "nobody of nobodies," and no one knew me from "Adam's off ox" because I was the last child born to a crop farmer who ran a very small Grade C dairy.

I grew up with my older sister Virginia, and two older brothers, David and Nathan. When I was a little boy our family was very poor but our parents always put us first. My brothers and I always went to school with starched jeans and spotlessly clean clothes. We always had plenty to eat and the very best of what our parents possessed. Since we always had what we needed, we did not know how really poor we were. Dad worked on the farm and off of the farm as a painter and carpenter. My mother worked at the hospital as a nurse's aide, and later after we were raised, she went back to college and became a licensed practical nurse.

My first memories of going to church include my mother practicing songs with me and praying with me, and the preacher lifting me up on a chair behind the pulpit to sing special music about Jesus. I have told you all this to remind all of you Christian parents that your children's musical training really matters. No matter what you have or do not have, the things that matter are not "things". Whatever it takes, make sure that your children receive a quality music education and that you provide them opportunities to give their musical talents back to the God who gave them to your children.

I am grateful that Dr. John I. Page and his wife, Virginia, took me to church fellowship meetings and to retirement communities to sing the gospel as a little child. I was extremely blessed to have a pastor and his wife that cared about a little boy who had some musical talent. I am also grateful that in July of 1967 Dr. Page invited me to an altar of prayer where I confessed my sins and wept my way into the loving arms of my forgiving Savior Jesus Christ. I will forever be thankful that I was given a Christian upbringing, and that as a child I was given musical training and many opportunities to give my musical talents back to God.

Every child is given musical talent by our loving Heavenly Father. Mothers and fathers, you have the responsibility to give your children an opportunity to develop their musical talents and at an early age give those talents back to God. That is what really matters, because children learn musically by doing. If you want your sons and daughters to give their musical talents to God in adulthood, make sure their early memories of going to church include musicing unto Him.

## How I Began this Philosophical Journey

In July of 1967 I attended the Eastern Kansas Camp with my mother, Anna Mayme Wolf, who has now gone to heaven. The evangelist was Dr. C.E. Cowen, who preached a very powerful, lucid gospel message. As I mentioned earlier, Dr. John I. Page came to me and invited me to step forward and give my heart to the Lord. I came forward that Sunday evening and bowed at an old wooden altar at the front of that open air tabernacle. I was tired of trying to control my life. I confessed my sins with much godly sorrow, gave my heart to the Lord Jesus Christ, and by faith in the merits of Christ, received the Lord Jesus Christ as my personal Savior. I began a spiritual journey that evening that has made all the difference in my life.

I later graduated from Pittsburg State University in Pittsburg, Kansas and accepted a teaching position at Kansas City College and Bible School in Overland Park, Kansas. I believe it was during my first year of teaching that I attended a music seminar by Dr. Frank Garlock that took place at a Christian School in Merriam, Kansas.

During Dr. Garlock's seminar the Lord impressed upon my heart to engage in serious study of music found in the Bible and to develop a coherent and congruent Christ centered music philosophy. The Holy Spirit used Dr. Garlock's firm regard for what the Bible has to say about music to cause me to start the twenty-five year study that resulted in the book *Music of the Bible*, and later *Church Music Matters*. I will forever be indebted to Dr. Garlock for his faithfulness to the Lord during that seminar. Without his faithfulness to deliver the message of Christ-centered musicing I might not have started on this marvelous musical part of my spiritual journey.

### Why I Include Transliterations and Strong's Numbers

Many music directors and music educators have not had the opportunity to study Greek and Hebrew and biblical Aramaic while they were in an undergraduate or graduate music degree program in college. For this reason I do not write any of the Bible language words and/or definitions in Hebrew, Aramaic or Greek characters. There is a multitude of Bible study books that include the keyed numbers found in *Strong's Exhaustive Concordance*. Because I include Strong's keyed numbers, those who read my philosophical writings have an immediate connection to scholarly sources which are keyed to *Strong's Concordance* without the hassle of having to compare the characters of the Hebrew, Aramaic or Greek words that are found in the many Bible study works.

Many times I read books and periodical articles by authors who contend that a passage of Scripture has a certain meaning, but when I study it, I cannot substantiate that it actually has the meaning a particular author purports. It would be a great help if all authors would identify exactly which Hebrew, Aramaic, or Greek word that is being referenced by the use of Strong's keyed numbers, and also transliterate the particular words for the reader who is not able to read the original biblical languages.

All words found in any language have meaning based on how they are used in sentences. Words mean something, and the writers of Scripture, who were inspired to write sentences under the direct (plenary) inspiration of the Holy Spirit, wrote exactly what they meant to say. It does not make any sense to suppose that an inspired writer of Scripture would have used words that meant what he did not intend to say. Misunderstandings of Scripture are most often the result of the reader not having a grasp of the original language; an understanding of the meaning of the words; or an understanding of how the inspired writers used these words in the context of writing Scripture.

When I commit my thoughts to pen and ink, it is possible that I spend more time with the English dictionary, Bible language dictionaries, and lexicons than I do writing my own thoughts. My writings are far from inspired, but that does not mean that I do not labor over each word, phrase and sentence. I would be greatly offended if my readers were to suppose that I had intended to write the opposite meaning of my intent.

So, if a writer expects readers to trust his supposed meanings of the original Bible words in his writings, that author must treat the ancient inspired writings of the Old and New Testaments with much respect. Changing the Holy Writ to merely fit modern thinking is a very dangerous writing technique. As Revelation 22:18-19 warns, "For I testify unto every man that heareth the words of the prophecy of this book, If any man shall add unto these things, God shall add unto him the plagues that are written in this book: And if any man shall take away from the words of the book of this prophecy, God shall take away his part out of the book of life, and out of the holy city, and from the things which are written in this book." Therefore, a writer has an obligation to the original meaning of the inspired words that were used in the Bible. When I expose and define original passages of the Bible that are thousands of years old, I endeavor to always identify the original words, as well as give keyed numbers, so that the reader may do personal language studies to establish whether my interpretations are valid or not.

Although I have used Strong's keyed numbers and some of his definitions in the preparation of this book, I did not use all of them because they do not always take into consideration the context of a particular Scripture passage and other historical considerations that sometime influence the meaning of words. I always consider various lexicons, dictionaries and sources like the *Encyclopedia*

*Judaica* and monumental historical works like the English translation of the *Babylonian Talmud* to consider extrabiblical considerations of what the Scriptures mean in historical context. Other study helps that I use extensively are *Practical Word Studies in the New Testament, Theological Lexicon of the Old Testament, Theological Wordbook of the Old Testament, Vine's Expository Dictionary of Biblical Words, The New Brown-Driver-Briggs-Gesenius Hebrew-English Lexicon, Theological Dictionary of the New Testament, Girdlestone's Synonyms of the Old Testament, The New Thayer's Greek-English Lexicon, The New Englishman's Hebrew and Chaldee Concordance*, and *The New Englishman's Greek-English Concordance*.

**Why I Use Lexical Forms of Words**

As I mentioned earlier, many Church musicians and Christian music educators do not read Greek, Hebrew or Aramaic. For this reason I have chosen to include in my writings the lexical forms of the words (except in direct quotes of other authors) and their keyed numbers found in Strong's Concordance. A lexical form is an abstract unit representing a set of word forms differing only in inflection and not in core meaning. Bible lexicons provide definitions and meaning of Biblical words found in the original Greek, Hebrew, and Aramaic languages used in the Bible. Lexicons help those who do Bible word studies to understand the origins and root meaning of the ancient languages used in the Bible. Lexicons often give the context and cultural meaning intended by the authors of the Bible.

When a student who does not know how to read Greek, Hebrew, or Aramaic is reading an English translation of the Bible, the only way to find out what a particular word means in the original language is to look it up in a lexicon. Lexicons use what is called "lexical forms of words," which means that this language source deals with the vocabulary of a language rather than with grammatical and syntactical aspects. The grammatical and syntactical aspects are largely determined by context. Ultimately, words only have exact meaning in the context in which they are used. A lexicon or dictionary only gives the range of possible meanings.

## About the Bibliography

The bibliography for this work is by no means a reading list of works that I approve as representative publications of the beliefs presented in this philosophical discussion. I have included works that were either cited or were influential in the planning and writing this book. A great number of the works listed in the bibliography are partially or completely in opposition to the philosophical and biblical principles presented in this work.

## About the Two Indices

This work has two indices. One is for proper names and other words and phrases. The second index consists of transliterated Hebrew, Aramaic, and Greek words from the Old and New Testament that are cited in this work.

## Symbols and Abbreviations

| | |
|---|---|
| AV | Authorized King James Version, the KJV |
| CME | Christian music education |
| CMEP | Christian music education philosophy |
| *Ibid.* | The abbreviation for *ibidem*, which means "a further reference to a work which was just cited." |
| KJV | King James Version, the AV |
| *Kosmos* | Words like this are transliterations of Hebrew, Aramaic, and Greek words used in the Bible. They are an attempt to spell out these words literally in English. |
| ME | Music education. |
| MEAE | Music education as aesthetic education |
| NT | New Testament. This abbreviation does not refer to any version of the Bible. |
| OT | Old Testament. This abbreviation does not refer to any version of the Bible. |
| SME | Secular music education refers to music education in a setting where Christ and the Bible are not revered and considered the central focus of all educational endeavors. |

*YHVH* (also *YHWH*) This tetragrammaton is of uncertain pronunciation since it was not pronounced by the ancient Jewish community for centuries, because it was considered to be too sacred to be pronounced. Therefore, the vowel sounds are now uncertain. It was translated Jehovah by the King James scholars and as Yawveh, Yahweh or Yahovah by others.

\* An asterisk indicates that the next word or words are defined in the "Word Meanings" at the end of the chapter.

# PART ONE

# Getting Started with a Music Philosophy

# 1

# Music Philosophy In and Beyond the Genesis Record

### How did Music Begin?

WE KNOW FROM GENESIS 1:1 that, "In the beginning God *created". From this *truism let us explore the philosophical presupposition that in the beginning God created music. Many church musicians do not start with this necessary philosophical basis. On the contrary, many Christian musicians believe that there is no answer to the question, "How did music begin?" They fail to recognize the evident answer found in Genesis 1:1, "In the beginning God created..."

God did not need to create music because He is and always has been without need. In His divine wisdom and sovereignty He chose to create music because He desired to create it. So He thought it into existence— that is creation. God did not create music to fulfill His destiny, because He has no destiny. Since everything that God has ever done is perfect, He did not need to create music to make His creation more perfect. Everything that He created before and after He created music was perfect. Although this is difficult for a musician to conceptualize, God's creation was completely perfect with or without music. Think about it: God's creation did not get better and His creative work does not get better. We as Christian musicians do things to perfect our musical skills in our long journey toward the development of our God-given musical gifts. God did not take a long or short musical journey. He simply thought and absolutely nothing became something— music. That is creation.

God truly created music. Although the word *created* is used loosely by many musicians, man never actually creates music, or anything else for that matter. God took nothing and made something— that something was music. Music composers and arrangers only "construct"— they only are capable of "arranging" or moving God's created musical building blocks into new artistic patterns. A contractor who builds a building takes created materials and uses them to construct something. He always takes "something" and constructs with these materials. No matter how great a building a contractor constructs or how much *creative effort he exerts, what he puts together is not truly a creation. We will discuss "creativeness" further in chapter eleven under the topic, "Creativity and the Christian Musician".

Earlier I said that God did not create music because He was destined to do so. God did not create music because it was in His destiny or future. God very clearly explained this to Moses when He declared in Exodus 3:14, "And God said unto Moses, I AM THAT I AM: and he said, Thus shalt thou say unto the children of Israel, I AM hath sent me unto you." God did not say, I was God in the past or I will be God in the future, but rather *hayah asher hayah* (1961, 834, 1961) which means, according to Dr. Clarke's research, "The Vulgate translates I am who am. The Septuagint, I am he who exists. The Syriac, the Persic, and the Chaldee preserve the original words without any gloss."[1]

Therefore, God does not have a beginning or end, but rather in His own words He simply explains, "I AM."

**Did God Create the Building Blocks of Music?**

Was music made as a part of God's objective acts of creation? Again I remind us that Genesis 1:1 tells us, "In the beginning God created..." We know from the words *Elohiym bara eth* (430, 1254, 853) in verse one that the supreme exceeding God absolutely made or created music from or of Himself. Some Christian music philosophers have believed that since music is "of or from God" it has always been a part of His moral nature and therefore did not have to be created in His objective acts of creation. They sometimes use John 1:3, "All things were made by him; and without him was not anything made that was made," as support for their belief by saying that God made things that needed to be made but He did not need to make music so He did not make it. This faulty belief is predicated on the theory that since music was already in, of, or from God, it was part of His moral nature at the time of the creation and therefore without need of His creative work.

This faulty theory effectively lets the Christian musician who is seeking autonomy off the hook philosophically. If God did not objectively take nothing and make music out of this "nothingness" then what does Psalm 146:6 mean, when it so clearly states that it was God "Which made heaven, and earth, the sea, and all that therein is: which keepeth truth forever"? Strong says that *asah* (6213) means "to do or make" something. Is there any logical reason why music is not a part of this "all" which is mentioned here? St. John 1:3 and 10, Ephesians 3:9, and Revelation 4:11 all attest to the belief of a complete creation, and especially Colossians 1:16, "For by him were all things created, that are in heaven, and that are in earth, visible and invisible, whether they be thrones, or dominions, or principalities, or powers: all things were created by him, and for him."

So, we are drawn to the logical conclusion that out of the chaos, emptiness and confusion reported in Genesis 1:2, God created music as part of His creation. God chose to create music because in His perfect will He desired that it should be a part of His perfect creation. In His objective acts of creation, God created the mathematical ratios that are the basis of what music is and what it will be like when a musician arranges the music part of music into artistic musical patterns. Because of this God has authority over how we arrange and use His musical building blocks. When Christian musicians get rid of the sense of music ownership many Church music problems disappear.

A non-descript and fuzzy music philosophy derived from a misunderstanding of the significance of Genesis 1:1 will give rise to a faulty musical ministry *praxis. This means that if God, by virtue of ownership, does not become Lord over all of a Christian's musicing, as an art form and as a musical offering to God in that musician's music ministry, it will not be very long until God will not be Lord over any of that Christian musician's musicing. A faulty music praxis will eventually result in a music ministry that has become anthropocentric* rather than Christocentric.

# 1: Music Philosophy In and Beyond the Genesis Record

When Christian musicians realize that they do not own music, it is much easier to recognize that they are musical servants with responsibilities rather than rights. Music was created because God willed that it should exist. Therefore, it is not farfetched to come to the logical hypothesis that He still has a will concerning music. Again we should remember that God created the formal properties of music, i.e., the nuts and bolts of music that make it what it is capable of being. However, what a musician does with the formal properties of music is a different matter. When we, as musicians, face Him whose eyes are as a flame of fire, we will give a stewardship account of what we did with His musical building blocks.

We know that God created the mathematical ratios that form the basis of the musical scale as an intentional part of His six day creation, because He created everything. The Genesis record in chapter 1:31 explains that at the end of the sixth day of creation "God saw everything that he had made, and, behold, it was very good." Therefore, as I have stated many times in my philosophical writings, we know with certainty that in the beginning God created music. In verse thirty-one God's opinion is that the system of music He created was very good. I do not know about you, but for me, I trust God's opinion since He *embodies absolute truth concerning all aspects of music. So, when His Word said that God created we know that music was created in a good condition. God created music and, as He conceived it to be, it was very good. It was very good because His Word attests that it was.

One may honestly ask, "What is God's opinion concerning music?" This is an honest question so it deserves an honest answer. Part of God's ultimate and perfect opinion concerning music is found in the more than 600 references to music in the Bible. Many doctrines are only mentioned a few times in the Bible, but music is so important to God that He mentions it hundreds of times in the inspired infallible Word.

So, the concept that God does not have anything to say about sacred and secular music is false. As a matter of fact, this faulty view actually denies God's authority over the whole of creation, which includes the whole of music. It behooves all of us to study His Word in order to discern His will concerning music. It is also safe to conclude that all music matters very much to God. Although it is presumptuous to claim to know exactly all that God thought when He thought music into existence, we do know from His infallible *inspired Word more about how to *music unto Him than many Christians suppose.

As we have already considered, music is not the original concept of primitive mankind, but rather the concept of God who is Alpha and Omega, the beginning and the end. To assume anything less is false and has no basis in or outside of Scripture. In the beginning God created the mathematical ratios that form sound or tone, the basis of music. As we have stated before, man did not evolve into existence, and likewise music did not evolve into existence. Although mankind has developed music over the thousands of years since creation, these advancements in the way that the building blocks of music are fitted together are not actually creations. They are only constructions or artistic arrangements of God's creation.

## Knowing Based on the Genesis Record

The Genesis record does not have much to say about music in very ancient times. However, we are not completely left in the dark concerning the beginnings of music since we have the mention of Jubal and his music instruments. As early as Genesis 4:21 we learn that Lamech's wife Adah gave birth to Jabal, "And his brother's name was Jubal: he (Jubal) was the father of all such as handle the harp and organ." You will notice that he was referred to as the "father" but never as the "creator" of music. Genesis 4:21 refers to Jubal as the father (*ab*, 01) and not as the one who created (*bara'*, 1254) music. The Bible calls Jubal the handler (*taphas*, 8610) or manipulator of music, but never refers to Jubal or anyone else as the creator of music.

The harp (*kinnor*, 3658) mentioned here was a hand held lyre (not a harp) and the organ (*ugab*, 5748) was a reed instrument (not an organ or pan pipe as some suppose). By the time of Jacob (Genesis 31:27) we have record of songs (*shiyr*, 7892). The frame drum translated tabret (*toph*, 8596) in the KJV which was a small breast drum, and the lyre (*kinnor,* 3658) that was again translated harp in the KJV. For a thorough discussion of ancient musical instruments mentioned in the Bible, read Chapter Seven of my book *Music of the Bible in Christian Perspective.*

A review of Scripture (much of it later than the Genesis record) reveals that during Israel's early period of nomadic life, instrumental music was well developed. I will say again that music's beginning can be traced back to creation, but most of its mention in the OT was recorded after the Book of Genesis. You may wonder what I am trying to establish philosophically by nailing down the facts of music's beginnings in God's creative acts and its early mention in Genesis. A simple answer is that there are ancient landmarks of musicing recorded in the Bible and their origin is found in God's creative work, i.e., "in the beginning God created..."

There is another concept of God's creation recorded in the book of Genesis that we should discuss at this point. As I said before, Genesis 1:31 records the fact that when God created music its condition was very (*ma'od,* 3966) good (*towb,* 2896). In other words, His music creation was not merely good, but it was exceedingly good or beautiful. The Hebrew word *ma'od* is a superlative term. To God, music was not "just there," but rather it was exceedingly good when used as He intended. *Towb* connotes not only goodness but also beauty. Although it is difficult to fully ascertain what is meant by beautiful, it is possible to understand that God created music for His glory and also created it to be exceedingly beautiful and wonderful. We can also justly conclude that this creation which was *ma'od towb* was exceedingly valuable to mankind. It was very beautiful, valuable, meaningful, and had the ability to be very efficacious either for good or, if perverted, for evil.

It stands to reason that God created the building blocks of music to be exceedingly good and that it is the objective of Satan to pervert them by negating their "goodness." Since in this instance *ma'od towb* also means that the elements of music were created to be the very best, we may safely deduce that it is the will and work of Satan to pervert a proper arrangement of those elements (building blocks) of music that make them exceedingly "good. " Satan is capable of influencing a composer's arranging of the building blocks of music. When Satan has an influence that produces a perversion (incongruent ordering of the building blocks), then this perversion does not produce "good music."[2] I do not know about you, but I do not want to agree philosophically with the belief that Satan's influence on music is good although it is perverted, or that Satan's influence on music makes it better. I find it hard to imagine how any thinking Christian musician could agree with those who believe that anything for which Satan is responsible is good, or that he does not negatively influence performers, arrangers, and performers.

It is possible for a composer who is not a Christian to order the building blocks of music in a fashion that will make them congruent with the purposes of sacred musicing. However, it is the responsibility of the Christian composer, arranger and performer to study music thoroughly and be filled with the Holy Spirit. Without such understanding it will be difficult to guard against the influence of Satan. Romans 8:6-8 instructs Christians to be filled with the Spirit "For they that are after the flesh do mind the things of the flesh; but they that are after the Spirit the things of the Spirit. Because the carnal mind is enmity against God: for it is not subject to the law of God, neither indeed can be. So then they that are in the flesh cannot please God." Furthermore, 1 Corinthians 2:14 explains, "But the natural man receiveth not the things of the Spirit of God: for they are foolishness unto him: neither can he know them, because they are spiritually discerned." However, 1 Corinthians 2:6 promises that Christ can guide the Christian's musical endeavors, "For who hath known the mind of the Lord, that he may instruct him? But we have the mind of Christ."

The way a composer or arranger organizes and utilizes the building blocks of music will give them the propensity to either be *congruent or incongruent with the purposes of sacred musicing to a high and holy triune God. It is not the building blocks of music that are good or evil, but rather it is how they are arranged and performed that gives them positive or negative meaning. To be more specific, it is not diatonic seventh chords, incomplete dominant ninth chords, augmented sixth chords, Neapolitan sixth chords, syncopated rhythms, push beats, dynamics, or hemiolas that are profane. It is the way that a composer, arranger or performer uses them that determines their appropriateness or inappropriateness. There is no such thing as an evil chord, dynamic or rhythm *per se*, but every astute performer, composer or arranger understands that they may be used inappropriately in a given situation. Furthermore, the inappropriate *juxtaposition or *amalgamation of styles of music is capable of making subtle, or not so subtle, jest of the very thing that a Christian musician is supposed to be expressing while musicing unto God.

## God Intended for Music to be Under Man's Supervision

It is possible that the beginnings of musical knowledge can be traced to Genesis 1:26 where Adam was commanded to "...have dominion (*radah*, 7287) over the fish of the sea, and over the fowl of the air, and over the cattle, and over all the earth (*erets*, 776), and over every creeping thing that creepeth upon the earth." Also in verse twenty-eight he is admonished to "replenish (*male* 4390) the earth (776) and subdue (*kabash*, 3533) it." The words *dominion* (7287) and *subdue* (3533) used in Genesis 1:26 mean to *subjugate or to conquer. The word *earth* (776) used in Genesis 1:26 is the broad term used for the world as opposed to the word *earth* (*adamah*, 127) used in Genesis 1:25 which means the soil. Note that God not only put the soil under man's supervision but also the *erets*, i.e., the world around him and *male*, i.e., presume influence over it.

So, Adam was given the command to conquer and bring under his control the world around him which doubtlessly included music. We know from Genesis 2:19-20 that Adam was given tremendous insight and knowledge. Although these passages say absolutely nothing about music, it is possible that he also had unusual insight concerning music.

We know from the authority of the Genesis record that God intended for man to subjugate, subdue and presume influence over all of His creation, which certainly included music. We also know that God set man over the personal works of His creation. Hebrews 2:7-8 states, "Thou madest him a little lower than the angels; thou didst set him over the works of thy hands: Thou hast put all things in subjection under him, he left nothing that is not put under him. But now we see not all things put under him."

Albert Barnes stated, "It was the original appointment (Gen. 1:26) that man should have dominion over the lower world, and be its absolute lord and sovereign. Had he continued in innocence this dominion would have been entire and perpetual. But man fell, and we do not see him exerting this dominion."[3] If Adam and Eve had not fallen, we probably would not be having so much debate over music philosophy in the twenty-first century.

## Is All Music Created Equal?

Writers like Greg Scheer claim that they are not interested in the musical style debate, but every musician whom I have had the privilege of knowing or reading their books or articles about music styles has taken a position on styles of music. Even the writers who have decided not to decide have in reality taken a position on musical style because they have come to the faulty pluralistic conclusion that all music that has ever been composed is equal. So, when Scheer made the statement, "I take the position that 'all musics are created equal,'" it stands to reason that he definitely, by that statement, chose to enter the style debate.[4] As a musician, surely he does not really believe that all creative music efforts are equal. If one were to ask him if the music of J.S. Bach was equal to compositions that I wrote for my undergraduate music theory class, I am sure that he would vote for Bach. What he was doubtlessly meaning at the time he wrote his book was that when one is referring to religious music, the music part of the music does not matter.

The musician who does not take a *cosmopolitan liberal pluralistic view of music style runs the risk of being considered "out of touch", "musically bigoted" or at least to have been "hiding under a rock" philosophically. It seems a bit strange that a writer may believe in a prescriptive approach to secular music without applying the same principles to sacred music. Various authors who have addressed secular music in the late twentieth and early twenty-first centuries have devoted much of their writings to the belief that the music part of secular music matters. While they have not been accused of stifling creative efforts, those who believe that the music part of sacred music matters have been accused of being musically bigoted.

Every college or university that has a quality music degree program takes a prescriptive approach to music. They prescribe which music is appropriate for study and performance. They decide which music is of a poor quality, good quality, or fine quality. Also, in their prescriptive decision making process they are able to show adequate proofs for their choices. However, when it comes to sacred music, some Christian musicians have come to the conclusion that there is no such thing as a quality musical offering to be presented to God, or worse yet, they follow the notion that all music offerings are equal in their nature and value. Although we hear much about worship music being a musical offering that is explicitly performed and offered unto God, it appears that some Christian musicians do not understand the biblical concept of the sacrificial system.

What we do not often hear about is where Christian musicians get the concept of offerings presented to God. This concept is taken from the Old Testament (it is also mentioned in the New Testament). This sacrificial system is mentioned in Jeremiah 33:11— "The voice of joy, and the voice of gladness, the voice of the bridegroom, and the voice of the bride, the voice of them that shall say, Praise the LORD of hosts: for the LORD is good; for his mercy endureth for ever: and of them that shall bring the sacrifice of praise into the house of the LORD. For I will cause to return the captivity of the land, as at the first, saith the LORD."[5]

From these and other Scriptures we get our understanding of the sacrificial system and its connection to the presentation of our musical offerings unto God. Among the many sacrifices presented unto God was the sacrifice of praise. There were also sacrifices made as atonement for sin. When Jesus shed His blood on Calvary He became our permanent sacrifice for sin and therefore superseded the need for the shedding of the blood of animals for remission of sin. However, I see no place in the New Testament where Christ's sacrificial death did away with the need for Christians to present God with musical sacrifices of praise, and I have no philosophical objection to referring to our sacred musicing as sacrificial musical offering.

This sacrificial system mentioned in the Old Testament was very prescriptive in nature. For instance, Leviticus 4:2-3 states, "Speak unto the children of Israel, saying, If a soul shall sin through ignorance against any of the commandments of the LORD concerning things which ought not to be done, and shall do against any of them: If the priest that is anointed do sin according to the sin of the people; then let him bring for his sin, which he hath sinned, a young bullock *without blemish* unto the LORD for a sin offering" (emphasis added). Notice that this offering was prescribed by *YHVH* to be a lamb "without blemish."

" The sacrificial system instituted in ancient Israel was quite involved and included various prescribed sacrifices which were acceptable for different occasions and under different circumstances. A careful study of the requirements for these sacrifices reveals that every sacrifice had the prescriptive requirement of being the best sacrifice the worshiper had to offer.

Why all the philosophical fuss over the sacrificial system of the Old Testament? In order to refer to worship music as musical offerings presented to God, a Christian musician should believe in the concept of presenting God the best suited musical offering possible. Therefore, the notion that since all music is supposedly created equal it does not matter what kind of musical offering one presents to God, is not congruent with the biblical concept of musicing unto God. Every honest minister of music or music educator who is knowledgeable of music composition and music theory will have to admit that all the creative efforts of composers and arrangers are not on the same level of musical quality and profundity and therefore not of the same value and suitability as musical offerings.

As I mentioned earlier, references to the Old Testament sacrificial system appear in the New Testament in Hebrews 13:15— "By him therefore let us offer the sacrifice of praise to God continually, that is, the fruit of our lips giving thanks to his name." (For more references to the sacrificial system, also see Romans 12:1, Philippians 4:18 and 1 Peter 2:5.) So, since there are references to the concept of sacrifices made unto God in the NT, without any reference to this concept not being compatible with Christian worship, I see no philosophical problem with worship leaders referring to their worshiping by musicing unto God as musical offerings. There is no logical philosophical reasoning behind the notion that these musical offerings should not be the very best offerings that a Christian is capable of presenting. If one accepts the concept of musical offerings presented in the Bible, then it stands to reason that not all musical offerings, regardless of what they represent, how they are presented, and what they contain, are necessarily equal in their nature or value.

Although the quality of the music we bring to God as an offering matters, musical offerings are not solely about quality musical performance or high quality musical art forms. Amos 5:22-23 states, "Though ye offer me burnt offerings and your meat offerings, I will not accept them: neither will I regard the peace offerings of your fat beasts. Take thou away from me the noise of thy songs; for I will not hear the melody of thy viols." God declared that He would not accept Israel's musical sacrifices because of their spiritual condition and referred to their musical offerings as *noise*. God was referring to the spiritual condition of those who "leave off righteousness in the earth" rather than, at least in this case, the quality of their music. I am drawn to this conclusion by what is recorded in Amos 5:12, "For I know your manifold transgressions and your mighty sins: they afflict the just, they take a bribe, and they turn aside the poor in the gate from their right." The Bible lesson is clear that our musical melodies and our instrumental music will be considered to be noise by our heavenly Father if we attempt to music unto him with sin in our hearts.

Now I will answer the question, "Is all music created equal?" First, based on the conclusions drawn earlier in this chapter, only God can create. Man always takes something that already exists and uses his God-given gift of creativity to construct musical compositions in new and wonderful (or not so wonderful) ways. Odd as it may seem, the spiritual condition of the creative musician's heart does not always dictate the nature and value of a musician's creative musical works. It is sometimes difficult to reconcile the statement above with Luke 6:45 which states, "A good man out of the good treasure of his heart bringeth forth that which is good; and an evil man out of the evil treasure of his heart bringeth forth that which is evil: for of the abundance of the heart his mouth speaketh." An evil heart condition may cause a composer to produce music that is not suited for worship. However, that musician could artistically arrange the formal properties of a piece of music in such a way that it is appropriate and useful for Christian worship.

No composer is a creator in the truest sense; the musician did not create elements of music from nothingness, but rather artistically ordered or reordered God's building blocks of music in new and fresh ways. Since God's creation is an orderly creation, in the realm of music theory and aesthetics the possibility exists that there is a good, acceptable, and even perfect ordering of the formal properties of a given music composition. So, composers who use personal creative gifts well may produce music that is appropriate and fitting for worshiping our awesome, wonderful, triune God regardless of their spiritual condition.

Quality sacred music is not entirely about a high level of artistic quality or intricate musical working out of the formal properties of the music. Also, acceptable musical offerings presented to God, although they must be the Christian musician's best possible offerings, are not about high art or exceptional artistic musical performances. In Isaiah 29:13 the man of God stated, "Wherefore the Lord said, Forasmuch as this people draw near me with their mouth, and with their lips do honour me, but have removed their heart far from me, and their fear toward me is taught by the precept of men." These people went through the procedures of worship, but their musical offerings were not acceptable unto God. Although composers who are not living in personal relationship with God may be able to use their artistic efforts to compose music that is appropriate for public worship, these same musicians are not able to worship with that music because God said they "have removed their heart far from me." No matter how well musicians who do not love and serve Christ have artistically ordered the building blocks of music, their attempts at worship will fail since true worship is not about high musical art.

While we are discussing whether or not all music is "created" equal, the concept of simple and complex music should be considered. It is a biblical principle of musicing that a Christian musician must present God the best musical offerings possible. All music is not equal in its nature and value, and styles that are antagonistic by association to the principles of the changed life of a Christian are not well suited to represent the moral nature of a perfect and holy God. Also, not all music is equally appropriate and useful as a worship vehicle because of its nature. However, the concepts mentioned above are not controlled by whether the music is simple or complex.

There are many situations in which a simple musical vehicle is more appropriate than a long intricate working out of musical themes, chord structures, and complicated organizational patterns. Sometimes the proper concomitant to the simplicity of the gospel message is simple music. However, it should be pointed out that by the term *simple* I am not referring to banal music (see chapter thirteen). The simplicity of a piece of music does not necessarily connote that it has a lack of artistic quality.

If Christian musicians avoid all of the more intricate and developed sacred music, they run the risk of not supporting the majesty, glory, and honor of our awesome triune God with music that is more capable of representing these great spiritual themes of the Bible. Sometimes Christian musicians seem to forget why some musical works are referred to as *sacred classics*. A classic is by definition a work of art with recognized and established value; in this case it is an artistic musical work that has proven itself over time to be a quality vehicle for the sacred content that it embodies. A musical work of this nature is a more intricate and often a more complicated working out of the formal properties and structure of the music. These sacred classics have the capacity to deliver more designated and embodied meaning than a work of less musical stature. One of the concepts that I am stressing is that the greater the working out of the music the greater the payoff in aesthetic value. Also the greater one understands the import of the embodied meaning of this music, the greater will be the understanding that the performer and the auditor receives. This conclusion is gathered from understanding that all quality music has a greater amount of understandable embodied meaning in the music and designated (referential) meaning which is given to the music from outside of the formal properties of the music itself than the more simple vehicles does.

## God Created Sound

If you have read the first chapter of St. Paul's Epistle to the Colossians you will remember that in chapter one, verse sixteen, it states that God created the visible (*horatos* 3703) and the invisible (*auratos* 517) part of music. Christian musicians are much more familiar with God creating the visible than they are with His creating the invisible. Twenty-first century Christian musicians are often much more fascinated with God creating the musical notation (the *te 'amim*) of the OT than with the importance of God's creation of sound.

We get caught up in discussions of the possibility that Moses came down from the mountain with the *te 'amim* engraved on the tablets. We may *postulate that Jehovah possibly revealed them to Moses and that Moses added them to the Decalogue. We may wax eloquent in our notion that Moses developed the system of notation used in the Old Testament since he could have learned about musical notation from the Egyptians. (We know from Acts 7:22 that "...Moses was learned in all the wisdom of the Egyptians, and was mighty in words and deeds.") An even wilder hypothesis is that he learned notation from the Sumerians or the Akkadians since we know that they had written notation at least 1400 to 1500 years before the earliest surviving Greek fragments in a written notation.[6]

However, although we now know much more about the history of world music, it is still an abstract thought to many Christian musicians that God created sound, i.e., the invisible part of music. It is what I call the "music part of music." You cannot touch it, or see it, but it is very much there. The *auratos* gives music life and great power. It gives our musicing the ability to function, develop, come "alive", and be efficacious. Therefore, Christian musicians should give very serious consideration to the sounds (*aoratos,* i.e., the invisible part of music) that we connect to the *Logos Christos*.

### Endnotes

1. Adam Clarke, *Genesis- Deuteronomy.* Vol. 1 in *Clarke's Commentary,* (Nashville, TN: Abingdon Press, *n.d*), 306.
2. Garen Wolf, *Church Music Matters,* (Salem, OH: Schmul Publishing Company, Inc., 2005.), 68-77.

3. Albert Barnes, *Hebrews to Jude*. vol. 13 in *Barnes Notes on the New Testament*. (Grand Rapids, MI: Baker Books, 1998), 59.
4. Greg Scheer, *The Art of Worship*, (Grand Rapids: Baker Books, 2006), 11-12.
5. Other references to the sacrificial system include Leviticus 7:12; 1 Chronicles 16:8, 34; 2 Chronicles 5:12-13; 7:3-6; Ezra 3:11; Psalm 107:22; 116:17; 136:1; Isaiah 12:4; Jeremiah 7:34; 16:9; 25:10; and 33:7.
6. Garen Wolf, *Music of the Bible in Christian Perspective*, (Salem, OH: Schmul Publishing Company, Inc., 1996), 322-323.

## Chapter One Word Meanings

**Amalgamation**— in this case it refers to the combining of incongruent styles of music in a musical composition.

**Anthropocentric** – focused on man as the center of existence.

**Congruent**— in harmony or agreement with something else.

**Cosmopolitan**— being at home with many notions or views of what religious music should be like.

**Create**— the phenomenon of taking nothing and making something.

**Creative**— having the ability to produce new things or to think of new ideas and to use them in productive new ways to construct something from elements that already exist.

**Embodies**— in theology it means that God actually is truth.

**Inspired**— as used here, this word means God breathed, i.e., directly from God.

**Juxtaposition**— here refers to the placement of two or more incongruent styles of music, either one following the other or overlapping the other. This is often done in jest by the arranger or as an inept attempt to pander to the style wishes of the audience.

***Logos Christos***— the Word of Christ. Some writers refer to it as the Word of God, i.e., the Bible.

**Music** – an active verb that means to engage in music making, as coined by author David Elliott.

**Praxis**— of or pertaining to action based on a specific mode of behavior or purposeful way of doing something; in this text often referring to one's purposeful way of using music as a secular art form or in one's church music ministry.

**Subjugate**— to bring music under man's dominion or control.

***Te'amim***— the graphic signs below and above the Hebrew text of the Old Testament that form a precise music notation.

**Truism**— a philosophical statement that is obviously true.

## Chapter One Questions for Discussion

1. Explain how music began and support your answer with Scripture.

2. Explain the difference in meaning of the words *create* and *creative*.
3. What does the author mean by the term "building blocks of music"?
4. Discuss the belief that God doesn't have anything to say about sacred and secular music.
5. What is the significance of the fact that the Genesis record refers to Jubal as the "father" (i.e., the *ab*) of music but never its creator (*bara*)?
6. Discuss philosophically the difference between the terms "the development of music" and "the evolution of music."
7. Discuss the philosophical significance of God's creation being *ma'od* (3966) *towb* (2896).
8. Discuss the author's statement, "If one believes that Satan's perversion of music produces 'good music', then that person has just bequeathed Satan the ability to produce "perverted good" music."
9. Discuss the significance of the author's statement, "It stands to reason that God created music to be exceedingly good and that it is the objective of Satan to pervert it by negating its 'goodness'."
10. Discuss the significance of the quotation from Albert Barnes, "It was the original appointment (Gen. 1:26) that man should have dominion over the lower world, and be its absolute lord and sovereign. Had he continued in innocence this dominion would have been entire and perpetual. But man fell, and we do not see him exerting this dominion."

## 2

# Why Develop a Philosophy of Music?

### A Christian's *Worldview of Music

THERE WAS A TIME in my career when I believed that a music philosophy was always developed before the formation of a music worldview. Now I understand that worldview, and specifically music worldview, is the window through which musicians view what they believe is the truth about the nature and value of music. All Christian musicians have a music worldview, but being a Christian does not ensure that one's worldview of music is truly Christian. I define music worldview as how a musician perceives the whole of music in terms of what that musician considers the reality of what is right and wrong, appropriate or not appropriate concerning music.

This *presumed reality is then woven into a Christian's music philosophy. What is woven into the musician's philosophy from worldview will strongly shape how the musician views and deals with music in relationship to being in the world. Certainly, every Christian is in the world, but simply being in the world does not mean that a Christian is "of the world", i.e., is squeezed into the world's mold philosophically. Hopefully, the Christian will not be convinced by those who are not Christians to view the world and music as they do. The way that Christian musicians view the world will strongly influence the way they view music in this world

In St. Paul's Epistle to the Romans (12:1-2). he strongly admonishes Christians, "I beseech you therefore, brethren, by the mercies of God, that ye present your bodies a living sacrifice, holy, acceptable unto God, which is your reasonable service. And be not conformed to this world: but be ye transformed by the renewing of your mind, that ye may prove what is that good, and acceptable, and perfect, will of God." The words "not conformed" (*me suschematizo,* 3361, 4964) teach us that in the process of presenting ourselves to God we must not let ourselves be fashioned into the pattern of the world's paradigm. It is interesting to note that the original meaning of the word *paradigm* first appeared in English sometime during the 15th century and meant "an example or pattern". However, since the 1960s the word *paradigm* has developed the meaning of a framework containing a person's basic assumptions and ways of thinking and knowing.

## The Christian Musician Thinks Differently

The word *transformed* (*metamorphoo* 3339) used in the second verse of the twelfth chapter of Romans connotes the complete change that takes place when a Christian presents himself or herself as a living sacrifice to God. After this transformation, the Christian looks at life and music differently than the world looks at it. So perhaps the import of not being conformed is resisting the world's paradigm of life and *ipso facto* music and musicing.

The word *renewing*, used in the same verse, is derived from *anakainosis* (342). It means a complete renovating or reordering of one's thinking or paradigm (using its current meaning) about the realities of life. This renewing of one's worldview is necessary in order to prove (*dokimazo* 1381) that the Christian musician's philosophic worldview is *amenable to the will of God.

As a Christian musician reads God's Word and as the Holy Spirit gives the musician understanding of the many verses concerning music and musicing found in the Bible, a *Christocentric music worldview is developed. St. John 16:13 explains, "Howbeit when he, the Spirit of truth, is come, he will guide you into all truth: for he shall not speak of himself; but whatsoever he shall hear, that shall he speak: and he will shew you things to come." I am not claiming that this verse in the Bible has any esoteric meaning that is exclusive to the Christian musician, but I am contending that the truth contained in this verse extends to Christian musicians who are developing that window through which they will view the whole of music and musicing that we call a Christian musical worldviewThe Holy Spirit and God's Word will guide

## 2: Why Develop a Philosophy of Music?   43

the earnest Christian musician into "all truth" (*pas aletheia*, 3956, 225 thorough truths or verity).

A Christian musician's worldview and, as a *concomitant of this view the musician's musical worldview, will shape that individual's music philosophy. The way that a musician perceives music's place and importance in education, church, home, and *community will determine what he or she considers the reality of the nature and value of the whole of music. Christian musicians cannot develop their music philosophy beyond how they view music in the larger pictures of church, home, and community.

Often what musicians say they believe about music and how they actually music are somewhat different. This *disparity is generally caused by the musician's worldview of music and, based on the reality of that view, what the musician believes music will or will not do to the whole life of a Christian. Furthermore, based on the notion many Christians have, that music is not capable of harming a Christian spiritually, a Christian musician's worldview may become clouded by *skewed perception and thereby cause the development of a false view of music's power to affect the whole life of a Christian.

### Direction Determines Destiny Philosophically

One of the most unfortunate twenty-first century dilemmas involving Christian music philosophy is that many Christian musicians have not developed a series of systematic written beliefs concerning the nature and value of the whole of music. Many Christian musicians believe that music philosophy is somewhat like Jell-O gelatin with too much water mixed in it and therefore it is not capable of *solidifying into a *cohesive whole.

These musicians fail to realize how important it is to know where they are going musically. Remember, direction determines destiny. Musically, these musicians want to go west to Kansas City, Missouri but fail to realize they are going east on Interstate 70 toward Baltimore, Maryland. No matter how sincere they are about going to Kansas City, they will never get there going east from Indianapolis, Indiana. Beginning with a faulty premise will take the Christian musician in the wrong philosophical direction so that the rest of that musician's faulty conclusions topple like dominos all lined up in a row.

Those who conclude that music is amoral have to incorrectly assume that in the beginning God did not create music in a personal, real, objective way. They believe that God sees music from a distance through rose-tinted glasses. Since they believe that God does not have an ultimate opinion concerning music, He is not "there" when it comes to music.

A logically thinking Christian musician who believes in a real music creation rather than some kind of musical evolution is led to the systematic conclusion that because music "is" it is a part of God's real creation. Therefore, God is "there" concerning music. If God is "there" concerning music in the twenty-first century, then He cares about it in a most objective way. I repeat, God is "there" concerning music! Never forget that because God is actually "there" concerning music He is more than willing to guide us musically in this century. James 1:5 contains a wonderful philosophical promise: "If any of you lack wisdom, (*sophia*, 4678) let him ask of God, that giveth to all liberally, and upbraideth not; and it shall be given to him."

## Defending Philosophy Biblically

Philosophy is generally understood to be the pursuit of wisdom which is realized through logical reasoning. It is employed to critically analyze one's fundamental *presuppositions and beliefs about some area of life. Philosophy investigates the nature, value, principles, knowledge, and causes of that discipline. After logically and critically analyzing one's systematic beliefs, hopefully a unified field of wisely developed knowledge is established that becomes a system of values and beliefs by which one operates within that discipline. To the Christian this pursuit is always deeply grounded in Bible principles.

It seems only logical to not only find out what the word *philosophy* means, but also if it is ever mentioned in the Bible, before one attempts to write a book about music philosophy. The English word *philosophy* is only used once in the AV in St. Paul's First Epistle to the Colossians. He warns in chapter two, verse eight, "Beware lest any man spoil you through philosophy (*philosophia* 5385) and vain deceit, after the tradition of men, after the rudiments of the world, and not after Christ." The word *philosophia* is derived from *philosophos* (5386), a word that comes from the two Greek words *philos* (5384) and *sophos* (4680) which mean one who is fond of wise things, i.e., loves wisdom.

So let us consider philosophy's mention in the Bible. *Philosophia* is used only once in the New Testament in Colossians 2:8 and is translated philosophy in the AV; *philosophos* is also only used once in Acts 17:18 and is translated philosophers in the AV; *sophos* is used 23 times and is translated wise, wiser, wise men, and wise man in the AV. The word *wise* (*sophos*), as it is used in the Bible, means having knowledge, good judgment, and wisdom when it is referring to men and "all wise" when it refers to God. The English word *wisdom* is used about fifty-five times in the AV New Testament. The word *wisdom* is found in 266 verses in the AV Old and New Testaments combined. The exact number of references is not important, but it is important that the Bible speaks so often of wisdom.

It seems logical to deduce that there is much support in the Bible for a Christian musician to establish systematic beliefs about the nature and value of the whole of music based on wisdom found both in and out of the Bible. Much of the wisdom concerning music and musicing may be found in the Bible. However, I do not claim to believe in *sola scriptura* as the only source of wisdom concerning music philosophy. I do, however, believe in *sola scriptura* in the sense that Scripture alone is the authoritative rule of faith and practice and that what the Bible does teach us about music is authoritative.

There are many other sources of knowledge that also help the Christian musician develop a congruent music philosophy. I am often reminded of Jesus' parable of the steward in Luke 16:8 which states, "And the lord commended the unjust steward, because he had done wisely: for the children of this world are in their generation wiser than the children of light." Although this parable had absolutely nothing to say about music, there is a principle in Jesus' parable that applies to us all. Stewardship requires getting the job done with the help of others.

Jesus was not commending the unjust steward for his unjustness.

Jesus said in Luke 16:9, "And I say unto you, Make to yourselves friends of the mammon of unrighteousness; that, when ye fail, they may receive you into everlasting habitations." It is difficult to know all that Jesus was teaching in this statement, but it appears that He was saying that we can gather wisdom from people who are not Christians. However, Christians are warned in Colossians 2:8, "Beware lest any man spoil you [i.e., lead you astray] through philosophy (*philosophia*, 5385) and vain deceit (*kenos apate*, 2756, 539, i.e., empty delusion), after the tradition of men, after the rudiments of the world, and not after Christ."

## What is a Music Philosophy?

What is a music philosophy? It is *a series of systematic beliefs concerning the nature and value of the whole of music*. What is a Christ-centered philosophy of music? It is a series of systematic beliefs (statements) concerning the nature and value of the whole of music in which Christ has preeminence— thus we use the term *Christocentric*. Christ's teachings are at the center of this philosophy which is the antithesis of a humanistic music philosophy where man is the center of all philosophic endeavors. If we are going to keep God at the center of our beliefs concerning the nature and value of all of music endeavor, then we must, as Colossians 2:8 warns, "See to it that no one takes you captive through hollow and deceptive philosophy, which depends on human tradition and the basic principles of this world rather than on Christ" (NIV).

In order to discuss the development of a philosophy of music we must be able to define what it is. Many church musicians and music educators that claim they do not have a music philosophy are outspoken about what should or should not happen in church music and in music education. Although they declare that they do not have a philosophy of music, they do have one; it just is not systematic, thorough or written. These beliefs should be written and they should be systematic. A Christian musician who does not want to be ashamed must "Study to shew thyself approved [i.e., tested or approved 1384] unto God, a workman that needeth not to be ashamed, rightly dividing the word of truth" (2 Timothy 2:15).

# 2: Why Develop a Philosophy of Music? 47

Since philosophy is the love and pursuit of wisdom, Christian musicians must not develop a music belief system based on the rudiments (*stoicheioin,* 4747) of this world. To paraphrase this passage of Scripture, do not let the world (*kosmos,* 2889) spoil (*esomai, sulagoges,* 2071, 4812) or seduce you when you develop your philosophy, by arranging or ordering it the way the world orders or arranges the philosophical principles of music and musicing. God (*thesis) orders things a certain way and the world, controlled or arranged by Satan (*antithesis), has confused or rearranged the order of things. Do not let the world take you captive by believing the empty delusion caused by what it believes to be the nature and value of music.

Without systematic guiding principles a Christian musician will likely make musical choices that are faulty. Biblical principles that relate to musicing must be the foundation of a philosophy of music. The Christian musician must be careful to analyze the fundamental grounds and concepts that govern all music and musicing to be sure that all philosophical beliefs are Christocentric. Furthermore, all of a Christian musician's philosophy of music must be in alignment to the matrix of God and His Word, which is His divinely inspired guidebook for Christian musicians.

## A Music Philosophy Is a *Belief System

A music philosophy is a belief system by which a musician governs musical activities. Utilizing a philosophy of music will help a musician make wise musical choices. Music philosophers refer to a music philosophy as a belief system because it systematically justifies a musician's musical choices. If it is not biblical it is without doubt faulty, and if it is not systematic and congruent with other Christian beliefs, it is incomplete at best.

Someone, along with Frank Peretti, needs to herald the message that there is a matrix of "This Present Darkness." A *matrix* is something from which something else develops or exudes. On one side there is God's matrix and on the other, the matrix of this world, which is influenced by Satan. Matthew 6:24 explains that "No man can serve two masters: for either he will hate the one, and love the other; or else he will hold to the one, and despise the other. Ye cannot serve God and mammon."

Christian musicians must realize that both God's plan for music and Satan's plan to pervert it exist in the twenty-first century and that they are at war with each other. Simply put, a musician will be constrained to follow some matrix because it is impossible to go in two directions musically at the same time. Christian musicians should understand that all philosophical thought comes from some matrix and that all musical actions will exude from that philosophical matrix. The idea that all musical philosophical thought comes from God is faulty. The *nemesis of God-given principles of musicing is Satan's musical matrix, developed from his desire to pervert God's creation which, of course, includes music.

For centuries philosophers held on to the hope of a unified field of knowledge, and for the most part, that field of knowledge shared a congruent epistemology and methodology. Georg Hegel changed philosophy forever. His philosophical influence reached beyond philosophy in general and changed how some music philosophers thought about music. Francis Schaefer made two observations about Hegel's influence on philosophical thought that are important to our discussion of music philosophy. "He changed the rules of the game in two areas: *epistemology*, the theory of knowledge and the limits and validity of knowledge: and *methodology*, the method by which we approach the question of truth and knowing."[1] When Hegel changed epistemology by altering the limits and validity of "knowing", he created a plethora of confusion concerning what is valid about the nature and value of music. Second, he forever altered *synthesis thinker's ability to "know" what the biblical or classical principles are concerning musical ministry.

When Hegel altered methodology by his new synthesis-thesis, he nearly destroyed progressive contemporary Christian musicians' ability to communicate effectively with traditional church musicians. Why? Thesis thinking musicians think in terms of thesis (right) and antithesis (wrong). Synthesis thinkers think in terms of a "truth" that is somewhere in between truth and error. They never think in terms of right and wrong. These two diametrically opposing philosophical views

## 2: Why Develop a Philosophy of Music? 49

march to the beat of a different drum. For decades, secular music education philosophy has left no room for the terms right and wrong when it comes to working music education praxis.

Synthesis and thesis thinking music educators not only *think different things* about music education, they also *think differently* about music education. What this means is they have different thinking processes and different connotation words for the very same aspects of music education and all musicing in general. The same observations can be made of the same kinds of thinkers when applied to music ministry.

Another major difference is the methodology or the way that synthesis thinkers go about the process of "knowing". A common misunderstanding is that synthesis thinkers who are modernists, postmodernists or post-postmodernists do not have a sense of "knowing". This is far from accurate because they "know" that there are no absolutes, and there is no right and wrong, no appropriateness or inappropriateness in church music, or any music for that matter. They "know" that it is impossible to know that something is wrong or right on the basis of a thought (thesis) and its opposite (antithesis). They "know" that the truth of what is right in music is always somewhere in between right and wrong in that mystic amalgamation called synthesis. They "know" that this "new truth" produces a new thesis which is a synthesis-thesis.

**Is There Philosophical Truth Concerning Music?**

Christian musicians who utilize synthesis thinking "know" that we who are traditional thesis thinkers cannot know the truth, and that they can "know" the truth which is a connotation truth based on truth and error. Their "knowing" brings order to their otherwise absurd musical surroundings, since it authenticates their music philosophy by the very act of their free will which is autonomous.

So, when the epistemology and the methodology are changed, music philosophy and music praxis become non-discussible (or at least they need no defense), not only because they are autonomous, but also because the connotation words used in explaining this new philosophy of music have drastically different meanings than their traditional counterparts. So "knowing" does not stop with *synthesis thinking. "Knowing" only changes its *truth basis.

In the midst of the relativism that was so wide spread in the 1960s, Francis Schaeffer succinctly explained his truth basis.

> "It is an important principle to remember, in the contemporary interest in communication and in language study, that the biblical presentation is that, though we do not have exhaustive truth, we have from the Bible what I term 'true truth'. In this way we know truth about God, true truth about man and something truly about nature. Thus on the basis of the Scriptures, while we do not have exhaustive knowledge, we have true and unified knowledge."[2]

The student of music philosophy needs to know, as we enter the twenty-first century where relativism now reigns, that Christians who were biblical thesis thinkers did not cave in to synthesis thinking in the twentieth century

Robert Berglund divided the process of finding truth that is not specifically found in the Bible truth as being divided into two categories, "*Revelational truth* is the area of knowledge verifiable by experience but not by scientific method (i.e., a believer's faith). Empirical truth is the area of knowledge verifiable by scientific method."[3] Christian musicians understand that revelational truth refers to having the Holy Spirit's guidance but sometimes they are not as familiar with verifiable empirical scientific truth. The scientific method may be defined as a research method that isolates a problem and then gathers relevant information about the problem. Utilizing this method enables one to develop a hypothesis based on the data and test it empirically. Being equipped with the true truth of the Bible and revelational and empirical truth is absolutely necessary before one communicates with the relative both-and synthesis truth which many twenty-first century Christian musicians believe.

There is little hope that these *synthesis-thinking musicians who believe in a relative truth that is found somewhere between truth and error will dialogue with a conservative in traditional thesis connotations, so it is necessary for the conservative to understand how synthesis thinkers think. If we do not talk to them on their terms there will be little or no communication! If we are ever going to communicate with musicians whose music praxis is based on non-traditional forms of church music, we must understand how they think. Many sincere rock-based church music and music education programs are carried out by musicians that have never committed their philosophical basis of music to pen and ink. Those who have, quite often do not base their philosophy on Bible truth.

If a conservative Christian musician, who believes in the current appropriateness of traditional forms of music, is ever going to be able to communicate with a musician who is convinced that rock-based music is a better vehicle for praising God than traditional forms of sacred music, the conservative musician must help that musician to think differently. Harshly criticizing a person's personal faith and music philosophy is a fatal approach. It is doomed from the outset because it is a negative, demeaning, demoralizing, and often de-Christianizing methodology. Instead, we as conservatives should use a positive approach to help liberal musicians change the way they think.

**Thinking Before we Act**

Conservative Christian thinkers need to think before they speak. Cutting, harsh words are hard to take back. There is never a second chance to make a first impression. If conservative musicians want to wrap their musical robes around themselves they can, but if they do, they will never be instrumental in helping musicians who are pluralistic synthesis thinkers change their thinking.

When I was doing research for my book *Church Music Matters,* I would read a book by a conservative and immediately think, "This is good, this is exactly what I believe." Then I realized that I do not like to read after those who do not agree with me. Through my reading the Holy Spirit was able to whisper to me, "You are not a good listener." As a matter of fact, I have found out that not only was I not a good listener, sometimes I would not listen at all! I wasn't the slightest bit interested in knowing exactly how a synthesis thinking musician thinks.

Through all the above thought processes, as I searched my heart, I came to the realization that if my philosophical writings were ever going to help a musician who disagreed with my philosophical and praxial* views, I must proceed with a heart without rancor. If I am half as interested in helping others think differently, I must be kind in what I write and what I say. 1 Corinthians 13:4a says, "Charity (*agape* 26 love) suffereth long, and is kind..." If my music philosophy is going to be not only Christocentric but also Christ-like, it must be developed in such a way that in following its precepts I suffer long and am kind.

## Why Musicians do What They Do

This book is largely about how people think. If one wishes to gain insight into why musicians do what they do, then one must learn not only "what they think", but also "how they think". As has been stated, modern, postmodern, and post-postmodern synthesis thinkers not only think different things about music, they also think differently than the thesis thinkers do about music. They think from a different epistemology.

The reason one must know how they think is that understanding their way of "knowing" will enable a thesis thinker to discuss the non-discussible with the synthesis thinker. Remember that the non-rational, non-logical autonomy of synthesis thinkers removes all need or responsibility for discussing or defending philosophical basis of musical thought since they consider themselves free independent thinkers without responsibility to anyone or any philosophy. Many times these Christian musicians believe that they are on a winding musical journey with God that results in constant philosophical change. If such musicians are in leadership positions, *leadershift is considered a strength rather than a confusing and upsetting dilemma for others who are trying to follow their musical direction.

One approach to discussion is for the thesis thinker is to start by stating as clearly and precisely as possible exactly what one believes philosophically about the nature and value of music. It is a mistake to start by asking postmodern or post-postmodern man to prove anything about music philosophy. Instead, offer biblical examples, warnings, admonitions and absolutes concerning music. Remember that to twenty-first century man music philosophy is often non-discussible, non-rational, non-logical, and without congruent explanation. Many Christian musicians in this century believe that the Bible contains but does not necessarily embody truth, or is the whole truth or true-truth. To these musicians truth is mixed with error. It is often hard for the thesis thinker to understand that many Christian musicians actually believe that the Bible not only contains truth concerning music but that also it contains error. These synthesis-thinking musicians have a non-rational, non-logical autonomous faith in Christ that is not totally Bible based. Their autonomous faith goes beyond the truth of Scripture since synthesis faith is based on their personal encounter with Christ that does not come under the scrutiny of Scripture. These musicians may not even believe in the deity of Christ, the Trinity, the virgin birth, a literal hell, eternal punishment, the witness of the Spirit, a personal relationship with Christ, a literal creation, or original sin. So, it is important to operate from the presupposition that the Bible is the infallible, completely accurate, inspired Word of God and that it does not contain a mixture of truth and error.

### "True Truth" Not Exhaustive Truth

Francis Schaeffer often spoke and wrote of what he called "true truth". He was famous among Christian conservatives for his belief that we could have knowledge of this truth. 1 Corinthians 13:12 gives us some clarification of how we now "know" when it states, "For now we see through a glass, darkly; but then face to face: now I know in part; but then shall I know even as also I am known." According to A.T. Robertson, the word *epiginosko* (1921) which was translated "shall I know" could be more accurately rendered "I shall fully (*epi-*) know."[4] The import of this verse is that, although at this time our knowledge is not exhaustive and is therefore incomplete, when we see God face to face in Heaven our knowledge will be exhaustive.

Although the Bible does not give us exhaustive truth about music, it does give us true truth about music. What the Bible does say about music is accurate and true because it "…is given by inspiration of God, and is profitable for doctrine, for reproof, for correction, for instruction in righteousness" (2 Timothy 3:16). Because it is "God breathed" it is completely true. Perhaps in past generations it may not have been necessary to remind church musicians and music educators that the references to music in the Bible are completely true, relevant and profitable to all musicians, but it certainly is in this post-postmodern world.

It was only a few generations ago that the United States was known for its strong *Judeo-Christian ethic. Now whether or not the Bible is accurate in what it teaches about music and musicing is almost a moot point to many Christian musicians, because the basis on which they develop a music philosophy does not include what the Bible says about the nature and value of the whole of music. Although they may quote a few verses in the Bible that mention music, what they say and what they do is often diametrically opposed.

Christian musicians must realize that all the truth we have available to us in the Bible is congruent truth. The reason that so many Christian musicians' music philosophies are not congruent is that much of their study has been isolated from the context of the whole of Scripture. Francis Schaeffer stated, "We have studied our exegesis as exegesis, our theology as theology, our philosophy as philosophy; we study something about art as art; we study music as music, without understanding that these are things of man, and the things of man are not unrelated parallel lines."[5] Because of this isolation of the various disciplines, more and more Christian musicians see no problem with studying music as music without bringing it into amenability with the Lordship of Jesus Christ. It is no wonder that there are so many *incongruencies in the way that many twenty-first century Christians music.

The way that a Christian *musicer musics is influenced by basic knowledge and understanding of the nature and value of music. Furthermore, the musicer's perceived understanding of music is influenced by that musician's worldview of music, whether that worldview is based on truth or error. If a musician's music worldview is inconsistent with the principles of the separated, changed life of a Christian, then it is incongruent no matter how well the musicer musics.

## We Know that We Know Only in Part

So, since we are very aware as Christian musicians that "we know in part" as 1 Corinthians 13:9 tells us, what do we do with what we know? The word *know* used in this verse is derived from *ginosko* (1097) which means to be aware, understand, or to be sure. Again, let me say that although we do not have exhaustive knowledge from the teachings of the Bible, we have congruent knowledge. Therefore, we can know from the truth basis found in the Bible. We can utilize the principles of musicing that are taught in Scripture to build a Christocentric music philosophy. Having partial knowledge should not keep Christian musicians from using the true truth that they do know and understand. Since the Bible does not answer every question concerning church music and music education, a long broad study of music is absolutely necessary if a Christian is to understand the nature and value of music at its deepest levels.

1 Corinthians 13:12 sheds more light on our knowledge and understanding, "For now we see through a glass, darkly; but then face to face: now I know in part; but then shall I know even as also I am known." Donald Metz believes that "The word darkly (*ainigmati* 135) actually means a 'riddle' and thus suggests an enigma or an obscure intimation. Hence the word as the apostle uses it means obscurely, darkly or imperfectly."[6]

We know that an enigma is something that is mysterious, puzzling, or difficult to understand. So, the Christian musician should not be discouraged by the fact that the apostle stated, "now we see through a glass darkly," or that he changed to the first person and further explained that "now I know in part." The Apostle Paul explained that in this life we often have to gain understanding and knowledge by looking through a mirror at things that are puzzling. The Christian musician should not be discouraged that Scriptures about music, which are 2000-4000 years old, are often difficult to understand. The musician must recognize that many of the precepts taught in the Bible that do not concern music are just as difficult to understand as those that concern music. However, that fact has not deterred biblical historians, exegetes and commentators from writing multiplied thousands of volumes on other things that are taught in the Bible. It is unfortunate that so few Christian musicians have written about the music of the Bible in the last 200 years. Instead they have concentrated on the problems we have with our musicing rather than with the positive things that the Bible teaches about music.

Raymond Brown explains that although St. Paul uses the imagery of seeing through a mirror dimly when he writes about knowing, "He does not mean that our knowledge is inadequate but that it is limited when compared to what we will know in the future."[7] When we get to heaven and are ushered into God's presence we will have perfect knowledge, but that does not mean that we cannot trust the knowledge that we have in this life. Some of the things we read in the Bible about ancient music and musicing have now, centuries later, become somewhat esoteric and are to us, because of our lack of knowledge, only indications or hints of what actually happened in ancient Israel. They are mere intimations to us because we read the Old and New Testaments through Western eyes and Western understandings.

For instance, we understand *heptatonic scales with half steps between three and four and seven and eighth in light of the music of the *Occident. When we study an ancient musical scale that seems to be a major or minor scale because of its construction, we expect that scale to follow the rules of music theory of Western Europe. This is possibly why so many musicologists before Suzanne Haïk-Vantoura were not able to successfully decipher the *te'amim* of the Old Testament. One of the main impediments to European theorists deciphering the *te'amim* was also the fact that in the music of the Occident the tonic is always the first note of the musical scale. In the music of the Bible the tonic is medial, i.e., the third note of the scale rather than the first note.

Why I am discussing music theory in the middle of a discussion of music philosophy in Christian perspective? We tend to view ancient Bible music and musicing through the dark glass of the rules of Western music. Some of what we read about music in ancient Israel will require reading the works of Jewish music scholars. They are practically the only scholars who have consistently studied the music of the

Old Testament over the last 2000 years. However, reading and believing the works of Jewish music scholars has been a pill too difficult for most twentieth and twenty-first Christian musicians and Protestant exegetes of Scripture to swallow.

If anyone knows what happened musically in ancient Israel, it is those who have for centuries studied the music of the Bible. In reading the exotic hypotheses of Christian musicians and Protestant biblical scholars over the last 100 years, one will see very clearly that music of the Bible was not their expertise or in many cases their interest. In many instances Bible scholars have failed to make any mention of verses of Scripture that are concerned with music. So, it is of little wonder that we are in such a mess concerning the value of what is written in the Bible about music and its application to twenty-first century musicing inside and outside of the church.

Let me reiterate the fact that although we do not have complete exhaustive truth from what is written in the Bible about music, what was written is completely accurate. In modern translations of the Bible, most translation teams have not included a music scholar and certainly not a student of ancient music. The problem has not been that there were errors in the *consonantal text. The problem has been that because the language scholars who have prepared our modern translations have not understood music of ancient Israel and their neighbors, they have perpetuated many of the misunderstandings of music found in earlier translations.

**Music Study is Essential**

It is the responsibility of every Christian performer, music educator, and worship leader to "Study to shew thyself approved unto God, a workman that needeth not to be ashamed, rightly dividing the word of truth" (2 Timothy 2:15). We also have the responsibility to study the many word study sources available to us today. There are more of these treatises available to us today than there has ever been in the history of Western civilization. There is also a myriad of great scholarly writings about the ancient music of Bible times that have been written by Jewish historians and musicologists. So, when we apply what Timothy is saying here to the field of music, we must study

God's Word thoroughly enough that we are not ashamed (*anepaischuntos* 422) of what we believe and teach (expounds *orthotomeo* 3718) philosophically about music because it is correct and *irreprehensible.

Christian musicians tend to avoid the works of the Jewish music scholars simply because of the many theological differences and because there is a general tendency to only read and respect the works of Christian musicians. Almost all the accurate knowledge of Bible music has been reported by Jewish scholars and other secular musicologists that have not given a clear profession of faith in Jesus Christ. Although the study of music in the Bible is not necessarily a strict study of ancient Jewish music, the musicians mentioned in the Bible were most often Jews. So, it is logical that one should read the works of scholarly Jewish historians and musicologists. Because most of the Christian writers over the past centuries have not been music scholars or musicologists, they most often say little or nothing of value about the mention of music in the Bible. However, there are a few exceptions to this tendency and these writers are quoted often in my writings.

## Is All Scripture Inspired and Accurate?

It is important to understand that postmodern and post-postmodern Christian musicians do not believe 2 Timothy 3:16 when it asserts, "All scripture is given by inspiration of God, and is profitable for doctrine, for reproof, for correction, for instruction in righteousness." Many of them believe that the references to music in the Bible have outlived their relevancy. Remember that the Bible will stand all the tests of validity and reliability since it is a timeless true truth and not merely "truth-and" or "some-truth" or merely a work "containing truth".

The word *inspiration* in this verse is translated from *theopneustos* (2315) which is a *hapax legomenon,* so we do not have other context to help establish its meaning. It means that all of the Holy Writ has come to us through inspiration which is God breathed. This means that God directly influenced the human writers of Scripture and therefore, all of the God breathed words are the exact words that God intended to be written. So, the thesis of the conservative Christian musician is that the true truth of the Bible concerning music is to be trusted to be accurate in the twenty-first century.

After explaining this thesis, invite the synthesis thinker to express thoughts or opinions about the statements about music that are mentioned in the Bible. Be sure to give the synthesis thinker opportunity to completely express his or her philosophical basis. Then ask questions like, What are your presuppositions concerning the Bible and its relationship to truth? On what basis do you derive your music ministry philosophy? On what basis do you exclude profundity, sacred vs. profane, suitability and appropriateness in religious music? What parts of the Bible do you consider to be authentic? On what basis do you "know" that the Bible is not accurate and divinely inspired?

This discussion of how twenty-first century musicians think is by no means complete, but it gives ideas of how to proceed with a discussion of why this musician believes what he or she believes. The objective here is not to argue with the synthesis thinker but rather to get this musician to express his or her way of "knowing." Many times it will help the synthesis thinker to explore his or her belief system. It is not only important for you to understand how this musician thinks but it is also extremely important for the synthesis thinker to be aware of his or her own presuppositions that serve as a basis for music ministry philosophy.

Remember it is not the responsibility of the conservative synthesis-thinking musician to change the thinking of modern and postmodern and post-postmodern man. Our responsibility is to be Christ-like, kind and patient. The most we can do is to present our beliefs, and to help others to explore theirs. It is the work of the Holy Spirit to guide Christian musicians into all truth.

It is a basic presupposition of this book and all my writings that all musicing is based on some philosophy and that this philosophy is fundamentally based on some matrix. Music philosophy is the foundation from which all musical actions exude. A sound philosophy of music ministry is founded on principles much deeper than mere likes and dislikes since it is based on God's matrix.

A word of caution is in order for those who are conservative in their philosophical positions concerning music. It is arrogant for anyone to believe that he or she has a corner on truth as though no one else can have knowledge of music's nature and value. There are areas where the Bible is silent about music and musicing and scientific method has produced no logical evidence to support a particular musical position. In such cases, tolerance is in order. The fact that the Holy Spirit has checked a Christian about a musical choice is not concrete evidence that no other Christian musician should music in that way. Christian musicians must always try to understand the difference between personal musical convictions, which are not necessarily a mandate for all Christian musicians, and biblical principles of musicing that are not negotiable.

## Is a Written Music Philosophy Important?

I am surprised that there are so few Christian musicians who are publishing material on church music and music education philosophy. I am thankful to those individual Christian musicians, churches, Christian schools, Christian colleges and universities, who have committed their philosophy to pen and ink. In such cases these writers' philosophies are often a well-developed series of systematic statements (beliefs) concerning the nature and value of the whole of music that serves as a basis for that person's or organization's direction in music. Many of these well thought out philosophies of music ministry and/or music education have proven adequate to serve as everyday guides for all their music actions. At the personal level, these well thought out, congruent, Bible-based music philosophies have served as a concomitant of these Christian musicians' whole life philosophy.

It is unfortunate that so many Christian musicians have never taken the time to write out their music philosophy. The result is often a philosophy that is in practice haphazard or at least a homespun way of "doing." As I mentioned earlier, some Christian musicians whom I have met in my travels over the past thirty years deny that they even need a written music philosophy. They often hide behind the excuse that they are not trained music philosophers or that they have never even had the opportunity to study music philosophy. What they do not know is that everyone has a philosophy of music. Even in the smallest of communities there is often a barbershop or a feed store with some chairs for philosophers. Just bring up the subject of music and these grass-roots philosophers, who may not know the names of the lines and spaces, will tell you exactly what is right and wrong with music today.

Every Christian should have a written philosophy of music and it should be Christocentric. How does one go about developing a Christ-centered Bible-based philosophy? St. John 4:21-24 emphasizes that a philosophy of worship must begin with truth.

> "Ye worship ye know not what: we know what we worship: for Salvation is of the Jews. But the hour cometh, and now is, when the true worshipers shall worship the Father in *spirit* and in *truth*: for the Father seeketh such to worship him. God is a Spirit: and they that worship him must worship him in *spirit* and in *truth*."

Truth is essential in the development of a Christocentric philosophy. Jesus said in St. John 14:6, "I am the way, the truth, and the life: no man cometh unto the Father, but by me." The Pharisees admitted in St. Matthew 22:16, "Master, we know that thou art true, and teachest the way of God in truth..." One of the major problems of music philosophies today is that so many of them are just not based on the truth of the Bible. Much too often one may hear statements like, "The reason I do what I do is because this is just how things are, here where I minister," or "I'm in Rome, so I have to do as the Romans do." I would be quick to admit that ministers of music must be aware of where they are ministering. However, music ministry must be based on truth, not error. St. John 16:13 reminds us that God will make truth known to the Christian when he states, "Howbeit when he, the Spirit of truth is come, he will guide you into all truth: for he shall not speak of himself; but whatsoever he shall hear, that shall he speak: and he will shew you things to come."

Proverbs 23:7 warns us, "For as he thinketh in his heart, so is he." There is no doubt that the Christian musician who is constantly captive to what the world thinks about music will eventually shape a music philosophy after the "synthesis" thinking of the world. Philippians 4:7-8 gives us the answer to a Christ centered mindset:

> "And the peace of God, which passeth all understanding, shall keep your *hearts* and *minds* through Christ Jesus. Finally, brethren, whatsoever things are *true*, whatsoever things are honest (venerable), whatsoever things are just, whatsoever things are pure, whatsoever things are lovely, whatsoever things are of good report; if there be any virtue, and if there be any praise, *think on these things*."

The Scriptures given above are admonishments to Christians to guard their thinking.

If musicians follow a path of philosophical pursuit independent of God's truth the result will likely be a philosophy void of correct judgment. Romans 1:28 tells us, "And even as they did not like to retain God in their knowledge, God gave them over to a reprobate mind, to do those things which are not convenient." The word *echo* (2192), rendered retain in this verse, means "to keep" or "hold on to" something. Because they did not recognize God in their knowledge or in other words because they did not acknowledge or hold on to His truth in their philosophy, they were given over to a mindset that was void of good judgment (*adokimos* 96).

What should be the basis of a Christian musician's philosophy? Colossians 3:15-16 gives the answer:

> "And let *the peace of God* rule in your hearts, to the which also ye are called in one body; and be ye thankful. Let the *word of Christ* dwell in you richly in all wisdom; teaching and admonishing one another in psalms and hymns and spiritual songs, singing with grace in your hearts to the Lord."

Notice that music philosophy that gives "the peace of God" must be based on the *logos Christos* (3056 5547), i.e., the Word of Christ. Hebrews 1:2 explains that God "Hath in these last days spoken unto us by his son, whom he hath appointed heir of all things, by whom also he made the worlds." St. John 1:1 tells us, "In the beginning was the Word, and the Word was with God, and the Word was God." Verse 14 of that chapter identifies Jesus as the Word when it says, "And the Word was made flesh, and dwelt among us." No true knowledge of Christ may be derived independently of his Word. Therefore, a Christian's philosophy must be Scripture based and must follow biblical principles. All music philosophy must come under the Lordship of Christ. Failure to compile these biblical principles and commit to a written philosophy will allow the Christian musician to be unaware of inconsistencies in personal philosophy and praxis.

**Music Philosophy Must Please God**

How should a Christian musician develop a philosophy of music? The first thing to do, in my judgment, would be to read the more than 600 references to music in the Bible. The safest place to study music is in the infallible inspired Word of God. It would seem that Christians would start by reading the Bible and studying its many examples of worship through music. Studying how music was used for therapy, false and true worship, harlotry, weddings, funerals, and public entertainment, should be the basis for understanding how music was used in public and private worship as well as on secular occasions in the history of ancient Israel and their neighbors.

Read Revelation 19:12-13 and you will see that Christ, our judge, "whose eyes were as a flame of fire," was called "The Word of God". So, since we will be judged by the "Word of God", it behooves us to not only build our music philosophies upon it but also follow it in the enactment of our duties as Christian musicians.

Every honest Christian musician that I have met wants to please the people to whom he or she ministers. However, music ministry is not ultimately about pleasing the people, but rather pleasing God. Galatians 1:10 brings us face to face with the dilemma of pleasing men or God. "For do I now persuade men, or God? Or do I seek to please men? For if I yet pleased men, I should not be the servant of Christ." No honest church musician would say, "I hope the people hate the music we sing this morning." Rather we all hope that our music ministry is accepted by the body of believers as well as by the seekers who attend our church services. However, even if the crowd believes that we are their enemy when we sing the truth to them, we are not. Read Galatians 4 and you will see that St. Paul dealt with the importance of telling the people the truth.

Romans 12:2 warns us that we must "...prove what is that good, and acceptable, and perfect will of God," and Ephesians 5:10 states, "Proving what is acceptable unto the Lord." Both verses reinforce the importance of what God thinks. Have you ever mused over the truism that God thinks about music? Yes, God thinks about music. Not only does music matter to us, but it also matters to God.

## Wise Choices of Secular and Sacred Music

A Christian musician's responsibility does not end with sacred music but it also extends to secular music. It does not seem to occur to some Christians that the whole of music must come under the lordship of Christ. I define secular music as that which pertains to temporal matters rather than with spiritual matters. So, secular music is music that is not religious in nature. Sacred music is that which is hallowed by religious association. Secular music that is anti-Christ, blasphemous, or irreverent does not belong in the life of the Christian. However, music that is not religious but is clean and wholesome in nature does belong in the life of a Christian. Secular music that is concerned with that which relates to life in general is many times of a wholesome nature. If it is of a morally sound nature it is amenable to the Lordship of Christ. Christians may include all secular music that passes the tests and conditions of Christ-centered living.

When it comes to the matter of secular and sacred music it is not either-or but rather wise choices of both. Although it would appear to be simpler philosophically for the Christian to only include the use of sacred music, there is no biblically sound reason not to include secular music that is amenable to the Lordship of Christ. There is no biblical conflict created by a Christian including clean secular music as well as sacred music. The two do not oppose each other. There is not anything inherently opposing about music that addresses itself to religious matters and music that does not address itself to religious matters.

One of the unfortunate philosophical positions of some Chris-

## 2: Why Develop a Philosophy of Music? 65

tian musicians is that all religious music is appropriate in the life of a Christian and conversely that all non-religious (secular) music is inappropriate in the life of a Christian. On the surface it would seem that including only religious music would greatly simplify music philosophy. This faulty praxis only complicates matters since it removes all need and responsibility for the Christian to prove what is "acceptable unto the Lord." This paradigm has spawned generations of Christian musicians who believe that there are no absolutes, rules, or standards of sacred or secular music. To them, there is only one guideline – it has to be religious in nature. Under this mindset, sacred and secular music is a standardless art that does not have to be evaluated or pass any tests of suitability and appropriateness or correctness or incorrectness.

A Christian musician without a well-defined congruent Bible-based music philosophy is like a ship in the middle of the sea without a compass. Since a Christian music philosophy must transcend regional cultural boundaries, it cannot be based totally on environment, community, or traditions but rather on that which is compatible with what the Word of God teaches. If we are to survive in the twenty-first century, Christians who are church and Christian school musicians must develop carefully defined music philosophies that are congruent with the Bible principles. These principles must serve as the foundation of music philosophy. These standards must be systematic and must cover the nature and value of the whole of both sacred and secular music.

### Endnotes

1. Francis Schaefer, *Escape from Reason* (Downers Grove, IL: InterVarsity Press, 1968), 41.
2. *Ibid*, 21.
3. Robert Berglund, *A Philosophy of Church Music* (Chicago: Moody Press,1985), 4.
4. Archibald T. Robertson, *Epistles of Paul.* Vol. 4 of *Word Pictures in the New Testament*, (Nashville: Broadman Press, 1931), 180.
5. Schaeffer, *Escape from Reason*, 12.
6. Donald Metz, *I Corinthians.* Vol. 8 of *Beacon Bible Commentary*, (Kansas City,

MO: Beacon Hill Press of Kansas City, 1968), 445.
7. Raymond Brown, *1 Corinthians.* Vol. 10 of *The Broadman Bible Commentary*, (Nashville: Broadman Press, 1970), 374.

### Chapter Two Word Meanings

**Amenable**— a Christian musician's beliefs are affected and controlled by what is taught in the Bible.

**Antithesis**— as used in this book, the opposite of the original thought, i.e., the thesis which came originally from God and is therefore true truth. The opposite of true truth is error which is its antithesis.

**Belief system**— is a fixed congruent set of beliefs that form a basis for a music philosophy.

**Christocentric**— connotes a music philosophy that is centered on doing the will of Christ.

**Cohesive**— that which tends to unify, harmonize, or be consistent.

**Community**— is defined in this book as joint participation; common character or activity; social state or condition under which musicing takes place.

**Concomitant**— that which naturally accompanies or is associated something else.

**Consonantal text**— the original text of the Hebrew Old Testament without the vowel points.

***Hapax legomenon***— is a term that is used only once in Scripture.

**Heptatonic scale**— a scale that consists of seven pitches per octave.

**Incongruencies**— tenets of a philosophy that are incompatible with what is suitable or appropriate.

**Irreprehensible**— that which is free from blame or reproach.

**Judeo Christian ethic**— refers to an ethic that is based in the common foundations of Judaism and Christianity.

**Leadershift**— a concept of looking at business propositions in community. Without solid reasoning these leaders shift, seemingly changing "for the sake of change." The problem with this leadership notion is that God never makes truth a matter of the newest bright ideas of twenty-first century Christians.

**Musicer**— This term, coined by David Elliot, refers to the one who is the doer of the music, i.e., the performer.

**Nemesis**— as used in this case, a source of harm or ruin.

**Praxial**— refers to the action of carrying out an intentional way of doing something

**Presumed reality**— to take for granted that what the musician believes about music is true without evidence or proof that this belief represents reality about music.

**Presuppositions**— things that one supposes or believes in advance; an antecedent condition.

# 2: Why Develop a Philosophy of Music?

**Skewed**— biased or distorted in such a way that a concept is regarded as inaccurate, unfair, or misleading.

***Sola scriptura***— the Protestant Christian doctrine that the Bible is the supreme authority in all matters of doctrine and practice.

**Solidifying**— in this usage it means making strong or united.

**Synthesis-thinking**— the consideration of thesis and antithesis in the Hegelian method in which the answer is always derived from a combination of both thesis and antithesis called synthesis.

**Thesis**— as used in this book, the original thought which came from God and is therefore, true truth.

**Truth basis**— the presumed facts about something that form the foundation for what a musician believes about music.

**Worldview of Music**— a particular philosophy of life or conception of the world as it relates to how a musician views music, i.e., a philosophical window through which a musician views music.

## Chapter Two Questions for Discussion

1. How does a Christian musician's worldview differ from a nonbeliever's worldview?
2. Why does a Christian musician think differently about music than a nonbeliever?
3. Why does a Christian musician need a biblical defense for a music philosophy?
4. In simple terms explain what a music philosophy really is practically.
5. Explain what the author meant by stating that a music philosophy is a belief system.
6. Discuss your view of whether or not there is truth concerning our musicing unto God.
7. Discuss your view of whether or not all Scripture is inspired and accurate.
8. Explain why or why not a written music philosophy is important to the Christian musician.
9. Explain why a Christian's philosophical views of both sacred and secular music must be pleasing unto God.
10. Explain how a Christian should go about making wise choices of both sacred and secular music.

# 3

# The Underpinnings of a Music Philosophy

## Building on the *Presupposition that God Created Music

IN CHAPTER ONE WE DISCUSSED the fact that God created music. Now we need to consider that in the beginning music was created *by Him* and *for Him* and not for us alone. Since He cares about us in a personal way, God also created music for our education, edification and our enjoyment as a part of His very excellent creation. However, the Bible teaches that the main reason that God created music was so that we might worship Him in a very personal way. Since we know that in the beginning God created music in a very personal way, we are able to accurately deduce that music is very personal to God. "The Bible says, first of all, that in the beginning all things were created by a personal infinite God, who had always existed. So what is, therefore, is intrinsically personal rather than impersonal."[1] Why should one care philosophically whether music was or was not personal or impersonal to God? If music is personal to God then music matters to God. If it matters to God then He cares about how the musicer musics with this personal creation. Since He cares about music, musicing, and the musicer, He without doubt has standards of correctness and incorrectness concerning all music.

So, let us explore the philosophical presupposition, based upon the truth of the Bible, that in the beginning, God created music. Many church musicians do not start with this necessary philosophical basis. On the contrary, many Christian musicians believe that there is no answer to the question, "How did music begin?" They fail to recognize the evident answer found in Genesis 1:1, "In the beginning God created." The fact that God created music is no joke, but rather it is so obvious that it is a truism.

God thought about music. The fact that God thought about music should be evidence to us that God still thinks about music. We know that God never experiences the fickleness of leadershift because He explains in Hebrews 13, "Jesus Christ the same yesterday, and today, and forever." Since God thinks consistently about music, we know that He has a changeless opinion concerning music. Therefore, it behooves us to study his Word to see what His thoughts are about music.

God truly created music. Although the word *created* is used loosely by musicians, man never creates music. God took nothing and made something— that something was music. Music composers and arrangers only "construct"— they only are capable of arranging God's musical building blocks into artistic patterns. A contractor who builds something takes created materials and uses them to construct something. He takes "something" and constructs with these materials. He never takes "nothing" and makes "something". No matter how great a building he constructs, it is not a creation. For a much more thorough discussion on this topic read Chapter One of my Book *Church Music Matters*.

### The Significance of Music's History

During the past century music theorists and historians stubbornly resisted the fact that the ancient Hebrew Scripture helps us to identify the beginnings of music. Scholarly sources like *The New Oxford History of Music* report, "It is very difficult to say anything definite about the origin of music, because the phenomenon is quite outside the range of our observation. Even in those primitive civilizations that still exist there is no race so primitive that it can be considered a relic of the beginning of human culture."[2] The problem with this statement is that we should not look for the origin of music in any existing remnant of early civilization but rather in the Old Testament Scriptures. It is true that the Pentateuch is relatively silent as to the specifics of the beginnings of music. However, we do know that God imparted musical knowledge to man before the Flood. As we discussed in chapter one, Genesis 4:21 explains that Lamech's son Jubal "was the father of all such as handle the harp and organ."

As we have discussed earlier, "In the beginning God created" everything—that certainly includes music. Every theory on which a music philosophy is established starts with a whole laundry list of presuppositions. A Christian music philosophy also starts with presuppositions. These include the belief that God created music and that He created it in a very good condition. God owns music. God created music for his glory. God created music so that we may music in a way that will bring honor and glory to his name. God created music for the edification of man. God created music not only as a science but also as a fine art. God created music so that we could enjoy the beauty of "created music". God expects the Christian musician to "subdue" music.

## Retaining God in Our Musical Knowledge

In 1960, Donald Grout published his famous book, *A History of Western Music*. In this treatise, Grout is careful not to be specific concerning the origins of music. He attributes the beginning of Western art music to the Christian church. He also states that "Greek mythology ascribed to music a divine origin and named its inventors and earliest practitioners gods and demigods, such as Apollo, Amphion, and Orpheus."[3] He also mentions Old Testament references to music but does not recognize Bible music as authentic knowledge concerning the beginnings of music, or that it is older than the extant Greek notated music fragments.

In 1971, Edith Borroff published *Music in Europe and the United States*. She begins her treatise on music history with, "Speculation on the beginnings of music is endlessly fascinating, but no certainty is ever likely to come to it."[4] Although Borroff was unaware of it, the Old Testament has authentic knowledge about ancient music notation.

In 1990, K. Marie Stolba published *The Development of Western Music: A History*. She begins this treatise on music history by reminding history students that "Plato placed the origin of music in creation, and numerous legends present music as a gift of

## 3: The Underpinnings of a Music Philosophy 71

the gods or the invention of one of them."[5] She began Chapter One by acknowledging the music of Ugarit and the *te'amim* (musical notation) of the Bible.[6] Finally a college text was published with an excerpt from the Old Testament including the *te'amim*. Although it has taken centuries for music historians to come to an understanding of the truth, musicology has forced music historians, at least partially, to retain God in their knowledge. (See Romans 1:28.) However, although currently published music historians give shallow lip service to the music of the Bible, some are still ignoring the historical, archeological and musicological evidences of specificity of the music of the ancient world and specifically that the deciphering of the *te'amim* has brought to the melodies of the Hebrew Old Testament. Mark Bonds' *A History of Music in Western Culture* (2003) is an example of a current refusal to even make mention of the musical findings that have been well known since 1976. For example, Bonds perpetuates the musicological ignorance of the second half of the twentieth century with his statement, "The precise nature of the music of the Old Testament describes remains largely a matter of speculation..."[7]

### Evidence that Demands Our Attention

As we just discussed, by the time Stolba's book was published there was evidence that, based on current knowledge of *Ugaritic and Hebrew music notation, what we know as Western music possibly did not start in the West, but rather in the Near East. If musicologists had listened to Plato, who believed that music's beginnings date back to the time of creation, they could possibly have avoided much of this misconception over music's origin.

Most certainly the *te'amim* (musical notation below and above the text of the OT Scriptures) and the Ugaritic notation have proven precise written music notations long before the existing Greek written music fragments. So, after much confusion, musicologists are now face to face with the fact that the notation of Bible music is authentic and that it is very ancient. Since the ancient Hurrian *diatonic *heptatonic scale of Ugarit dating to about 2000 BC has been deciphered by Dr. Ann Kilmer, and the two heptatonic scale systems in the OT have been deciphered by Suzanne Haïk-Vantoura, ancient world music has been connected to Western music.

As I mentioned earlier, music historians now realize that the Ugaritic *cuneiform notation on clay tablets that are now 3500 years old are 1400 to 1500 years older than the Greek musically notated fragments on *papyrus found in Oxyrhynchus, Egypt. Also, musicologists now know that Bible music notation is at least 3000 years old. So, depending on when the *te 'amim* system was developed, written Bible music may be much older than the 3000 years date given by Stolba.[8]

Why all this fuss about music history, and what does it have to do with music philosophy? The import of this discussion is simply that in the beginning God created music, and based on what we now know about the *te 'amim* found in the Bible, God placed His approval on at least the prosodic system being organized as a diatonic heptatonic scale and the psalmodic system as a heptatonic scale. It is my belief that under inspiration, God possibly revealed the *te 'amim* to the ancient Bible authors, who wrote both music and words as a unit or a musical *melos. It is also possible that God could have revealed the *te 'amim* to Moses on Mt. Sinai. So, if musicologists and Christian authors who write on Church music would treat the ancient musical notation of the Old Testament with respect like Stolba has, they would have many more answers to music's beginning and ancient use in both secular and sacred music.

The written Bible notation (i.e., the *te 'amim* above and below all of the OT text) is without doubt musical evidence that demands our attention and respect. Again, I want to say that music began when God created all things. When YHVH revealed it to mankind is still a mystery. "For now we see through a glass darkly; but then face to face: now I know in part; but then shall I know even as also I am known" (1 Corinthians 13:12).

## Does Satan Have the Power to Pervert Music?

Does Satan have the power to influence musicians to take God's creation of music, which Genesis 1:31 tells us was "very good," and rearrange it until it is no longer very good? The answer is Yes. Satan's influence is responsible for the perversion of many things that God created for His glory and our good. For instance, when Satan twists sex and marriage into his perverted form it is no longer the wholesome wonderful thing that God created for us. Since we know this, why do we struggle with the concept that Satan can pervert music? It is the work of Satan to twist, pervert, and destroy the original work of God's creation. That is what Satan does! So, any praxial view purporting that all music is good, no matter how its formal properties are arranged, is a faulty view.

Can we trust Satan? The answer is Yes, we most definitely can. We can trust him to always be Satan. He never takes the day off. He is very busy working on music every day. Can we trust him to influence musicians who arrange the building blocks of music which belong to God? Yes, we can. We can trust that this music will be corrupted by his perverse influence that permeates it. It is not easy to always tell whether Satan has influenced the arrangement of the building blocks of music. If it was easy we would not have such a plethora of confusion about religious music. 2 Corinthians 11:2-3 warns, "For such are false apostles, deceitful workers, transforming themselves into the apostles of Christ. And no marvel: for Satan himself is transformed into an angel of light."

## No Musical *Absolutes— A Flawed View

What would lead a Christian musician to believe that when it comes to music making there are no absolutes or standards of correctness? Some musicians honestly believe that music is completely a matter of personal taste and is a standardless art form. There is room for taste in church music, but musicing unto God is not all a matter of a musician's musical tastes.

All philosophical thoughts concerning music and all music making comes under the absolute authority of our Lord and Savior Jesus Christ. The philosophical view that Christian musicians are free to do whatever they wish with their musicing is a flawed autonomous view. Regardless of their theology all committed Christian musicians should be careful Christian musicians in what they think, what they say and what they do. If they are committed to being Christ-like in everything they do, that tenderness toward God will include their musicing. Having tenderness toward our Lord and Savior Jesus Christ will cause them to be careful in their musicing, and in their philosophical musical viewpoints.

There is another aspect of Colossians 1:16, quoted earlier, that merits discussion here. All things were not only created *by* God, but also *for* God. God created music for His glory, not for man's aggrandizement. Any *praxial view of music philosophy or music making that is humanistic is an autonomous view and therefore a non-biblical view. In Colossians 1:1-8 we are reminded "...that in all things he might have the preeminence." God must have the preeminence in our music making. Men like Diotrephes, who was mentioned in 3 John verse nine, have always hindered the work of God by seeking to be preeminent in the church. Beware of the church musician who is *enamored with self.

## Humanism and Christian Music Philosophy

The attitude of a sincere Christian musician should be that "He must increase and I must decrease. He that cometh from above is above all: he that is of the earth is earthly, and speaketh of the earth: he that cometh from heaven is above all" (St. John 3:30-31). Musicing is neither about the performer nor musical talent. Spirit-filled music making should be Christocentric and not self-centered. Musicing does not begin and end with self, but rather it begins and ends with God, who is above all.

Both secular and religious *humanism purport that the end of all human endeavor should be the *actualization of one's human potential. This self-centered philosophy has spawned generations of Christian musicians who believe one's highest development must be the actualization of self. What this means simply is that in the maturing process a Christian performer recognizes human potential and ability to make music and uses it to empower self. A Christian musician should become aware of the musical gifts that are God-given, and should develop these talents in order to use them for God's glory. However, all music endeavors do not begin and end with self, but rather they begin and end with God.

This ability to music effectively includes the performer's charisma or the ability to move a crowd with a musical performance. There is a sense in which it is empowering for a Christian performer to actualize his or her potential in order to move or manipulate a crowd through music making. Capturing an audience's attention until it is completely drawn to one's persona is addictive and is a major source of self-satisfaction. Holding the emotions of a crowd in the palm of the performer's hand, so to speak, is an enormous source of self-aggrandizement. However, this mindset is humanistic and not Christocentric.

Bennett Reimer, who is one of the most influential music philosophers in the U.S., stated that "…the arts may be conceived as a means of self-understanding, a way by which a human's sense of his nature can be explored, clarified, grasped. Many words have been used to describe the value of insight into one's nature as a responsive organism: 'self-unification' (John Dewey); 'personal identity' (Susan K. Langer); 'individualization' (Leonard B. Meyer); 'individualization' (Carl G. Yung); 'self-actualization' (Abraham B. Maslow); 'integration of the personality' (Paul Tillich). All these terms signify the humanizing value of self-knowledge."[9]

This long list of general philosophers and music philosophers is proof of the fact that a great host of influential music philosophers are strong humanists. They believe that music begins and ends with SELF. What is even worse is that those on the list believe that a musician can and should derive life's significance from the arts.

Now you know why I so strongly emphasize that "God made music" and "God owns music." We derive much of life's significance from the Bible and from a personal relationship with Jesus Christ our Savior. I have devoted much of my life, and all of my adult life, to the study of music education, music in the Bible, and philosophy of music. None of my studies have ever brought me to the conclusion that we derive life's significance from music or any of the fine arts. I am reminded of a verse in 1 Corinthians that explains, "For after that in the wisdom of God the world by wisdom knew not God…" (verse 21a), and also 2 Timothy 3:7, that talks about people who are "Ever learning, and never able to come to the knowledge of truth."

## Endnotes

1. Schaeffer, *Escape from Reason*, 86.
2. Egon Wellesz *The New Oxford History of Music*, Vol. I. (London: Oxford University Press, 1957), 5.
3. Donald Grout and Claude Palisca, *A History of Western Music*, (New York: W.W. Norton & Company, Inc., 1988.), 3.
4. Edith Borroff, *Music in Europe and the United States*, (Englewood Cliffs, N.J: Prentice Hall, Inc., 1971), 3.
5. K. Marie Stolba, *The Development of Western Music, A History*, (Dubuque, IA: Wm. C. Brown Publishers, 1990), 3.
6. Ibid, 5.
7. Mark Evan Bonds, *A History of Music in Western Culture*, (Upper Saddle River, NJ: Prentice Hall, 2003), 1.
8. K. Marie Stolba, *The Development of Western Music*, 5.
9. Bennett Reimer, *A Philosophy of Music Education*, (Englewood Cliffs, NJ: Prentice Hall, 1989), 25-26.

## Chapter Three Word Meanings

**Absolutes**— values and principles that are universally valid and that may be considered without relation to other things.

**Actualization**—psychological theories of the quest for realizing one's human potential.

**Cuneiform**— refers to wedge-shaped characters (marks) that form a precise alphabet used in the various ancient writing systems of Mesopotamia, Persia, and Ugarit. It is believed that this form of writing began in Sumer.

**Diatonic scale**— a scale with eight notes in an octave and half steps between scale degrees 3 & 4 and 7 & 8. This is true of the prosodic scale system found in the OT, even though the tonic is medial (i.e., the third note of the scale rather than the first). The psalmodic scale system of the OT is a seven note scale with no repeated note. The Ugaritic scale is seven note diatonic scale with half steps between 3 & 4 and 7 & 8.

**Enamored**— in this case means the musician who is filled or inflamed with self-love.

**Heptatonic scale**— a musical scale with seven pitches per octave. The psalmodic and prosodic scales found in the OT are both seven note scales. The Ugaritic scale is also a seven note scale.

**Humanism**— a system of philosophical thought that attaches prime importance to human rather than divine or supernatural matters, and supposes that problems can be solved using reason instead of religion. It also often centers on the importance of human self-actualization rather than on a life of service to God.

**Music**— a verb, coined by David Elliot, referring to what the performer actively does, i.e., the action produced by the musicer (performer).

**Papyrus**— a paper-like material made from the papyrus plant.

**Praxial**— actions in music education that are goal oriented.

**Presupposition**— a belief that is required as a necessary antecedent condition to a discussion.

**Ugaritic notation**— musical notation from the ancient city of Ugarit, located in western Syria on the Mediterranean Sea.

### Chapter Three Questions for Discussion

1. Do all musicians base their music philosophies on presuppositions? Explain your answer.
2. Explain the author's view of what a Christian musician's philosophical presupposition should be.
3. Discuss the dangers of realizing that it is empowering for a Christian performer to actualize potential in order to move or manipulate a crowd through music making.
4. Why is it important for every Christian musician to study music history?
5. Explain your beliefs about what it means for Christian musicians to retain God in their beliefs about music and musicing.
6. Explain the significance of the deciphering of the Ugaritic music and the *te 'amim* of the Old Testament.
7. Discuss your beliefs about whether or not Satan has the power to pervert music.
8. Discuss your beliefs about whether or not there are absolutes concerning musicing unto God.
9. Explain what secular and religious humanism purports and how this affects how a musician musics unto God.
10. Does a Christian musician derive life's significance from performing the fine arts? Please explain your answer.

# 4

# Building a Christocentric Music Philosophy

## Is Your Musical Ship Driven by the Wind?

JAMES 3:4 STATES, "BEHOLD also the ships, which though they be great, and are driven of fierce winds, yet are they turned about with a very small helm, whithersoever the governor listeth." On one occasion when I visited my son-in-law Mark Mander and his wife Deanna, my oldest daughter, I walked by the sea shore in Northern Ireland in the early morning. That day the waves were crashing against the sea wall as they sent the sea spray high into the air. Although it was an awesome sight, I was very glad that I was on dry land rather than in a boat that morning.

We are reminded in James 3:4 that ships, although driven in one direction by the wind, are easily turned around by a very small rudder. A horse may also be turned to the left or right or completely around by simply tugging on the bit in his mouth. It is odd that a ship or a powerful horse can be turned completely around at the will of the one in control, but sometimes Christian musicians override the gentle checks of the Holy Spirit when He nudges them to make a correction in their music philosophy.

This passage clearly teaches that the musician needs the Lord's help in governing musical choice. If a sailor can easily turn a ship around in fierce winds and huge waves, the Christian musician should be able, with the "tugs" of the Holy Spirit, to control musical actions as a result of direct obedience to God and a well-developed Bible-based music philosophy. As I have often said, every action is an exercise of a philosophy. In the same way, every musical choice is a testimony of a belief about the nature and value of music.

## Are They Biblical Principles or Personal Preferences?

What the music educator firmly believes about the nature and value of music at its deepest levels should exude from that musician's musical convictions. A musical conviction is the strong feeling of being sure that what that musician believes about music is true and therefore must be followed. A musical preference is different in that it is a greater liking for one musical alternative over another. As the reader can see there is a dramatic difference between the two terms.

I am not only passionate about my philosophic music convictions, I am also passionate about the philosophical preferences that I have which I earnestly believe are important to excellence in musicing. However, there is something that I have learned over the years that has helped me— some of my preferences do not matter enough to cause me to break fellowship with other musicians who disagree with me. In light of what spoken words do to relationships, most musical preferences really do not matter as much as we think they do when the waves of adversity and disagreement are blowing. At these times we need Christian musical friendship more than having our way musically. We need to let the blessed Holy Spirit be our rudder to help us stay out of "foot in mouth disease" and remain on course musically.

I am not saying that my philosophical preferences do not matter. I am simply acknowledging that my relationship with other Christian musicians matters more than most of my musical preferences. They matter enough for me to disagree agreeably with my Christian colleagues who are of a different opinion about music education and church music preferences. So, I must very carefully differentiate between my musical preferences and Biblical principles of musicing which are not negotiable.

## God Owns Music

A discussion of developing a Christocentric music philosophy must begin with the fact that God created music and therefore, He owns it. Christians should get rid of the sense of ownership of music because the sense of our ownership will cause us to operate independently of the Lordship of Christ. It is imperative that all philosophical bases begin with God's creation and ownership, which of course includes music.

To the Christian, all forms of music come under the ownership and Lordship of Jesus Christ. Colossians 1:16 teaches, "For by him were all things created, that are in heaven, and that are in earth, visible and invisible, whether they be thrones, or dominions or principalities, or powers: all things were created by him, and for him." St. John 1:3 further explains that "All things were made by him; and without him was not anything made that was made." Once there was no music. God was before music. God wanted music so He made music. No one else made music. Therefore, no one but God has true ownership of music. The Christian musician should get rid of the sense of ownership of music. No Spirit-filled musician, or any musician for that matter, has the right to claim personal ownership. Remember that no musician has ever taken "nothing" and made "something", but merely arranges God's musical building blocks. Musicians "construct" but they cannot create.

Why all this fuss over ownership? Our *autonomous God made music. As Christian musicians, we must give Him preeminence in all things—that of course includes music. Any other philosophical belief will lead down the long slippery slope toward a humanistic philosophy of music. Christian musicians are not autonomous and therefore no part of our musicing is autonomous.

The core of my music philosophy is based on a single, fundamental *premise which the reader must understand when reading my philosophy of music: *God owns music.* In order to understand the nature and value of both sacred and secular music at their deepest levels, a music philosopher must not only know about God but also know God by having a personal relationship with Him. 1 Corinthians 2:12-16 explains:

> Now we have received, not the spirit of the world, but the spirit which is of God; that we might know the things that are freely given to us of God. Which things also we speak, not in the words which man's wisdom teacheth, but which the Holy Ghost teacheth; comparing spiritual things with spiritual. But the natural man receiveth not the things of the Spirit of God:

for they are foolishness unto him: neither can he know them, because they are spiritually discerned. But he that is spiritual judgeth all things, yet he himself is judged of no man for who hath known the mind of the Lord, that he may instruct him? but we have the mind of Christ.

Knowing God personally gives the musician the ability to "compare spiritual things with spiritual" because the Spirit-filled musician has the "mind of Christ"—a condition that the worldly music philosopher does not have. The unbroken consistent wisdom of the Holy Spirit guides the musician who seeks the "mind of Christ" in making musical decisions.

The Christian musician must constantly be *cognizant of the fact that the world is not a friend of grace. The worldly music philosopher that does not love God with all his heart, soul, and mind is not seeking to accomplish the same musical goals as the Christian musician who believes that God created and owns music, which He created for His glory and our *edification.

1 Corinthians 2:13 explains the source of a Christian musician's wisdom, "Which things also we speak, not in the words which man's wisdom teacheth, but which the Holy Ghost teacheth." It is not egotistical for the Christian musician to believe that God's wisdom is of a higher and more profound character than man's wisdom. The wisdom of the Holy Spirit is freely given to musicians who know God and retain His wisdom in their philosophical basis. Romans 1:28 explains why one should not trust the wisdom of worldly music philosophers. "And even as they did not like to retain God in their knowledge, God gave them over to a reprobate mind [i.e., a mind void of judgment], to do those things which are not convenient." The Greek word *echo* (2192), that is translated "retain" in this passage of Scripture, means "to hold" or to "hold on to" something, as a valuable or a valuable tested possession.

## Good and Perfect Musical Gifts

James 1:17 explains that "Every good gift and every perfect gift is from above, and cometh down from the Father of lights, with whom is no variableness, neither shadow of turning." At first reading of the first chapter of James, it seems that this verse was merely dropped into this passage of Scripture without direct connection to the rest of what James was teaching. However, as one studies this chapter it becomes apparent that James is teaching that all good gifts emanate from God.

One of the perplexities centers on the apostle's use of the words *agathos dosis* (18, 1394) and *teleios dorema* (5046, 1434) which were translated good gifts and perfect gifts in the AV. What is the significance of the apostle's use of the Greek words *dosis* and *dorema*? What is the significance of good gifts and perfect gifts? Finally, what does this verse teach us about gifts given to us from God?

*Agathos dosis* means a beneficial giving [of God] *and telios dorema* means a perfect bestowment [of God] in the context of completeness. The words translated good and perfect in the AV reflect gifts [given to us by God] that are beneficial and complete. This application given in the Book of James extends to Christian musicians.

No Christian musician is self-sufficient and autonomous. All of the special gifts that musicians possess are given to them by our wise and all-knowing Heavenly Father. In St. John 3:27, "John answered and said, A man can receive nothing, except it be given him from heaven." Romans 11:29 teaches, "For the gifts and calling of God are without repentance." 1 Corinthians 4:7 asks, "For who maketh thee to differ from another? and what hast thou that thou didst not receive? now if thou didst receive it, why dost thou glory, as if thou hadst not received it?" 1 Peter 4:10 also teaches that "As every man hath received the gift, even so minister the same one to another, as good stewards of the manifold grace of God." Romans 12:6-8 explains, "Having then gifts differing according to the grace that is given to us, whether prophecy, let us prophesy according to the proportion of faith; Or ministry, let us wait on our ministering: or he that teacheth, on teaching; Or he that exhorteth, on exhortation: he that giveth, let him do it with simplicity; he that ruleth, with diligence; he that sheweth mercy, with cheerfulness."

The aforementioned Scriptures iterate the fact that no musician is self- made. The beneficial and perfect gifts that Christian musicians exhibit in their professional endeavors are given individually to them by our Heavenly Father who never makes a mistake. Therefore, it is no wonder that God's Word declares that they are "without repentance." I have told my college classes over the years that when we face Him whose eyes are as a flame of fire, we will give an account of what we did with the musical gifts which God has given to us. (See Romans 11:29, Revelation 19:12 and 20:12.)

As a Bible college music teacher for over forty years, I have seen very talented music students that headed down a dangerous philosophical path. It did not take them long to find out that they were talented enough to proceed without God's help. They would deny that they were "religious humanists" but they acted as owners rather than good stewards of their musical gifts. Secretly, or sometimes openly, they held ownership to music especially when it came to matters of musical style and performance style. Like Thomas Aquinas, they followed a philosophical path in their musical pursuit that was independent from the Lordship of Christ. Remember that Aquinas believed that man was fallen in matters of grace but that he was not depraved when it came to matters of nature— which included music.

### *"True Truth" Comes from God

Postmodern and post-postmodern music philosophers believe that all truth about music can be true and not true at the same time (post-postmodern music philosophy is too much in the state of development for one to make a conclusive analysis of what this new philosophical notion purports.) Simply put, postmodern musical belief can be likened to the notion that a burner on a stove can be hot and not hot at the same time, i.e., the notion that the truth about music is always relative. It appears at this early stage of the development of post-postmodern belief that it is not built on the notion that there is any relative truth.

In contrast to postmodern and post-postmodern musicians, the Bible believing Christian musician believes that truth from God's infallible Word should be retained in Christian music philosophy. The musicer's preferences may change but Bible-based musical principles are non-negotiable because they are true truth. Romans 1:28 explains the philosophical problem that arises when one does not believe in this true truth: "And even as they did not like to retain God in their knowledge, God gave them over to a reprobate mind, to do those things which are not convenient." Notice that this passage of Scripture uses the words "did not like" that are translated from *dokimadzo* (1381) *ou* (3756) *dokimadzo* (1381). So, the import of this phrase is that that they did not test or discern God's knowledge in developing a truth basis.

Unsaved music philosophers could retain the evidence of God's Word in their music philosophy, but as is mentioned in Romans 1:28, they most often do not like to consider what the Bible says about music so they do not consider it in their truth basis. Matthew Henry, referring to Romans 1:28, said, "The blindness of their understanding was caused by the willful aversion of their wills and affections. They did not retain God in their knowledge because they did not like it."[1] I am in no way trying to indicate that a Christian musician cannot learn from a music philosopher who is not a Christian. I am, however, warning the young Christian musician who is trying to develop a congruent Christocentric music philosophy to be extremely careful not to accept what man's wisdom teaches over what the Holy Spirit teaches, because the two are often in disagreement with each other.

## Developing a Unified Music Philosophy

According to Francis Schaeffer, up to the time of Kierkegaard, philosophers had always hoped "…that they would be able to construct a unified field of knowledge."[2] There are two ways in which Christian musicians may develop a consistent, congruent, unified system of beliefs concerning the nature and value of the whole of music. They must utilize Bible-based epistemology (theory of and limits of "knowing") and methodology (the method used for coming to a knowledge of truth).

The first requirement is that the musician must believe that there is objective truth concerning how to music unto God, and that we are able to know and appropriate that truth. Second, that Bible knowledge concerning music is not dispensational, but is relevant to all generations of musicians. 2 Timothy 3:16-17— "All scripture is given by inspiration of God, and is profitable for doctrine, for reproof, for correction, for instruction in righteousness: That the man of God may be perfect, throughly furnished [*exertizo* 1822- equipped fully] unto all good works." The Bible did not say that the Word *was* profitable but that it *is* profitable.

What does "all Scripture" mean? Does it mean all passages except those mentioning music? Are these ancient musical writings profitable in the twenty-first century? Are they inspired or not? Are they too difficult or too *esoteric for us to understand? The Scriptures on music are there, and since God is there we have objective truth concerning music. The question is, What are we going to do with this truth? James 3:13 asks, "Who is a wise (*sophos* 4680) man and endued with knowledge among you? let him shew out of a good conversation [i.e., lifestyle] his works with meekness and wisdom (*sophia* 4678)." The wisdom is there and the validity is there. It is our responsibility to use this knowledge to form a congruent music philosophy.

**What is a Christocentric Music philosophy?**

We have established that a music philosophy is a series of systematic beliefs concerning the nature and value of the whole of music. Now we need to establish what a Christ-centered philosophy of music is. *It is a series of systematic beliefs concerning the nature and value of the whole music in which Christ has \*preeminence.* Christ is at the center of this philosophy, which is the antithesis of a humanistic music philosophy. Remember that for the music philosopher who is a humanist, music begins and ends with self; any insight or understanding that is derived from making, writing about, or listening to music, gives insight into the humanness of life. It supposedly gives the musician insight into the meaning of human existence.

If we are going to keep God at the center of our beliefs concerning the nature and value of the whole of music, then we must, as Colossians 2:8 warns, "Beware lest any man spoil (*esomai* 207) you through philosophy (*philosophia* 5385) and vain deceit, after the tradition of men, after the rudiments (*stoicheioin* 4747) of the world, and not after Christ." Note that the Greek word *kenos* (2756) means empty, and *apate* (539) means delusion. So the warning in this Scripture verse is to avoid empty delusions produced by false philosophical beliefs.

Since philosophy is the love and pursuit of wisdom, Christians must beware lest they develop a belief system in music based on the "rudiments of this world." In this passage of Scripture St. Paul is warning the Colossian Christians not to let the world (*kosmos* 2889) spoil (seduce, corrupt, lead away— *sulagogeo* 4812) them into developing philosophical thought patterns in the way the world ordered or arranged them. In other words God (thesis) has ordered things a certain way and the world, influenced and controlled by Satan (antithesis), has confused or rearranged or reordered many things. This philosophical reordering has the power to influence how we music.

So, do not be taken captive by the world's delusional views on the nature and value of music. Do not let the humanistic music philosopher lead you to believe that the most important thing that music accomplishes in our lives is the authentication of our humanness. We are human— we are in the *kosmos* (2889) but we are not of the *aion* (165). Therefore, Christian musicians should look at the nature and value of music differently than worldly musicians.

## The Essence of a Musical Praxis is "Doing"

The Christian musician must be careful to analyze the fundamental grounds and concepts that govern all musicing to be sure that they are Christocentric. Furthermore, all of a Christian musician's fundamental systematic beliefs concerning the nature and value of the whole of music must be in alignment to the matrix of God and His Word, which is His divinely inspired guidebook for Christian musicians. It should be pointed out that there are many Bible principles that apply to a Christian musician's music philosophy other than only those Bible verses that specifically mention music or musicing.

The Bible is not necessarily the only source of truth concerning music. Much of what a Christian believes about music should come from a long broad study of every aspect of music and musicing. So, what a Christian does musically will come from a life-long study of music both inside and outside of the Bible. However, everything that a Christian believes philosophically about music and musicing must be congruent with biblical principles of musicing and with the changed, separated life of a Christian. As I explained in chapter two, the reason philosophers refer to a philosophy as a belief system is that it is a systematic approach to why we do what we do. If a Christian music philosophy does not follow biblical principles it is faulty. If it is not systematic it is likely that it will be incomplete at best. Every musical choice reflects a philosophical belief about music.

The real essence of a musical praxis is "doing." That is the reason I am so concerned about what we do with the great God-given art form of music. It does not matter very much what musicians believe about music or musicing if they do not follow this belief system when musicing or listening to music. Musical action is profoundly affected by philosophical belief. Christian musicians must understand why they value (esteem) the types of music they listen to and perform and consider the essential nature of all the musics allowed in their "whole life" musical praxis.

### Testing One's Music Philosophy

Is the Bible all we need in the development of a unified, *congruent, thorough, and useful Bible-based music philosophy? No. We need not only to know much of what the Bible teaches about music, but also to understand music education, music history, church music, music theory and composition, and music *performance practice. Why then do I keep mentioning Bible principles of music? Biblical principles are not all we need but they are the foundations of the development of our music philosophy. When we are developing the details of our musical beliefs, the Scriptures are the looking glass through which we always view the whole of music.

Why do I continually talk about the "whole of music"? If a music philosophy does not include the "whole" of music it will surely have a "hole" in it. 2 Timothy 2:15 admonishes the Christian to "study to shew thyself approved unto God, a workman that needeth not to be ashamed, rightly dividing the word of truth." The Greek word *spoudazo* (4704), translated study in this verse, means to be earnestly diligent. According to Jamison-Fausset-Brown, the word *dokimos* (1384) means "tested by trial, as opposed to 'reprobate'". So, St. Paul admonishes the Christian to study diligently to test all philosophical beliefs so that one's praxis will be approved by the Lord before it is set into action in the church, music classroom, or performance hall.

In order to develop a series of beliefs or convictions about music, it is necessary to become knowledgeable of the nature and value of music and to retain knowledge from God's Word in the development of a philosophical belief system (Romans 1:28). Study of the varying music philosophies published today must be in light of Bible principles of musicing. One must be aware of what a particular music philosopher believes, not only about music, but also about God and about living life. A music philosopher's inwards beliefs about God will be evidenced in that philosopher's outward writing and musicing.

## All Musical Actions Exude from a Philosophy

All music ministries, musical performances, and music pedagogies are based on some philosophy, and this philosophy is fundamentally based on some *matrix. Music philosophy is the basic foundation from which all musical actions exude. A sound Bible-based Christocentric philosophy of music will always be founded on principles much deeper than mere likes and dislikes, since it will be based on Bible principles of musicing.

Wise Christian musicians commit their music philosophy to pen and ink. A well-developed series of systematic statements (beliefs) concerning the nature and value of the whole of music will serve as a basis for a person's direction in music. The reason we care about musical direction is because musical direction determines musical destiny. A well thought out philosophy of music will serve as an everyday guide for all music action. Articulating one's music philosophy will bring an inner peace and will serve as a concomitant of one's whole-life philosophy.

Many Christian musicians have never taken the time to write out their music philosophy and therefore their music philosophy is many times incomplete and homespun. As I mentioned earlier, some Christian musicians whom I have met in my travels over the years deny by their actions or their words that they need to have a written music ministry or music education philosophy. They often hide behind the excuse that they are not trained musicians or that they have never had the opportunity to study music philosophy. What they do not know is that everyone has a philosophy of music and all one's musical actions exude from that belief system.

Even in the smallest of communities there is often a barbershop or a feed store with some chairs for "philosophers." Just bring up the subject of music and these grass-roots armchair philosophers, who may not know the names of the lines and spaces, will tell you exactly what is right and wrong with music today.

### Proving Music's Acceptability to God

Many Christian musicians act as if the Lord does not really care about music philosophy or music making. Some Christian musicians believe that all forms of music making and all music philosophies are acceptable unto the Lord and, furthermore, that there are no absolutes in music philosophy or music making.

Ephesians 5:10-11 admonishes that we walk as children of light, "Proving (*dokimazo* 1381) what is acceptable (*euarestos* 2101) unto the Lord. And have no fellowship with the unfruitful works of darkness, but rather reprove them." So, we know from Scripture that a Christian musician has the responsibility to prove by testing what is or is not acceptable or well pleasing to the Lord. In spite of this fact, many Christian musicians in the twenty-first century still believe that all forms and styles of music making are acceptable unto the Lord. Since they feel free to pursue their philosophical music journey by themselves, they act as autonomous musicians.

Now in the twenty-first century, an increasing number of Christian musicians have come to the conclusion that there are no "musts" or "absolutes" in our religious journey, since God only watches the musicer music from a distance through rose tinted glasses. Are there any "musts" or "absolutes" in the Bible about our walk with the Lord? Christ said in St. John 3:7, "Marvel not that I say unto thee, ye must be born again." In Matthew 5:20

Christ stated, "For I say unto you, That except your righteousness shall exceed the righteousness of the scribes and Pharisees, ye shall in no case enter into the kingdom of Heaven." This list of absolutes could be multiplied by many, many verses, all of which are *very absolute*. I am often shocked that so many Christian musicians believe so strongly that none of the more than 600 references to music mentioned in the Bible constitute absolutes or objective truth concerning music and the musicer's musicing. Romans 1:28 talks about people "Who changed the truth of God into a lie, and worshipped and served the creature more than the Creator..." The word *ktisis* (2937) which was translated creature in the AV means "a created thing". Music is a created thing, so it is an absolute truth that if a musician worships music such worship is idolatry.

As I mentioned in Chapter One, when God created music it had the capacity to be very beautiful, valuable, and meaningful, and had the ability to be very *efficacious either for good or, if perverted, for evil. If God created music to be exceedingly good then it is the objective of Satan to pervert it by removing its goodness. Genesis 1:31 explains the condition of everything that God created, "And God saw everything that he had made, and, behold, it was very good. And the evening and the morning were the sixth day." The words *very good* were translated from the words *maod* (3966) and *towb* (2896). So, one may rightly deduce that God did not create music to be only in good condition, but rather to be in an exceedingly excellent condition, since *towb* is a superlative term which means "in the very best condition".

Since music was created in such a way that it had the *propensity to function in such a way that it might be used to bring glory to His wonderful name, we may safely conclude that it was and still is the work of Satan to pervert those elements of music that make it exceedingly the best. If one believes that Satan's perversion of music produces "good music", then that person has just bequeathed Satan with the ability to produce "perverted good" music.[3]

## All Musicing Should be Discussable

The discourse in Ephesians 5:6 states simply, "Let no man deceive you with vain words: for because of these things cometh the wrath of God upon the children of disobedience. And have no fellowship with the unfruitful works of darkness, but rather reprove them." Christians must not be deceived by the "vain words" (*kenos* 2756), i.e., hollow words, of the world's dialogue about music. In verses ten and eleven St. Paul explains that the Christian's responsibility is "Proving what is acceptable unto the Lord. And have no fellowship with the unfruitful works of darkness, but rather reprove them."

Modern, postmodern, and post-postmodern men have often erroneously come to the conclusion that musical matters are non-discussable; they believe that music is part of the natural world, and therefore a part of man's non-fallen natural autonomous ownership. The Greek word *dokimazo* (1381) rendered proving in the above verse in the AV means to test or to examine. It is important to carefully examine what and how one is musicing before the Lord and make sure that all musicing is well pleasing and fully acceptable unto our Lord and Savior Jesus Christ. It is always a wise decision to prove first and do second.

Simply put, although a multitude of Christian musicians believe they do not have to prove anything about "their" music to anyone, this philosophical belief is faulty. Even though many believe that musicians do not have to prove what is "acceptable unto the Lord" when it comes to music philosophy and practice, the Bible teaches very clearly that they do.

As a Christian musician, you may believe with all your heart that you are autonomous when it comes to your musicing, but when you face Him whose eyes are as a flame of fire, you will give an account of what, when, why and how you have musiced before God. Now you have the opportunity to make sure that your religious musicing unto God is acceptable unto Him and that your secular musicing does not bring reproach upon His moral nature. You will give an account for all of your musicing regardless of whether it is sacred or secular.

## Recognizing that All Music Has Purpose

John Coblentz believes that there are several reasons why people sing. According to him these purposes are to worship, to testify, to teach, and to express.[4] Those who believe that music is powerless to express meaning would purport that only words express meaning. However, Coblentz goes on to say, "A serious composer is interested in writing music which communicates clearly, and he structures melodies and chords which are expressive and supportive of the themes he is communicating."[5] I agree that words and the music part of music both express or communicate meaning. So, an understanding of the nature of music will include recognizing what the composer or arranger is expressing and thereby teaching and communicating through the music part of the music. Chapters six and seven will discuss this aspect of music philosophy more thoroughly.

### Endnotes

1. Matthew Henry, *Acts to Revelation.* Vol. 6 of *Matthew Henry's Commentary*, (McLean, VA: MacDonald Publishing Company, n.d.), 372.
2. Schaeffer, *Escape From Reason,* 35, 42.
3. See *Church Music Matters*, Chapter Five.
4. John Coblentz, *Music in Biblical Perspective*, (Kalona, Iowa: Calvary Publications, 1986), 7-9.
5. Ibid, 18-19.

### Chapter Four Word Meanings

**Autonomous**— able to act completely independently of the control of others.

**Cognizant**— the condition of having knowledge or being aware of something.

**Congruent**— as used in this book, it means a music philosophy that matches or is in agreement with the musician's Christian values.

**Disparity**— a lack of similarity or equality.

**Edification**— the instruction or improvement of a person morally and intellectually.

**Efficacious**— effective musicing in that it is successful in producing a desired result.

**Esoteric**— a word or a terminology that is likely to be understood by only a few people who have a specialized knowledge.

**Matrix**— something such as a situation or a set of conditions from which something else develops.

# 4: Building a Christocentric Music Philosophy

**Melos**— a term used of ancient music that connotes a melody and a text composed at the same time as one unit.

**Performance practice**— historically informed performance in which the musicer adheres to the aesthetic criteria of the period in which the music was composed.

**Postulate**— to suggest or assume that something is true as the basis for one's reasoning, discussion, or belief.

**Praxial**— actions in music education that are goal oriented.

**Premise**— a stated philosophical basis on which reasoning proceeds.

**Propensity**— an innate inclination or a natural tendency to behave in a particular way.

**Preeminence**— the state of being superior and thereby surpassing all others.

**"True Truth"**— a term coined by the Christian philosopher Francis Schaeffer, which means God's immutable truth.

## Chapter Four Questions for Discussion

1. Discuss how the Christian musician can keep from being over-influenced by what the world currently considers to be important in music.
2. Explain the differences between musical preferences and biblical principles of musicing.
3. Discuss your musical preferences and biblical convictions, and how you differentiate between them.
4. Discuss what the author means by saying, "God owns music," and the significance of this philosophical belief to the Christian musician.
5. Explain the postmodern belief that all truth about music can be true and not true at the same time.
6. Give a statement from the text that explains what a music philosophy is and discuss what that statement means.
7. Explain the significance of 2 Timothy 3:16 to the Christian musician who is developing a music philosophy.
8. Discuss what it means to develop a Christocentric music philosophy.
9. Explain what the author meant by the statement, "The essence of a musical praxis is doing."
10. Explain the statement, "All music has purpose," and how this belief will affect a Christian musician's music philosophy.

PART TWO

**Understanding Music Philosophy**

# 5

# Developing a Philosophy of Music Education

## A Music Education Credo

THE MORE THAN 600 references to music in the Bible are given by inspiration of God and are profitable for doctrine, reproof, correction, and instruction (that includes music and musicing) today. The Bible provides timeless, relevant, and practical spiritual guidance for twenty-first century musicians. The principles of musicing set forth in the Bible are relevant for developing a music education philosophy and praxis. The only completely safe teacher of Christian music education and music philosophy is the Holy Spirit, who is willing to guide Christian musicians into all truth concerning music education in this century.

There are absolutes concerning music education and its place in a Christian organization's ministry. A prescriptive Christian music education philosophy must be built on Bible principles of musicing, profundity, appropriateness and standards of correctness. There is room for taste in music in the context of music education, but the use of music in education is not all a matter of personal taste since it must be congruent with the principles of a changed life. God thought music into being. He owns it and His Word addresses it specifically. Therefore, we should study God's Word to *ascertain what He thinks about music and musicing. The Old Testament teaches that it is the responsibility of Christians to educate their own musically so that good causes in music may be served. His Word commands us to instruct our children in "the songs of the LORD" (1 Chronicles 25:7).

Although Christian musicians live in this present evil world, they are not of this present world system. Therefore a philosophy of Christian music education should be of a higher renovated character than secular, humanistic philosophies of music education. A Christian music educator's music philosophy matters to God, and although there is much evil in this century, conservative Spirit-filled musicians can effect changes in Christian music education that will have a positive influence in this century. Parents, churches, Christian schools, and Bible colleges who have a Chistocentric music philosophy can and should catechize the next generation of Christian musicians.

## Music's Historic Place in Education

Music had an important place in education in the ancient civilizations of Sumer, Akkad and Egypt. It was also important in ancient Israel since the time when the first and second books of Chronicles were written. 1 Chronicles 25 states, "Moreover David and the captains of the host separated to the service of the sons of Asaph, and of Heman, and of Jeduthun, who should prophesy with harps, with psalteries, and with cymbals... So the number of them, with their brethren that were instructed in the songs of the LORD, even all that were cunning, was two hundred fourscore and eight" (verses 1 and 7). Music education in ancient Israel was the responsibility of the Chief musicians Asaph, Heman, and Jeduthun (and their sons and brethren). The Hebrew phrase *yad ab shiyr* (3027, 01, 7892), translated in verse six as "under the hands of their father for song" in the AV, means literally that the Levite musical sons studied sacred music under the hands of their God-fearing fathers who were chief Levite music directors and music educators. Music education in Israel was uniquely different than in the cultures of its neighbors. In verse seven in the AV the Hebrew phrase *lamad shiyr JHVH* (3925, 7892, 3068), translated "were instructed in songs of the LORD," speaks directly to the fact that the Levite sons received training specifically in sacred music. It is important to note that the essence of music education in ancient Israel was preparation for music ministry.

Music historians have established that music was also a vital part of education in the ancient Egyptian culture. It had a prominent place in the medieval educational quadrivium of mathematics, astronomy, geometry and music. Since it has had an important place in education for such a long period of time, Christian school and college administrators need to recognize that music education is vital to a Christian education. It is not merely a public relations tool for recruiting students and raising money for the educational institution. Since verses like 1 Chronicles 16:23, Psalm 96:1, and Psalm 144:9 command us to sing and play music unto God, it stands to reason that it is our responsibility to teach our children and youth to do so properly. With this in mind, it seems strange that so many Christian elementary, secondary schools and Christian colleges and universities graduate students with little or no music classes.

Christian higher education must give music its historic place, since musicing is a primary means of worshipping God and a concomitant to the preaching of God's Word. Therefore, not only undergraduate music majors, but also others such as ministerial, missions, and education majors need a dedicated study of music before they enter the world of work. College students need a serious study of music because in adult life they will be catechizing and educating worshipers. Since all worshipers will be involved in worshiping God with music, knowing how to worship will require knowing how to music unto God. Only an educated music teacher who has a personal relationship with Christ is capable of teaching others how to love and worship God through music.

**Music's Place in an Academic Curriculum**

A well-articulated Christian Music Education Philosophy (CMEP) must define music's place in a Bible-based educational philosophy. Traditionally in the USA, music education has been justified in academics on the basis of its aesthetic qualities. In the late twentieth century performance based (*praxialists) and listening based (MEAE) music education received criticism for not meeting the requirement of being *assessable. It is not easy to assess students' aesthetic experiences because they are clearly in the affective domain, which deals with attitudes, likes, dislikes and emotional responses to music. However, music education not only deals with the *affective domain but also with the *psychomotor and *cognitive domains.

A student who weeps when listening to a piece of music may

be having an aesthetic experience with the music or may be responding to negative memories that the music arouses mentally (i.e., the arousal theory). That student may be responding to the *import of the music at a very deep aesthetic or emotional level, regardless of their level of knowledge about the nuts and bolts of music. As a matter of fact, even evaluative tools like call charts, fill in the blanks tests, and essay tests do not effectively evaluate the level (i.e., the depth of aesthetic knowing) of aesthetic experiences of individual student listeners and performers.

So, the question arises: do we have to effectively evaluate students' aesthetic or pleasurable experiences with music in order for music to be justifiably placed in an academic curriculum? There are very effective tools for evaluating music in the cognitive and in the psychomotor domains. Therefore, a well-articulated series of beliefs about the nature and value of music education must include the philosophical justification of music in an academic curriculum on the basis of all three domains.

There are many reasons for a Christian music educator to develop a thorough understanding of the nature and value of music and how to apply these philosophical principles in Christian elementary, secondary, and post-secondary music education. Understanding the nature and value of music at the deepest levels will illuminate our understanding of the place music education has in a Christian education.

Christian musicians who work in the larger scheme of Christian education must understand specifically what it means to musically educate children, young people and mature adults. As I have said before, no person has received a thorough Christian Music Education (CME) unless that student is able to read, write, perform, and evaluate music in order to be able to make wise choices of sacred and secular music in the context of living a Christ centered life. A music education praxis that does not deal with all of the aforementioned domains will not yield graduates who understand the true nature of music from a Christian perspective.

Students will not gain these skills by merely being in listening-based music classes or by playing and/or singing in a performing group.

CME must provide opportunities to develop a wide variety of the music skills described in the national music education standards. A quality music education curriculum must provide balanced music class offerings that are centered in student learning. Student learning must include and be focused on music experiences that involve the aesthetic, cognitive and psychomotor domains. As we have discussed earlier in this chapter, assessment must take place in all three educational domains even though evaluative processes may be complex and difficult to administer in some situations. CME must fulfill academic requirements if it is going to earn academic respect in the Christian education community. In a high quality academic setting music classes must be centered on student learning that is assessable.

The time has come in the educational community when music education can no longer ride in the first class section of education and only pay coach fare. If music educators want music classes to be considered "academic" instead of "extra-curricular" then all music classes and performing organizations must pay the price educationally by undergoing the academic rigors of assessment. Astute Christian administrators are beginning to demand "proof of academic life" before they are willing to pay the ransom of shared time, in an already over-crowded class schedule, and money, in the context of shrinking Christian education budgets. Although it goes against the philosophical concept that music educators often have that Christian education must include music at any cost, Christian education as a whole is now faced with the reality of doing more with less.

## Why Christian Music Education?

Is the Christian school a conviction or a preference? If a Christian education (CE) is a mere preference then it is not a necessity, and Christian music education is most certainly not a necessity. Every parent, Christian school teacher and administrator must know why they and the students are involved in a Christian school. Although I do not want to be overly simplistic, I can see no reason for Christians to deny their children a Christian education. As I have pointed out so many times in my writings, 1 Timothy 5:8 states, "But if any provide not for his own, and specially for those of his own house, he hath denied the faith, and is worse than an infidel." This extends to the education of one's household. It also pertains to the music education of our own. Every Christian parent must remember that when Lot chose the well-watered plains of Jordan near Sodom and Gomorrah, he made an excellent choice for his cattle and a poor choice for his children.

Perhaps I should define the terms "educational preference" and "educational conviction". Educational preference, as it will be used in this discussion, is defined as a greater liking for one type of school over another. An educational conviction is the strong belief that it is the responsibility of Christians to train their own, and that this can only be done properly through a Christ centered education in the context of a Christian school. With these definitions the reader can see clearly why many Christians feel convicted that the Christian school is a must.

It is puzzling to me that a number of Christians feel strongly that we must have Bible colleges and Christian universities, but that our children should attend public schools. Certainly, if our college age young people need a CE, our children who are in the process of making life-long decisions need the shelter and philosophical support of a Christian school. For these reasons a CE is a necessity and not merely a preference, if our children and young people are going to develop a Christocentric whole-life philosophy. Anyone who denies the power of a Christian teacher's long term influence on students does not understand the philosophical power of teacher/student relationships.

## Defending Christian Music Education

With the introduction above, we are now ready to defend CME. 1 Chronicles 25:6-7 gives us information about how the Levite musicians in the ancient Hebrew culture felt about training their own musically. It states, "All these were under the hands of their father for song in the house of the LORD, with cymbals, psalteries, and harps, for the service of the house of God, according to the king's order to Asaph, Jeduthun, and Heman. So the number of them, with their brethren that were instructed in the songs of the LORD, even all that were cunning, was two hundred fourscore and eight." This teacher, scholar relationship (verse eight) was considered to be vital to the music education of their Levite sons. Notice that these musical sons were said to be "under the hands of" (*yad ab shiyr* 3027, 01, 7892) their fathers, who were themselves trained musicians. Although there are several possible shades of meaning in these Hebrew words, including possible reference to the ancient use of *cheironomy, we do know that their chief Levite fathers trained them personally to music unto *YHVH*.

The reason that the ancient Levite musicians considered it necessary for their Levite sons to receive a God centered music education was because, as 1 Chronicles 25:1 explains, "Moreover David and the captains of the host separated (*badal* 914) to the service (*abodah* 5656) of the sons of Asaph, and of Heman, and of Jeduthun, who should prophesy with harps, with psalteries, and with cymbals..." The significance of this statement is that David and the captains of the hosts had separated the Levite sons to prophesy with music. These young men had been separated, set apart, or distinguished for a life of musical service to God.

The word *separated* is translated from the Hebrew word *badal* (914) which connotes separation by way of selection. They would not submit their "separated" musical sons to the musical influence of Israel's godless neighbors. As was mentioned earlier, they instructed their musician sons "in the songs of the LORD" because their Levite sons were called to guide Israel's musicing in the generations to come. These Levite musicians were instructed (*lamad* 3925), i.e., made to be expert, in the songs of *YHVH*. This educational process was carried out "under the hands of their father for song." Hence we rightly deduce that in this century it is still necessary for our sons and daughters to receive a music education under the direct supervision of God-fearing Christian music educators.

Before developing a music education program, each Christian educational institution must answer the question, "Why should students receive a CME?" Certainly a music educator who is a *"Philistine" will educate those whom he comes in contact with to be "Philistine". If he did not seek to *inculcate every student with his philosophy, which will be without doubt not a Christ centered Bible-based philosophy, he would not be a good Philistine. Therefore, it is a great philosophical mistake to suppose that a musician who is not a Christian will instill biblical principles of musicing in the minds and hearts of our children. It is a fact that they will not emerge from a "Philistine" music teacher's tutelage instructed or expert in the songs of the Lord.

There are a wide variety of other reasons to support CME philosophically. One of the obvious justifications for teaching music is that music is one of the valuable and useful fine arts. Another reason is it can enrich the lives of the students who are involved in performing it, listening to it, and learning about its theory, history, and performance practice. A third justification is that student performers can be involved in enriching the lives of others with their musicing. Although all of these reasons are valuable justifications for teaching music they are not the main reason for including music in the curriculum of a Christian school, Christian college or university. The main philosophical justification for music education in the curriculum is that the Bible teaches so strongly that it is the responsibility of Christians to train their own.

Christian music educators who are committed to Christ have different music education goals for their students than worldly musicians do. This fact alone is reason enough to defend CME. However, Christians must answer several questions such as:

1) Are there real differences between CME and secular ME?
2) What are the goals of secular music education (SME) and CME?
3) What makes CME different from SME?
4) Are there enough differences between them to justify a CME and do these differences matter?

The answers to these questions will determine if a CME is a mere preference or a deep conviction.

A Christian music education philosophy (CMEP) must exude from Biblical principles of musicing. A congruent Bible-based music philosophy will help to instill in the lives of our children and young people an understanding of excellence in music. (See Philippians 1:9, 10.) An applied CMEP will serve as a guide for our youth in their development of the belief that music expresses real life meaning and therefore is not amoral.

Since the Bible is clear in its teaching that we are to be sepa-

## 5: Developing a Philosophy of Music Education 105

rated from that which is a part of this world's system (*aion*— see Romans 12:1, 2; 1 John 2:15-17), our music should exemplify this principle of separation. It is unreasonable to expect music educators that are not Christians and are a part of this present world's system to provide our children and youth with a Christocentric music education. Thus CME is not an option but rather a necessity as we begin the twenty-first century. Christian parents and Christian music educators must realize that the world is not a friend of grace.

Although everything about CME is not different from SME, there are fundamental differences that put the Christian music educator and the worldly music educator at *loggerheads philosophically. We know that there are a wide variety of acceptable styles available to the believer in both sacred and secular music that can be taught and performed in both SME and CME settings. However, the Christian music educator's musical emphasis is directed to help students acquire a taste for God honoring music styles. The purpose of CME is to prepare students to enter adulthood with enriched musical concepts that will enable them to use music as a concomitant to Christ centered living. It is also the purpose of CME to give students who wish to use music as their chosen profession a quality music education. When it comes to quality music education, a Christian music educator should have as high or higher expectations for their students as those of educators who are involved in SME.

Another justification for the Christian school and college is that our children and young people deserve to study music in an atmosphere that is not *saturated in the philosophy of this present world. As I have told my undergraduate music education classes so many times, when it comes to musicing, we are educating our students to function in the world (*kosmos*) but to function outside of this present world's system (*aion*). St. John 17:15 explains, "I pray not that thou shouldest take them out of the world (*kosmos* 2889), but that thou shouldest keep them from the evil." The Greek word translated as evil here is *poneros* (4190) which connotes keeping from the influence of that which is spiritually detrimental.

When it comes to the music education of our own, we have

the responsibility of providing music education and music performance opportunities in an environment that will protect them from harmful influences during their formative years. The music with which students engage should build their faith in God instead of filling their minds with the evil of this present world system. Since music with or without words communicates meaning, Christian parents cannot trust unregenerate music educators to make musical choices for our children.

Students should be able to enjoy and participate in musical activities at the elementary, secondary, and collegiate level without having to listen to and perform music that is offensive and contrary to their Christian beliefs. Engaging in music activities should be a vital educational and social part of a student's education at all levels. Memories from these musical experiences should be happy ones instead of being remembered as times of spiritual guilt and separation from other students. No Christian student should ever have to refrain from participating in musical activities because of the type of music being performed, uniforms, immodest costumes, offensive language, or inappropriate staging.

### What is the Essence of Music Education?

A Christian music educator must decide exactly what music education is. Is it performance? Is it an appreciation of music? Is it philosophical? Is it theoretical? Is it practical? Is it a historical knowledge of music? Is it an understanding of music theory? Is it a cultural aesthetic? Is it a multicultural knowledge and understanding of music? Many music educators give lip service to all of the aspects of music education mentioned above, but when their actual music education praxis is observed and evaluated, not very many areas of music education mentioned earlier are being carried out.

So, it is the responsibility of each Christian music educator to understand the *intrinsic nature, the indispensable quality, and the essential character of music education that formulate justifications for including it in the larger scheme of Christian education. Since music, like many of the other fine arts, is an abstract phenomenon, the Christian music educator must understand music's

## 5: Developing a Philosophy of Music Education 107

nature and value at its deepest levels in order to defend music on an aesthetic and utilitarian basis.

Every music educator has to decide whether music performance is merely one of the goals or the major goal of a CME, or if music appreciation classes provide aesthetic experiences that are successful in accomplishing the necessary goals of music education. Those who follow this praxis believe that listening, appreciating, and evaluating music are the realistic goals of music education in general, and that music performance organizations are for only a few talented students.

A very important question to be answered by all Christian music educators is whether or not every student needs to learn the *nuts and bolts of music. Is it essential for every student to be musically literate? A musically literate student knows how to read, write, perform and evaluate music. Any other music praxis is the outgrowth of a music education philosophy that purports that students may be sufficiently educated musically by primarily having aesthetic experiences through music listening, appreciating and evaluating.

Some music educators have accepted a philosophical position that supports the notion that being a music lover is education enough for the majority of students. The goal of this praxis is to educate students in music through the process of musical likes and dislikes that are *predicated on the student's musical tastes. These educators believe and purport that students are able to make lifelong choices concerning which styles of music are "the best" by learning a series of techniques for evaluating music. This philosophical belief accepts the notion that the majority of students do not learn best by doing but rather by listening and evaluating. To these music educators, knowing may be accomplished by active evaluating and by having aesthetic experiences through evaluating and listening.

Those who believe in a listening-evaluating praxis are seldom against performance organizations and private applied music lessons; rather they tend to believe that in many schools applied music and music performing organizations are over-stressed in school music education programs. They tend to point out that very few students are headed toward a music performance career. Therefore, the inordinate cost of music, instruments and proper facilities cannot be justified in an age of budget cuts and curriculum downsizing.

They are quick to point out that a highly mobile population has caused a condition in music education that makes it nearly impossible to educate students in reading, writing, and performing music. The reason for this educational hypothesis is that student populations in any given school situation are too fluid for systematic music education in music fundamentals, music history, music performance practice, and multicultural music education.

These music educators are aware that elementary schools, middle schools, junior high schools, and senior high schools have students in each grade that are educationally at many different levels. Therefore, they believe that traditional general music classes that require learning the nuts and bolts of music are impractical. They also tend to believe that the listening-evaluating-appreciating music education praxis is much more realistic than attempting to teach all students to read, write and perform music.

Some music educators who believe in listening, appreciating, and evaluating music education give lip service to the national standards of music education even though they are aware that these standards very clearly specify that every student must learn the nuts and bolts of music which are, of course, reading, writing, and performing music. Although aesthetic music education is stressed it is not the prime objective of these standards. Listening, appreciating, and evaluating are also a vital part of the national standards but these are only part of what is supposed to happen in a quality music education at the elementary and secondary level.

### Critical Thinking vs. Being Critical

As was mentioned earlier, my philosophical writings are largely about how musicians think. Thought shapes musical action, and action affects the long term direction. Musical direction determines musical destiny. We are not only what we eat, but we are also what we think and do musically.

Making daily musical decisions shapes the tenor of every Christian music educator's music praxis. All music education praxis exudes from music philosophy. Let me repeat that a music education philosophy is a series of systematic statements (beliefs) about the nature and value of the whole of music education. That understanding of music's nature and value gives the music educator an inner peace that is absolutely essential to following a congruent musical praxis. There is a peace that comes with being in the center of the Lord's will and teaching with a foundation of the biblical principles of the changed life of a Christian musician. Without that inner witness of the Holy Spirit, a music educator is destined to be driven about by the latest trends of what is popular in the world's opinion.

Furthermore, a Christian music education philosophy must be Christocentric; Christ's teachings must be at the center of a Christian music educator's musical beliefs. A Christian's music philosophy may be systematic, but if it does not follow the clear teachings of the Bible, it will be faulty. There is objective truth concerning music education. That truth is always Bible-based and congruent with the separated life of a Christian. Christian music educators must always consider what their music praxis will do to the whole-life of their students because no one musics in a vacuum. Proverbs 23:7 reminds us that, "For as he thinketh in his heart, so is he." All musicing is referential; students will muse on what they perform and listen to, and it will have an effect on their whole-life.

At the fundamental level a CMEP should be the result of a Christian musician's Bible-based thinking that has been developed into a music praxis. A music educator's thinking should be impregnated with critical thinking that is Christ centered. There is a vast gulf between being critical and being a musician that builds all philosophy and praxis as a result of careful critical thinking. I know that the terms *critical* and *critical thinking* are connotation words. So, let me define the terms very carefully. I define critical thinking as careful, disciplined thinking that is informed, clear, and rational and therefore backed by evidence. Furthermore it is the process of carefully conceptualizing musical and biblical evidence into congruent music education philosophy and praxis.

I define being critical as the inclination to judge severely without disciplined thinking that is the result of careful consideration of the biblical and musical facts. It is often the product of prejudice and a lack of musical understanding which comes from a lack of a long careful study of music in the Bible and music theory, history and performance practice that has taken place over many centuries. The term "critical thinking" should not be confused with the process of being unjustifiably critical.

Merely being a Christian and a talented, gifted practicing musician does not necessarily qualify a person to employ "critical thinking" about music education. One of the major difficulties of modern Christian elementary, secondary, and collegiate music education is that many of those who make the major decisions in these Christian educational organizations are not qualified musically to make curriculum and policy decisions concerning the musical education of Christian young people. Let me reiterate that simply being a Christian school or Christian college administrator does not qualify one to make music curriculum decisions. A wise Christian administrator always collaborates with a team of educators that are qualified in their field of educational endeavor.

## Music Education Philosophy must be Positive

"Critical thinking" about music education will of a necessity recognize pitfalls and shortcomings of various music education philosophies of the past one hundred years. However, identifying the problems of music education philosophies does little to solve these problems. The attitude that all musical endeavors until the present day have been faulty is shortsighted and lacks honesty. There is nothing wrong with proposing changes to current music education philosophy and praxis, but to deny the vast history of successful music education around the globe is an egotistical position. A careful Christian music educator will not get caught up in the faulty belief that almost everything done in music education is worldly, incongruent, or not adequate in some way.

Bennett Reimer stated, "And yet, having acknowledged the inherent limitations of any philosophy, it must be maintained that some philosophy— some underlying set of beliefs about the nature and value of one's field— is absolutely necessary if one is to be effective as a professional and if one's profession is to be effective as a whole."[1]

The way to keep from becoming a negative and unjustifiably critical music educator is to remain positive in one's thinking. Philippians 4:8 sums up the philosophical matter well: "Finally, brethren, whatsoever things are true, whatsoever things are honest, whatsoever things are just, whatsoever things are pure, whatsoever things are lovely, whatsoever things are of good report; if there be any virtue, and if there be any praise, think on these things."

If an undergraduate CMEP is going to lay the foundation necessary to accomplish its fundamental purpose, it must include much more than a long list of do's and don'ts. Music educators who enter the profession must know what to do and what not to do, but as necessary as teaching techniques are, they are not the *sine qua non* of music education. For instance, knowing how to conduct music patterns and having the ability for the left and right hand to function independently are almost worthless techniques unless the actions of the arms, hands and fingers are guided by a passion for the essence of the music, its nature and value, and its essential meaning in the context of musical performance. Understanding the nature and value of the music being performed by students should be guided by a strong and unified music philosophy.

All music education should exude from a passion for teaching. This only comes through a well-developed and unified understanding of why the music being taught to students is valuable to them in the context of their musical journeys. The music educator must understand why the music is valuable to students' understanding and love for the art of music. Again, such an understanding will come through a music philosophy that illuminates the nature and value of the specific piece of music being taught, and the nature and value of the students' music education at large.

A list of music education procedures does not instill a passion for teaching in the music educator. It is a unified and congruent music philosophy that will illuminate the music educator's understanding of the deepest levels of meaning of music that one teaches. A musical praxis will exude out of this educator's congruent music philosophy. This praxis must be impregnated with the conviction that music education in general, and the learning and performance of particular selections of music, are worthwhile and are deeply meaningful experiences to the students involved. Anything less will result in a perfunctory grinding out of the music in very lackluster and lifeless performances.

A biblical, solidly Christian, and clearly articulated philosophy of music education will do more to solve the many problems of music education than long lists of musical behaviors or problems concerning popular music, rock music or contemporary Christian music. A clear congruent CME philosophy will reveal the deepest levels of music's nature and value in the whole-life of a Christian.

A well written CME will consider the why, how, when, and to whom of music education. It will illuminate the deepest purposes for teaching music. It will consider music's importance in the overall educational system of a Christian school, college or university. It will also consider the philosophical issues essential to the process of insuring that an educational program is truly biblical, practical and thorough. It will also deal with the educator's truth basis concerning music's value to the institution, the students, and most of all how music is valuable to God's kingdom. A thorough CMEP will illuminate, for the music educator and the students, how and why the music education curriculum will equip those being educated to serve this present age musically.

## There is No Substitute for Musical Skill

1 Samuel 16:17— "And Saul said unto his servants, provide me now a man that can play well, and bring him to me." Because of King Saul's disobedience God rejected him as king. God then allowed an evil spirit to greatly trouble Saul. Saul's servants said, in verse sixteen, "Let our lord now command thy servants, which are before thee, to seek out a man who is a cunning player on an harp: and it shall come to pass, when the evil spirit from God [i.e., allowed by God] is upon thee, that he shall play with his hand, and thou shalt be well."

God opened a door of ministry to David because he was an accomplished musician. Today God still opens doors of music ministry to those who have prepared musically to be "cunning players." The words *cunning* (*yada* 3045) and *player* (*nagan* 5059)

## 5: Developing a Philosophy of Music Education 113

mean that David was accomplished or was able to perform well on his musical instrument. Because there is such a great need for musicians who can "do," I am constrained to only accept a musical praxis that trains all students to read, write, perform and evaluate both sacred and secular music.

God uses musicians who have practiced until they are musically aware and have become skillful on their instrument. There is no substitute for a thorough, broad study of music. Those who apply themselves to musical study have greater doors of musical opportunity opened to them than those who struggle when they perform on their musical instrument. All those who make decisions concerning music education must have an understanding of music. Such understanding is only given to those who are musically literate, i.e., are able to read, write, perform and evaluate music. On this philosophical basis we reject a music philosophy and praxis that is solely appreciation-listening based. Being a music lover does not qualify one to make decisions concerning a CME.

The sixteenth chapter of 1 Samuel is the oldest extant account of music therapy. 1 Samuel 16:23 states, "And it came to pass, when the evil spirit from God [allowed by God] was upon Saul, that David took an harp, and played with his hand: so Saul was refreshed, and was well, and the evil spirit departed from him." David was very well prepared musically. This Scripture tells us that he *nagan im yad* (5059, 5973, 3027), i.e., he played with his open hand as opposed to playing with a pick in the closed hand. It is believed that the *kinnor* (3658) was usually played with a pick but David played with his fingers, indicating that he could play skillfully. Also, 1 Samuel 16:18 states that one of Saul's servants had seen David play the *kinnor* and reported that he was a cunning player (*yada*, 3045 *nagan* 5059). *Nagan* means to play with the fingers rather than merely playing with a pick, thus supporting the belief that David was a very skillful player. *Yada*, in this instance, also connotes knowledgeable and discerning playing.

So, with all of this in mind, we can understand that one of the main reasons that David was given the opportunity to minister musically to King Saul was that David was prepared musically. As mentioned earlier, God allows musicians to serve Him in as great a capacity as they are capable to do, based on their spiritual and musical preparation. Therefore, one should plan for life-long continued music preparation in order to be able to give God the best that a Christian musician is capable of giving musically.

## Submitting Music Education to Christ

Mark 6:35a states, "He [Jesus] answered and said unto them [His disciples], give ye them to eat." After Jesus taught the people, his disciples wanted Jesus to send those He had taught away so the people could go somewhere and buy something to eat. The disciples were overwhelmed at the enormous task of feeding about 5000 people. The job was too costly and too big for them, but it was not too big for Jesus.

Christian musicians are often just as overwhelmed at the tasks before them. Eighty thousand dollars for a new organ; seventy-nine thousand dollars for a new grand piano; as well as responsibility for an elementary choir, a junior high choir, a high school choir, and an elementary general music program; music appreciation, and music theory classes; beginning, intermediate and advanced band and orchestra rehearsals; an Easter pageant; and a Christmas production with a special choir, orchestra, sets, lights and drama— all these are definitely too much pressure and too much work and responsibility for any music educator. However, many Christian music educators find themselves with all or most of the aforementioned list of responsibilities.

In the midst of a busy music career it sometimes seems that Jesus is saying, "Do it all yourself. " What we often forget is that although the Lord does expect our meager musical "loaves and fish, " God blesses our work and provides for the "five thousand. " God takes whatever we have and when He has blessed it, it is enough and it will be sufficiently proper to accomplish the music education task.

It is our responsibility to give of our best educational and musical efforts to the Master, and it is His responsibility to bless our music education ministry so that it will be effective. Jesus said that it is our responsibility to provide for our own household. However, He does not expect us to do it with our own strength or power. We are required to give those who are under our tutelage the best that we have, but we must remember that our teaching and our musicing will only accomplish the desired task if we will let Him "bless and break" our efforts so that they will feed all those who are under our musical instruction.

**Training Our Own**

1 Chronicles 25:6 tells us, "All these were under the hands of their father for song in the house of the LORD, with cymbals, psalteries, and harps, for the service of the house of God according to the King's order to Asaph, Jeduthun, and Heman." The Levite sons were under their father's "hands for song" (*yad shiyr* 3027, 7891). This Scripture is probably a reference to *cheironomy*, i.e., the use of hand signs to designate pitches to the Levite musicians. So, these musicians were under the hands of their father who was a *cheironomer, or at least knew how to teach others the ancient art of cheironomy. Now many centuries later, young people are under our hands for song like the Levite sons in ancient Israel. The conducting gestures used by the conductor actually place these ministering Christian musicians under his or her hands.

It is an awesome responsibility to have children, young people, and adults who are depending on us for musical and spiritual leadership. Chapter twenty-five of 1 Chronicles is a discourse about the chief musicians who were music directors, and the young musicians who received musical training and leadership from godly musicians like Asaph, Heman (Ethan), and Jeduthun. These Levite men taught musical matters in the context of service to Elohiym, the supreme exceeding God.

The Christian music educator has an awesome responsibility, like Heman, to be the King's "seer" or a beholder of a vision of God's kingdom (see 1 Chronicles 25:5). As a Christian musician you are responsible to pass that vision on to those with whom you minister and those who are "under your hands." 1 Chronicles 25:3 states, "Of Jeduthun; Gedaliah, and Zeri, and Jeshaiah, and Mattithiah [and Shimei, mentioned in verse 17], six under the hands of their father Jeduthun, who prophesied with a harp, to give thanks and to praise the LORD."

This Scripture is an example of a musician in ancient Israel who was wise enough to musically educate his own sons. According to 1 Chronicles 25:7, "So the number of them, with their brethren that were instructed in the songs of the LORD, even all that were cunning, was two hundred fourscore and eight." These ancient musicians did not send their children to the Philistines to receive music lessons. They trained their own because they had musical *massa* (4853) or burden for the musical training of his own household, like Chenaniah mentioned in 1 Chronicles 15:22.

The concept of training our own is not only an Old Testament concept, but also a New Testament principle. 1 Timothy 5:8 states, "But if any provide not for his own, and specially for those of his own house, he hath denied the faith, and is worse than an infidel."[2] Although this New Testament verse does not specifically mention music education, The concept mentioned here is broader than the care of widows.

One more concept is note-worthy in this passage of Scripture. 1 Chronicles 25:1 records, "Moreover David and the captains of the host separated to the service of the sons of Asaph, and of Heman, and of Jeduthun, who should prophesy with harps, with psalteries, and with cymbals..." The musical sons of Jeduthun prophesied *(naba, nabiy* 5012, 5030— to sing by inspiration as a prophet) with the harp. It is significant that the six sons were taught to sing by inspiration while they played the harp, psaltery, and cymbals by their God-fearing chief musician father. He taught his sons to give thanks, i.e., hold out their hands in avowal and thankfulness to God. He also taught them to praise (*halal* 1984) and to show or to boast about the self-existent, eternal God as they sang and played by the inspiration of God.

Many parents who love and serve the Lord do not recognize the great need for the next generation to be "instructed in the songs of the LORD. " As a matter of fact, some Christian parents do not recognize that their children need any music education at all. Many parents who are not Christians are more consistent in training their children musically than some Christian parents. Assuming that an astute music educator recognizes the necessity of quality music in elementary and secondary education, we are now ready to consider the necessity of a study of music philosophy at the elementary and secondary levels. It is one thing for a plumber to know how to turn the water on and off, but it is entirely another for him to know why water comes out when the water faucet is turned on. It is amazing that so many elementary and secondary Christian music educators are satisfied to teach mainly the appreciation of music to these students without teaching then to know philosophically why a type of music should or should not be included as a part of the student's life-long music listening and performing. Far too many music educators have the philosophy that music students should, after being guided through listening and analyzing experiences (with a few visual aids), have a life-long appreciation for a type of music.

Students have the right to know why an educator believes that a style of music is appropriate or inappropriate, good or bad, helpful or harmful to them spiritually. Understanding music at this level comes through an understanding of the formal properties of the music; the style of the music; the intent of the composer or the arranger; the text (if it is vocal music); and the current associations that the music has or does not have with subcultures that are not compatible with the principles of a changed life of a Christian. During the elementary and secondary years students must be presented with the musical and philosophical tools that are necessary to make wise life-long choices of both sacred and secular music.

By the time a student enters a college or university, it is much too late to introduce them to music philosophy. Becoming musically literate before entering college or university is absolutely necessary. However, a deep congruent philosophical understanding of the nature and value of music will do more to prepare pre-college students to enter college with the ability to make wise choices of both sacred and secular music than any other aspect of their music education. This is not to say that all the other aspects of a Christian elementary and secondary music education are not also necessary— because they are.

There must be a pre-collegiate, pre-secondary philosophical music education that will equip these students to understand the nature and value of the whole of music at its deepest levels. This does not mean that an elementary level student should be taught music philosophy at the same level of difficulty as a college student. Music educators should simply apply the principles of *curriculum spiral sequence to the study of music philosophy.[3] Only an understanding of music's significance will equip students who are entering post-secondary education to make educated, biblically based congruent musical decisions in adult life.

Almost all of a Christian youth's philosophical presuppositions concerning the musics that will be included in his or her lifelong decision making will be established long before the student ever enters a college or university. The age old maxim, "If you want to change a world's music philosophy, teach elementary music; if you want to change nothing philosophically teach music at the college level," is probably a much more accurate statement than most music educators are willing to admit. Someone has said that college music students only remember about five percent of a college music professor's lectures. In Matthew 13:13 Jesus made this statement about teaching adults: "Therefore speak I to them in parables: because they seeing see not; and hearing they hear not, neither do they understand." Once an adult has established a philosophy it is very difficult to effect any musical change. Probably only the blessed Holy Spirit will be successful in making much change in college student's musical actions.

### Music as a Part of the Larger Educational Picture

There is a vital need for music education in the Christian school before students enter college. If the music classes are going to be a part of a congruent educational system, then every educational institution must have a written educational philosophy, and their music departments must develop a music education philosophy that is congruent with that philosophy. There is not only a need to have a written series of systematic statements concerning the nature and value of music education, but there is also a need to continually reevaluate and revise this document in light of the goals and objectives of the larger educational organization.

It is one thing to have a series of basic beliefs about music education, but it is another to cultivate an educational institution's

## 5: Developing a Philosophy of Music Education

philosophy of music education as a way of improving the overall quality of education in a particular setting. Also, experienced music teachers need to be involved in the process of examining the institution's philosophy of education. Each Christian institution is unique and its music education philosophy and praxis should be a good match to that institution. Music educators should always be aware that they are a part of the big picture of the Christian school or college where they teach.

Musicians many times forget that learning about music and learning to music is always done within the context of a community. No one learns music in a bubble. The large educational atmosphere of the institution will greatly affect a student's musical likes and dislikes. If a music educator is going to have very much success in developing the quality of the musical tastes of the students, the general community atmosphere of the Christian school or college must be congruent with the changed life principles of Christian living that, of course, include music. Therefore, the Christian music educator must become a part of the larger community of the Christian school or college that has the same goals and purposes for developing the Christian character of each of its students.

Successful music educators have a tendency to isolate themselves in the process of getting the job done well. However, those who ignore the larger educational philosophy and praxis of the mother organization almost always have problems in the area of advocacy with administrators and board members of that institution. Administrators and educational boards of directors almost always have a mistrust of music departments that do not outwardly demonstrate that they are a willing part of the "big educational picture" and that they have a verbal and written regard for that overall educational philosophy of that educational institution.

### "Write this Song and Teach It"

In Deuteronomy 31:19 God instructed Moses, "Now therefore write ye this song for you, and teach (*lamad* 3925) it the children of Israel: put it in their mouths, that this song may be a witness for me against the children of Israel." Verse 22 states further, "Moses therefore wrote this song the same day, and taught (3122) it the children of Israel." The word *teach* in verse 19 and *taught* in verse 22 is *lamad* (3925) and means to goad or to instruct in order to make one expert. So, God told Moses to goad or instruct the people by teaching them a song.

God knew that Israel was going to rebel against Him. He promised that He would be angry with them and that He would hide His face from them. It is an awful thing for God to turn His back on the rebellious. God will not let sin go unpunished forever because He is a just God. As Christian musicians, we cannot condone sin. As true ministers of music our musicing must picture sin as ugly and awful. Therefore, it is our responsibility to educate our children and youth to discriminate between what is acceptable and what is unacceptable in the life of a Christian.

God still demands that our musicing should not only tell about His love, longsuffering and forgiveness, but also of His justice. Romans 6:23 very clearly teaches us that "...the wages of sin is death, but the gift of God is eternal life through Jesus Christ our Lord." Although it will not be easy, we must educate the next generation of Christian musicians how to music not only about God's love, but also God's judgment, which is tempered with His love and forgiveness. A truly Christian music educator will use music to goad or educate the next generation by telling them complete truth about the wages of sin. Although it is much more pleasant to sing only of God's love, God's justice is also a necessary part of an honest, complete Christian music education.

## A Philosophy that Covers the Whole of Music

A Christian philosophy of music education must concern itself with the nature and value of all of sacred and secular music. It is faulty to follow the notion that the way to deal with the whole of music (both sacred and secular) is to ignore half of it. Some Christian music educators seem to believe that music education in the Christian school and college can ignore secular music. Now this philosophy is simple, isn't it? Yes, it is— too simple. They seem to believe that secular music does not matter to a Christian because a Christian should only listen to and perform religious music. Why doesn't this music philosophy work? It does not work because they choose to believe that secular music does not affect them or their family spiritually. However, while they refuse to deal with secular music, their children purchase it and listen to it incessantly.

The reason we know that secular music must be included in a CME curriculum is because children are deeply involved with secular music at many levels. When Christian music educators ignore the whole of music by failing to include the study of secular music, their students do not develop the skills necessary to make wise choices of secular music. Hence they do not develop musical and biblical guidelines for the inclusion or exclusion of all styles of music in the changed life of a Christian. Another reason that the music educator must consider secular music is that it is a worthy use of leisure time and that there is much secular music that is worthy of serious musical study.

Many Christian music educators have left this part of music education up to the parents. The decision that is sometimes made by parents is for young people to get rid of all secular music that is of a questionable nature. Now we have a bona fide musical generation gap on our hands. The younger generation rebels and at this point, a series of yelling matches or serious misunderstandings will probably take place. These misunderstandings occur because music educators and parents have ignored the problem instead of developing a *lucid music philosophy that covers the whole of music.[4]

### Defining "Secular Music"

At this point a definition of secular music is necessary. Secular music deals with the temporal and does not address itself to religious matters. I never mean that it is proper to include anti-Christ music or music that promotes social or moral rebellion or error of any kind. If the music part of the music (words excluded) does not appeal to the lust of the flesh and if it is clean (words included), there is no scriptural basis for excluding it from the life of a Christian. This is not referring to secular rock music and other genres of destructive popular music in the definition above. They have become a meta-language of filth that should not be included in a music education program as good choices of secular music.

It would be much simpler if a Christian's musical choices only involved appropriate sacred music. However, the inclusion of only sacred music is much too simplistic and therefore is incomplete. Although there is nothing morally wrong with excluding all music except sacred music, it certainly will impoverish the artistic life of those we are seeking to educate.

Christ said in St. John 10:10b, "I am come that they might have life, and that they might have it more abundantly (*perissos* 4053)." Part of this *perissos* is the superabundance of life that is enjoyed by the Christian, who follows Christ's precepts and keeps all that is heard, seen, and done with the fine arts under the Lordship of Christ. The Christian is then free to fully enjoy the beauty and import of God's creation. Those who exclude the great classics, and other styles of music of an even lesser degree of import and profundity, only deny themselves some of God's purest pleasure afforded to those who enjoy the fine arts. A part of abundant living is being able, with God's guidance, to include many styles and types of music in the whole life of a Christian.

Ignoring the "whole" of music only creates a "hole" in one's music education philosophy. When a Christian music educator ignores the whole of music it stops communication between parents and children, teachers and students, and pastors and their parishioners. The greatest cause of the generation gap in music between parents and their children, and music educators and students, is the inability to civilly discuss wise choices in both secular and sacred music in an educated manner. Please note that these should be civil discussions. Remember, parents and music educators, it is a mistake to do the right thing in the wrong way.

### Philosophies of Utilizing the National Standards

When it comes to educating Christian young people musically, there is no substitute for knowing what it is that music educators wish to accomplish in the educational process. The Music Educators National Conference (now known as the National Association for Music Educators) produced the national standards for music education, most recently updated in 2014. Although the national content standards have been a source of unification among music educators, each Christian music educator must develop his or her CMEP in light of what the Bible teaches concerning music. There is no philosophical problem with Christian music educators molding the voluntary national standards into a Christocentric MEP. Hopefully music educators who are praxialists and believe that CME should be guided by "doing" or performing, and educators who believe in music education as aesthetic education, will both be able to successfully incorporate the content standards into a CMEP.

The key to a quality music education philosophy is balance. If a *praxialist ignores the standards because of the performance pressure of music performing groups, then educational balance will not be achieved. If a music educator who is an *aesthetician neglects learning the nuts and bolts of music, like reading, writing and performing music, because he or she believes that an aesthetic listening based music education program is the ultimate goal of CME, then the MEAE program will not achieve educational balance. Praxial music education can be a form of aesthetic music education, since there is probably not a better way for students to have aesthetic experiences with the art of music than by "doing", i.e., performing it. A CMEP that ignores music performance either partially or totally is without doubt a faulty philosophy and praxis.

Music educators are not in agreement concerning whether CME should follow a performance (praxialist) or a MEAE (aesthetician) music education philosophy. Educators from both educational views sometimes make claims that the other is not a truly balanced academic approach to music education. The problem is not primarily academic, but rather practical, because both music education plans provide for student evaluations which are of an academic nature. A praxialist may incorporate regular playing evaluations and the aesthetician may incorporate academic evaluations of listening, evaluating, and appreciating music at a level that is beyond mere tests that evaluate listening and enjoying music. Also many MEAE proponents can and do incorporate music performance in their music education praxis. So, the voluntary standards that have been available to music educators for decades are compatible with either a MEAE or a praxialist philosophy, but the way they will be achieved will be somewhat different. I suggest that you study the standards below in light of the educational view you support.[5]

## Utilizing the National Standards in a CMEP

In 2014 the National Music Standards were revised and expanded in the context of music literacy and artistic processes: creating, performing, and responding. There is nothing about the national voluntary standards that violate philosophical guidelines of a Bible-based CMEP. Therefore, there is no reason why any Christian music educator would be offended by any of them. These voluntary standards for music education should be incorporated into every Christian school's music philosophy and praxis. The inclusion of these music education standards does not preclude the use of additional spiritual and musical standards in a CMEP. Singing, performing on instruments, improvising, composing and arranging, and reading and writing music, listening discriminately, evaluating music and performances, music's relationship to other arts, and music's historical and multi-cultural relationships, are all necessary and valuable components of a CMEP.

One of the shortcomings of music education, both in secular and religious settings, has been the lack of educating students multiculturally. Christian musicians have too often viewed music through Western eyes. There are musics from many cultures that do not violate Bible principles of musicing. If a type of music does not violate Christian principles then it is redeemable in Christian culture. One of the objectives of a CMEP is to study musics from other world cultures and evaluate them in light of a Christocentric music aesthetic. All too often CMEP has excluded the study of any music that is not clearly Western and does not follow the rules of music of the *Occident. Christian music educators must not look at non-Western music through Western eyes but rather through Christian eyes, recognizing that many styles of music are redeemable if they do not violate biblical principles of musicing or are not closely related to anti-Christ culture.

Every Christian music educator should be reminded that the music notation of the entire Old Testament (the *te 'amim*) does not follow the rules of music of the Occident, yet no one could say that the music of the Bible does not follow its own precepts. All the Old Testament was notated long before and without the influence of the music of the Occident.[6]

So, every CMEP should include multicultural music study, at least in an evaluative manner. Since the goal of a CME is not the exclusion of all musics that are not from the music culture where the Christian educational institution exists geographically, any music that does not violate Christian principles is redeemable and usable in the specific culture from where that music originates. If Christian musicians are going to reach people from other world cultures, this musical and philosophical distinction must be recognized in a CMEP. If students never have the opportunity to apply Christian principles to other world music, they will not be able to make wise choices concerning music that is not Western.

A Christian musician who has been educated in one of the countries of the Occident and teaches music in a non-Western cultural setting must be equipped to function in that cultural setting. Everything that exists in a particular culture that is fitting in the context of a Christian philosophy of the fine arts should be utilized in that cultural setting. This philosophical belief extends to the use of other *world music. The Christian music educator should be cautioned that the associations which a type of music has in the context of a particular culture or sub-culture do matter. Therefore, music educators who are called upon to teach in a different culture than the one with which they are intimately associated should seek the advice of a musically educated Christian who lives in that culture and understands a particular music's cultural associations in that world setting.

Music teachers should be reminded that it is the responsibility of every Christian music educator to develop a Christian approach to the fine art of music instead of a Western cultural approach to music. Music, Western or non-Western, is not the doorway to God's kingdom and must not ever become the object of worship. God is the object of worship and He should never have to share His worth-ship with music performance, a musical performer or music as an art form.

## The Performance Emphasis Debate in Music Education

It was assumed for decades in the first half of the twentieth century that the ultimate culmination of educational efforts in music education was having the ability to "do" rather than merely to "appreciate". The philosophy of the MEAE enthusiasts that became influential in the late 60s and early 70s brought the music performance philosophy and praxis into question. Bennett Reimer wrote in 1970, "For music educators and for a large portion of the general public the terms 'music education' and 'performance' were synonymous. But just as every other part of the school curriculum has come under scrutiny in recent years, the performance program finds itself being examined according to changing conditions of education."[7]

From that time until now the music educators who support the MEAE philosophy have been in serious debate with music educators who believe in strong performance programs as the central culmination of the efforts of music education. The former group is called MEAE educators and the latter group has come to be known as the praxialists.

Bennett Reimer's music philosophy book, *A Philosophy of Music Education*, has had much influence on music educators, and so has David Elliot's Music education philosophy book, *Music Matters*. The writings of both of these music education philosophers have caused the music education profession at large to give much needed attention to what the goals of music education should be. As was mentioned earlier, the school music performance emphasis was criticized because of cost and scheduling problems, because it could not involve all students, and because of the argument that so few students ultimately choose music performance as a career.

MEAE emphasis has been severely criticized because in many situations it became a listening-evaluating based educational program. Probably its greatest criticism has been that the ultimate music education goals seem to be learning to have aesthetic experiences with music largely through music listening and evaluating rather than experiencing music personally through performing.

The debate is far from over, and although both sides have scrutinized the other philosophy and praxis legitimately, both sides could and should learn from each other. Sometimes performance programs exist and are heavily supported because of their participation at sports events and in school public relations efforts. Under such conditions the performance organization is not really educationally and philosophically supported by the strong educational conviction that every student should be afforded the opportunity to become a part of an organization that "does" music, but rather by the music organization's usefulness in sports events and public relations efforts.

Many of the MEAE programs are now heavily criticized because listening based music education programs produce graduates that often are not musically literate. When the emphasis is not on the nuts and bolts of music that enable all students to read, write, and perform music, students graduate without the academic tools necessary to be involved in active musicing in adult life. When one considers David Elliott's understanding of music, there is no wonder that the usual emphasis of MEAE proves to be inadequate to him. According to Dr. Elliott,

> "Music, then, is a four-dimensional concept at least. Music is a tetrad of complementary dimensions involving (1) a doer, (2) some kind of doing, (3) something done, and (4) the complete context in which the doers do what they do. Let us refer to musical doers as *musicers*, to musical doing as *musicing*, and to the musical 'something done' as music in the sense of performances, improvisations, and other kinds of audible musical achievements. Please note that the term *musicing* is a contraction for music making."[8]

152
St. John 16:13 assures the Christian musician, "Howbeit when he, the Spirit of truth, is come, he will guide you into all truth: for he shall not speak of himself; but whatsoever he shall hear, that shall he speak: and he will shew you things to come." The Holy Spirit is faithful to guide Christian musicians in the development of a philosophical *truth basis. "All truth" extends to the Holy Spirit's guidance in the process of developing a CMEP. Sometimes Christian musicians form philosophical beliefs, act on the basis of those

beliefs, and pray later when the going gets rough, but that is not God's perfect plan for CME.

This book will certainly not clarify everything about the deepest understandings of CME and whether MEAE philosophy or praxialist music philosophy should be incorporated into a CMEP. I would caution Christian music educators who are developing a CMEP that the ultimate goal of CME is the preparation of Christians to bring musical praise and honor to God. Therefore, it is the responsibility of CME to prepare all students to enter adulthood musically literate. The only way that Christians will be able to successfully pass Christian music values on to the next generation is for those adults to be able to read, write, perform and evaluate music in the context of Christian perspective. That makes CME distinctively different than secular music education (SME).

## Christian Musicians Who Know Teach More Effectively

Some Christian music educators who are not praxialists seem to live under the false impression that a music education praxis that requires musical performance as a major part of its goals is a late twentieth or early twenty-first century notion. But Aristotle (c. 384 BC— c.322 BC) had a philosophy of educating young people to be able to make quality judgments concerning music.

> "We must now return to the question raised earlier— must they learn to sing themselves and play instruments with their own hands? Clearly actual participation in performing is going to make a big difference to the quality of the person that will be produced; it is impossible, or at any rate very difficult, to produce good judges of musical performance from among those who have never themselves performed. And all that we have been saying makes it clear that musical education must include actual performing; and it is not difficult to decide what is appropriate and what is not for different ages, or to find an answer to those who assert that learning to perform is vulgar and degrading. Since, as we have seen, actual performance is needed to make a good critic, they should while young do much playing and singing, and then, when they are older, give up performing;

they will then, thanks to what they have learned in their youth, be able to enjoy music aright and give good judgments."[9]

Why should Christian music educators be concerned with musical performance in the process of developing a student's life-long preparation in music? As Aristotle put it centuries ago, performing is essential to the development of a person who will be able to make good judgments about music. One of music education's major problems in the twenty-first century is the failure to develop Christians who understand musical performance and what it is capable of doing to the whole-life of the performer and listener. The music appreciator must have the ability to perform, or as Aristotle asserted, it will be "impossible, or at any rate very difficult," to prepare a person to make quality life-long decisions of music's quality and value.

Although the world considers us to be bigoted, Christian music educators and Christian parents certainly have the responsibility to pass conservative music values to the succeeding generation. The fact is that although it is our responsibility, we cannot teach what we do not know. Christian education and public education have often failed students by not teaching them to know music for themselves. Knowing how to perform music is not the only goal of music education, but it should be one of the most important goals of any music education praxis.

It takes a community to raise a Christian musician, and it requires a number of successfully completed goals to properly prepare a person to make life-long quality decisions that are educationally and philosophically in congruency with Bible principles of musicing. Since this discussion is not a "how to," but rather a philosophical discussion, I will refrain from going into detail about how a church music director or a music educator should go about educating Christian youth in such a manner that they will be able to become, as Aristotle put it, a "good critic." I do, however, strongly support utilizing all of the objectives presented in the US National Music Education Standards of 1974 and the new presentation of these standards in June of 2014. I also assert that when Christian music education's goals are fine-tuned they will be somewhat different than those of secular public music education because, as Philippians 1:10 states, "That ye may approve [*dokimazo* 1381] things that are excellent [*diaphero* 1308]; that ye may be sincere and without offence [*aproskopos* 677] till the day of Christ."

Christian music educators must become aware that, although St. Paul was not referring specifically to music in this discussion, the principles being taught here extend to excellence of music in the life of a Christian. Excellence as described in this epistle to the Christians at Philippi means more than high quality performance. The word *diaphero* that he used in verse 10 has shades of meaning that connote tossing things about objectively: things that differ from or surpass other choices, things that are more excellent, and things that are of more value. Therefore, although Christian music educators should approve quality music performance they should only approve music that is of a higher and changed or renovated character that is congruent with the changed life of a Christian.

Plato also had much to say about correct musical judgment.

> "Afterwards, in course of time, an unmusical license set in with the appearance of poets who were men of native genius, but ignorant of what is right and legitimate in the realm of the Muses. Possessed by a frantic and unhallowed lust for pleasure, they contaminated laments with hymns and paeans with dithyrambs, actually imitated the strains of the flute on the harp, and created a universal confusion of forms. Thus their folly led them unintentionally to slander their profession by the assumption in music that there is no such thing as right and wrong, the right standard being the pleasure given to the hearer, be he high or low."[10]

So, those who suppose that the concept that there is right and wrong, and that which is legitimate and appropriate in music is only a late twentieth century desperate effort to fight new approaches to music and music performance, are sadly misinformed. As early as the lifetime of Plato (c. 420 BC— c. 348 BC), philosophers were considering the concept of what was right and wrong concerning music and judgments made on this basis. Of course, a Christian does not agree with much of Platonic thought (and Aristotelean thought),

## 5: Developing a Philosophy of Music Education  131

but there is no reason that a Christian musician should not give serious consideration to the fact that from ancient times until somewhere in the twentieth century, philosophers believed that there was such a thing as right and wrong concerning music and music performance.

At the risk of repeating myself, I must also add that the Bible is not silent concerning musical performance in the process of training our young people. The twenty-fifth chapter of 1 Chronicles begins by explaining that, "Moreover David and the captains of the host separated to the service of the sons of Asaph, and of Heman, and of Jeduthun, who should prophesy with harps, with psalteries, and with cymbals..." This verse makes it very clear that these Levite sons were separated to perform on instruments of music. They were commissioned and taught how to perform the music of the Temple.

Verses six and seven of the twenty-fifth chapter of 1 Chronicles give further explanation of this ancient music education process. "All these were under the hands of their father for song in the house of the LORD, with cymbals, psalteries, and harps, for the service of the house of God, according to the king's order to Asaph, Jeduthun, and Heman. So the number of them, with their brethren that were instructed in the songs of the LORD, even all that were cunning, was two hundred fourscore and eight." Notice that the chief Levite musicians instructed (*lamad* 3925), i.e., taught their sons to be skillful performers of the songs (*shiyr* 7892) of the Lord (*YHVH* 3068). This Scripture leaves no question about the specificity of their performance education—they were not only taught about this music but were also taught to perform the songs of the Lord. I have no doubt that they studied about the ancient didactic lyric poetry that was a part of their music ministry in the Temple, but the study and appreciation of this ancient lyric poetry was certainly not the end of the praxis of musically educating these Levite sons— they actually performed this music in the context of Temple worship.

### Endnotes

1. Reimer, *A Philosophy of Music Education*, 3.
2. kindred-cf. Cambridge KJV
3. See "Keeping Christian Music Education Academic" in chapter six. Also see

Isaiah 28:10&13.
4. See *Church Music Matters,* Chapter 13.
5. The 2014 music standards are available through the website for the National Association for Music Education.
6. See *Music of the Bible in Christian Perspective,* Chapter 8.
7. Reimer, *A Philosophy of Music Education,* 126.
8. David Elliott, *Music Matters: A New Philosophy of Music Education* ( New York: Oxford University Press, 1995), 40.
9. Piero Weiss and Richard Taruskin. *Music in the Western World A History in Documents* (New York: Schirmer Books, 1984), 11, quoting Aristotle's *The Politics* (part of 307—316).
10. Ibid, 7, quoting Plato's *Laws* (part of 700a).

## Chapter Five Word Meanings

**Aesthetician**— as used here, a person who is knowledgeable about the nature and appreciation of beauty in the fine arts.

**Affective domain**— refers to learning outcomes in music education that involve attitudes, motivation, and values.

**Assessable**— the vehicles used in the process of music education are capable of being evaluated in terms of student understanding and academic growth.

**Cheironomer**— a musically knowledgeable person in ancient times who used hand signs to designate pitches to another musician who was playing a musical instrument.

**Cognitive domain**— refers to the area of music study that focuses on the processes and the qualitative results as well as the ability to apply intelligence.

**Concomitant**— something that naturally accompanies or follows something else. As used here it is the belief that music accompanies preaching especially in a subordinate way.

**Curriculum spiral**— refers to Jerome Bruner's theory of cognitive growth, applied by teaching content at increasing levels of complexity throughout a student's education.

**Import**— the meaning or significance of a particular selection of music, especially when the meaning or the music is not directly stated.

**Inculcate**— to instill in someone an idea, attitude, habit, or way of doing by constant instruction.

**Intrinsic**— inherent and belonging naturally.

**Loggerheads**— those who are engaged in strong disagreement or dispute so much so that they are at an impasse.

**Lucid musicing**— a philosophy or way of musicing that is clear or congruent.

**Maxim**— a well-known statement expressing a general truth or fundamental principle.

**Nuts and bolts of music**— the essential elements necessary for reading, writing and performing music.

**Occident**— the countries of Europe and the Americas as contrasted with countries of Africa and Asia.

**Philistine** – direct enemies of Israel and of God; Israel would have never sent their sons to be trained by them.

**Praxialist**— one who follows a particular intentional way of doing something. Among music educators it has come to mean a music educator who follows the concept of "doing" music rather than merely listening, appreciating and evaluating music.

**Predicate**— to base or establish a belief on some concept.

**Proxy**— as used here, the authority to represent the parent as the one to educate a child musically.

**Psychomotor domain**— in music education, refers to learning that is demonstrated, and thus evaluated, by physical skills such as coordination, dexterity, manipulation, grace, strength, and speed. All of these actions demonstrate the use of fine motor skills.

**Sacred trust**— a calling that causes life-long devotion and service to God.

*Sine qua non*— the essential condition, action, or thing that is absolutely necessary.

**Spurious**— false, fake, or not being what it purports to be.

**Truth basis**— the body of statements and propositions on which a judgment has been made that they are true.

**Whole-life philosophy**— a philosophy that covers every aspect of a Christian's life and is congruent with the principles taught in the Bible. A whole-life philosophy is predicated on the belief that all aspects of a Christian's life must be Christ centered (under the Lordship of Christ) and that no aspect of a Christian's life is autonomous.

**World music**— music that originates from or is influenced by non-Western musical traditions.

### Chapter Five Questions for Discussion

1. Discuss the topic, "Why Christian Music Education?"
2. Explain your position on the place of music in Christian education.
3. In a paragraph or two give your defense for Christian music education.
4. Discuss the topic, "There is no substitute for musical skill."
5. Explain why or why not you believe that Christians have the responsibility to train our own children musically.

6. Please explain what you believe to be the essence of music education.
7. Discuss the author's belief that a Christian music education philosophy must cover the whole of music.
8. Explain whether or not you believe that there is any defense for the inclusion of secular music in the life of a Christian.
9. Explain how you would keep music education academic if you were in charge of a music education program in a Christian school.
10. Explain your position on whether or not teaching music is a sacred trust.

# 6

# Congruency in Music Education and Musicing

### Definitions of Terms Used in Music Education

PERHAPS THE PLACE TO START this portion of our philosophical discussion is with some definitions of terms. The term *congruent* is generally defined as meaning agreement, harmony, correspondence or conformity. Although the word *music* needs no general definition, technically it is a series of organized sounds and silences formed into a congruent whole. *Musicing* is a word coined by the music philosopher David Elliott in the late twentieth century. Elliott is correct in his belief that music education should be largely the act of musicing and is therefore a praxial art of "doing". Since at its core it is the act of making music, it is a different approach, somewhat opposed to the mainstream of aesthetic music education that is largely a "listening, enjoying and evaluating" based praxis.

Elliott has taught at the University of Toronto, Indiana University, and Northwest University as a visiting professor. He joined the New York University graduate faculty in 2002. He is the author of the book *Music Matters: a New Philosophy of Music Education, Praxial Music Education: Reflections and Dialogues* and other valuable publications on music education philosophy.

Also, before we continue, the word *praxis* needs to be defined. David Elliott stated, "As Aristotle used the word in his *Poetics, praxis* connotes action that is imbedded in, responsive to, and reflective of a specific context of effort.*"*[1] So, when the word *praxis* is used in this discussion it will refer to a specific way of "doing" or "musicing" that reflects the context in which one performs or listens to it.

Dr. Elliott asserts that musicing should take place through a praxial philosophy of music education. Elliott states, "The noun *praxis* derives from the verb *prasso*, meaning (among other things) 'to do' or 'to act purposefully.' But when we use *prasso* intransitively [i.e., a verb not taking a direct object] its meaning shifts from action alone to the idea of action in a situation."[2] Elliott believes that music is always performed in community. He says,

> "By calling this a praxial philosophy I intend to highlight the importance it places on music as a particular form of action that is purposeful and situated and, therefore, revealing of one's self and one's relationship with others in a community. The term praxial emphasizes that music ought to be understood in relationship to the meaning and values evidenced in actual music

making and music listening in specific cultural contexts."³

## Keeping Music Education Christian

Christian educational institutions have an obligation to keep music education Christian education. If they do not they cannot fulfill their mission. If Christian elementary, secondary, and post-secondary educational institutions are only different from secular institutions because they sing and play religious music, or because they use God or Christian in their name, they are not essentially different from secular schools, colleges and universities.

A congruent understanding of the nature and value of music education at its deepest levels can do more than anything else to keep CME (Christian music education) essentially Christian. As was said before, a series of systematic written beliefs concerning the nature and value of music that is truly Christian and is carefully applied to an educational institution's music praxis is necessary if music education is to become and remain Christian.

All one has to do is to search for Christian Music Education Philosophy on the Internet to understand that many Christian educational institutions do not publicize their CMEP (Christian music education philosophy) on their websites. Many of them may have written statements of music philosophy, but for some reason they do not consider it important to make these statements easily available. If a Christian institution is going to be intellectually honest it should make it completely clear to prospective music students that the nature of the Christian music education platform is different than the mainstream of public education.

How does an educational institution insure that the music education a student receives is truly a CME? Philippians 1:9-10 states, "And this I pray, that your love may abound yet more and more in knowledge (*epignosis* 1922) and in all judgment (*aesthesis* 144); That ye may approve things that are excellent; that ye may be sincere and without offence till the day of Christ; Being filled with the fruits of righteousness, which are by Jesus Christ, unto the glory and praise of God." Ephesians 5:8-11 states, "For ye were sometimes darkness, but now are ye light in the Lord: walk as children of light: (For the fruit of the Spirit is in all goodness and righteousness and truth;) Proving what is acceptable unto the Lord. And have no fellowship with the unfruitful works of darkness, but rather reprove them."

This passage in the first chapter of St. Paul's epistle, written to the Philippian Christians by his scribe Ephaphroditus, includes some words that have been the source of much discussion over the centuries. In verse nine Paul uses the words *knowledge* (*epignosis* 1922-discernment) and *judgment* (*aesthesis* 144-perception). One of the ways to keep CME on course biblically is to allow the Holy Spirit to guide and increase the Christian's musician's philosophical discernment and perception. This discernment and perception concerning the deepest levels of the nature and value of music, which one gains from studying first the Bible and then many other sources that are congruent with what the Bible teaches, will enlighten the music educator in what is really important in the music education process of those being educated musically.

Another phrase used in verse ten of the same passage is "that ye may approve (*dokimazo* 1381) things that are excellent (*diaphero* 1308)."[4] The word *dokimazo* connotes approval that is the result of discerning examination. The word *diaphero* comes from two Greek words *dia* (1223) and *phero* (5342) these terms put together mean a bearing through or carrying through until something is of a higher value or character. This approval comes by carrying through or testing and is made possible by the Holy Spirit's gift of discernment (verse nine) that gives the musician the wisdom to approve music which is of a higher value (verse ten).[5] Spirit-filled musicians (verse eighteen) have the wisdom given by the Holy Spirit to guide their music philosophies into goodness, righteousness and truth (Ephesians 5:19; also see 1 Corinthians 14:15 and St. John 4:23-24).

Educational truth and musical truth will come to the Christian music educator as the blessed Holy Spirit enlightens that musician's understanding of the many divinely inspired Bible texts that concern music and music education. Knowing musical truth will also be made possible by allowing the Holy Spirit to guide and direct the Christian's pursuit of musical knowledge. Ephesians 5:8-10, discussed above, explains that Christian music educators have the ability to develop a CMEP and have the assurance that they are doing the right thing the right way because they are guided by truth.

The last portion of Philippians 1:10 makes another statement that is worthy of discussion, "...that ye may be sincere (*heilikrines* 1506) and without offence (*aproskopos* 677) till the day of Christ; Being filled with the fruits of righteousness, which are by Jesus Christ, unto the glory and praise of God." The word *heilikrines*, that was translated *sincere* in the AV, means to test something in the sunlight to see if it is genuine. Some commentators believe that this word especially refers to the testing of precious metals or gems to see if they were pure. So, St. Paul meant that if something was going to be inoffensive (*aproskopos*), it needed to be tested to see if it would lead someone into sin. Certainly music is no exception to this rule of Christian living.

## Keeping Christian Music Education Academic

As has been mentioned earlier, if Christian music educators wish for music classes and performance organizations to be considered with the same respect as other academic classes in the curriculum, music classes and performing groups must actually be of an academic nature. If students who graduate from Christian schools are going to be considered educated musically, they must be musically literate. Students must learn music literacy in music classes and performance organizations and this learning must be systematically evaluated. Music literacy requires that each student must be able to read, write and perform music.[6]

Jerome Bruner believed that readiness theory was faulty. He stated, "We begin with the hypothesis that any subject can be taught effectively in some intellectually honest form to any child at any stage of development."[7] So, the question is not *when* students are ready to be taught music reading, writing and performing. It is rather *how* to teach these concepts in an intellectually honest fashion that is compatible with their understanding as they pass through different levels of musical and intellectual development.

Isaiah 28:10 explains, "For precept must be upon precept, precept upon precept; line upon line, line upon line; here a little, and there a little." Elementary music education should start teaching kindergarteners and first graders the nuts and bolts of the formal properties of music. However, these elements of music reading, writing and performing music must be approached at the students' level of intellectual development.

So, when one considers the word *tsav* (6673) which has been translated precept in the AV and was in a discussion of how children learn, it naturally connotes a little or simple concept. It is generally believed by Bible exegetes that the word *kav* (6957), which is translated here as line, refers to some kind of measuring line. *Kav* signifies the line that a mason stretches out to build each layer of stones. "After one layer or course is placed, he raises the line and builds another; thus the building is by degrees regularly completed. This is the method of teaching children, giving them such information as their narrow capacities can receive; and thus the prophet dealt with the Israelites."[8] So, a music educator should not try to teach the nuts and bolts of music to kindergarten and lower elementary students at the same cognitive level as upper elementary, junior high and high school students.

At each grade level musical principles must be taught, as Isaiah states, "precept upon precept" and "line upon line." In modern times this educational method is known as "curriculum spiral". Philosophically this connotes that in elementary music education the instructor teaches the same musical concepts from the national standards each year but at a more advanced level. Since this is not a "how to" book, but rather a discussion of some of the philosophical principles that should enshroud the whole of music education, I will not discuss how the Christian music educator should approach the process of curriculum spiral sequence.

During the second half of the twentieth century many music educators accepted the notion that playing music which has been learned by rote, on Orff instruments, recorders, rhythm band instruments, or learning and singing choral music, without being able to utilize conventional counting or note reading, was evidence enough that a student was musically educated. This may be an excellent way to teach music by rote to children who are in kindergarten or the lower elementary grades; however, during the upper elementary grades students need to learn conventional methods of reading notes and rhythms.

"Orff-Schulwerk" was first developed in the 1920s in Bavaria, Germany to be used with adult music and dance students. As far as the record shows, Carl Orff never intended for the use of these instruments to become a complete music education system, or for their use to preclude learning conventional counting and music reading. The use of these quality instruments should not circumvent the process of teaching mid to upper level elementary students how to utilize conventional methods of music reading. There are a host of musical concepts that can be effectively taught through the use of Orff instruments. However, somewhere in the curriculum spiral the transition to conventional rhythmic and melodic reading must take place.

At the kindergarten and lower elementary grades, counting with little nonsense syllables used in Zoltan Kodaly's system is an intellectually honest way to teach rhythm. However, when sixth graders are still utilizing only these syllables and do not know how to systematically and educationally count and subdivide beats, the music instructor is following a faulty education philosophy and praxis. When students enter beginning band or orchestra and cannot utilize conventional methods of reading notes and counting rhythms, including some subdivision of beats, something is philosophically wrong with what has been taught in the elementary general music classroom. Perhaps elementary general music instructors should consider themselves to be in charge of a "preparatory department" for musicing in adulthood.

## Can Music Transform the Musician?

After decades of humanistic music education, music philosophers are searching for ways to transform student's lives through musicing and the praxis of doing music. From David Elliot's perspective, "fully understood, praxis combines several integrated themes: (1) active reflection and critically reflective action dedicated to (2) human well-being and flourishing, (3) the ethical care of others, and (4) the positive empowerment and transformation of people and their everyday lives."[9] This pungent article is a plea to music educators to expand their music praxis beyond mere performance for enjoyment to include the four areas mentioned above.

Humanism as a philosophic foundation and humanistic music education as the basis of music praxis has never given satisfactory answers to the needs of depraved men and women. As I read this well-written article, with much good intent, on what Elliott called "artistic citizenship", I found myself agreeing with much of what he was saying. However, I was strengthened in my conviction that Christian music education is not merely a preference but rather a necessity.

The place that I began to part philosophic agreement with Elliott's answers to human need is his fourth point, "the positive empowerment and transformation of people and their everyday lives." My thoughts were immediately drawn to St Paul's statement in Romans 12:1 and 2: "I beseech you therefore, brethren, by the mercies of God, that ye present your bodies a living sacrifice, holy, acceptable unto God, which is your reasonable service. And be not conformed to this world: but be ye transformed (*metamorphoo* 3339) by the renewing (*anakainosis* 342) of your mind, that ye may prove what is that good, and acceptable, and perfect, will of God."

There is no place in the Bible where it teaches that people will experience a *metamorphoo* through community efforts with music. Although there is no quarrel with Elliott's belief that musicians can serve positive causes with their musicing, students' lives will never be eternally transformed by musicing. Human need and condition can only be transformed by the *metamorphoo* of the mercy and grace of God being applied to a person's heart.

When music educators and music philosophers only address music and music education as a fine art, they would not necessarily address the music student's spiritual condition. However, when they speak of people experiencing transformation and empowerment through service, and fail to mention the transforming work of Christ, we must part philosophical company with such an incomplete hypothesis. The only thing that will change a music student's empowerment and essential inner condition is for that student to be born again and experience the empowerment of the Holy Spirit. Any praxis or philosophy that addresses personal human transformation without salvation is denying the power of God and therefore is faulty.

We are once again brought face to face with the philosophic differences between secular music education philosophy and Christian music education philosophy. The separation of church and state in the USA requires a philosopher who deals with human condition to deny, by omission, the power of God. For this reason, among many others, I am drawn to the strong conclusion that for the Christian, a Christian music education under godly music instructors is a must.

## The Precursor of Instrumental Music Education

Arguments for and against the use of instruments in public worship have been considered for centuries without final resolution. This discussion is a necessary prelude to building a CMEP since so much of the goal of a CME is utilitarian. It would not make much sense to include learning to play a musical instrument if the Bible condemned the use of musical instruments in public worship. The Church Fathers interpreted what the Bible says about the use of musical instruments in worship.

Marvin Vincent discussed the opinions of some of the Church Fathers on both sides of the issue.

> "Some think that the verb here has its original signification of singing with an instrument. This is the dominant sense in the Septuagint and both Basil and Gregory of Nyssa define a psalm as implying instrumental accompaniment; and Clement of Alexandria, while forbidding the use of the flute in the agape, permitted the harp. But neither Ambrose nor Chrysostom mention it in their *panegyrics upon music, mention instrumental music, and Basil expressly condemns it. Bingham dismisses the matter summarily, and cites Justin Martyr as saying that instrumental music was not used in the Christian church."[10]

One can see from the writings of the Church Fathers that they were of differing opinions concerning the use of instruments with vocal music. The greatest impetus for supporting the use of instruments in worship is the fact that the worship examples in the Bible record very clearly that instrumental music was a part of ancient public worship and is therefore definitely an ancient land-

## 6: Congruency in Music Education and Musicing 143

mark of worship.

Whether or not the Church Fathers supported the use of instrumental music in worship is not the *sine qua non* of historical musical worship. Although every Christian musician would be interested in what happened musically in the Early Church, their beliefs and policies should never be considered a higher authority than what is recorded about musical worship in the Bible.

Although Hiram Bingham may have dismissed the matter of instrumental music as a part of public worship *precipitately, the Old Testament accounts of music record the use for instrumental music in worship repeatedly. Music is mentioned in the New Testament though it is not mentioned nearly as much as in the Old Testament. Although writers argue about the meaning of Ephesians 5:19, Colossians 3:16, 1 Corinthians 14:26, and James 5:13, as well as the mention of singing psalms, the meaning of words like *psalmos* (5568) and *psallo* (5567) have strong meaning for both vocal and instrumental music.

The fact that the Septuagint (LXX) considered psalm singing to connote vocal and instrumental music should be ancient evidence enough that there was no question about the Holy Writ supporting the use of instruments. At the time of the Greek translation by the seventy scholars, it was proper biblically and historically to accompany singing with musical instruments. St. Basil the Great of Caesarea is reported to have expressly condemned instrumental music, but he, along with St. Gregory of Nyssa, admitted that psalm singing as recorded in the Bible included (implicated) the use of instrumental accompaniment. For a very thorough study of this topic please read the chapters on vocal and instrumental music in *Music of the Bible in Christian Perspective*.

What are the implications of the ancient writings and opinions of the Church Fathers about the use of instrumental music with music worship? To say the least, the Church Fathers did not agree with each other, and from the ambiguity of some of their writings, it becomes apparent that they had much difficulty interpreting the Hebrew Old Testament writings and early OT translations like the LXX. It seems that perhaps their own opinions and worship traditions clouded their views of how to interpret what the OT actually said about the use of musical instruments with singing in worship.

## Instrumental Music in Christian Music Education

As was just mentioned, there is an age old argument among Christian musicians about the use of instruments in public worship. There is absolutely no objection to singing without the use of musical instruments. Those who have chosen to worship God without using musical instruments have done so in the fear of God. Although I have not made the same conclusions as they have, I respect their view and understand that they have not decided to exclude the use of musical instruments to in any way be contentious. So, I have no quarrel with those who do not use instruments as a part of public worship, providing they do so on the basis of religious, musical, or worship preference rather than biblical mandate.

*A cappella* singing by a congregation is often a very worshipful experience. On the contrary, all of us have experienced public worship in which a set of drums have almost completely covered up the singing of words to God by a congregation. We have also had to suffer through songs like "Silent Night" being introduced by a mighty drum roll or a trumpet fanfare, or a great hymn like Wesley's "Arise, My Soul Arise" accompanied by a monotonous rhythmic drum figure played over and over, which is completely inappropriate to hymn style.

Those who have chosen to sing without instruments are philosophically more biblically accurate than those who worship with a praise band with all the instruments amplified to such decibel levels that an observer can see mouths moving but cannot hear a word of the attempted praise offering of the congregation. The question is not to use or not to use instruments in worship, but rather how a musician uses musical instruments in musicing unto God.

With that introduction, the use of musical instruments is so connected and entwined with singing in both the Old and New Testaments that no reason can be found, based upon the Holy Writ, to exclude the use of musical instruments in public worship. But their use must have properly controlled volume, be tastefully performed, be appropriately orchestrated, and be properly utilized as a *concomitant to, and not the master of, congregational singing.

There is also no Bible-based prohibition of performing instrumental music alone as a part of public worship. After spending nearly a half century studying the use of instruments in the Bible, I have concluded that the Bible records the use of instruments alone and with singing in bringing praise and honor to God both inside and outside of ancient Temple worship. Furthermore, after extensive study of music in the New Testament I find no biblical justification for the exclusion of musical instruments when worshiping God either publicly or privately.[11]

Philosophically, an instrumental music education is vital and necessary to a quality CME (Christian music education). Even a music education that is considered a basic CME should include some training in instrumental performance. Certainly a thorough quality music education program must include the opportunity for students to play and perform in an instrumental music organization.

### Aesthetic Experiences in Education and Worship

Those of us who know the philosophical tenants of MEAE (music education as aesthetic education) are aware that the mainstream of MEAE purports that music should be understood in terms of the aesthetic qualities of the music without regard for the context in which one is listening to or performing it. No one can perform or listen to music in a bubble or vacuum. All active musicing or music listening is done in the context of community. In other words, every performer or listener brings something to the performing or listening experience—something the individual contributes and something that is derived from community. Therefore, no one listens or performs without both internal and external influences. Music educators and philosophers label these influences as intrinsic and extrinsic. The intrinsic properties are the formal properties of the music and the extrinsic influences are those that are derived from the world around the performer and listener which may be labeled "community".

The fact that more than the formal properties of the music and words are involved in all music performance or listening has been glossed over by a host of Christian music educators. Christian community does and should affect all of a Christian's musical experiences; the influences of this present age or system also affect us.

Although many Christian musicians deny it, all of us are affected by the influences of the world system around us. As mentioned earlier, the terminology "world system" means the *aion* (165) not the *kosmos* (2889). *Aion* is defined as the system of this age and *kosmos* the physical world in which we all live.

Many church musicians and Christian music educators have accepted the mainstream beliefs of music education as aesthetic education (MEAE). They have modified the MEAE beliefs into a philosophy that purports that the Christian has "religious aesthetic experiences" with the music that are somewhat like aesthetic experiences. To them, the importance of musicing and listening is communication alone. These musicians believe that if the music sounds good it should be performed and listened to because liking it sanctifies it.

To illustrate what I mean by the discussion above let me quote what Geisler and Feinberg stated, "There is a close association, and sometimes an overlap, between a religious experience and a moral experience, as well as between religious and aesthetic experiences... There is also a close connection between religion and art. Some contend that recreation and religion often have the same origin in ritual (the kinship between a holiday and a holy day is used to support this). And, often an aesthetic experience (beautiful music or mountaintop scenery) can be used to evoke a religious experience."[12] Although music and *ipso facto* aesthetic experiences with music are certainly not intrinsically wrong, it is dangerous to equate what happens when the Holy Spirit visits the human in worship, and thereby communicates with a Christian, with aesthetic music experiences.

Music can, should, and has historically been used as an aid to worship. However, it is like opening *Pandora's Box when one connects "holiday" with "holy day", and aesthetic musical experiences with what happens when the Divine visits the human in musical worship. No matter how valuable musical aesthetic experiences are to the wholesome whole-life of an individual, they are in no way equal in value to what happens when God tabernacles with His people in worship.

Comparing aesthetic experiences to religious experiences opens the philosophical door to worshiping the creature (created things) rather than the Creator. (Romans 1:25) Aesthetic experiences with music are worlds apart philosophically from what happens when a Christian musician takes the journey from the natural to the supernatural and communicates with God. Once a Christian musician considers worship to be an event, religious musicing becomes, at its worst moments an entertainment, and at its best moments an artistic aesthetic experience.

When a Christian cries, "Abba Father" (Matthew 14:36) and God witnesses by His Spirit and His Word that "I will never leave you nor forsake you" (Hebrews 13:5 NKJV); and the God who spoke worlds into existence promises, "I will be their God and they [Christians] shall be my people" (Ezra 37:27), this experience should in no way be compared with "holiday". When musical worship becomes "holiday", God has to share His worth-ship with pianists, organists, choirs, bands, orchestras, instrumental and vocal soloists. When this philosophy is put into practice, post-postmodern musical performers take God's worth-ship out of worship musicing, and replace it with the worth of the created thing (music) and the creature (the performer). When the music and the performer become preeminent, they soon become autonomous as they increase in value and *ipso facto* eclipse the Creator.

St. John very carefully explains in John 3:30-31, "He must increase, but I must decrease. He that cometh from above is above all: he that is of the earth is earthly, and speaketh of the earth: he that cometh from heaven is above all." Without this philosophical understanding of the Christian musician's place in light of eternity, music ceases to be the handmaiden of God's Word, and usurps a worth and authority that in Christian worship only rightly belongs to God.

How a musician perceives music is partially influenced by community. Romans 14:7 reminds Christians, "For none of us liveth to himself, and no man dieth to himself." Yes, the writer of the letter to the Romans was referring to the eating of meats, but the same is true of our performing and listening to music. What we believe and bring to a musical experience will influence how we perceive and respond to it. So there is no doubt about it: community does influence a music's meaning and thereby its influence on the performer or listener.

The previous experiences that a person has had with a genre of music will cause it to exert meaning on a religious performance in that genre. The former context that one associates with a particular style of music will of necessity cause it to communicate meaning, and that will convey both musical and spiritually related meaning. The music part of music, as a result of the arrangement of its formal properties and the context or community within which it is performed or heard, will communicate meaning to the performer and the listener. So, music performed or heard in the context of community does matter. Music matters because the combination of these factors contributes greatly to the communicated meaning of all music performed and heard.

Now let us return to the belief of the MEAE enthusiasts that all music should be understood in terms of its aesthetic qualities. One of the problems of this thesis is that a concomitant of this belief is that aesthetic qualities control music's meaning (or value, if one does not believe that music has meaning). A concomitant of the "aesthetic qualities" theory is the belief that the more aesthetic qualities a piece of music possesses, the more value or import it contains.

One of the apparent *anomalies with the aforementioned philosophical belief is that it is possible that a very simple genre can and often does communicate much meaning and thereby may possess great value. It should be pointed out that the aesthetic qualities in a piece of music are capable of effecting its nature and value. Music that is well composed or arranged will possess aesthetic qualities that are valuable to the listener and performer, but that does not mean that aesthetic qualities are the only qualities with which one should evaluate or esteem a music genre.

One of the sides of this multi-sided musical coin displays the formal properties of the music. To the strict formalist, these formal properties are the only side of the musical coin that matters. To them, all music should be perceived and understood strictly from this viewpoint. The formal properties of any music are very important to what any type of music offers to the listener or performer. Much of music's meaning is expressed through these formal properties. But they are not the only part of a music that expresses meaning. Other factors like context, community, previous musical experiences, the import of which the performer and/or listener brings to the music experience, the aesthetic qualities of the music, the text, and the associations that the music has with other factors, all have an effect on the music's communicated meaning, which is both embodied and designated.

## In the *Kosmos* but Not of the *Aion*

What these factors mentioned above represent and communicate will definitely affect the whole-life of the performer and the auditor. Therefore, understanding music's communicated meaning becomes a very complex phenomenon. Ephesians 2:2 reminds us that "Wherein in times past ye walked according to the course [*aion* 165] of this world [*kosmos* 2889], according to the prince of the power of the air, the spirit that now worketh in the children of disobedience." Based on the import of this Scripture, a Christian music philosopher does not need to build a new conspiracy theory because the Bible has already identified one for us. The system of this present evil universe in which we live has its own course and this course includes music, the purpose and import of which is most often not a friend of grace.

This Scripture passage is an admonition to Christians who once followed the course (*aion*) of the system of this world (*kosmos*) to no longer follow the system of the "prince of the power of the air," who is without doubt Satan. The system of Satan in this present age is *circumambient*— it is everywhere. To deny the circumambiency of Satan's system and to deny that it includes music and its designated and embodied meaning is certainly short sighted on the part of Christian musicians. If the Christian musician believes this Scripture that states emphatically that Satan's system encompasses the air (*aer* 109) and is therefore circumambient, then that musician should also believe that it permeates every area of life around us that is not protected by the Holy Spirit. There is no logical argument that religious music escapes this influence.

The significance of this discussion so far is that there is a philosophical influence exuding from "the prince of the power of the air," and that this terminology is a reference to Satan's matrix. There is not a single philosophical argument that would successfully refute this conclusion, which is based on the premise Scripture, that Satan's system or matrix includes music. If Satan permeated every area of life except music, he would be less than Satan. It makes no sense that Satan would work very hard to pervade every area of life except music.

The Christian music educator should not be depressed by the knowledge that Satan is the prince and power of the air and that he is constantly influencing music educators around us. Remember that Ephesians 2:2 states that "In times past ye walked according to the course of this world." Christian musicians are not controlled by Satan's influence because they no longer follow the course of this world. Christians must remember that, like the seven Asian churches which are mentioned in Revelation 1:4-6, we are given the promise, "Grace be unto you, and peace, from him which is, and which was, and which is to come; and from the seven Spirits which are before his throne; And from Jesus Christ, who is the faithful witness, and the first begotten of the dead, and the prince of the kings of the earth. Unto him that loved us, and washed us from our sins in his own blood, and hath made us kings and priests unto God and his Father; to him be glory and dominion for ever and ever. Amen."

### Congruency in a Christian's Music and Musicing

Now let us consider congruency in a Christian's music, music performance and music listening. Earlier in this discussion congruency was defined as the following: agreement, harmony, correspondence or conformity. Romans 12:2 warns all Christians— which of course includes Christian musicians— "And be not conformed to this world: but be ye transformed by the renewing of your mind, that ye may prove what is that good, and acceptable, and perfect will of God." The English word *conformed* is translated from the word *suschematizo* (4964) which means to conform or fashion to the same pattern of the world (*aion* 165) system. How could Scripture be any clearerThis requirement extends to every area of a Christian musician's life. A Christian musician is commanded to not be in agreement, harmony, correspondence, or conformity with the music of the world's system. If our music conforms to the world system it is not congruent with the Bible commandment to not be conformed.

Conversely, the Christian musician is commanded to be transformed (*metamorphoo* 3339) which means to make a complete, thorough and dramatic change in the form, appearance and character. This is extremely difficult for many Christian musicians to accomplish because they have not had a complete (*anakanoisis* 342) renovation of mind. The *People's New Testament Commentary* explains, "Two things we learned from this chapter [Romans 12] (1) there is a divine wisdom or mystery or philosophy. (2) This divine wisdom, or mystery, is an absurdity or perplexity to the world, but the wisdom of God to the saints."[13]

If a Christian musician chooses to only music in those styles that are philosophically congruent with the mind of Christ, this kind of musical restraint will be considered foolish by non-believers and Christian musicians who have not had a complete *anakanosis* of mind. Worldly musicians will consider it foolish that the conservative Christian musician is constantly "proving what is acceptable unto the Lord" (Ephesians 5:10). Furthermore, they will not understand that the careful, wise Christian musician proves every composition before performing it and acknowledges the command in verse eleven, "And have no fellowship with the unfruitful works of darkness, but rather reprove them."

**Musical Truth Found in the Bible**

All Christian music educators should be concerned about the authenticity of what they use in the instructional process. Should a Christian music educator refer to Scripture as an historical and philosophical basis for musical convictions? At least two concepts are important to the process of Christian music education. First, what the Bible has to say about music and musicing is relevant to music education in the twenty-first century. Second, the music educator should quote Scripture and treat it as authoritative truth concerning music. Many music educators are overly concerned about whether or not they are qualified to quote both Old and New Testament Scriptures that mention music because they are not sure what they mean or how they are applied to modern day musicing. It is true that the Bible does not deal with every aspect of music that twenty-first century Christian musicians encounter. Although the Bible does not provide us with exhaustive truth concerning music, what it does tell us is always true. As Francis Schaeffer wrote,

> "It is an important principle to remember, in the contemporary interest in communication and in language study, that the biblical presentation is that, although we do not have exhaustive truth, we have from the Bible what I term 'true truth'. In this way we know true truth about God, true truth about man and something truly about nature, thus on the basis of the Scriptures, while we do not have exhaustive knowledge, we have true and unified knowledge."[14]

Every reference to music mentioned in the Bible, as 2 Timothy 3:16 states, is "...given by inspiration of God, and is profitable for doctrine, for reproof, for correction, for instruction in righteousness." It is the Christian's responsibility to follow the admonition in 2 Timothy 2:15: "Study to shew thyself approved unto God, a workman that needeth not to be ashamed, rightly dividing the word of truth."

In order to have true and unified knowledge, one should be careful not to try to prove a point with Scripture without regard to context. It stands to reason that such use of Scripture does not result in biblical accuracy or what Schaeffer called "true truth". However, one should be careful to not assume that one who quoted it is using it without regard to how it was used by the original author. We should also remember that New Testament authors quoted verses from the OT to support their arguments. Jesus quoted Deuteronomy 8:3 when he was being tempted by Satan (see Matthew 4:4 and Luke 4:4). So, it isn't quoting Scripture that constitutes proof texting, but rather misrepresenting the original intent of Scripture or the principle that the original Scripture represented.

For example, an author stating that a Christian musician should not music unto God with carnal songs, based on the use of *pneumatikos oide* (4152 5603) in Ephesians 5:19, does not constitute the unwarranted use of Scripture, which is called *proof texting,* because lexicographers generally agree that *pneumatikos oide* means spiritual, i.e., non-carnal songs. As we know, indiscriminate quoting of Scripture to try to prove a point will many times result in incorrect conclusions, but so will trusting the usual meaning of an English word or words used in a Bible translation without regard to the meaning of the word or words used in the original text. Words have meaning but their meaning is greatly influenced by how they are used in sentences. However, how a writer interprets what words mean in context is many times a matter of opinion.

There are many factors that should affect how a writer will arrive at a musical conclusion, such as musical worldview, general academic knowledge of music history and theory, knowledge or lack of knowledge of ancient musical instruments; ancient species of music mentioned in the Bible; music worship practices in the first and second ancient Jewish Temples; the meaning of musical terms used in the Bible; the ancient Jewish sociological and cultural limitations of the use of women in Temple music; the meaning of the biblical accents *(te'amim)* found below and above the OT texts; secular music and musicing mentioned in the Bible; ancient biblical principles of sacred and secular music and musicing mentioned in the Bible; and an understanding of the music of the nations and cultures that surrounded ancient Israel.

So, why does a Christian music educator care whether or not ancient cultures utilized harmony? Furthermore, why does it matter whether or not Bible music includes harmony? There are several reasons why a music educator should know about the music of ancient Israel and their neighbors. One reason is that a great host of educators still believe that the music of ancient Israel and their neighbors was written only in the pentatonic scale, or worse yet, some weird synthetic scale, and that it could not have possibly been heptatonic or diatonic, or have exhibited any characteristics like half steps between the third and fourth and seventh and eighth degrees of the scale. Even the well-known fact that some of this music exhibited the use of octaves, harmony, and ornamentation is still sometimes adamantly denied by writers.

With these glaring misconceptions about ancient music still believed and taught by multitudes of Christian (and secular) music educators, it is of little wonder that they do not consider Bible music to be relevant to the process of music education. Certainly such music educators will not teach that Bible music is an authentic source of truth concerning music and musicing. Christian music education needs to get rid of the notion that information about music found in the Bible and other ancient extra-biblical sources is strictly dispensational and outdated.

**Moral Implications of Music**

When a music educator teaches that music has moral implications, what that teacher is saying is that when one arranges the formal properties of music into a congruent whole, which we call a musical composition, it has moral implications both inside and outside of the music itself. Some Christian music educators and music philosophers object to the philosophical belief that music has moral implications. They sometimes also object to the belief that the formal properties of music have moral implications since they believe that music is amoral or that it is incapable of indicating anything at all.

Christian music educators sometimes believe those who purport that music is moral are saying, for instance, that an incomplete dominant ninth chord or an augmented second chord is either evil or good. There is also a myth that the use of any syncopated rhythms is evil. Although there may be some conservative Christian music philosophers who purport such hypotheses, that certainly is not what most Christian music philosophers, educators and performers believe and put into their writings or performance practice.

However, they are saying that an astute Christian musician will observe that the way the formal properties of music are put together in a music composition definitely does have strong moral implications. Certainly, this argument will never be settled until Jesus returns, "For now we see through a glass, darkly; but then face to face: now I know in part; but then shall I know even as also I am known" (1 Corinthians 13:12).

The fact that we do not have exhaustive truth and knowledge about the moral implications of music does not mean that we should blindly follow every musical fad, fashion and current trend that the world considers proper for worship. Surely conservative Christian musicians should be able to exercise some wise discretion when it comes to the appropriateness of the music we use in public and private worship and also in our *secular musicing. This discretion must be taught in the early elementary music classroom. It is a huge educational and philosophical mistake for music educators to depend on good philosophical concepts to be "caught" from what happens in churches and concerts by Christian artists. Music philosophy must be directly taught and this educational process must begin in the early elementary music classroom if one expects to effect positive behavioral musical changes in the next generation of our youth.

### The World may Consider You to be a Fool

If you are a conservative Christian you will be considered a fool by non-believers and by much of the church world at large. 1 Peter 4:4 states, "Wherein they think it strange that ye run not with them to the excess of riot, speaking evil of you." The words *excess* and *riot* are translated from *anachusis* (401) which means "license" and *asotia* (810) which connotes, among other things, the condition of not being saved, or actually being debauched. You will be considered strange and foolish if you refuse to take license or to debauch sacred music in an effort to be trendy in your music ministry.

You have to make a choice to conform your musicing either to the spirit of this age or to the scrutiny of the demands of Bible principles of musicing. If you choose to conform to worldly musical trends that follow the philosophical spirit of this age, your musicing will not be congruent with the moral nature of God or to Bible principles of musicing.[15] Philosophically, a Christian musician cannot "have his cake and eat it too."

## Be Ready to Fall Down

Daniel 3:5 states, "That at the time ye hear the sound of the cornet, flute, harp, sackbut, psaltery, and dulcimer, and all kinds of music, ye fall down and worship the golden image that Nebuchadnezzar the king hath set up." This ancient admonition sounds like a twenty-first century admonition to worship whenever and whatever is going down musically at a particular time. The Hebrew men Shadrach, Meshach, and Abednego refused to violate their conscience musically or spiritually. Twenty-first century musicians are at times put in a place where they will have to take a stand. The Bible lesson in this Scripture is very clear. These three men would not worship the Chaldean image and they would not worship with "all kinds of music" merely because they were pressured to conform. The result was that they got themselves thrown into a fiery furnace. Sorry! These men took a stand about worship style and idol worship which incurred the wrath of those who were in charge. Those in authority were so mad that they heated the furnace seven times hotter than normal. So, if you take a stand musically and spiritually, get ready to enter the fiery furnace.

These Hebrew men maintained a meek and quiet spirit, which included a good attitude, and God honored them and took care of them. You may feel that you are in the fiery furnace because you refuse to go along with worship that does not follow Bible principles of musicing unto God. However, you must stay cool in the midst of the hot furnace. If you do, God will take care of you. God cared so much for Shadrach, Meshach, and Abednego that He got into the furnace with them.

## Does God call Music Teachers?

Students who are in a music education degree program often wonder if teaching music is a sacred trust and therefore a calling of God. During my lifetime I have seen very little written on the subject of whether or not music teaching is a calling of God like being a pastor or a missionary. Also, I have never had the privilege of hearing anyone (except myself) give a lecture on music teaching being considered a *sacred trust. 1 Corinthians 12:28 states, "And God hath set some in the church, first apostles, secondarily prophets, thirdly teachers, after that miracles, then gifts of healings, helps, governments, diversities of tongues."

First of all, before we answer the question, "Does God call teachers?" it is necessary to identify the Bible definitions of the words *teacher* and *teachers* and *false teachers*. In 1 Corinthians chapter twelve, verses twenty-eight and twenty-nine both use the word *didaskalos* (1320) which means a master or instructor. [2] Peter mentions false teachers (*pseudodidaskalos* 5572) which has the connotation of *spurious teachers. The same Greek word is translated master several times in the AV. Sometimes it was referring to Jesus and others who were also referred to as "master." It was translated once in James 3:1 as "many masters" (*pokus didaskalos* 4183 1320).

Of special interest is Ephesians 4:11 which refers to pastors and teachers (*poimen, didaskolos* 4166 1320) as one instead of different callings. Because of this reference some believe that being a teacher is a concomitant gift of a pastoral calling rather than a separate calling. The fact that God endows some pastors with the gift of teaching does not preclude God calling others to be teachers. This seems perfectly clear from 1 Corinthians 12:28, where the inspired writer is careful to include teachers among the various classifications of callings. The words "God hath set" clearly indicate that God places (*tithemi*, 5087) or calls Christians into these several ministries including those who are called with specificity to be teachers without any indication that they are also pastors.

Also noteworthy is Romans 12:6-8 where it states, "Having then gifts differing according to the grace that is given to us, whether prophecy, let us prophesy according to the proportion of faith; Or ministry, let us wait on our ministering: or he that teacheth, on teaching; Or he that exhorteth, on exhortation: he that giveth, let him do it with simplicity; he that ruleth, with diligence; he that sheweth mercy, with cheerfulness." Among the long list of gifts that Christians are given by the grace of God, teaching is specifically included. It is interesting to note that this Scripture passage instructs Christians to keep doing what God gave them the gifts to accomplish. The teacher is instructed to keep teaching, i.e., "he that teacheth on teaching (*didasko en didaskalia* 1321 1722 1319). It seems self-evident that God would not instruct teachers to keep on teaching unless He considers teaching to be a sacred trust, i.e., a calling.

So, to the question, "Does God call teachers?" the answer is definitely yes! If God calls teachers and instructs them to keep teaching, then He calls Christian music teachers and instructs them to keep teaching music. God not only calls music teachers but also beseeches them to present their bodies as a living teaching sacrifice. Also, according to Romans 11:29, teaching for the called music teacher is not an option, "For the gifts and calling of God are without repentance." The reason for this logical conclusion is that the Greek word *ametameletos* (278) translated "repentance" here in the AV means that when God bestows gifts and callings they are irrevocable.

## Conclusions about Congruency in Our Musicing

Those who know me best know that I often contend for the value of traditional sacred music in this century (I also contended for the same in the last century). I have often said that what a musician really believes is revealed in his or her music and in the way that a musician musics unto God. I believe in a conservative lifestyle but I also believe that being a conservative Christian musician goes far beyond how a musician dresses or looks when he or she musics unto God.

However, before I elaborate on lifestyle and its relationship to a Christian's musicing, perhaps the first order of business should be to give a clear definition of the terminology *conservative Christian musician*. An accurate definition of a *conservative Christian musician* is one who holds to and highly regards traditional attitudes and values about sacred music and is therefore cautious about but not necessarily antagonistic to change or innovation in sacred music and musicing. We should also consider that this conservative musician is first a Christian and secondarily a musician, artist, performer, music director, music educator, composer, arranger, and church musician.

The conservative musician's entire life and musicing should be ultimately a sacrifice of service unto God. Sacred and secular music are not one and the same and therefore secular music is not always suitable to be used in worship. When a Christian lumps the whole of music into an erroneous musical stew pot, enormous philosophical problems occur. Although philosophical consideration of music must include both sacred and secular music, treating them both as some kind of indiscriminate glob as though they were the same is a huge philosophical mistake.

Before we venture any farther into what I call the "whole of music" we should define the terms *sacred* and *secular* music. We will define the term *sacred* as, "music connected with God or dedicated to the purpose of extolling and worshiping the triune God and hence worthy of and deserving veneration." Many dictionary definitions consider religious and sacred music to be the same phenomenon. Religious and sacred music are not the result of a single perception of all composers, arrangers and musicers. Musicians who consider religious and sacred music as equals try to make an erroneous philosophical amalgamation of these two distinct "musics" that are the result of two different perceptions and hence are unlike, although somewhat similar on the surface.

Since the conservative Christian musician does not have a pluralistic view of God, there is philosophically no possibility of a plurality of gods or musicing unto a plurality of deities. Much of religious *world music* does not address or concern the only true God. Although such music is religious in nature, because it in some way or another addresses religious things, it cannot possibly be considered sacred music by a Christian musician. So, a music composition that may be rightfully considered *sacred music* is music that is inseparably connected to the only true God, is theologically accurate, and is suitable to the awesomeness and solemnity of the worship of a triune God. It is not sacred if it is connected to a plurality of gods, to religious function, to music performance, or merely to religious acts or processes.

*Religious music* is that large and indiscriminate conglomeration of musical compositions that are concerned with some form of religious usage. Religious music may address itself to any god or to any false religion. It may also address itself to any form of religious-pseudo-speak, or it may concern itself with the performer or the formal properties of the musical composition itself. Such music and musicing is in direct violation of the clear Bible principles of sacred musicing taught in Ephesians 5:19, "Speaking to yourselves in psalms and hymns and spiritual songs, singing and making melody in your heart to the Lord." Sacred music and sacred musicing, as taught in this passage of Scripture, is directed toward God and is ultimately for His glory rather than an artist hawking his or her musical wares before an audience who is enamored by the performer's artistic abilities. Although it is performed before an audience and to an audience, i.e., "to yourselves," sacred music is ultimately sung "to the Lord. " We must never forget that sacred music is God music— it is always addressed to God and is about extolling God rather than about aggrandizing the performer or worshiping or admiring the artistic content of the music.

We must be concerned about Christian musicians who receive the preeminence when they are performing what they call worship music. Remember that God has declared in Isaiah 42:8, "I am the LORD: that is my name: and my glory will I not give to another, neither my praise to graven images." Many Christian musicians who consider themselves to be conservatives have subscribed to the popular musical idol philosophy. As a result of accepting this worldly philosophical view, worship leaders draw the listener to themselves rather than to Christ— thus they become an idol to the audience rather than a humble servant of Christ. It is impossible to successfully worship the Creator of music while God is being upstaged by heady highminded musicians who are performing the artistic medium that God created for His glory.

Now we should consider what is meant by the tem *secular music*. This term simply means music that does not address spiritual matters; it is not addressed to deity or to sacred acts of worship or adoration of the one true God. There is absolutely no philosophical problem with a conservative Christian musician performing secular music as long as it is not antagonistic to the changed life of a Christian. Furthermore, there is nothing wrong with a performer receiving praise for a secular performance. Honoring a performer for a secular performance is perfectly in order because God is not the object of this performance. Christian performers must never forget that while God is not the object of secular performance, He is the creator of music and therefore philosophically music as an artistic form ultimately belongs to Him. So, Christian musicians should not act like they own music. All music in the life of a Christian musician belongs to God and therefore comes rightfully under the Lordship of Christ.

Christian musicians who are conservative in lifestyle are to be commended because such appearance reflects a wholesome public image and a proper image of a representative of our Lord and Savior Jesus Christ. However, Christians hiding behind a conservative lifestyle while performing instrumental or vocal music that, by its moral implications, is not a proper representation of the God whom they are musicing about, is incongruent with the principle of a changed life of a Christian. Hence, when a Christian performs such music it becomes a form of hypocrisy. Conservative music refers to the *music part* of the music that they perform as well as the words or physical actions that accompany the music part of the music.

If a musician believes in separation from the world and believes that this difference must be shown outwardly, that musician should not perform religious music that is strongly representative of the world and a worldly lifestyle. I have never been able to understand why some Christians believe in separation in every area of life except music style. Such a haphazard approach to separation from the spirit of this world [i.e., *aion* 165] is a very incongruent music philosophy and must seem quite inconsistent to non-believers who are watching everything that Christians do. There are several perplexing questions about what is currently happening in the realm of church music. How can a musician in good conscience believe 2 Corinthians 6:17, which very clearly commands, "Wherefore come out from among them, and be ye separate, saith the Lord, and touch not the unclean thing; and I will receive you," and make no definite separation in the way he or she musics unto God? Is separation from the world a misnomer when it comes to a Christian's musicing? How can Christian musicians ignore over a half century of serious concern by a host of careful believers who have observed the alarming changes that have been made and are currently being made in church music? Why do so many musicians take their musical cues from liberal church musicians—and worse yet, nonbelievers who write and perform religious music that are not concerned in the slightest bit about spiritual things or the direction of church music?

I am concerned about the writings of Christian musicians who consider themselves to be conservatives and at the same time are supporting massive musical style change. They claim that these huge changes are necessary because traditional church music and the musicians who perform it are out of touch with reality, not seeker sensitive, outdated and incapable of being an efficacious means of musicing unto God. Although there is much evidence that the musicing of many church musicians is no longer efficacious, there is no body of evidence that the culprit is the music itself. Although there is much "death" in the musical city, this death is not caused by traditional sacred music but rather by the spiritually dead musicians who are doing the musicing.

Christian musicians must constantly reevaluate what it means to truly be conservative. Christian musicians who call themselves conservative musicians must realize that one of the most important things about following a conservative philosophy is being consistent about lifestyle and that this congruency most certainly must include the way Christians music unto God.

It is puzzling that so many Christian musicians in the last quarter of the twentieth century and now in the twenty-first century have believed that the formal properties of music have absolutely no power or ability to communicate anything at all. By accepting this erroneous notion, in their minds they have reduced music's power to the potency of diluted vanilla extract. Furthermore, they have done so without a shred of musical or philosophical logic. Why can't Christian musicians observe obvious actions, reactions, and outcomes that are triggered by music's power? I have found after studying music philosophy seriously since 1967 that the age old quip is true, "There is none so blind as he who will not see."

Some Christian musicians have failed to recognize that when a genre of music has been set into motion it does its own communicating, because the music part of music has great power to influence the listener for either for good or evil. Therefore, Christians need to realize that the concept that music has great power is not a novel notion hatched up by conservative Christian musicians who are overprotective of traditional church music. Musicologists are aware that since Plato and Aristotle philosophers have believed that the musical mode makes a difference because it communicates meaning to the listener. Furthermore, no music philosopher, ancient or modern, has made any sensible hypothesis or produced musical evidence that would discredit these ancient musical observations that resulted in the theory that music does have power.

For centuries music philosophers have written about their convictions that music has power to communicate moral values to the auditor. They have elaborated on how music goes about strengthening or weakening these moral values. Philosophers have not always agreed about the way music communicates its power to the listener, but historically, until the twentieth century, they have almost universally believed that music does have great power to communicate.

So when a musician connects music's power to God by marrying it to the worship of a holy triune God, that power definitely makes a reflection on the auditor's perception of who God is, what He is like, and what He is capable of doing. Although music cannot change God's moral nature, it can change the listener's perception of His moral nature when a musician, in an unsystematic manner, connects a music style to worship music that represents anything but wholesome moral or Christian values. What is often done in jest by a composer, an arranger, or a performer can become a tool for Satan to distort the auditor's view of who God is.

Also, when church musicians have an attitude of respect for the kinds of musics they use to honor the triune God, this respect permeates the place of worship in a positive way. Conversely, when worship leaders have a *laissez- faire* attitude about styles of worship music, worship becomes more and more folksy and familiar. As the quality of worship styles are lowered so is the mental image of a high and holy God. Perhaps this is happening because it is much easier for musicians to bring God down to where the congregation that they are ministering to is living spiritually than it is to get the worshipers to strive to conform more and more to the image of God. It is difficult to minister musically to people who do not seem to care much about deep spiritual living. However, there is right and wrong, good, better, and best when a Christian considers and utilizes various styles of music in worship.

Plato once wrote in his *Laws* about those who were ignorant "about what is right and legitimate in the realm of the muses. " He observed that they were

> "Possessed by a frantic and unhallowed lust for pleasure, they contaminated laments with hymns and pæans with dithyrambs, actually imitated the strains of the flute on the harp, and created universal confusion of forms. Thus their folly led them unintentionally to slander their profession by the assumption that in music there is no such thing as right or wrong, the right standard of judgment being the pleasure given to the hearer, be he high or low."[16]

It should be evident to any serious Christian musician that some things that can be realized through the art of music are too secular to be properly connected with our worship of our holy and most awesome God! Not everything that a musician is capable of doing with the great art of music is suitable or appropriate for worship merely because it is performed by a Christian. Christians therefore need to recognize the difference between secular and sacred music and learn how to utilize both in their lives. As I have often taught my college students, the use of sacred and secular music is not "either/or" but rather wise choices and usage of both. It is perfectly proper for a Christian to ride a bicycle to get to church, but it is not a proper thing to ride it down the center aisle of the sanctuary. Why can't musicians have the same common sense about worship music?

When a Church musician connects a music to God this connection becomes an inseparable one. A musician cannot separate inappropriate musical performance which he or she musics for personal enjoyment or aggrandizement from the fact that this music and its performance is antagonistic to the purposes of worshiping God. When a composer or arranger, either in jest or unwittingly, amalgamates musical styles and musical performance techniques that are incongruent with the awesomeness and solemnity of worshiping a holy triune God who is high and lifted up and is sitting upon a throne in heaven, the result is most unfortunate. Also, when a minister of music combines styles of music that are inappropriate for worship, just because he or she has the power to do so, what occurs in the sanctuary is not worship but a mere hawking of that musician's musical wares. Such pseudo-religious performance jesting is sacrilegious. Robert Berglund explains that "Worship is never an act of man based upon his own merit with the intension of satisfying man's desires. It satisfies God's command first, and then the experience benefits man. One does not worship because one enjoys it or it feels good (aesthetic reasons). One worships God because He is worthy, and He expects it."[17]

### Endnotes

1. Elliott, *Music Matters*, 14.
2. Ibid, 14.
3. Ibid, 14.
4. See "Christian Musicians Who Know Teach More Effectively" in chapter five.
5. See Cambridge KJV margin.
6. See the discussion of national standards in chapter five.
7. Jerome Bruner, *The Process of Education*, (Cambridge: Harvard University Press, 1960), 33.
8. *Clarke's Commentary*, Vol. 4, 123.
9. David Elliott, "Music Education as/for Artistic Citizenship", *Music Educator's Journal*, 99, no. 1 (Sept. 2012).
10. Marvin R. Vincent, *Vincent's Word Studies in the New Testament*, Peabody, MA: Hendrickson Publishers, n.d.), 269-270.
11. For a thorough study of the use of singing with and without musical instruments and the use of instrumental music alone in the Bible read chapter seven of *Music of the Bible in Christian Perspective*.
12. Norman Geisler and Paul Feinberg, *Introduction to Philosophy: A Christian Perspective (*Grand Rapids: Baker Books, 1980), 341-2.
13. *Power Bible 5.9* (Bronson, MI: Online Publishing, Inc.), CD-Rom, Romans 12:2.
14. Schaeffer, *Escape from Reason*, 21.
15. For more on Bible principles of musicing, see *Music of the Bible in Christian Perspective*.
16. Piero Weiss and Richard Taruskin, *Music in the Western World*, 7.

17. Berglund, *A Philosophy of Church Music*, 38.

## Chapter Six Word Meanings

**Anomalies**— things that are abnormal or incongruous, or do not fit because they are not consistent.

**Circumambiency**— an encompassing or surrounding influence.

**Concomitant**— a phenomenon that naturally accompanies or follows something else.

**Pandora's Box**— a Greek myth in which a large jar given to Pandora contained all the evils of the world.

**Panegyrics**— public speeches or written texts that praise someone or something.

**Precipitately**— to dismiss something carelessly or with abrupt or unwise speed.

**Secular**— music that is not religious or addressed to God; not necessarily music that is antagonistic to a Christian's lifestyle or beliefs.

**Occident**— the countries of the West, i.e., Europe and the Americas, as contrasted with countries in the Orient.

## Chapter Six Questions for Discussion

1. Define the word *praxis* and discuss its meaning in the context of music education.
2. Define music education as aesthetic education.
3. Discuss your beliefs about how one keeps music education academic.
4. Explain what it means to philosophically keep music education Christian.
5. What did the author mean by saying that the Christian musician is in the *kosmos* but is not of the *aion* and how does this relate to the Christian musician?
6. Explain your beliefs concerning whether or not the Bible contains musical truth.
7. Discuss aesthetic music experiences in light of performing music in Christian community.
8. Does music have moral implications? Explain your answer.
9. Explain why the world considers the conservative Christian to be a fool when it comes to music choices of music and musicing.
10. Explain a biblical position on whether or not God calls music teachers.

7

# Musicing Without a Congruent Music Philosophy

## What may Happen if We do not Develop a Music Philosophy?

EARLIER WE DISCUSSED the importance of developing a music philosophy. As we know, there is a need for all individuals, churches, Christian schools, Christian colleges and universities to develop a series of systematic statements concerning the nature and value of the whole of music. Although there are many websites representing churches, Christian colleges and universities, many of them say absolutely nothing about music philosophy, let alone publish a systematic Bible-based music philosophy. Those who have thought out what they actually believe about the nature and value of music, and have published their philosophic views concerning the deepest levels of what God honoring musicing is all about and why this music is estimable to them, are to be applauded.

Every Christian organization that is responsible for music and musicing must understand music at its deepest levels if they are going to have an effective music witness in this post-postmodern world. It is one thing for an individual to not bother to think through music's nature and value philosophically. It is entirely another to try to guide others in the area of music's nature and value without a thorough understanding of musical truth. One of the reasons that many Christian organizations fail to develop a music philosophy is that they do not believe that there is any objective truth or Bible basis concerning music's nature and value. Some Christians have the notion that music philosophy is somewhat like Jell-O gelatin, i.e., that its meaning cannot be pinned down because it is never stable or solid.

A surprising number of Christians believe that the references to music in the Bible are somehow *dispensational and have out lived their meaning. Although they would not admit it, they seem to believe that 2 Timothy 3:16 means, "All scripture [unless it is addressing music] is given by inspiration of God, and is profitable for doctrine, for reproof, for correction, for instruction in righteousness." One of the reasons that so many Christian musicians are without answers concerning the nature and value of the whole of music is that they have not developed an epistemology (the theory and limits of knowing) and methodology (the system used to establish knowing).[1]

So, an institution that does not have a congruent philosophy of music many times will go in a musical direction without much understanding or knowing. Such an organization either tries to cater to everyone's likes and dislikes or the exact opposite—they cater to whatever direction the music leader is going at that moment in his musical journey. When leadership tries to cater to everyone's musical tastes the potpourri of music that ensues does not please anyone thoroughly.

### What may Happen if We Resist all Change in Music?

By definition, a conservative tries to "conserve." The Christian musician who is biblically conservative is concerned about holding on to our biblically based music values. Notice that I said *biblically* based music values, not *traditional* music values. Traditions change and there is nothing inherently wrong with man's traditions being changed. The mere fact that some music tradition has been associated with a certain fellowship of believers certainly does not make it true truth, or even a valuable worthy tradition.

The Karaites, a Jewish sect that came into being at the beginning of the eighth century, were characterized by their belief that the Scriptures were the only source of religious law. They chose to accept the Scriptures as the only true truth to the exclusion of *Rabbinical Judaism. So, the Karaites were scriptural traditionalists who fought against some of the traditions established by rabbinic law. What resulted was a fight over tradition. Rabbinic Judaism was contending for the long collected traditions which had been laid down in layer after layer, and the Karaites purposed to "build up a wall around the Torah."

What we can learn from this ancient fuss over tradition is that we need to be sure the traditions we contend for are truly ancient Bible *landmarks of musicing unto God. It is possible that some of our musical "sacred cows" might be better left dead than resurrected. Not everything that the previous generations of church musicians have done musically was based on solid musical foundations or actual ancient landmarks of worship. However, all that being said, much of what they did do is time honored and if these principles of music worship are abandoned the church will certainly be impoverished musically and spiritually.

## What may Happen if We do not Resist Destructive Change?

First of all, a Christian musician should not resist change merely because it involves new music or a new way of musicing unto God. Every new method and all new music must meet the biblical and musical criteria of musicing unto God. We know that God does have an opinion about the appropriateness of the musical offerings we bring unto Him. (See Genesis 4:4 and Leviticus chapters 4 and 5 and Romans 12:1.) It goes without saying that it is sometimes very difficult to discern whether or not something new will meet the biblical criteria of musicing unto a triune God. However, most of the time it is not as difficult as one might suppose.

To a conservative minister of music, new music and new techniques are suspect until they are tested and pass all the Bible principles of musicing unto God, proven to be appropriate ways of worshiping a high and holy triune God. For that matter, a conservative musician tests all old music and music methods to make sure they meet the same standards mentioned before using them to worship God. Earlier I mentioned the Karaites passion to "build up a wall around the Torah." Similarly a conservative music minister must have a passion for "building up a wall around musicing unto God." If true ministers who music unto God do not protect our Bible-based musicing in worship, it will not be very long (it just takes one generation) until we will not recognize public music worship. Those who are not careful in their approach to music utilized in worship will soon lead the church down every musical rabbit trail that appears along their musical path. The ultimate end will surely be destructive musical change.

It is believed by some ancient music scholars that the Levite musicians of ancient Israel kept the musical notation (the *te 'amim*) in the abbreviated manuscripts called the *Serugin* because they feared that the music melodies of the OT would be *vilified. Modern day ministers of music have the same responsibility to protect church music in the fear of the almighty God who thought music into existence. If we do not conserve the integrity of music worship, who will?

I sometimes think about the milk cows my father kept in the west pasture of the farm where I grew up years ago. My father always kept the hedge brush cut down and the pasture sowed with fescue, red clover, brome, and other grasses so that our milk cows would have quality grass to eat. However, I remember coming home from school in the evening and seeing some of our cows with their heads pushed through the tightly stretched barbed wire fence. I saw their necks bleeding as they incessantly pushed through the barbed wire trying to get to a wild onion just outside the fence. There was absolutely no need for them to reach for the onions because there was high quality nourishment inside the fence. This is the mental picture I get of many post-postmodern church musicians today. There are wonderful old and new hymns and worship choruses available to them, but they are incessantly reaching outside of the quality musical provisions available to them for a musical "wild onion."

Some present day church musicians seem to have no interest in being careful which styles of music they use in musicing unto God. It isn't that they have set different limits of which styles of music they consider appropriate for worshiping God, but rather they are no longer setting any limits. They have no interest in "proving what is acceptable unto the Lord." When a postmodern church musician makes no difference between what is proper and not proper for the awesomeness and solemnity of worshiping the Trinity, music ministry becomes independent of the Lordship of Christ.

## What may Happen when we Become Trendy with our Musicing?

First, it would be a good idea if we would define the term *trendy*. Something is considered to be trendy when it has the predilection to follow a current dominant movement. The near opposite of trendy would be the inordinate passion to only revere what is seriously antique. All of us have seen both extremes in church music. There is nothing inherently wrong with new music, and likewise there is a large repertoire of time honored church music that is still valid, useful, and meaningful today.

If new and old music are both proper for public worship, then is this discussion much ado about nothing? There are problems with dropping everything in music that is traditional for that which is in vogue at the moment. Churches have made sudden musical decisions, like one church in central Ohio that made some very rash decisions in an effort to become trendy. A friend of mine visited their sanctuary and was informed by the pastor that one of the church members had cut all the wires to their $80,000 organ. When asked if they had a piano, the pastor pointed to a large object covered up at the side of the church platform. Further inspection proved that it was their nine foot grand piano. Both of these fine musical instruments had been replaced with a $4,000 keyboard and a drum trap set in one desperate effort to become seeker sensitive. The musical instruments went first but I understand that the church's fine sanctuary choir was the next thing to disappear from the sanctuary.

Although it is possible to be seeker sensitive without a church choir, piano or organ, they do not keep a fellowship of believers from caring about folks who are not Christians. So what happens to the church next after the ministering music organizations and the quality music instruments get the axe? What happens if a church desires to have a ministering concert pianist come for an instrumental worship service? Do you ask this artist to humbly play your electronic keyboard? Once a fellowship of believers heads down the path of following music trends, there is no stopping place. The church becomes a hostage of the latest musical notion.

We should not allow the church to get squeezed into the world's latest trendy notion of what the church can or cannot do musically in public worship. Although there is certainly nothing inherently wrong with doing something new musically in worship, doing something new will not necessarily fix all the church's worship problems. A church should not drop everything time honored in a desperate effort to be more like the world or make musicing unto God a trendy experience. If you do you will probably be left out in the musical cold when the trendy winds began to blow in another direction.

### What may Happen if We do not Sing at all in Worship?

Singing is without doubt an "ancient landmark" of worshiping God. No body of believers has the right to deny worshipers the privilege of responding to God through musicing unto Him. Admittedly, over many centuries the church at large has had a tendency to vacillate when it comes to congregational singing. Regardless of what a particular church thinks about the necessity of responding to God through singing at a particular time, singing has been a Bible principle of worshiping God since ancient times.

The Bible repeatedly commands Christians to sing unto the Lord. Psalm 30:4; 96:1, 2; 98:1, 4; 135:3; 1 Chronicles 29:30; 2 Chronicles 16:23 are just a few of the verses that command us to sing unto the Lord. As a matter of fact, singing unto the Lord is one of the Bible absolutes of musicing. The Hebrew is so very clear in these verses that it seems no one has been able to translate around this biblical principle— singing is a definite part of worship for God's children from ancient times until this very day.

Some ministers have mistakenly considered singing to be almost the whole of public worship. Throughout the Bible, singing was a part of worship but not the end of worship. One of the Bible principles of musicing is that singing since the time of ancient Israel has been the handmaiden of the Torah. The *te'amim* were placed above and below all of the OT Scriptures in order that the entire OT could be sung.

Nehemiah 8:8 has, over many centuries, become an esoteric reference to the intoning the Scrolls with the use of the *te'amim*.

The Hebrew word *parash* (6567) which has been rendered

distinctly in the AV means to separate or literally to disperse. Intoning (singing) the Holy Writ with what we now know to be a precise music notation (the *te'amim*) helped in bringing preciseness and understanding to God's written Word. The same verse uses the Hebrew word *biyn* (995) which has been translated in the AV with a group of English words "and caused them to understand." So, when we bring all these thoughts together we can see that singing the Word of God helped to bring greater understanding to the hearer. Now you know the "rest of the story" about ancient intoning of Scripture. There is a very valid reason for singing God's Word if our musicing helps to make the Word more clear to the congregation.

This also brings to mind that there is great responsibility placed on those who lead musical worship, to make absolutely sure that all of the music sung is biblically accurate. That was probably the reason John Calvin was so adamant about singing psalms, and it was exactly why John Wesley once instructed the society of Christians called Methodists to "Sing no songs of your own composing." In review, we have considered that the commandment to sing unto the Lord is clear in Scripture. There is no doubt that we should sing biblically accurate songs in our public worship. If we do not we will certainly impoverish those whom we lead in worship.

### What may Happen if We do not Distinguish Between *Sacred and *Profane Music?

There is not much use for a church musician to distinguish which music is sacred or profane if he or she does not make a sincere effort to exclude that which is profane from music worship. If the criterion for a music inclusion is the will of the people, the church's musicing will constantly be enduring the music minister's leadershift. Dr. Richard S. Taylor put the whole matter in proper perspective when he explained,

> "The fact that some people may like this or that is not sufficient reason for the church to use it. The church should lead the way in such standards, not abjectly follow every fad and custom

which happens to be 'in' at the moment. The Church has no business adopting the philosophy, 'If you can't lick 'em, join 'em.' We should be governed by basic and eternal principles. There are music forms, whether secular or sacred, which create moods of pensiveness, or idealism, or awareness of beauty, of aspiration, and of holy joyousness. There are forms of music which create moods of recklessness and sensual excitement. Surely it doesn't take much judgment to know which forms are most appropriate for religious function."[2]

Only the essential nature and value of a piece of music gives it the honor of being considered as sacred music. Therefore, each piece of music must pass the tests of Bible principles of musicing before it makes its way into the repertoire of worship. As Christian musicians carefully consider the nature and value of all the music used in musicing unto God, a clear line of demarcation between what is truly sacred and what is profane will become evident. It is the volumes and volumes of music that is "sort of" or "kind of" that is so difficult to categorize into that which is or is not appropriate for sacred function. So, since there is such a multitude of religious music that is biblically accurate, appropriate and clearly to be classified as sacred, the short answer is "when in doubt leave it out." There is absolutely no excuse for using any music that is questionable stylistically or inaccurate theologically.

## What may Happen if We try to Cater to Everyone's Musical Tastes?

No musician that I know ever thinks, "I'm going to sing this song just to annoy the congregation." Every sensitive ministering musician desires that the congregation will enjoy and appreciate the church music ministry. However, the Bible is very clear about whom we should please. Galatians 1:10 states, "For do I now persuade men, or God? Or do I speak [sing] to please men? For if I yet pleased men, I should not be a servant of Christ."

Any music praxis that is based on pleasing the seeker or the believer is a faulty praxis. There is nothing inherently wrong with Christians or those who attend worship services who are not Christians being pleased with our musical offerings, but our worship praxis must be built on pleasing God. So, pleasing God with one's musical offerings is a Bible principal of musicing. In my writings on music I have often discussed the fact that the unregenerate cannot truly worship God. However, if we can capture their interest with styles of music that are appropriate for worship, we have a better opportunity to present the gospel through our musicing.

I have also often mentioned that the Holy Spirit can use worship music to convict the sinner. When the Holy Spirit is doing His "office work" of locating and convicting the unregenerate man or woman, they will probably be anything but pleased by the music that is convicting them of the awfulness of their sins. Just like the pastor's preaching of Christ crucified does not make the sinner joyful, the effectual fervent singing of Christ crucified will not make the unregenerate comfortable in the presence of a just God who will not overlook sin and rebellion against Him.

A music praxis that is developed to make the sinner feel okay is just not okay. Man outside of the forgiveness of sins and the grace of God is far from okay. Effectual anointed musicing should never be psychologically designed to connote that "I'm okay and you're okay." The philosophical notion that worship music should be about "us," "me," "my," and "mine" is nothing less than religious humanism, which is no better than secular humanism. As we have pointed out many times, worship music is about God and our response to Him. The notion that the church should cater to my likes and dislikes is essentially humanistic music philosophy. Under this praxis, music begins and ends with "me." With this type of thinking, man receives the preeminence. Such humanistic thinking violates the teaching in Colossians 1:18, "And he is the head of the body, the church: who is the beginning, the firstborn from the dead; that in all things he might have the preeminence." *Proteuo* (4409) which is here translated *preeminence* means "to be first." Christ must always be first. Therefore sacred musicing should never be about the performer's talent or musical likes.

So, to sum this all up philosophically, we should worship God through our musicing in a manner that will be pleasing unto God. Furthermore, being seeker sensitive is not about singing music that unregenerated man will like. It is totally different to sing music that a sinner will understand than it is to build a music worship praxis on music that the sinner will like.

### What may Happen if We try to "Retask" Music Styles?

*Retasking music styles is a pseudo-religious philosophical musical notion that originated in the last quarter of the twentieth century. The *epitome of this notion is that "we should not let the Devil get all the best tunes." First of all, who established the fact that the Devil has use of all the best tunes? This discussion is certainly not the platform to list all the thousands and thousands of wonderfully composed musical compositions that have been used for God's glory over many centuries. So, the little quip used by CCM enthusiasts merely shows their lack of knowledge of the history of church music and sacred concert music.

Furthermore, the inept comparisons of G.F. Handel's Italian soprano duets (which he later rearranged into the marvelous four part chorus "For unto us a child is born") with hard rock music (in which the music part of the music was composed to appeal to the lust of the flesh and later supposedly sanctified to represent the love of our Lord and Savior Jesus Christ) again shows a complete misunderstanding of Handel's compositional style. There was absolutely no *contradistinction in the compositional style of his soprano duets and the message or the music of his oratorio *Messiah*. To put it very clearly, there was absolutely nothing about the words of the original duets or the musical style of the music part of the music of these works that brought attention to the lust of the flesh. Also, the well-known fact that parts of *Messiah* were *eclectic is certainly no evidence for *retasking hard rock music as worship music.

While we are on the subject of retasking music, the written statements of CCM enthusiasts that John Wesley's book *A Collection of Thirty-six tunes, set to music, as they are sung at the Foundry* (1742) were bawdy drinking songs are simply ludicrous, since we know that they were songs composed during the time they were worshiping in the old foundry which was close to where Wesley's church and home now stand in London. These songs had absolutely nothing to do with the rough drinking foundry workers.

So, Handel's arrangements of previously composed music and Wesley's Foundry Collection are not proof comparisons that justify CCM's strong desire to utilize inappropriate *juxtaposition of a music style with religious words. Retasking styles of music that have traditionally been antagonistic to the changed life of a Christian is risky and simply the wrong way to music unto our Lord and Savior. The objection is on the basis of style, the music part of the music, and also the *associations* that surround the use of some styles of music.

## What may Happen if We Remove the Ancient Landmarks?

The last thing that I would ever wish to do would be to spend my time preparing books on music philosophy that always predict gloom and doom for the future of church music and Christian music education. However, the musical discourse of Ephesians chapter five, verses fifteen and sixteen warn Christians to "See that ye walk circumspectly, not as fools, but as wise, Redeeming the time, because the days are evil." When I was being trained in the US Army, our instructors drilled us on the concept that, when we were part of a patrol, everyone must walk circumspectly. That means that as the patrol advances every patrol member must be looking at all times and that the patrol as a whole must be looking in all directions at all times. Certainly that training has proven valuable to me over the past forty years as a conservative Christian musician. Every time in my life that I have made the conscious decision to exercise caution instead of disregarding time honored principles of musicing unto God, I have been thankful later.

What will we have of value after we remove all the time honored principles of musicing from public worship? One thing is for sure: we will not recognize public worship in one generation if we as Christian musicians do not exercise some musical caution about adding the profane and subtracting everything traditional from our music worship. There are Bible principles of how to music unto God. We may deny that they are in the Bible or we may consider them to have outlived their relevance, but that will never change the fact that they are there and they are profitable to us in this century.

We know that the kind and quality of music matters to God. We know that according to God's Word, (see Amos 5:23; Isaiah 5:12; 14:11) He reserves the right not to hear some music, and He considers other music to be noise and states that He will not hear such musicing.[3] So, we may remove all traditional ways of musicing from our so called "worship" but if we do we will be worshiping "we know not what" (St. John 4:22). We will also be impoverished spiritually by removing these time honored Bible principles of worshiping through music.

### Endnotes

1. See *Church Matters,* chapter three,
2. Richard S. Taylor, *A Return to Christian Culture* (Minneapolis, Minnesota: Dimension Books, 1975), 85.
3. If you have further interest, I have discussed these and other Bible principles of musicing in the books, *Music of the Bible in Christian Perspective* and *Church Music Matters.*

### Chapter Seven Word Meanings

**Contradistinction**— as used here, a musical statement that contradicts another and therefore is logically incongruous.

**Dispensational**— the belief that God deals with people in different ways during periods of history so that, for instance, a music reference in the OT is not relevant to the twenty- first century musicing.

**Eclectic**— in this case it means that Handel borrowed from his own musical compositions composed in the same musical style although these previous works were secular.

**Epitome**— a typical or ideal example.

**Juxtaposition**— placing things side-by-side; in this case it means pairing an incongruent style of music with religious words.

**Landmark**— this reference to the words "ancient landmark" simply connotes that there are ancient principles of musicing found in the Bible that are worth preserving.

**Profane music**— music that treats sacred things with irreverence or disrespect

**Rabbinic Judaism**— the normal form of Jewish belief that developed after the fall

# 7: Musicing Without a Congruent Music Philosophy

of the Second Temple in 70 AD. It is the belief that Moses received the first five books called the Torah (written law) and that God also revealed Oral Law through the Talmud which is as authoritative as the written Torah.

**Retasking**— to change the work or mission of a genre of music like rock music to cause it to perform a new task.

**Sacred music**— music that meets all the requirements of being theologically correct, respectful of God, and appropriate and congruent with the purposes of worship.

***Serugin***— were the ancient abbreviated manuscripts of the Old Testament.

**Vilified**— as used in this context, it means any changes in the musical notation (*te'amim*) of the Old Testament that could have happened by accident or on purpose by succeeding generations of Levite musicians who did not understand their significance.

## Chapter Seven Questions for Discussion

1. Discuss why so many Christian organizations do not publish their philosophy.
2. Explain why you do or do not believe that Christian musicians should resist all musical change.
3. Discuss which types of musical change should be avoided.
4. Explain what the author means by "destructive musical change."
5. Give several reasons why it is not a good idea for a Christian organization to build a music philosophy on trendy music styles.
6. Defend singing in public worship from a biblical position.
7. Discuss the meaning of the terms *sacred* and *profane* music.
8. Discuss your position on whether or not the church and Christian school should try to cater to everyone's musical tastes.
9. Explain why retasking musical styles for use in public worship is problematic.
10. Are there ancient Bible principles of musicing and are these so-called landmarks relevant to musicing in this century?

# Part Three

# Meaning in Music

# 8

# Does Musical Sound Communicate Meaning?

## Is Music Communicative?

THE CONCEPT OF MUSICAL COMMUNICATION has been a buzzword for over a half century among Christian and secular musicians and music philosophers. Christian musicians have traditionally had a sincere desire to make sure that the music they use in public ministry connects so that it will communicate meaning to both Christians and the unchurched. Many who have advocated change in the music utilized in children's ministry as well as teen and adult ministry have based their musical philosophy on both style and text. However, a confusing incongruity has occurred. Those who have advocated complete style change have often at the same time purported that the music part of music does not matter since it does not communicate meaning to the hearer, and furthermore, that only text communicates meaning.

It is difficult to understand how something that does not communicate meaning is so vital to music ministry. If the music part of music does not communicate meaning, then one should ask, why all the fuss about the necessity of drastic style changes? Why cause so much division over traditional church music if only words matter? Wouldn't it be much better to simply write new words with current urban imagery and set them to traditional church music? If communication is the issue, then changing the word pictures created in the mind from descriptions and figures of speech so that they will communicate meaning more clearly to the listener is understandable. However, many times new worship music does not succeed much or any better than hymns and gospel music at producing urban mental images that are \*germane to the understanding of an urban unchurched audience.

## 8: Does Musical Sound Communicate Meaning? 183

The problem is much deeper than new urban imagery or esoteric meaning in hymn texts. Those who consider all the music part of traditional church music to be completely *anathema are making a style statement. Whether they will admit it or not, philosophically these musicians do believe that the music part of music communicates meaning. What they will not admit is that if it does communicate meaning it is in no way neutral, benign, and without any communicative power. Furthermore, if the music part of music does communicate meaning, then it has the power to communicate either positive or negative meaning.

Conservative Christian musicians definitely believe that music is communicative and powerful and that it is in no way neutral. Musicians and philosophers have contended for hundreds and even thousands of years that the mode makes the difference in appropriate or inappropriate music, making it good or bad music. This philosophical belief has existed from the time of the ancient Greek philosophers until now. Traditional musicians have believed that the Bible, the history of church music, and good common sense all dictate that there is a difference in sacred and profane music in terms of the meaning, both designated and embodied, that each communicates.

Christian musicians need to use terms like appropriate-inappropriate, usable-unusable, correct-incorrect, good-bad, and a multitude of other terms that may be used to try to make some philosophical designation for the use or disuse of particular types, styles, or genres of music (*genre* refers to the type of music and *style* refers to the way in which the genre is performed.).

Many Christian musicians and Christian organizations have become totally silent philosophically in an apparent attempt to get along with others. Thankfully, there are those who are succinctly and positively publishing their personal and organizational music philosophy statements. Without these noble philosophical writings it would appear that the entire Christian world is in agreement with current music philosophy trends. Also, these philosophical statements are very helpful to Christian music education students, and to church music students who are in the process of developing and writing their personal CME philosophical statements. The reason that written philosophical statements are so vital at the personal and professional level is that they become guidelines for what an individual and a musical organization does musically. Remember that all musical praxis exudes from a music philosophy.

### What does "Joyful Sound" Mean Philosophically?

This chapter is largely a discussion of musical sound and its relationship to the Christian musician. First let us consider musical sound as mentioned in Psalm 89:15. It states, "Blessed is the people that know the joyful sound: they shall walk, O Lord, in the light of his countenance." What does the Bible mean by speaking of joyful sound? As one can see, this verse does not include the word *music* or the words *musical sound*. However it does use the words *joyful sound* which were translated from the Hebrew word *teruah* (8643). The word *teruah* is derived from the word *ruwa* (7321) which has several shades of meaning, but it primarily means a mighty shout or sound of acclamation and great joy. The word *teruah* in Psalm 89 is dealing with musical sound. Also in the heading, the Psalm is identified as didactic, i.e., a *"Maschil* (4905) of Ethan the Ezrahite." So, one can justly conjecture that part of what is to be learned in his teaching song (*maschil*) will be realized by an understanding of the joyful, i.e., musical sound.

There has been heated discussion, disagreement and confusion among Christian musicians about musical sounds in religious music for over a half century. Although we will not settle the issue once and for all in this philosophical discussion, I hope that this discussion of musical sound will be valuable to you as a Christian musician. Although this discussion will be full of beliefs concerning musical sound, I will support them not only by logic but also with God's infallible inspired Word. Since both qualities and kinds of sound exist, the *onus is placed on the Christian's ability to discern which sounds are and are not "joyful sounds" and consequently are appropriate or not appropriate sounds for a Christian to use in presenting the joyful Christian message.

It is important to note that Psalm 89:15 teaches that those who are able to know or discern which sounds are appropriate to use in musicing unto God are able to do so because they walk in the light of God's countenance. The word *know* (*yada* 3045) means the ability to ascertain, comprehend, or perceive. We can assume that since there are those who are capable of perceiving which sounds are proper for musicing unto God, then there are also those who are obviously unaware of the sounds that are "joyful sounds." As Christian musicians are faced with "everything is appropriate" music philosophies, they must be aware that such philosophies are not biblical.

The Hebrew word translated "walk" (*halak* 1980) in Psalm 89:15 means "to behave" or "be conversant." The words *in the light* are translated from the word *owr* (216) which means, among other things, "continually" or "perpetually" in Jehovah's countenance (*paniyn* 6440), i.e., face or favor. There are several conclusions that could be drawn from this verse. It most probably means that those who are able to discern which sounds qualify as "joyful sounds" must continually or perpetually be living in God's favor or presence. If this is correct *exegesis, it is no wonder that worldly musicians sometimes call evil good and good evil when it comes to the sounds they music unto God.

Psalm 89:15 states, "Blessed is the people that know the joyful sound: they shall walk, O LORD, in the light of thy countenance." First, let us look at the meaning of the word *know*. It is translated from the Hebrew word *yada* (3045) which means ascertain, comprehend or literally recognize something. If one is able to recognize proper sounds, then it is possible that there are improper sounds that a Christian should be able to recognize. Also, because the Bible teaches that there is "joyful sound" then there are also sounds that musicians may use in musical worship that do not qualify as "joyful sound."

Second, we should consider the words "joyful sound." They are translated from the Hebrew word *teruah* (7321) which means a great sound of acclamation. (We know that *teruah* means a great sound or joyful shout of acclamation rather than noise because it is used here in a positive sense.) From the context of this verse, those who recognize the sound that brings acclamation and praise to God are "blessed" (*esher* 1835). This Scripture connotes that only those who ascertain the sounds that are truly "sounds of acclamation" are blessed or are filled with true happiness.

Based on the authority and import of this Scripture, we are drawn to the philosophical conclusion that it is the responsibility of each Christian musician to gain the knowledge necessary to ascertain what "the joyful sound" is. Accomplishing this difficult task requires understanding of the internal formal properties of each selection of music that is listened to or performed. The formal properties of music communicate a message to everyone who performs or listens to them.

### Does Music Affect the Whole-life of a Person?

It is not popular to contend that Christian musicians have the responsibility to make wise choices about all the musical sounds that they use in secular or sacred musicing. However, Psalm 89:15 and other scriptures back up the philosophical hypothesis that the formal properties of every piece of music do have the potential to affect the whole-life of the performer and the auditor. Therefore, it is philosophically and morally dangerous for a person's mind to be filled with the sounds that exude from the formal properties of a piece of music without having a thorough understanding of what a particular piece of music is capable of doing to that person's whole life. It is not that a musical composition has *subliminal meaning or that the notes or chords by themselves have secret meaning, but when a composer or arranger organizes the elements of music into a congruent whole that we call a musical composition, that composition does have moral implications.

We are constantly warned that we should not eat anything without knowledge of what it has the potential to do to our body, because there is such a strong belief that "we are what we eat." We are not only "what we eat" but also "what we listen to and perform musically." Since sound, and especially combinations of sounds, communicates meaning by arousing moods, passions, feelings, memories, etc., Christian musicians have the responsibility to be aware of how sound affects their whole life and how it affects those who hear the music they perform.

## Moses and Joshua Heard before They Saw

The musical discourse in Exodus 32:17-20 is a discussion between Joshua and Moses about the musical sounds that they heard when they were returning to the camp of the Israelites. Note that their first reaction was caused by what they heard, not what they saw. Although I will not thoroughly consider this Bible example of musicing, I simply wish to point out that the sounds produced from the formal properties of this "idol worship music" greatly disturbed both Joshua and Moses. Remember that they heard before they saw the people musicing. These men of God were aware from the sounds they heard that there was something wrong with the worship music they were hearing as they approached the camp of the Israelites.

They were so disturbed by what they heard that they discussed the sounds that they were hearing. When they saw the people musicing around the golden calf, Moses was convinced that it was certainly a very carnal form of worship. It is evident that if this musicing had been a representation of "the joyful sound" that Joshua and Moses would not have been so upset by what they heard before they saw the people musicing around the golden idol. If the people were musicing with appropriate sounds they would not have referred to their worship sounds as noise (*kowl* 6963).

We should observe that Moses had just spent time on Mount Sinai in the presence of Jehovah. When he left the presence of God, where he received the Ten Commandments and no doubt spent time worshiping in the presence of the Giver of the Decalogue, he was in a position to recognize the genuine from the false, i.e., sacred from profane musical sounds of worship. Twenty-first century Christian musicians should learn from this example that living in the presence of God will keep us in tune with "the joyful sound" and that there is a difference between sacred and profane musical sounds.

Ephesians 5:19 makes this statement: "Speaking to yourselves in psalms and hymns and spiritual songs, singing and making melody in your heart to the Lord." Note that the words "spiritual songs" are used in this example of Bible principles of musicing unto God. The Greek words *pneumatikos* (4152) and *oide* (5603) mean spiritual, i.e., non-carnal songs. Notice that the author of the letter to the Ephesians was very careful not to use the Greek word *oide* by itself. If he had that would have admitted all melodies, sounds and songs. We know further that St. Paul, who was a linguist, was referring to the formal properties of the music and not just words that are sung, because he follows the words *psalmos* (5568), *humnos* (5215), *pneumatikos oide (4152 5603)*,, and *ado* (103) with the words "making melody" (*psallo* 5567). The word *psallo* means to touch the parts of a stringed instrument, i.e., to play a melody on a stringed instrument.

Note that the Greek word *ado* is a direct reference to singing. The Greek word *psallo* does not refer to singing directly but rather to accompanying singing (*ado*). When Paul used the word *psallo* he was without doubt referring to the sounds produced from the formal properties of the music when it was produced on a musical instrument. St. Paul used the word *pneumatikos* to signify that it was necessary to use non-carnal sounds when musicing unto the Lord. So, conversely there are sounds which may be produced from the formal properties of carnal music that do not please God. This Scripture is a Bible proof that musical sounds do communicate meaning. If musical sounds were (and therefore are) incapable of communicating meaning, St. Paul would not have clearly stipulated the use of *pneumatikos oide*, i.e., spiritual or non-carnal songs produced by touching the parts of a stringed instrument. Remember that St. Paul was a linguist and would never have used a word that meant exactly what he did not wish it to mean.

### Is Musical Meaning Inside or Outside of Music?

Much could be said at this point about what constitutes * "carnal music". Almost all Christian musicians would agree that words on carnal themes are never appropriate for use in sacred music. The problem comes when musicians discuss the formal properties of a piece of music that are considered to communicate carnal or suggestive meaning. First of all, if music philosophers are *strict* (absolute) formalists, absolute expressionists, or symbolists, they will most likely contend that if music does have meaning (some of the aforemen-

## 8: Does Musical Sound Communicate Meaning? 189

tioned schools of philosophy do not clearly purport that music has any meaning inside or outside of itself), its meaning is in no way related to life outside of the art of music.

If it seems to the reader that these aforementioned music philosophies are confusing, it is because they are both conflicting and confusing. One of the reasons tobe drawn toward the referentialist viewpoint is that the music part of music, and all the concepts that surround the formal properties of music, definitely have a great potential to affect the whole-life of the performer and the auditor. One should remember that music referentialists believe that musical meaning takes reference, at least partially, from the extra-musical world of concepts, actions, emotional states, and character.

Leonard B. Meyer asserted that the meaning that comes from music will tend to have at least some connection to meaning which is found outside of the formal properties of the music. All musicing, i.e., "doing" and listening to music, is affected somewhat by the references one brings to the great art of music from the world outside of music. Although some of music's meaning is cerebral (intellectual), some of its meaning is emotional (aroused from the sounds).

Those who believe that music's essential nature, its essential meaning, and its real value are music's and music's alone will not admit that any of this meaning is imported from the world around us, because they believe that music is a *closed system. I do not believe any of the above theories because, although I am not a strict referentialist by definition, still, association from the outside world does affect the music we listen to and perform. Although Christian musicians can and should learn from the major schools of music philosophy of the twentieth and twenty-first centuries, they do not have to align a Christian music philosophy with any of them. A Christian musician does not have to swallow the tenants of the various schools of music philosophy hook, line and sinker in order to develop a congruent Bible-based music philosophy that uses parts of one or more of the philosophic schools.

The mainstream absolutists believe that musical meaning lies exclusively within the work of music itself. In other words, to most absolutists music is not about anything because its meaning is its own and thereby it is a "closed system." Remember that these absolutists believe that music's meaning only lies in the perception and understanding of the musical properties inside of the music and the resultant influences created in its closed system which in no way relates to real life.

Another school of absolute music philosophy called *absolute expressionism* disagrees with the mainstream of absolutism and teaches that music's relationships are capable of exciting feelings and emotions in the listener and performer. This belief has become known as *arousal theory*. Some music philosophers believe that these feelings and emotional meanings are actually embodied (found in the music) or are designated or referential (assigned) to the music. This school of music philosophy has merit and should be considered seriously by the Christian musician.

Still another school of music philosophy called *formalism* teaches that music has no meaning at all. These philosophers believe that music is enjoyed simply by appreciation of its formal properties or structure and technical construction. These *strict formalists* believe that music does not have a subject or meaning beyond the combinations of notes we hear. They contend that music communicates nothing else but its sounds and that these sounds have no relationship to life outside of the music. This philosophical belief is what I call the "music sound is benign and in a bubble" theory.

Christian musicians have fallen into this philosophical pit by the thousands in the late twentieth and early twenty-first centuries. This philosophical viewpoint became the easy way out of taking the responsibility of discerning just what on earth the "joyful sound" is philosophically. It became the basis for a musical philosophy and praxis that released the Christian musicians from the responsibility of knowing if the musical genres they use in their secular and religious musicing are carnal forms of musicing and if they have a positive or negative effect on the performer and auditor. Because of this belief their often unwritten and unspoken thesis became "There is nothing sacred about the music part of music", i.e., its formal properties do not matter when musicing unto God or in their secular musicing.

Not every music philosopher believes that music is part of a closed system or that it never refers beyond itself. Davies said,

> "If music never referred us beyond itself, so that all that was involved in understanding music was an appreciation of its structure, its texture, the thematic relationships, and so on, then the nature of musical understanding (and, thus, of musical 'meaning') would raise few philosophical difficulties… But music does refer beyond itself, in that the listener usually reveals her understanding of the music through her appreciation of, and response to, what is expressed in music (in those places where the music is expressive), such difficulties cannot be dismissed in discussing the nature of musical meaning. I do not wish to claim that all music is expressive of emotions. But the importance attached to the appreciation of such expressiveness, where it occurs, as indicating that the listener understands the music, clearly suggests that the conceptually interesting difficulties in describing music as expressive of emotion are of central importance in a consideration of the philosophically interesting cases of musical meaning."[1]

So, the argument about what music does or does not say is still a matter of great philosophical concern in this century. Those who believe that music is not capable of saying anything at all would have us believe that referentialism, or any other philosophy that purports that music can and does refer beyond itself to the real world, are beliefs of the past that have been proven to be false by those who are "in the know" philosophically. Part of music's meaning is found inside of music in its formal properties and part of music's meaning is derived from beyond or outside of itself, because all musicing is experienced in reference to community, which expresses real life meaning.

## Denying Transmittable Meaning

In order to be free of any philosophical restraint, a Christian musician needs only to believe that in the context of musicing unto God the music part of music says nothing, represents nothing, means nothing and is incapable of exerting any positive or negative influence on the performer or auditor. This lackluster music philosophy allows the use of a music praxis based on the belief that "anything goes, anything works, and anything is appropriate" for public or private worship or in secular musicing.

This philosophical pursuit is called a "praxis" because it is an "on purpose" way of musicing, regardless of whether or not it is thought out or written. With this intentional denial of the existence of transmittable musical meaning, a musician is free to music without any restraint. This praxis allows any musical style to be used in music worship because those who follow this philosophical pursuit falsely believe all music styles are appropriate to represent the "joyful sound". With the acceptance of this false belief, the musician is free to become autonomous in philosophy and practice.

The discussion of musical sound sooner or later brings up the heated debate over whether music is or is not capable of arousing passion. Ancient music philosophers generally believed that music could and would arouse passion in the performer and the auditor. More recently, secular music philosophers have batted this philosophical ball around rather unsuccessfully in the last half or the twentieth century. Early writings in this century have not done any better in solving the questions concerning the arousal theory. Those who disagree with arousal theory and the referential theory are absolutists, many of whom *uncategorically deny that music has any meaning outside of itself because they believe that music is in a bubble or music is a closed system.

It is amazing that any Christian musician could honestly climb on the absolute formalism band wagon and deny that music has the power to arouse passion in the performer and the auditor. The Bible is so very clear that there is a war between the flesh and the spirit, and this war is caused by our enemy Satan. The Bible is also very clear that a Christian must control passion by being sure that the flesh is kept in subjection. 1 Corinthians 9:27 states, "But I keep under my body, and bring it into subjection: lest that by any means, when I have preached to others, I myself should be a castaway." This has to include the kinds of passions that are capable of being aroused through musical sounds.

Because there are so many excellent published writings on the dangers of the many styles of contemporary Christian music

(CCM), I will not thoroughly discuss arousal theory and its relationship to religious music in the context of this discussion. Christian musicians who trifle with the arousal theory in the form of sexual arousal caused by religious music are playing with fire. Further, those who present sacred things with sexual meaning transmitted through music (sexual innuendos), are sadly misguided and they are doing the work of God deceitfully— a practice that the Bible directly condemns in Jeremiah 48:10.

## Is Music a Closed System?

The belief that music is a *closed system* is a spurious notion because, as a closed system, music would be independent of any outside influences. If music was not related to real life it would be completely amoral and independent of any moral jurisdiction. That condition would allow the Christian musician to become autonomous in musicing. There is no aspect of a Christian's music philosophy that may be allowed to become autonomous simply because we are accountable to God in every area of our life. Therefore, it is not believable that God, who in the beginning created music, created it as a closed system. God created the mathematical ratios that produce sound so that we could worship Him with these sounds. He also created these ratios that produce pitches so that these sounds could become a part of the abundant life that the Christian should enjoy. This "abundant life" or *perissos* (4012) which is mentioned in St. John 10:10 means that God has created music, among many other things, in superabundance or exceedingly and abundantly above and beyond the necessary things for mere existence.

As can be expected, Satan is always present in this dark world to assist men and women in messing up God's wonderful creation called music. Any philosophical belief about music that denies that God intends music for our good, and that Satan intends to use his influence to pervert it so that music can aid in our spiritual failure, is simply a naïve and over-simplistic misguided belief system.

In the Book of Genesis it is stated very clearly that ALL of God's creation, which without doubt had to include music, was created in a very good (*ma'od towb* 3966, 2896) condition (see Genesis 1:31).

God always gives man a choice. If man had not listened to Satan he would not have fallen from that wonderful state where he walked and talked with God in the Garden of Eden (see Genesis chapter three). However, he listened to Satan, fell spiritually when he disobeyed God, and took on Satan's sinful rebellious nature. Since man has a choice today, he can either arrange musical sounds in ways that honor God or that feed the lust of sinful men and women, and that can be a source of spiritual failure of Christians.

1 Corinthians 14:7 states, "And even things without life giving sound, whether pipe or harp, except they give a distinction in the sounds, how shall it be known what is piped or harped." This Scripture has been subjected over the centuries to a plethora of confusion of opinions concerning its meaning. We know that the Greek words translated giving sound (*didomi phone*-1325, 5456) in verse seven mean something that yields sound. The words "give a distinction in the sounds" (*didomi, diastole, phthoggos* 1325, 1293, 5353) mean to yield a distinction of musical notes in the process of utterance of musical sounds.

Although the use of this musical reference in the fourteenth chapter of 1 Corinthians is in the middle of another discussion, it is still a musical reference. Verse six explains that distinct speaking brings about clear communication. Likewise, verse seven explains that clear production of musical sounds brings about a clear musical communication which establishes message and meaning. Therefore, one may safely conclude that music is at least a *meta-language in that it communicates meaning in an *analogous manner to language. Musicians are cautioned by this verse that clear production of musical tones will insure a clearly communicated musical message and meaning much like clear language communicates an *understandable message.

We are not saying that clearly spoken language and clearly produced musical tones function exactly alike. However, because they have the ability to function in somewhat similar ways, we conclude that music functions as a meta-language. The import of the use of this musical reference in 1 Corinthians 14:7 is that clearly produced music can and does communicate meaning to the performer and the auditor. Therefore, the music part of music does matter because it communicates real understandable meaning. A careful look at verse seven reveals that the inspired Word of God teaches that music that gives a clear distinction in its sounds has the potential to cause the performer and the auditor to "know", i.e., gain information and meaning, from the musical sounds.

If music was totally benign, knowledgably mute, sealed in a bubble, and therefore helpless to communicate any meaning, the writer of this first letter to the Corinthian Christians would not have used the Greek word *ginosko* (1097) which means "to perceive" or "to understand". As I said earlier in this discussion, music alone (music without text) is not capable of communicating exactly like a spoken known language, but it does have the power and ability to communicate meaning— thus the term meta-language is applied here to music being able to "say something" or communicate meaning.

### The Visible and Invisible Parts of Music

I have often mentioned in my philosophical writings the importance of Colossians 1:16, which states, "For by him are all things created, that are in heaven, and that are in earth, visible and invisible, whether they be thrones, or dominions, or principalities, or powers: all things are created by him and for him." There are two words in this Scripture that are of great importance to our discussion. They are "visible" (*horatos* 3707) and "invisible" (*aoratos* 517).

When it comes to God's creating music there is the portion that one is able to see (*horatos*) and the portion that one cannot see (*aoratos*). The musical score is a part of music that one can see and musical sound is a part that one cannot see. Although the written part may communicate meaning to the trained musician who is capable of audiating it [i.e., the ability to see pitch, rhythm and harmony on the musical score and hear them in one's mind], it is the sounds that are what really matter to the rest of the people who are incapable of audiating it in their minds. Music that is still on the page of the score, if it doesn't have words, may very well be considered to be neutral to those who cannot read music. However, when sounds are produced from that score they take on life and communicate meaning to everyone who hears and performs them.

In Colossians 1:16 there is a list of things that were created by the exceeding God (*Theos* 2316). Included in this list is the word *exousia* (1849) which, among other things, means delegated influences. The invisible part of music belongs to this category. Colossians 1:16 explains that all these categories of creation were made by the exceeding God for the exceeding God. God, in His creative power, gave music the delegated authority to influence mankind with musical sound. Composers, arrangers, performers, and conductors have been given the delegated authority to influence all those who hear them produce sound. Because God always gives mankind a choice, all those who compose, arrange, perform, and conduct music may influence others for good or evil with the musical sounds that they produce.

So, *ipso facto* musicians are able to influence others with the message, or understandable meaning, that a particular sound communicates to the auditor. If musical sound was incapable of communicating understanding, then the music part of music would not have any value as a ministering or general musicing tool. However, there is entirely too much evidence that music has the power to communicate "knowing" to the performer and the auditor to ever convince that musical sound is impotent and incapable of having any positive or negative influence.

## Those who Understand Receive the Most Meaning

Roger Scruton's statement should be considered at this point in our discussion of musical "knowing" and "meaning".

> "The meaning of a sentence is what we understand when we understand it. Constraints on understanding are therefore constraints on meaning... If music has meaning, then that meaning must be understood by the one who understands the music. Hence the concept of musical understanding displaces that of musical meaning: we have no idea what musical meaning might be until we have some grasp of the distinction between the one who hears with understanding and the one who merely hears."[2]

It is a very dangerous thing to take one or two isolated statements of a music philosopher's writings and suggest exactly what is meant by these statements. So, I will not attempt to lock down exactly all that Scruton meant, but merely use these famous quotes as a springboard for discussion.

Music does communicate meaning, and the person who will receive the greatest meaning (understanding) from a particular music will, without doubt, be the person who has the greatest understanding of that musical genre and *ipso facto*, its meaning, import, communication, or message. Constraints on one's understanding of a piece of music will affect the amount of meaning its musical sounds will communicate to the performer and the listener. The strong belief that musical sounds are a "mirror of life" or an "imitation of reality" is as ancient as Plato and Aristotle— and so are the various arguments against such a philosophical thesis. Thus, it is not far-fetched to contend that musical sounds do have the potential to affect the whole-life of all who hear and perform them.

Therefore, this leads to the conclusion that those who have a thorough understanding of music that arouses physical passions, such as rock music with its incessant driving forward propelling directionality, will possibly receive more harm because they have the greatest understanding of this music's content and intent communicated to them through sounds. This is not to say that the music will not also have a negative influence on all who hear it. Because sounds penetrate the mind and the emotions, this music will exert influence on all who hear and perform it.

This does not put a premium on a Christian's ignorance of a particular genre of music; it is merely stating that those who are the most entrenched in worldly carnal styles of music will possibly be the ones who experience the greatest emotional and spiritual damage from performing and listening to it. This is all the more reason to not pander to the worldly seeker's addictions to spiritually harmful styles of music. Christian musicians also must be aware of the sound addictions that some seekers have. It gives strong impetus to the church to provide the un-churched seeker a diet of "new song" (see Psalm 40:3 et al.), which will be music of a higher renovated character, than the music with which they have surrounded themselves. There is no doubt about it; many sinners will need a renewing of their minds (see Romans 12:2) which will not be possible if church music sounds feed their sinful lusts by triggering that lust and passion.

### Does a Formalist Believe in Music's meaning?

At this point in our discussion I find it germane to return to the school of music philosophy called *formalism*. When considering the well-known philosophy of *strict formalists*, it is generally understood that they believe that the meaning of "absolute music" (music without words) is meaningless outside of the music itself. That means that in the real world, the "meaning" of the musical sounds produced from the music written on the score are actually meaningless marks on the page since they supposedly have no meaning in the extra-musical world, i.e., the real world around us. They are incapable of communicating anything practical or referential.

Peter Kivy made a statement about strict formalists' musical beliefs that is worthy of our consideration in this discussion of sounds produced by music. "But isn't that exactly what the formalist is saying that absolute music is? Isn't she saying that the symphonies of Beethoven, the string quartets of Haydn, the organ fugues of Bach are 'meaningless noise'? And what greater condemnation could there be of a human enterprise? You spent your life making meaningless noises."[60] Surely if religious music is to be considered amoral because it is part of a closed benign system that is incapable of communicating meaning, then Christian musicians spend their lives producing meaningless noises.

The "music sounds are amoral" theory just does not make any logical sense philosophically. Musical sounds do matter because they communicate meaning to everyone who hears or performs them. Furthermore, there is no evidence either in or out of the Bible that would support the theory that musical sounds are a part of a closed system. If this was true, contrary to the teaching of the Bible, the musician could live and die to himself when it comes to the task of producing musical sounds.

So, in conclusion, we are brought back to the thought that every Christian musician has the responsibility to "know" what the "joyful sound" is, to make continuing distinctions between sacred and profane religious music, and to music unto one another and unto God with non-carnal combinations of sounds. I will bring this discussion to an end with the admonitions found in Ephesians 5:15-19.

> "See that ye walk circumspectly, not as fools, but as wise. Redeeming the time because the days are evil. Wherefore be not unwise, but understanding what the will of the Lord is. And be not drunk with wine, wherein is excess, but be filled with the spirit; Speaking unto yourselves in psalms and hymns and spiritual songs, singing and making melody in your heart to the Lord."

## Is Musical Style Involved in the Communication of Meaning?

Traditional thinking Christians who are conservative in their music philosophy are concerned about making sure that the musical styles that they use in musicing unto God are suitable vehicles. Although it is not popular or politically correct to use the terms "good" and "bad" in conjunction with religious musicing, the terms are appropriate. When considering appropriate vehicles, we are talking about the music part of the music and not merely the texts of religious songs. There is a continuum along which music genres move that places them somewhere between excellence in quality and appropriateness and ineffectiveness, to the point of being ineffective music vehicles for representing God's perfect moral character and being communicators of spiritual values.

Richard S. Taylor put it this way: "The difference in good and bad church music is the emotion generated. On the one hand there is that which is selfward and manward; on the other that which is Godward, upward, and decisive. This is why in all the various possible forms, sooner or later a line is reached beyond which the music ceases to be a good conductor of spiritual edification, and instead becomes a conductor of fleshly stimulation."[4] As I have often told college students, I am not as concerned about exactly where a Christian musician draws the line to which Dr. Taylor referred as I am about the fact that Christian musicians are, in many cases, no longer drawing any philosophical lines at all. The fact that the musical "light bulb" of style is not suddenly on or off makes it much more difficult to discern when a musical style is too worldly or sensual to be a proper vehicle for sacred musicing.

There are a host of twenty-first century musicians who deny that there is such a phenomenon as right or wrong vehicles for sacred musicing. The reasoning behind the belief that there is no continuum from right to wrong is the philosophical musical fallacy that the music part of music does not matter. The obvious conclusion deduced from this fallacy is that any consideration of what is good or bad in church music is "much ado about nothing" spiritually and musically. Robert Berglund put it this way: "The notion that there are neither right nor wrong styles of music used in the church today seems indefensible in light of the obvious stylistic meanings and the contradiction to the changed life premises of Scripture."[5]

The Christian musician who does not wholeheartedly believe in the changed life principles so clearly taught in the Bible will not believe in the Bible concept that a Christian's music and musicing must be of a higher renovated character. Many Scriptures in the Old and New Testament teach the "new song" principle, including Revelation 5:9 which states, "And they sung a new song (*kainos ode*), saying, Thou art worthy to take the book, and to open the seals thereof: for thou wast slain, and hast redeemed us to God by thy blood out of every kindred, and tongue, and people, and nation." The new song (*kainos* 2537 *oide* 5603) mentioned in this verse has the meaning of being new in character rather than only being new in relationship to time.[6]

So, the changed life premises taught in the Bible should lead Christian musicians to the belief that sacred music should be of a higher renovated character than the music of the world produced by composers who do not know Christ and are in many cases producing music that appeals to the lust of the flesh. Galatians 5:16 teaches this principle when it states, "This I say then, Walk in the Spirit, and ye shall not fulfill the lust of the flesh." 1 John 2:16 also teaches very clearly, "For all that is in the world, the lust of the flesh, and the lust of the eyes, and the pride of life, is not of the Father, but is of the world."

Berglund also touched on another concept that is particularly germane to the discussion of appropriateness of church music with his mention of style implications. We all recognize music by its style. Style recognition involves the communication of auditory musical information incorporated in instrumental and/or vocal tones that are systematically distinguishable to the listener. This auditory information is communicated to the listener from the structured execution of a particular music. Thus it becomes recognizable as a particular musical style. Robert Berglund believes that "...it is through musical style that music assumes much of its meaning to the listeners. Certainly in vocal music concrete meaning is arrived at by texts. But as far as music is concerned, meaning, both concrete and abstract, designative and embodied, is generally arrived at through style. In other words, as people are aware of style and its implications through conditioning and psychological associations along with their intuitions, music assumes meaning."[7]

Music finds its place in the multiplicity of style classifications by the way the composer arranges its formal properties. All music has purpose and that purpose causes it to take on stylistic characteristics that are the means of communicating its meaning to the listener. Every astute composer desires to draw the listener into the emotion and meaning expressed in the music. For this reason, a Christian musician must become familiar with what the composer or arranger, through the music part of a particular style of music, is attempting to communicate to the auditor.

Although it is true that every garage or basement musical group is not necessarily a skillful communicator of a particular style of music, many of them are because they apply the style patterns to the building blocks of the music they are composing, arranging and performing— thereby the music becomes a communicator of the desired meaning. Since the time of the Coryville jazz groups in New Orleans, Chicago jazz, and Kansas City jazz inventions, jazz has been successful in transmitting sexual meaning to its listeners. The same success may be said of the rock 'n' roll of Elvis Presley and those who followed him in that style. Probably the most successful communicators of sexual meaning have been the many sub-styles of rock music that have developed since Presley. For a Christian musician to make a claim that the aforementioned music styles were and are not capable of communicating their desired meaning is naïve and short sighted. To contend that these styles of music were and are benign and therefore not capable of communicating meaning is to deny music's great power which is delivered with the help of these style meanings. The music part of music molded by style becomes a powerful communicator of musical meaning which is related to the real world around all of us.

### Endnotes

1. Steven Davies, *Themes in the Philosophy of Music*, 121-122.
2. Roger Scruton, *Understanding Music: Philosophy and Interpretation*. (New York: Continuum US, 2009), 34.
3. Peter Kivy, *Introduction to a Philosophy of Music* (Oxford: Clarendon Press, 2002), 137.
4. Taylor, *A Return to Christian Culture*, 89.
5. Berglund, *A Philosophy of Church Music*, 12.
6. See "A Study of Song in the Bible", *Music of the Bible in Christian Perspective*, Chapter Three.
7. Berglund, *A Philosophy of Church Music*, 22.

### Chapter Eight Word Meanings

**Analogous**— similar or comparable in certain respects, performing a similar function but having different abilities that make them only partially alike.

**Anathema**— in this case, something that a church musician dislikes because it is not an effective tool for musicing the gospel since its imagery is not understood by an urban unchurched audience.

**Arousal Theory**— the theory that music arouses in us feelings of emotion.

**Carnal music**— relates to music that purposefully appeals to crude bodily pleasures and appetites.

**Closed system**— This terminology comes from the belief that music's meaning belongs to music and music alone and has no relationship to the real world outside of music's "bubble".

**Exegesis**— refers to critical explanation or interpretation of a text in the Bible.

**Germane**— something that is relevant to the subject under consideration.

**Meta-language**— as used here, it represents a symbolic system that is beyond (not quite like) language. It is also a form of language or set of terms used as

# 8: Does Musical Sound Communicate Meaning? 203

analogous to another language.

**Onus**— in this context refers to something that is one's duty or responsibility.

**Plethora**— as used here an excessive amount of confusion.

**Subliminal**— a musical stimulus which is below the threshold of conscious perception.

**Understandable meaning**— in this work, connotes that music's meaning can be understood in relationship to the real world around the musician. This belief is in opposition to the notion that music has meaning but that its meaning is its own and has no relationship to activities, situations or conditions in the real world outside of music.

**Urban imagery**— visually descriptive or figurative language that would be understood by those who live in the inner city.

## Chapter Eight Questions for Discussion

1. Explain why you believe that music is or is not communicative.
2. Discuss the meaning of the statement in the Bible, "Blessed is the people that know the joyful sound," in light of a music philosophy.
3. Explain why you do or do not believe that music has the ability to affect the whole-life of a person.
4. Explain how Moses and Joshua knew that something was terribly wrong in the camp of Israel by the music they heard before they actually saw what was taking place.
5. Discuss why you do or do not believe that musical meaning is not only found inside but also outside of music.
6. Discuss the question, "Is music a closed system?"
7. What is the significance of the Greek words *horatos* (3707) and *aoratos* (517) in light of a Christian music philosophy?
8. Explain what the author meant by the statement, "Those who understand the music receive the most meaning."
9. Discuss your position on the belief of *strict formalists* that the meaning of "absolute music" (music without words) is meaningless outside of the music itself.
10. Does music have the power to refer beyond itself? Explain your answer thoroughly.

# 9

# Can We Understand Music's Meaning?

## Reading (Singing) Distinctly Gave the "Sense"

Nehemiah 8:8— "So they read [*qara 7121*] in the book in the law of God distinctly [*parash 6567*], and gave the sense [*sekel 7922*], and caused them to understand [*biyn 995*] the reading [*miqra 4744*]."

THIS PASSAGE OF SCRIPTURE has troubled many Bible expositors for centuries. They have often queried, "What made the reading of the scrolls of the Law 'distinct'?" They have also wondered how the Levite musicians were able to "give the sense" of the meaning of the Law. It has also been a great mystery what type of rendering of the scrolls by the Levite musicians actually took place. We know from verse seven that the Levites were among those who "...caused the people to understand the law..."

This Bible reference has become an esoteric reference to the Levite musicians intoning or singing the Law by the use of the *te'amim* (the biblical musical notation) which is found above and below the text in some Hebrew Bibles. This intoning, *cantillating, or singing is what made the Levite rendering of the Law "distinct", i.e., more understandable to the people.

The word translated "read" in this verse is taken from the Hebrew word *qara* (7121); it sometimes connotes reading the scrolls, and at other times it means to call out or to proclaim the Torah. This proclaiming is commonly understood by Hebrew scholars to mean the intoning or singing of Scripture.

Note that the Bible does not say that the Levite musicians gave commentary (i.e., explanation that was something like the

*Halakhah and *Haggadah from the *Midrash) on the content of the scrolls, but merely about their type of "reading," which most likely refers to the singing of the Law through the use of the *te'amim*. We know with certainty that this rendering was performed so distinctly (*parash* 6567) that it separated or gave specificity to the meaning of the text making it possible for the congregation to understand "the reading" of the Torah.

One may legitimately ask, "What should we learn from this text in the Book of Nehemiah?" Christian musicians in the twenty-first century need to be aware that proper musical rendering of the good news of the Bible is an ancient landmark of musicing and can make the message of Scripture more understandable to modern hearers. The musician must perform sacred music in such a way that the modern-day worshiper will be aware of the "sense" of the message in order to understand it distinctly. Anything that distracts or obscures the Bible message should be avoided. The music part of the music should be the handmaiden (helper) of God's Word, not a hindrance. The formal properties of the music should be congruent with the good news of the gospel.

### Is Music's Meaning Related to Real Life?

For our discussion of music's meaning, see a portion of 1 Corinthians 14:15, "...I will sing with the understanding also." This portion of Scripture is small but its meaning is huge. *Absolute formalists* and *absolute expressionists* believe that all of music's meaning is to be found in the music. They contend that there is no understanding of music outside of the music itself. The absolutists claim that music is a closed system with its own esoteric meaning which is not related to real life. The staunch formalists purport that music understanding, i.e., meaning, is an intellectual experience with the formal properties of the music. Most of them deduce a sort of humanistic self-meaning as an end to this understanding.

Music has meaning both inside and outside of itself, i.e., its formal properties have a relationship to the world outside of music. My belief is somewhat like Leonard B. Meyer's concept of *embodied* and *designated* meaning. That makes me a hybrid referentialist that got kicked out of "Formalist" school because I believe all music has meaning inside and outside of itself. Maybe Kivy would call me an "enhanced referentialist"— or maybe not. It is an oversight to contend that all music and all musicing is incapable of saying anything at all. Music with words and without words has the ability to communicate meaning that is related to or is suggestive of real life. The music part of music not only conveys a message but as Dr. Frank Garlock has said for years, "the music is the message."

Music always has a purpose and it always says something. It always has meaning both inside and outside of itself because no musicer musics in a vacuum or in a bubble. If we fail to understand this philosophical concept, we can erroneously believe that music does not have real life meaning and that it is futile to try to understand music— especially in reference to the world outside of the music. Christian musicians must remember that, unless the musicer is locked alone in a soundproof room, musicing is always done in community.

The performer and the auditor always bring something from real life to the music experience. No performer or listener can wipe the mental slate clean of what they have experienced previously in community before experiencing a particular musical performance. Also, what they experience from a musical performance will be influenced by the embodied and designated meaning of the music part of the music.

Leonard B. Meyer made this statement about designated meaning in music: "Though the perception of a relationship can only arise as the result of some individual's mental behavior, the relationship itself is not to be located in the mind of the perceiver. The meanings observed are not subjective. Thus, the relationship existing between the tones and the things they designate or connote, though a product of cultural experience, are real connections existing objectively in culture."[65] There are real objective connections between music and culture, community, and what the formal properties of the music communicate. These meanings are very complex since they include a combination of designated (referential) meaning and embodied (actual intrinsic) meaning.

If the strict formalists were correct in their belief that music's meaning is its own meaning that relates to real life outside of music, then essentially music would have little or no meaning. If music is a closed system, it has no practical meaning to the performer or hearer that is understandable. Furthermore, if music cannot be perceived in a form that is understandable outside of itself, it has little or no practical meaning. Under this notion when a person hears music it has only an academic meaning. since the only experienced emotion that can be derived from performing or listening is an emotional response that results from an academic understanding of the music's formal properties. This reduces the art of music to mathematical ratios, arrangements of the elements of music and to a mental understanding of music's form. Under such conditions, the aesthetic joys of emotionally experiencing music in community are drastically curtailed since the emotions that are aroused by the music do not come from the music's communication to the listener but only from the listener's academic understanding of the formal properties of the music.

### Musicing with the Musician's Intellect

Although I have introduced the philosophical concept that we have the ability to understand music's meaning, this topic will need to be discussed much more thoroughly throughout this book. 1 Corinthians 14:15 sheds more light on this thesis: "...I will sing with the understanding also." The word *nous* (3563) means, according to the Strong's Greek Dictionary, "With the intellect, i.e., the mind; by implication meaning, or understanding." The Bible tells us that we can and should music with understanding. When discussing this verse most Bible commentators major on the argument concerning known or unknown language. They fail to recognize that this mention of singing is a Bible principle of musicing used advisedly by St. Paul.

Note that the word *psallo* (5567) used here means, according to Strong's Greek Dictionary, "from *psao*— to rub or touch the surface; to twitch or twang, i.e., to play on a stringed instrument." Paul was no doubt referring to both instrumental and vocal music in this passage of Scripture. He was instructing the Corinthian Christians to music with understanding both vocally and instrumentally. St. Paul, who was a linguist, understood that *psallo* connoted both instrumental and vocal music, and therefore, he would never have used this Greek word if it meant precisely what he did not want to say. Also, if he had wanted to refer only to words sung without instrumental accompaniment he would have used words that meant only singing.

The Bible instructs us that part of the meaning of musicing both vocal and instrumental music should be an understanding of the music which is both inside (intrinsic or embodied) and outside (extrinsic or designated) of the composition itself. This means that part of the understanding of the internal formal properties of the composition being performed and the various meanings of these properties are to be found outside of the music itself. This does not connote that the musician who is "doing"(i.e., the musicer) should not have an understanding of the internal embodied meanings of the music itself. He or she most definitely should understand the music's formal properties, its text, and how to interpret it aesthetically. However, music's meaning is not a totally esoteric meaning that is part of a closed system with no relationship to life outside of the music itself.

## Bible Music Increased the Performer's And Listener's Understanding

Our English word *music* is derived from the word *muse*, that means "to think". From as far back in history as there is a record of music, it has been considered by some cultures as not only an emotional but also an intellectual art form. Although the ancient music of the Bible was definitely an art form, it was not merely an art form to be consumed on man's desires and pleasures. The Ancient Hebrews did not consider it to be primarily an art form but rather a means of connection with YHVH.

The music of the Bible was not written by heady high minded composers who were seekers of musical artistic self-actualization, entertainment, fame and fortune. Music was created by *JHVH* as a means to honor and worship the blessed trinity. It was created for God's glory and man's edification, education and enjoyment as part of the abundant (*perissos* 4053) life God created for His created beings. There is also music mentioned in the Bible that did not honor God. However, the Bible does not put a premium or approval on such music. As a matter of fact, the Bible condemns it in Exodus 32, Amos 6, and Isaiah 23.

The previous explanation of music as an intellectual art form was discussed to point out that the types of ancient music of the Bible that followed Bible principles of musicing was designed at least partially to make one think. Since muse means "to think", the logical conclusion is that music was given to mankind, at least partially, in order to increase his understanding. Part of its purpose was and is understanding which is derived from outside of the music itself and, therefore, brought to the musicing experience. However, this does not preclude the importance of meaning inside of the art of music, which is very vital because of its ability to communicate understanding to all who perform or listen to it.

Whatever meaning was to be found inside of the formal properties of the music of the Bible was intended to be understandable outside of the music itself and *ipso facto* from real world meaning. Music of the Bible did not contain an esoteric set of secret symbols that magically gave music meaning which was "music's meaning alone," and therefore was not congruent with real life meaning. The experiences in musicing in ancient times included insight from knowledge of the music's formal properties and from what the performer or auditor brought to the experience of musicing from former experiences both inside and outside of music.

Likewise, in the twenty-first century everyone brings something to the experience of "doing" or listening to music. No one is capable of performing or listening to music in a vacuum. Neither is music a secret closed system that will only reveal its esoteric understanding to a few erudite professional performers, college music professors, and music philosophers. I also do not agree with the notion that music says absolutely nothing and cannot be experienced with understanding. No musician performs and no person listens in a bubble which has no connection to life itself.

## Do Those Who Understand the Music Receive More Understanding?

For the purpose of discussion let me quote Roger Scruton's statement again. "If music has meaning, then that meaning must be understood by one who understands the music."[2] Without agreeing with all Scruton meant by that statement, at face value, the statement is true. We can understand music and also its meaning, i.e., its import and its message. Where we would disagree is that the performer always brings something from outside of music to the experience of "doing", i.e., performing music, or to the experience of listening to music, and that all *understanding* which comes from inside of music can be *understood outside* of music.

The most important thing about music is that we EXPERIENCE it. It will never hurt or help us very much while it is merely left in the musical score. Although an astute musician may audiate music (hear the music in his mind as he sees it), it does not really come alive and have great power until one experiences it produced, performed, or recorded.

Scruton's statement is true, in that the person who stands to receive the most understanding from music is the one who understands its formal properties, its style, its "nuts and bolts," its melodic structure, its harmonic practice, its text, etc. Therefore, the person who stands to be influenced the most, either positively or negatively, by a particular type of music is the person who hears or performs it with the most understanding. However, all who music actively by doing, or passively by hearing, are affected either positively or negatively by what they do understand.

### What about Music that Has a Dual Intentionality?

We have been discussing the concept of understanding music's meaning. The question may be asked at this point in our discussion, What kind of understanding will be received when one juxtaposes two diametrically opposed styles, genres, or types of music? If a style of music evokes a specific meaning, then marrying the understandings of two diametrically opposed styles is incongruent.

Now we are in deep water philosophically. If we mix two musics incongruently and music A somehow gives us understanding of the "lust of the flesh" by exciting us sexually, and music B somehow gives us understanding from the words about the "love of our Savior Jesus Christ," which understanding will the performer and listener receive?

This musical amalgamation has a double or dual *intentionality. I want to make it clear that I do not believe in this terminology in the exact way as music philosophers like Scruton. Music A has a specific purpose and aim, so therefore its intentionality is different from that of music B, which has a diametrically opposed intentionality.

Therefore, the understandings received from the juxtaposition of these two musical purposes will at best severely muddy the waters of the message of this music. For this reason we are unable to have our musical cake and eat it too. We cannot sort out the bad and keep the good by "re-tasking" music that is of a dual intentionality. To explain the result of this musical amalgamation, we can use a concept from Francis Schaeffer's writings, which explains that when "nature and grace" do battle, "nature eats up grace."

## Does All Musicing Have Moral Implications?

When a Christian musician performs either sacred or secular music the implications of that music's message should not be contrary to the moral nature of God, because every Christian musician represents God. Although they do not have the power to damage the moral nature of God with music, they do have the power to damage God's reputation with those who hear the musician perform. So, how a Christian musics either sacred or secular music matters very much.

As already discussed, a Christian music aesthetic should be based on, among other things, the beauty that God intended it to have when He created it. God created the mathematical ratios that make sound possible, and He created it to have the potential to be, without doubt, beautiful. It is only reasonable that God created music in a beautiful condition because He intended it to be used for His glory and honor. Ugly, unreasonably dissonant and inordinately raucous and loud music would not possibly have been considered, by the all-wise Creator, to be in an exceedingly good condition.

Because music has the potential to communicate meaning to the mind of those who hear and perform it, Christian musicians have the awesome responsibility of making musical choices that will bring honor to God's name. The psychological and moral influence that music exerts upon the hearer has the potential to either lift up the auditor's human spirit or to harm it. Since music has this power a Christian musician cannot justly purport that music performance does not have moral implications.

Every Christian musician must remember that he or she is a Christian first and a musician second. If Christ is going to have preeminence in all things (Colossians 1:18) then every time that a musician performs religious or secular music in a way that brings reproach on the cause of Christ, that musician is in violation of Bible principles that govern all of a Christian's musicing. The philosophical issue is not secular and sacred music, but rather wise choices of both.

## Does Emotion, Communicated Through Music, Have Meaning?

I hesitate to write on emotional meaning in music. Some believe that the word spirit (*pneuma* 4151) is referring to the human spirit, while others believe that this word is referring to the spirit of Christ or the Holy Spirit. The Bible verse that they often refer to is 1 Corinthians 14:15— "What is it then? I will pray with the spirit, and I will pray with the understanding also: I will sing with the spirit, and I will sing with the understanding also." Adam Clarke referred to the Greek word *pneuma* as the "Spirit of God."[3] Henry J. Foster considered it to mean the "human spirit."[4] Joseph S. Exell referred to it as meaning the "Holy Ghost."[5] D.D. Whedon believed that *pneuma* referred to "My higher spiritual emotional nature."[6] R.C.H. Lenski believed it to mean "...my own spirit, the material part of my being in which my ego centers which is able to receive impressions from God."[7] Many of the Bible expositors made no attempt to identify the word *pneuma*.

As one can see, the meaning of the word *pneuma* has a drastically different meaning if it is interpreted as the human spirit rather than the Holy Spirit. If one interprets it to mean the human spirit it could be referring to singing with emotion, i.e., emotional meaning. If, on the contrary, one interprets it to mean with the influence of the Holy Spirit, it possibly would mean singing with the anointing and power of the Holy Spirit.

Now you can understand why I am reticent to base singing with emotion on 1 Corinthians 14:15. So we will have to continue this discussion carefully and without strong unrefuted biblical support. What about emotion in singing? Certainly stoic, unemotional poker-faced singing is not artistic musical performance. If *pneuma* used in the verse mentioned above refers to the human spirit (I am inclined to believe probably does not) then Scripture would support the idea that no one can sing sacred music effectively without the involvement of the human spirit, which produces emotion and *ipso facto* meaning.

Whether one is singing "Bold Intruders" from Mozart's *Cosi fan tutti*, "He Was Despised" from Handel's *Messiah*, or the gospel song "His Eye is on the Sparrow" by Civilla Martin, great emotion is required on the part of the singer if the musician's musicing is going to be effective. Whether the vocalist is musicing to a crowd of worshipers in a church or in an auditorium full of opera lovers, the greatest way to alienate an audience is to remove emotions from solo, choral or congregational singing.

The issue here is not that a Christian musician may not be able to find a Bible proof text for singing with feeling or intent. The issue is that unemotional singing of secular music cannot be effective, and singing sacred music cannot be efficacious, without the involvement of human emotion (understanding that sacred musicing necessitates the anointing of the Holy Spirit in order for it to be efficacious). The only aspect of singing that is of greater value than good vocal technique is the believability of the performance.

Much of the vocal music message is expressed through the unfolding of a text. However, in order for a singer to be effective in text exposition, the text must be expressed emotionally. This is a major part of what voice teachers call effective musicing or artistic vocal production. Notice that in 1 Corinthians 14:15, singing is volitional since St. Paul said "I will" in the first person. Regardless of which view a Christian musician takes on the meaning of the word *pneuma* in this context, it stands to reason that the singer, as an act of will, must purpose to seek God's anointing and engage the emotions that come from a human spirit that is responding volitionally to God who is worthy of all praise.

Emotional meaning does not merely happen because a song has a text. Whether the song is secular or sacred, text brought to life becomes very meaningful, and brings understanding to the hearer, through the doer's doing. This understanding is brought about through the singer's cognitive understanding of the meaning of the text and emotional rendering of that text vocally by engaging body, mind, and the human spirit in the musical performance. The singer, very much on purpose, chooses to express text meaningfully by engaging everything that has been mentioned in the discussion above.

Although removing one's self from the performance by singing in an inartistic manner without emotion is often an attempt at humility, it is a misguided attempt. If one takes the view that a Christian musician's singing is a musical offering unto God, then one must look at the sacrificial system to see what it required of the one making the offering. Without a lengthy explanation of the sacrificial system of the Bible, it simply required the best offering that the one presenting the offering to God could present. (There are nineteen verses in Exodus, twelve in Numbers, and eight in Ezekiel that mention an offering being without blemish.) A lackluster musical offering without emotion and meaning is not the best musical offering that a Christian vocalist is capable of presenting to God. I have often told choir members and soloists that it is not the best offering (in terms of musical perfection) that God will accept, but rather it is the best offering that the musician is capable of presenting (out of a pure heart that has pure intentions) that God will accept.

One reason that I have been so careful in my writing about emotion in musicing, and *ipso facto* its communicated meaning, is because it may seem to the reader that I agree with the philosophical notion that the performer is everything to sacred musicing. It may also seem that I believe that a humanistic approach to musicing is proper for the Christian performer. On the contrary, the Christian performer who is sold out to Christ believes like St. John, who declared in John 3:30, "He must increase, but I must decrease."

I most certainly disagree with musical performance that exalts self. It thereby denies the Bible principle of music ministry established in the Old Testament that the Levite musicians were to minister in the spirit of *sharath* (8334), i.e., in the spirit of humility like a servant or a menial worshiper. One of the Scriptures that teaches this principle of musicing is 1 Chronicles 6:31-32, which states, "And these are they whom David set over the service of song in the house of the LORD, after that the ark had rest. And they ministered (*sharath* 8334) before the dwelling place of the tabernacle of the congregation with singing, until Solomon had built the house of the LORD in Jerusalem: and then they waited on their office according to their order." Without this biblical philosophy of musicing unto God, it is possible to go through the process of religious musicing with the purpose in mind to glorify self and to display personal musical ability, rather than the sole purpose of presenting a musical offering to God as a response to who He is, what He has done, and what He will do in the future.

With all this in mind, Christian musicians can still hide behind the cross and lift up the Christ who died on the cross while giving an artistic performance. No musician has to exalt self when musicing with emotion and meaning. Although I have met performers who were haughty and high minded, some of the greatest musicians that I have had the privilege to meet were very humble, down to earth people. Musicing with emotion does not require the musicer to be self-centered or to not be Christ-like.

Refusing to music with emotion as a means of exhibiting outward humility, though perhaps well-meaning, is a misguided philosophical position, because real humility is not a mere act but rather a condition of the heart. Likewise, musicing for the purpose of *self-aggrandizement at the expense of musicing that lifts up Christ is also the result of a condition on a musician's heart. So, the Christian musician should not dumb down musical performance by inartistic unemotional performance that attempts to appear humble to an audience. Conversely, spiritual musical offerings are never about the musician or his or her ostentatious musical performance.

Regarding an over-humble approach to one's performance, I remember that one of my daughter's violin professors once said to her,

"A performer's false humility is a form of pride, too." Removing oneself emotionally from musical performance often has results in musicing that is detached and sterile. Trying to look, sound, or appear humble is a form of self-pride. Another of the many reasons that bland unemotional musical performance is ineffective is that it produces a musical ministry that is not believable. One of the most important aspects of sacred musicing is that it must be believable to an audience if it has any hope of being efficacious. If the Christian musician is singing about how much he or she loves the Lord in such a way that the audience believes that the one ministering does not really love the Lord, then that musician's musicing will not be effective. One of the main reasons that so many church leaders have become disillusioned with traditional church music is that many church musicians perform traditional music in a lackluster manner.

### Endnotes

1. Leonard B. Meyer, *Emotion and Meaning in Music* (Chicago: University of Chicago Press, 1956), 34.
2. Roger Scruton, *Understanding Music*, 34.
3. *Clarke's Commentary*, Vol. 6, 275.
4. Henry J. Foster, *I Corinthians*. Vol. 27 of *The Preacher's Homiletic Commentary*, (Grand Rapids: Baker Book House, n. d.), 309.
5. Joseph Exell, *I Corinthians*. Vol. 2 of *The Biblical Illustrator*, (Grand Rapids: Baker Book House, n. d.), 350.
6. D.D. Whedon, *I Corinthians – 2 Timothy*. Vol. 4 of *Commentary on the New Testament*, (Cincinnati: Walden & Stowe, 1882), 100.
7. R.C.H Lenski, *The Interpretation of St. Paul's First and Second Epistles to the Corinthians*. Vol. 7 of *Commentary on the New Testament*, (Minneapolis, MN: Augsburg Publishing House, 1937), 591-592.

### Chapter Nine Word Meanings

**Cantillating** — the process of intoning the OT Scriptures.
**Intentionality** — the fact or condition of some action being deliberate.
**Haggadah** — the book of readings for the Seder service.
**Halakhah** — the book of Jewish laws which was derived from the written and oral Torah.

9: Can We Understand Music's Meaning?   217

**Midrash**— an ancient commentary on part of the Hebrew Scriptures.

**Self-aggrandizement**— an action for the purpose of enhancing one's power, wealth, position, or reputation.

**Uncategorically**— coming to an absolute conclusion without exceptions or conditions.

### Chapter Nine Questions for Discussion

1. Discuss the meaning of the words in the statement in the Bible, "So they read [*qara 7121*] in the book in the law of God distinctly [*parash 6567*], and gave the sense [*sekel 7922*], and caused them to understand [*biyn 995*] the reading [*miqra 4744*]."
2. Explain why you do or do not believe that music's meaning relates to real life.
3. Discuss your position on the author's statement that "the performer and the auditor always bring something from real life to the music experience."
4. Discuss the philosophical significance of the statement in 1 Corinthians 14:15, "…I will sing with the understanding also."
5. Explain what philosophers such as Leonard B. Meyer meant by the terms *embodied* and *designated* meanings of a music composition.
6. Explain why you do or do not believe that experiences in musicing include insight from knowledge of the music's formal properties and from what the performer or auditor brought to the experience of musicing from former experiences, both inside and outside of music.
7. Discuss the significance of Roger Scruton's statement, "If music has meaning, then that meaning must be understood by one who understands the music."
8. Explain what the author meant by the statement that some music has a dual intentionality.
9. Discuss the psychological and moral influence that music exerts upon the hearer.
10. Does emotion, communicated through music, have meaning? Explain your answer by giving evidence to support your belief.

# 10

# Is Music a Language?

## What Can Music Say?

CERTAINLY WE ARE NOT going to solve the age-old argument of whether music is a language, a meta-language or no language at all. Most music philosophers agree that music does not communicate explicitly like spoken language. Music does not say what it means distinctly in a well-defined manner like a spoken language does. The music part of music, i.e., the formal properties of the music, cannot say, "It is raining outside" or "It is 27 degrees Fahrenheit outside." However, the fact that music does not function exactly like a language does not prove that it does not transmit a message or meaning to the auditor.

Laird Addis stated that in one respect, "...music is more like language than dreams and religious ideas. For language also, at least as sound and inscription, is not something mental even though its intentionality is more closely tied, analytically, to that of the literary intentionality, if there is such in music— at least in the new [i.e., in his] theory."[1] His new theory admits some likeness of music to language but is somewhat fuzzy about just what and how music communicates meaning. He looks backward to philosophers like Freud and Durkheim and their views of unconscious awareness and symbolism. But again he is quite fuzzy in how these philosophers' theories of unconscious awareness relate to music's ability to communicate. Music philosophers often exhibit nondescript explanations of what they believe music can or cannot say.

Music philosophers who are formalists generally believe that "Music's beauty, its essential nature, and its highest value are things that are music's and music's alone..."[2] The referentialist's position is that music's meaning must have connection to meanings outside of music. Symbolists believe that music's symbols are objects used to represent abstract insight into an understanding of the nature of human feeling.

As may be seen from the views just mentioned, music's way of "knowing" and its ability to communicate that knowledge is essentially different depending on one's philosophical view. Some who believe that music is a closed system will tend to believe that music has its own agenda, i.e., that the significance of music is not related in any way to life in general. Others who consider music to be a closed system believe that music symbols reveal the significance of human feeling which is in no way related to what the performer or auditor brings to musicing or music listening. The philosophical views of non-referentialists all tend to either be, or to have the propensity to become, autonomous philosophical views. When a musician develops an autonomous music philosophy, that musician will have a definite inclination or tendency to behave musically in a way that is independent of the Lordship of Christ; the emphasis is placed on the musicer rather on music's ability to communicate.

Those who have read very much of my philosophical writings know that I am always skeptical of any philosophical view that is autonomous or tends to lead toward autonomy. All real truth is a congruent truth that is related to real life. Therefore there is no aspect of true truth that is a part of a closed system which is not related to real life, or that is developed from a philosophy that is a law to itself, because its truth is part of an esoteric truth that is found in music's little non-related bubble. All music philosophy must submit to the Lordship of Christ.

Music has the power to communicate information, mood, emotion, and message to the listener and the performer. So, although music does not function exactly like written language, its function is at least analogous to language. Music has so much power to say something that in some ways it is beyond language in its ability to communicate information directly to the listener. Therefore, its power to affect the whole-life of a person should never be taken lightly. This fact places the *onus probandi* on every Christian musician.

## Does a Musician Bring Anything to the Experience of Musicing?

Every musician who performs music and every person who listens to music brings something outside of music to the music experience. All too little has been written about the multiplicity of emotions, opinions, or ways of communicating or "knowing" that each person brings from the outside world to a music listening or performance experience. Every person brings something to the worship experience, or the secular music experience, that adds to the amount of communication they will receive from performing or listening to a piece of music.

No one is capable of listening to or performing music in a vacuum and thereby escaping "knowing" or understanding the music. Music cannot be perceived by the human mind in a closed space or bubble which has nothing at all in it from life experiences. Music psychologists have shown for many years that a human fetus perceives music and responds to it before birth. Kinder-Music enthusiasts have shown us that the newborn infant can and will respond to music if proper stimulation is provided. Therefore, no one perceives music in a closed system without reference to the real world. This view places me, at least partially, in the camp of the referentialists who believe that all musicing and all listening to music is affected by the references one brings to the great art of music from the world outside of music. However, I want to make it clear that I am not contending that all of music's communication comes from outside of the music itself. On the contrary, much of music's communication comes from hearing and understanding its formal properties, its style and its historic perspective.

A Christian music aesthetic must be at least partially but not totally referential. Such a belief makes one's philosophical position to fall short of strict referentialism, I am not a strict referentialist because I do not believe that all of music's meaning is found outside of the music itself. Those who believe this believe that the music part of music is powerless to communicate without its references to things outside of the actual music. On the contrary, music's sounds, i.e., the music part of music, is very powerful. Where I part philosophical company with the non-referentialists is that I do not believe that music is a closed system, and therefore, a law to itself that is devoid of the possibility of any real-life meaning.

A Christian's study of the philosophy of beauty in secular or sacred music should be somewhat referential. Most secular philosophers consider aesthetics to be that part of philosophy that deals with beauty in music as distinguished from music's useful or moral value. Since the Christian must "know" in reference to God and His creative ownership of beauty in music, he or she must not develop a music philosophy independent of music's ethical or moral nature and value. If music has ethical or moral value it will always derive this ethical and moral value outside of itself and *ipso facto* from God. If a musician considers that music's communicated meaning does not have ethical and moral value because music is amoral and does not need to come under the Lordship of Christ, this meaning is in conflict with the moral nature of God and His divine ownership. In other words, all music has *moral implications and *ipso facto* ethical and moral value. What music communicates to the listener must not conflict with the ethical and moral nature of God. A Christian is not free to be involved in musicing that communicates carnal or anti-Christ understanding merely because it is "fine art."

### Does It Matter Whether Music is a Language or Not?

At this point in our discussion one may legitimately ask, "Why does it matter if music is or is not a language?" Certainly all serious music philosophers are greatly concerned about whether music is a language, a meta-language, or no language at all. Depending on whether a music philosopher is a formalist, referentialist, or symbolist, different conclusions will be drawn. But all philosophers are deeply concerned about whether or not music has meaning and how and what, if anything, it communicates in either a closed, symbolic or referential manner.

It seems that it is mostly contemporary Christian musicians who do not struggle with music's meaning. Many of them function without a clear understanding of the nature of the music part of music in relationship to what it is or is not capable of communicating. Without a clear understanding of the nature of music, the simplest philosophical praxis is to ignore music's power to communicate anything at all. So they choose to blindly ignore the efficacy of the music part of music by denying that it is a language, a meta-language, or that it has any power to communicate meaning and understanding. If music does communicate, they do not address what that communication does to the whole-life of the performer and listener.

Unlike the serious music philosopher who spends a lifetime studying the nature and value of every aspect of the music part of music, many Christian musicians, without any written scholarly basis, purport that only words are efficacious. Their writings do not consider, with scholarly philosophical basis, the nature and value of the formal properties of the music part of music. This seems strange and illogical since their main thesis is purported to be communication with the seeker.

The denial that music is a language or a meta-language does not solve the philosophical problems concerning communication and meaning. Although all serious Christian music philosophers are concerned with whether or not music is or is not a language, meta-language or has no language-like capabilities at all, the greatest concern is whether or not music communicates message and meaning. The Bible evidence that music does communicate information, meaning and understanding should sober all Christian musicians. The fact that the music part of music does communicate a message to all who perform and listen to it places the responsibility squarely on the musician rather than entirely on the words of songs.

What one believes about the music part of music's communicating power will affect the entire process by which a Christian musician approaches music ministry and music education. The Christian musician who naïvely assumes that the music part of music does not communicate anything at all will erroneously suppose that the music part of music does not matter. Have you ever considered why so many Christian musicians do not have a developed, systematic, philosophical basis for their beliefs concerning the nature of the music part of music's communicating power? Christian musicians should give music the same level of respect as non-believers do.

10: Is Music a Language?   **223**

## Does Music Communicate in an Effective Way?

We know with certainty that the music part of music is capable of communicating because Psalm 49:4 states emphatically, "I will incline mine ear to a parable: I will open my dark saying upon the harp." In the context of this Bible teaching there is no mention of words alone, although some exegetes assume that the word *chiydah* (2420) which connotes puzzles indicates that text was included. If text was involved the music part of the harp music helped to make communication and understanding of these dark sayings possible. Earlier I mentioned that the Christian musician who wrongly assumes that the music part of music is unable to communicate will also wrongly assume that the music part of music does not matter because it is benign and incapable of resulting in any moral implications. This erroneous assumption seems to be most often purported by Christian musicians. Perhaps they make this assumption in a feeble attempt to make the end justify the means in their philosophy and praxis.

I have often read quotes by rock, jazz, country and pop musicians and they are very strong in their belief that music communicates in very effective ways to the listener. I have not read a single quote from a pop, rock, country or jazz musician that would even slightly hint that music does not have power or the ability to communicate a message to the listener. However, a host of classically trained musicians deny that music communicates any meaning that is related to real life situations, i.e., the "bubble" philosophers. However, the mere fact that they are well trained musicians does not make their musical and philosophical assumptions correct.

From ancient to modern times, music philosophers have believed in general that "the mode made the difference" when it came to musicing and listening. However, modern, postmodern, and now post-postmodern man has not been unified in his belief about the nature, value and communicating power of music. Because music philosophers disagree about how and what music communicates, they are divided into referentialist and non-referentialist camps.

The communication matter was further complicated by the advent of the symbolist philosophers, who basically believe that music's symbols communicate in their own little bubble which does not relate to life outside of music's world. Although it is evident that I do not totally buy this philosophical theory, I do admit that they are possibly right in their belief that music does have the potential, at least in some situations, to communicate symbols to the performer and the auditor. However, I do not concur with the mainstream symbolists in their belief that music's symbols do not relate to life outside of music's little bubble, which they refer to as a closed system. Jimi Hendrix once said, "Atmospheres are going to come through music, because the music is a spiritual thing of its own... you can hypnotize people... and when you get them at them their weakest point you can preach into the subconscious what you want to say."[3]

### Do the Formal Properties of Music Communicate Meaning?

Aaron Copland wrote this about music's meaning:

> "My own belief is that all music has an expressive power, some more and some less, but that all music has a certain meaning behind the notes and that that meaning behind the notes constitutes, after all, what the piece is saying, what the piece is about. This whole problem can be stated quite simply by asking, 'Is there a meaning to music?' My answer to that would be, 'Yes.' And 'Can you state in so many words what the meaning is?' My answer to that would be, 'No.' Therein lies the difficulty."[4]

I partially agree with his analysis of music's meaning. Music does say something because it has great power— the greater the skillfulness of the work of the composer the more the music tends to accomplish its intended purpose and intended meaning. However, one cannot always say with great certainty how a listener will respond and will be affected by the music. I most definitely agree with his statement that music has meaning behind and beyond the organization of its formal properties. Since music's meaning can be behind and beyond the music's formal properties, it has the capability to be referential.

It has never made logical sense that, as many Christian musicians believe, words matter but the formal properties of the music do not matter. To them, only words are efficacious. If this were to be the case, which it definitely is not, why all the fuss about having to drastically change music style to fit the needs of the postmodern seeker? Isn't it self-evident that style greatly communicates a message to the worshiper or seeker? It also seems self-evident that, if the formal properties of the music communicate, i.e., send messages, to the listener, that it is possible to send messages that are incongruent with the spiritual message of the text or that do not congruently represent the moral nature of God.

Another concern is that it is not believable that the music part of a piece of "music alone" (i.e., instrumental music without words) can communicate the concept of sex to an audience if a secular jazz, pop, rock, etc. group performs it, and that it becomes neutral, benign, and completely docile and *ipso facto* is incapable of arousing passion when it is played by a Christian. The one who performs the music is not capable of sanctifying the music performance merely because he or she is a Christian. If the music is by its nature contrary to the moral nature of God, it is not amenable to the Lordship of Christ or acceptable when performed by a Christian musician.

If a fine art accomplishes carnal intent when performed in a secular setting, it is still carnal when performed by a Christian in a religious setting. However, one must discern whether or not it was the music part of the music or the risqué text, immodest suggestive body movements or immodest costuming that gave occasion to the arousal of sexual passion. As I have stated many times in my philosophical writings, a Christian musician must make wise decisions in both secular and sacred musicing.[5]

Furthermore, it is impossible to believe that a piece of music that is composed in a style that explicitly arouses sexual passion and the lust of the flesh is a better musical vehicle than traditional church music, which is composed in time honored styles that have proven to be God honoring. How can such a style represent the pure moral nature of a holy God when it is juxtaposed with religious lyrics? Believing such a thesis is without scholarly philosophical basis, because religious words are not capable of sanctifying the musical deed.

The objection is raised that many post-postmoderns believe that when a Christian composes or arranges religious music in styles that are most often utilized by secular musicians to arouse sexual passion, it will not send sexual messages or arouse carnal passion, because the music part of the music does not matter; it is incapable of communicating any moral import. Furthermore, these Christian musicians object because they believe that the musician, not the music, makes the difference. So, to them, the emphasis should always be shifted from the music to the musicer.

It is the responsibility of every Christian to make wise choices when considering both sacred and secular music. Furthermore, there is no logical or scholarly basis for a Christian musician to develop a philosophy and praxis that purports that "the end justifies the means," or that the intent of the musician is the only thing that matters when musicing either secular or sacred music.

### Endnotes

1. Laird Addis, *Of Mind and Music*, (Ithaca, New York: Cornell University Press, 2004), 100.
2. Wayne Bowman, *Philosophical Perspectives on Music* (New York: Oxford University Press, 1998), 194.
3. Robin Richman, "An Infinity of Jimis," *Life*, Oct. 3, 1969, p. 74,
4. Aaron Copland, *What to Listen for in Music* (New York: McGraw-Hill Book Company, Inc., 1957), 12.
5. See *Church Music Matters* for a more thorough discussion of wise choices of secular and sacred musicing.

### Chapter Ten Word Meanings

**Esoteric reference**— a reference that is understood by only a small number of people with specialized knowledge and understanding.

**Moral implication** — this term is concerned with the principles and rules of right or wrong conduct and the distinction between the principles of right and wrong.

### Chapter Ten Questions for Discussion

1. Since many music philosophers agree that music does not communicate explicitly like spoken language, do you believe that music is or is not a language? Explain your answer.
2. Discuss the author's statement that music's way of "knowing" and its ability to communicate that knowledge is essentially different depending on one's philosophical view.

3. Explain the significance of the statement, "Every musician who performs music and every person who listens to music brings something outside of music to the music experience."
4. Explain why you believe or disbelieve that a person is or is not capable of listening to or performing music in a vacuum, and thereby escaping "knowing" or understanding the music.
5. Do you believe that a Christian's study of the philosophy of beauty in secular or sacred music should be somewhat referential? Please explain your answer.
6. Why does it matter if music is or is not a language?
7. Explain your view of whether music is or is not a language, meta-language or has no language-like capabilities at all, the greatest concern is whether or not music communicates message and meaning.
8. Do the formal properties of music communicate meaning? Please explain your answer.
9. Do you believe that if a fine art accomplishes carnal intent when performed in a secular setting it is still carnal when performed by a Christian in a religious setting?
10. Why is it the responsibility of every Christian to make wise choices when considering both sacred and secular music?

# 11

# Creativity and the Christian Musician

## Real Creation Took Place When God Created

AT THE OUTSET OF this discussion it should be understood that real creation is not synonymous with a musician being creative, or his or her *propensity toward creativeness. In Chapter One we discussed the fact that man did not create music and that it did not evolve into existence. Music's beginning and its development over many centuries is a much different phenomenon when one compares the notion of some kind of musical "big bang," with no one knowing how it started, with the belief that music's beginning was a part of the creation as recorded in the first chapter of Genesis. Since evolutionists, both atheistic and theistic, refer to evolution in different terms than a creationist, it is unwise for those of us who believe in a real creation to refer to music's "evolution." The term *development* is a much better word to explain what has happened over the many centuries.

Earlier we established that although performers, composers, arrangers, and music directors are "creative," they are not capable of creating anything. We know from Genesis 1:1 that "in the beginning God created..." The lexical form of the Hebrew phrase "in the beginning God created" is *reshiyth elohiym bara eth* (7225, 430, 1254, 853). This statement is, as lexicographers tell us, rather unprecedented in the English language. At the first (*reshiyth*) the plurality of the supreme exceeding God (*elohiym*) through the formative process by entity and "self" created (*bara eth*). In other words *elohiym* the supreme God by Himself and through His own power took nothing and made something. In the truest sense of the word, that is actual creation. God took nothing and made music. No one but God has ever made something from nothing.

We know from Genesis 1:27 that mankind was created in the image of God— "So God created man in his own image…" The Hebrew word *tselem* (6754) which has been rendered image in the AV connotes an illusion, resemblance or a representative figure. So, Christian musicians were created by our Heavenly Father as representative figures or little shadows of an infinite God. We are made in His image, but we are not gods nor are we actually like God. I like to use the illustration of a person holding their hand directly below a bright light. The image of a hand that is seen on the floor is not a hand, but it is the image of the real hand that is above it.

What was said in Chapter One and again in this chapter is to point out that God created; He made us in His image, so we are called to be "creative" but we are in no way creators. Only God can take nothing and make something out of it. When a Christian musician exercises his God-given *"creativeness" he takes the building blocks of music, which were created by God, and arranges them into what is hopefully a creative musical composition.

When Christian musicians use terms like creation, creative, creating, creative effort, creative genius, creative ability, and creative talent when they are referring to the work of a musician, they are using the terms loosely. God has given many musicians unusual musical ability to perform, arrange, compose, and orchestrate music, but God has never given a musician the ability and power to start with nothing and form something out of that nothingness.

### The Composer is Somewhat like a Carpenter

The creative music composer or arranger is somewhat like a carpenter who takes building materials that exist as a part of God's infinite creative work and constructs or arranges them in a creative orderly fashion to "create" or, more properly, to construct a building. The construction may be beautiful, practical, aesthetic, and useful but it is not, in the truest sense of the word, a creation.

The same is true of the work of a composer or an arranger, who takes the building blocks of music (rhythm, melody, harmony, etc.) and places them into some order which is commonly referred to as a musical "creation." The musician may place his or her name at the top, the bottom, or any place in the middle of the musical score. To him or her, this may signify that the composition is his or her "CREATION" because this musician believes that it was "composed from scratch", i.e., from nothing. In reality this is not true, because the composer did not take nothing and turn it into something.

Now that we have reasonably established that composers do not create, we need to pursue the thought that Christian musicians are called upon by our Heavenly Father to be creative. From the introduction to this discussion, we know that God *"bara* (1254) *eth* (853)", i.e., took nothing and made something. Christian musicians, although they are not capable of making nothing into something, are responsible to be musically creative.

God expects all musicians to make imaginative use of the resources which He has made available to them through His creation. We know this because God expects Christians to be good stewards of the resources that he has given them. If one studies the Parable of the Talents in Matthew 24:14-30, Jesus very clearly taught that His servants are responsible to be good stewards of the resources given to them.

The English words *several* and *ability* found in Matthew 25:15 are derived from the Greek words *idios* (2498) and *dunamis* (2411). They connote one's own ability or might to utilize God-given resources, i.e., talents. There is absolutely no conflict here between a Spirit-led life and one's God-given power to utilize the fine arts in a creative manner. The servant who was afraid to be creative in his use of the talents given to him by his lord was said in verse 26 to be *poneros* (4190), i.e., culpable, and *okneros* (3636), i.e., slothful.

Although the Parable of the Talents does not directly mention music or creative use of the fine arts, they are included in the principle which Jesus was teaching. One of the servants failed to make creative use of the resources his lord had given him and *ipso facto* was found culpable for this failure.

Creative responsibility requires just that— responsibility. God-given resources are to be used, not only in a creative manner, but also in a responsible manner. When a Christian musician creatively musics unto

God, a freedom which God has given, that musician has the awesome opportunity and responsibility to creatively represent the moral nature of God. Conversely, there is not freedom to music in such a manner that the moral and perfect nature of God will be misunderstood or misrepresented. To put it another way, a Christian composer, arranger or performer is free to express creative freedom in the creative process as long as that freedom does not misrepresent the moral nature and reputation of the holy triune God.

When one's creativity in arranging the building blocks of music causes the musical vehicle to send a subtle (or not so subtle) message that is less than representative of the nature of the perfect and holy triune God, that music style or genre is inappropriate for sacred musicing. Music listeners and performers do not have to have doctorates in music performance or composition to be aware that a music style can make fun of its object. When a musician musics unto God in jest, the one who is musicing and those who hear it are aware that it is sending a less than honest message about our precious Lord and Savior Jesus Christ. Christian musicians in the twenty-first century must come to the sane understanding that the time to poke fun with music is never when we are presenting God a musical offering.

## "Music Alone" Expresses Meaning when Performed

Although the philosophical discussion of if or how music expresses either intrinsic or extrinsic meaning (see chapters eight and nine for this discussion) is too large a topic to thoroughly discuss in the context of this discussion of music creativity, it is necessary to inject at this point that music does express meaning. It expresses both intrinsic and extrinsic meaning. The way the building blocks are arranged into a musical composition expresses meaning when it comes alive in musical performance. It also expresses referential meaning which is outside of itself.

Instrumental "music alone" may be benign when in its written state if it is left dormant on the printed page of a musical score (and if no musician ever *audiates it). However, the mighty lion comes alive and roars when it is performed. Vocal music is not capable of being benign or dormant when it is merely in the printed state, because its words are capable of misrepresenting the moral nature of God when one reads them on the written music score. Not only is creative music "doing" a serious responsibility, but also creative music arranging and composing is a very serious responsibility. Christian lyric poets, composers and arrangers must be aware that it is possible, at least for vocal music, that it may be destructive by misrepresenting the moral character of God even before it is ever performed.

Music creativity is important to all music but it is especially important to sacred music. Creativity helps to keep our musical offerings to God fresh and alive. One of the most lethal things that can happen to worship music is complete predictability. When this happens to Christian worship boredom sets in and the congregation's minds begin to wander. This problem has been compounded in the late twentieth century and now as we have entered the twenty-first century by the three second (or less) attention span of many of those who attend worship. Without creativity and the anointing of the Holy Spirit upon that creativity there is little hope of holding a modern day congregation's attention.

### Christian Musicians Should Fear "Rutual"

What would happen to public worship if the pastor took a fresh new text from the Bible and preached the same exact message Sunday after Sunday? Most of us would not think that the different Scripture text read at the beginning of the sermon was enough to ward off boredom. Creative music worship should be a concomitant of the whole scheme of fresh creative worship services. Although it is outside the scope of this discussion, music ministers must be in constant search for new creative, wholesome, appropriate ways to worship the blessed Trinity through the church's musicing.

Those who believe and practice free worship should fear * "rutual" far more than ritual. I have found in my travels over the past forty-five years that those who practice free worship are often not very creative in the way they present their musical offerings unto God. Many of the free worship services that I have attended in recent years are caught up in very inartistically repeated patterns of singing the same sequence of praise chorus sequences Sunday after Sunday.

They pride themselves in the fact that they are not caught in the rut of singing the same hymns and gospel songs over and over, but they are doing the same thing with the new praise chorus sequences that they are singing.

I want to make it very clear that I am not against free worship or ritual worship. What I am advocating is the impregnating of fresh creative musicing into whichever style of worship a congregation of Christians is comfortable to utilize. God has always demanded the best offering that His people are capable of presenting to Him. Surely fresh new creative musicing fits into that "best sacrifice" concept, if church musicians will be cognizant of the fact that the creative process is always a responsible process. Any musical worship praxis that does not cause one to congruently music in such a way that God's moral nature, *worthship, and honor is preserved is faulty.

Many Christian music education programs experience the same problems that occur in church music. The music directors and classroom general music teachers are plagued with a lack of creativity. Without passion and the creative process, music education becomes very predictable. I remember my student teaching experience as an undergraduate student. I worked under two very different cooperating teachers. Loretta Crim was one of the most passionate and creative junior high school educators that I have ever met. Every day I was amazed at the creative ways that she presented choral music to her very large junior high choir. On the other end of the spectrum was an elementary general music teacher (who will remain nameless) that was unbelievably predictable. On Monday we reviewed page 26 and sang and/or played rhythm instruments on page 27. On Tuesday we reviewed page 27 and sang and/or played page 28. On Thursday we reviewed page 28 and sang and/or played page 29. As you can see her music praxis was devoid of any musical creativity whatsoever! Music teaching should be done with great passion that exudes from a systematic series of beliefs that congruently flow from a belief that creative musicing is of great importance to everyone in the music classroom.

## Creativity and Conservatism

A part of creativity in music is the use of one's imagination and original ideas in the process of composing or arranging the music part of a piece of music and thereby producing an artistic musical work. This artistic creativity does not have to be at loggerheads with Christian conservatism. Although "new song" mentioned in the Bible (Psalm 40:3) does not connote a new artistic musical work, there is no reason why Christians should not be continuously using their creative gifts to produce new sacred and secular musical compositions. Conservatism can cause one to not trust anything that is new or creative.

The Christian musician should never feel that conservative beliefs about music stifle creative efforts. The musician who fears and loves God and desires to creatively represent and reflect the moral nature of God has a freedom to compose and arrange sacred and secular music because that musician is living a life in the Spirit that guides all creative efforts. If that musician will obey the checks of the blessed Holy Spirit, He will guide his or her creative efforts. There is no dichotomy in these creative efforts because there is no opposition between God's will and that musician's creativity. Every effort of the Spirit-filled creative musician is guided by the Holy Spirit, and this musician will obey the checks of the Spirit in order that his or her creative work will be pleasing to God. I like to compare the example of spell check on my computer to the relationship of a Spirit-filled creative musician. Many times I make mistakes, but if I am faithful to run the spell check it will point out the necessary adjustments in my work that need to be made.

### Chapter Eleven Word Meanings

**Audiate**— a term coined by Edwin Gordon that means to mentally hear a sound without actually hearing it audibly.

**Creativeness**— is imagination or original ideas, especially in the production of an artistic work by a finite being. This term should not be compared to God's infinite creation, where He took nothing and created something.

**Propensity**— the inclination and natural tendency to behave in a particular way.

**Rutual**— This word is not found in a standard dictionary. It is my term for those who do the same things over and over in the worship service until they are caught in a deep rut of repetition.

**Worthship—** is the Old English word *woerthship* meant worthiness, and its modern derivation is worship. An act of devotion based on the Christian's knowledge of God's worth.

### Chapter Eleven Questions for Discussion

1. Discuss the significance of the author's statement, "The process of music's development over many centuries is a much different phenomenon than the notion of some kind of musical 'big bang' theory."
2. When a Christian musician exercises his God-given creativeness he takes the building blocks of music, which were created by God, and arranges them into what is hopefully a creative musical composition. Discuss how this statement differs from the humanist view of creativity.
3. Discuss why you agree or disagree with the author's belief that "The creative music composer or arranger is somewhat like a carpenter who takes building materials that exist as a part of God's infinite creative work and constructs or arranges them in a creative orderly fashion to 'create' or, more properly, to construct a building."
4. Explain why you do or do not believe that God expects all musicians to make imaginative use of the resources which He has made available to them through His creation.
5. Give philosophical justification for the author's belief that "When one's creativity in arranging the building blocks of music causes the musical vehicle to send a subtle (or not so subtle) message that is less than representative of the nature of the perfect and holy triune God, that music style or genre is inappropriate for sacred musicing."
6. Discuss why many music philosophers contend that music expresses both intrinsic and extrinsic meaning.
7. Discuss what the author meant by stating that "Instrumental 'music alone' may be benign when in its written state, if it is left dormant on the printed page of a musical score (and if no musician ever audiates it), but the mighty lion comes alive and roars when it is performed."
8. Explain why you do or do not believe that creativity helps to keep our musical offerings to God fresh and alive.
9. Explain what the author meant by coining the word *rutual* and why he connected it to free worship by saying, "those who believe and practice free worship should fear 'rutual' far more than ritual."
10. Explain why you do or do not believe that artistic creativity does not have to be at loggerheads with Christian conservatism.

# 12

# Aesthetics and the Christian Musician

### Aesthetics in A Christian's Music *Paradigm

CHRISTIAN MUSICIANS MUST BECOME aware of where they place the aesthetics of music in their musical paradigm. Although we will consider many more aspects of aesthetics in the life of a Christian musician, pinpointing where aesthetics is placed in one's musical paradigm, and ultimately in that person's music philosophy, is essential to the establishment of what that musician considers the nature and value of music to actually be.

The Christian should not develop an aesthetic approach to religion, but rather a religious (biblical) approach to aesthetics. Music aesthetics is by no means the *bellwether of Christianity. Having an *aesthetic experience with music does not form any proof, nor is it any indication, that the Holy Spirit has placed His anointing or approval on a musical performance or a performer. However, aesthetics and aesthetic experiences with music are important and must be considered in our discussion of both musical paradigm and music philosophy. Music's beauty is an important part of its nature, and will definitely affect what that music will communicate to the musicer and the listener.

A Christian musician should not admit or exclude a style of music solely on the quality of its aesthetic value. Notice that I did not say that one should totally ignore a style's aesthetic qualities that give it its value. However, the question at hand is not music's deepest aesthetic value but rather what effect it is capable of having on the whole life of a Christian. For instance, it has been a mistake to exclude the host of different styles of music that exist today from the musicing of a Christian based on the belief that these styles are not music at all or that they are not aesthetically high quality music. The issue is not whether a type of music is "musical junk" or that it is "not music at all" or that it is "not of enough musical quality" to be aesthetically effective. The problem with such statements that are often made is that they are simply not always accurate.

What really matters is much more complicated than mere musical or aesthetic quality—although musical and aesthetic quality does matter. What really matters is what a particular style of music communicates to the musicer and the listener and what that communication has the potential to do to a person mentally and spiritually. A piece of music that is not full of aesthetic meaning is not necessarily harmful to the musicer and the listener. So, whether or not the formal properties of the music are arranged in such a way to make that music aesthetically valuable is not reason enough to exclude a style of music as a whole or as a single musical composition from the life of a Christian.

### What is Music in Aesthetic Terms?

In the study of the aesthetics of music, one must define very clearly what music aesthetics really is. A standard definition of aesthetics may be explained as a set of principles concerned with the nature and appreciation of beauty in all of the fine arts. Because of this universally known understanding of what aesthetics means, musicians must understand that the study of the aesthetics of music traditionally deals with beauty in music rather than its popularity, usefulness, or utilitarian aspects. A music composition is the result of the composer or arranger's organizing sounds and silences into a musical thought or congruent whole so as to arouse emotions in the listener and performer in order to elicit some kind of intended response inside of the hearer. In some cases this response will hopefully be an aesthetic experience within the listener and performer's mind. What happens covertly inside of the hearer may or may not result in an overt response.

These organized sound colors, which are the result of combinations of vocal and/or instrumental sounds and silences produced from rhythms, melodies, and harmonies that are aesthetically pleasing or harmonious sounding to the listener, are considered to be music. Combinations that negate the musical elements of the combination of sounds and silences produced from rhythms, melodies and harmonies are considered anti-music. Although the result of this anti-music may have much shock value and therefore have some sort of value, either negative or positive, it is still considered philosophically *anti-music.

With this introduction in mind, the Christian music philosopher must, when developing a Christian music philosophy, remember that historically and biblically a Christocentric philosophy of music aesthetics must deal with beauty in music. Although there is room for what a Christian considers beautiful when evaluating music, what is beautiful is not completely a matter of taste. This is especially true when a Christian musician is considering either vocal music or instrumental music (music alone) that is intended to be sacred.

In light of Matthew 11:28, which states, "Come unto me, all ye that labour and are heavy laden, and I will give you rest," a Christian music aesthetic must deal with the concept of music having a forward directionality which consists of beginning, middle (climax) and end. Music must not only move from beginning through a point of tension, but also to a final point or rest. This aesthetic is extremely important in sacred music. Incessant tension without the finality brought about by rest is not consistent with the rest that the Bible message brings to those who find the rest found in a born-again relationship with Jesus Christ.

Great musical phrases, both sacred and secular, have for thousands of years moved from beginning through climax to a final moment or resolution and rest. Any music aesthetic that does not follow this pattern is upsetting to the human psyche. The human mind both consciously and unconsciously is able to cope with tension but release is vital to mental stability. When a musician understands the deepest levels of the essential nature of music's aesthetic, an understanding of what music with a forward incessant, propelling directionality is capable of doing to the human psyche is illuminated much more clearly. When a musician develops a sacred music aesthetic based on noise and/or upsetting amounts of volume; continuously misplaced rhythmic accent; and long periods of unresolved tension caused by unresolved dissonance, the upsetting psychological tension that results is in no way compatible with the message of the gospel, or to good mental health for that matter. Music that intends to overthrow all traditional conventions and expectations just for the novelty of upsetting the human psyche is not congruent with the good news and rest of the gospel of Jesus Christ our Lord. Remember that Jesus said in Matthew 11:28, "Come unto me, all ye that labour and are heavy laden, and I will give you rest."

## Aesthetics and the Beautiful

As was said before, aesthetics is that area of philosophy that considers the perception of the beautiful as distinguished from the moral or the useful. Christian musicians often wonder just where Christocentric music philosophy fits in to a Christian aesthetic. One thing is sure, God is interested in beauty. We know that He is since His creation is not only useful but also very, very beautiful.

As always, the Christian is concerned with where to start when building a philosophy of artistic beauty. One thing we know, that in the beginning God created everything that is beautiful. Since music was a part of His creation, we know from the Genesis record that the beauty that God created was very good. So therefore His creation of beauty was exceedingly beautiful. We have no logical or factual reason to believe that God created music with the propensity or intention for it to be grotesque, raucous, or ugly.

Any philosophical view of aesthetics that is built on the grotesque or ugly is faulty. We know that crude, ugly, unmusical religious compositions do exist, but they are the result of a mis-intention and a mis-arrangement of the building blocks of music. Never blame God for ugly, grotesque, unmusical compositions. The anti-music compositions of the twentieth and twenty-first centuries have not generally been produced by God-fearing Christian composers and arrangers who were writing music to honor God.

The AV translates Psalm 81:2 as, "Take a psalm, and bring hither the timbrel, the pleasant harp with the psaltery." The RSV translates verse two as, "Raise a song, sound the timbrel, the sweet lyre with the harp." The English words *pleasant* and *sweet* were translated from the Hebrew word *naiym* (5273) which means in this context delightful, pleasant, or sweet sounding hand held lyre (*kinnor, kinnore,* or *kinowre* 3658). The word *naiym* is almost always translated pleasant in the KJV and always connotes something that sounds or is pleasant. Therefore, it is reasonable to believe that when *naiym* refers to musical sound it represents beautiful or pleasant sound. From this conclusion, we may rightly deduce that beautiful sound is a Bible principle of music aesthetics.

## An Anti-music Music Aesthetic

We have very briefly introduced the philosophical discussion of aesthetics and the Christian musician. Now we are going to discuss very briefly some musicians in the twentieth century who were instrumental in the development of the philosophical notion that there are no absolutes in music. Musique concrète is an example of anti-music music composition. Pierre Schaeffer (1910-1995) composed music directly on tapes or discs from natural sources. However, these natural sounds were seriously distorted by playing them backward, changing the speed of the sound or by other editing abnormalities. In 1948, Schaeffer composed his *Concert des bruites* (Concert of Noises) and other original compositions. Pierre Schaeffer's music can be identified with the philosophy of surrealist painters, with its unmusical juxtaposition and chance techniques. He often took perfectly natural sounds and scrambled them in an indeterminable manner. (Surrealism will be considered later in this discussion.) Pierre Schaeffer, Henry Cowell, Jean Baronnett and Pierre Boulez were the early "inventors" of this anti-music distortion. These compositions included religious pieces like *Mass for Liverpool* and *The Apocalypse of John*.

Distortion is a form of anti-music. Distortion found its way into religious genres making subtle mockery of the awesomeness and solemnity of sacred music. One shocking aspect of this distorted religious music is that the narration of the Bible text is clearly understandable.

John Cage (1912-1992) became interested in anti-musical techniques like prepared piano and chance operations. Cage called his chance music indeterminacy. His composition which he titled *4'33"* (four minutes and thirty-three seconds) has become the ultimate composition of anti-music since his purpose was to compose music that said absolutely NOTHING! The performer simply sat at the piano for the designated period of time making absolutely no sounds.

## Aesthetics and Distortion

We have discussed very briefly the philosophical meaning of John Cage's anti-music composition *4'33"*. At this point in the history of music, serious music composition had philosophically destroyed an aesthetic of beauty and profundity in music. Cage had philosophically proved Igor Stravinsky's antithesis philosophical statement, "I consider that music is, by its very nature, essentially powerless to express anything at all..."[1]

The music philosophy of depraved man in the twentieth century closed the door on a music aesthetic based on beauty and musing, and replaced it with anti-music that is based on distortion and chance techniques. These composers opened the door for the philosophy that the music part of music is incapable of expressing any effective message, or perhaps any message at all. They also destroyed profundity in music since chance music is just as profound as the most thought-out composition by great composers like J.S. Bach. Now in the twenty-first century complete musical despair reigns. To these composers music says nothing, is incapable of being profound, and is ultimately incapable of expressing anything at all.

What does all this mean to church musicians and music educators in the twenty-first century? Why should we care what "serious academic music" composers do? The reason we care is that in order for us to know how contemporary Christian music derived its philosophical basis, we must understand the history of music. With these basic understandings of twentieth century philosophical despair in music philosophy, we are able to know how twenty-first century church musicians derive their synthesis music philosophy. The term *synthesis music philosophy* refers to the mixing of styles of music that were developed with the intent of appealing to the sexual appetites of depraved man with religious words. Sometimes this synthesis music uses music styles that have direct historical connection to the anti-music despair of the twentieth century. This music aesthetic also purports that the way to build a music aesthetic is to bring sound under the yoke of the music system of godless musicians so that Christian music will relate to the worldly desires of the seeker.

Many Christian musicians are incorporating elements of the anti-music despair in this century. They believe, like Stravinsky, that the music part of music is not efficacious, i.e., it is incapable of expressing anything at all. Furthermore, these Christian musicians believe that nothing is sacred or profound about the music part of Christian music. Finally, like the religious music of Pierre Henry, these post-postmodern Christians' religious music is grotesque and dissonant but the words are clear and clean! To them this sanctifies the deed! If the words are clean, nothing else matters.

Under this philosophy, religious music no longer has to be aesthetically beautiful. Although almost all Christian musicians who perform anti-music music would deny it, they do not believe in a music aesthetic based on any definable traditional standards of beauty. If they do believe in a Christian music aesthetic, it is most certainly a redefined beauty based on a synthesis somewhere in between beauty and ugliness. How did music degenerate in its aesthetic beauty from the music of J.S. Bach to the anti-music of composers like John Cage? Achille-Claude Debussy (1862-1918) was one of the early composers who started in the direction of despair music. He became interested in the literary works of the symbolist writers of the nineteenth century. These writers addressed their writings to a system of symbols and symbolic meaning as a negative reaction to naturalism and realism in literature. This school was non-literal and figurative, thus developing a network of vague images.

The music of Claude Debussy was highly chromatic, fluid and vague. Debussy's opera *Pelléas et Mélisande* was composed in symbolist style. Stolba explained, "The opera is an expression of Debussy's philosophy that music should be a free art, truly representative of the fact that it cannot be contained, but exists in time and is born on air. That freedom meant a relaxation of restrictions such as those that normally governed form, harmonic progressions, and rhythm."[2]

This vagueness was considered impressionistic and thus the connection was made with the vagueness of the visual art of Édouard Manet (1832-1883), Paul Cézanne (1839-1906), Hilaire Germain Edgar Degas (1834-1917), Claude Monet (1840-1926), and Pierre Auguste Renoir (1841-1919). The works of these painters are studies in the impression light makes on the subjects of these paintings. Often, light and subject seem to almost merge. The overall impression takes precedence over clarity, thus vagueness reigns.

## Aesthetics after Impressionism

Dadaism was another aesthetic movement that had a profound effect on music philosophy and composition. Dadaism was one of those movements that struck out at traditional aesthetic and moral values. This school of thought, starting around 1916, used chance techniques, was very irreverent and often employed irrational artistic absurdity. Proponents of Dadaism were Tristan Tzara (1896-1963), Jean Arp (1887-1966) and others.

This movement gave rise to surrealism which was formulated by André Breton (1896-1966) and made famous by Salvador Dali (1904-1989). The philosophy of surrealism came from Breton's automatism philosophy that what a person thinks, feels or wills is determined by physical changes. After French impressionism came a school of artistic thought that purported that, although one is fully conscious, actions come from subconscious images over which that person has no control. The problem with this philosophical thought is that it removed the artists' personal responsibility for their actions.

Another philosophical theory that affected composers of the twentieth century was existentialism. Introduced by Sören Aaby Kierkegaard (1813-1855), this theory was a literary movement rather than an artistic theory like Dadaism and surrealism. He believed that man was not a part of any *metaphysical scheme. He believed that each person must create (authenticate) his own being in his hostile environment by an act of his free will.

Composers of the modern era who were somewhat like the proponents of the "isms" mentioned above, struck out against all tradition and standards of correctness with their musical compositions in an attempt to authenticate themselves.

## Aesthetics and the Destruction of Musical Absolutes

Claude Debussy paved the way to the door of despair, and Igor Stravinsky (1882-1971) walked through it with portions of his ballet *Petrushka* composed in bitonality. His ballet *Le sacre du printemps* was composed in polytonality with the use of polyrhythms. His *Septet* (1953) and his ballet *Agon* (1957) were composed in Serial (12 tone) technique. So, by the end of his career Stravinsky had moved from conventional diatonic harmonic practice to Schoenberg's despair of 12 tone technique.

The ultimate expression of twentieth century despair in music composition was developed by Arnold Schoenberg (1874-1951). Although his earliest works were in post-romantic style, his compositions became more and more chromatic. Next, his works became very dissonant and pantonal, which defied the rules of traditional harmonic practice.

Schoenberg developed his twelve-tone (dodecaphonic) compositions. These works were based on a tone row using all twelve tones equally, thereby emancipating dissonance. This technique was the ultimate twentieth century expression of philosophical despair in music composition. It purported that all 12 tones should be used with equal emphasis with no regard to the rules of harmonic practice. Up to this time, music always flowed from consonance to dissonance which was always resolved into consonance.

What Schoenberg accomplished was the destruction of absolutes in music. To him nothing was profound, appropriate, proper, right or wrong in harmonic practice. He changed both the epistemology and the methodology of meaning in music composition. So, under his epistemology there are ways of "knowing" that involve new foundations and new limits. With this compositional methodology, he created a new way of dealing with the science of music. His new compositional procedures established a completely new way of musical "knowing" through his new rules and procedures.

No one before Schoenberg had ever been successful in completely negating the traditional way of "knowing" when it came to music composition. What musicians most often fail to recognize is that Schoenberg's dodecaphonic invention was deeply ingrained in a praxis that defied the philosophy that there was profundity in standard harmonic practice. To him nothing about music was profound and nothing mattered in music but the composer's free will. In his opinion, the only rules or standards of music that mattered were those rules and standards that the composer self-determined. To him the only thing that mattered about how a composer arranged the building blocks of music was the composer's self-actualized rules of how he wished to arrange the building blocks of music.

The purpose of all this discussion of progressive despair is to show logically how twentieth century music philosophy prepared the way for the autonomous philosophical practice of contemporary Christian musicians. As a matter of fact, the twentieth century secular composers' inordinate quest for musical freedom strongly molded the autonomous freedom philosophy of contemporary Christian musicians.

The parallels are astonishing. Both believe that music aesthetic is totally a matter of personal opinion. Both believe that rhythm and dissonance are extremely vital to their music. Both believe that the only artistic standards in music composition are those which the artist self-imposes. Both believe that the composer and the performer are autonomous. The godless worldly composers are not interested in what God thinks about music, and the Christian musicians who have followed this philosophical belief are not interested in the belief that God thinks about the music part of music. These Christian musicians believe that the music part of music is amoral and does not matter to God.

## Developing a Music Aesthetic

How does a Christian musician develop a philosophy of music aesthetics? Some Christian musicians who are referentialists believe that music derives most of its significance outside of itself. This is especially true when one considers sacred music. Referentialists believe that music's meanings are often not only outside of the music itself, but also are actual references to real life. Christian non-referentialists believe that music has meaning, but that its meaning is music's own meaning as part of a closed system that does not relate to life outside of the music.

Worship music normally exists as a means to an end. Music is a vehicle upon which the Word of God rides into the mind of the worshiper. However, as was just mentioned, an increasing number of Christian musicians believe that music is a closed system, and that its system of "knowing" and its significance comes from within itself with absolutely no cause and effect on real life outside of music. This philosophical belief allows a Christian musician to function independently of the Lordship of Christ. They believe that the music part of music's significance is in no way referential; it only refers to itself and may not say anything at all. This belief system allows an autonomous artistic approach to religious music.

The Christian musician who is developing a music aesthetic will be forced to come to philosophical grips with whether or not music has a cause and effect on the performer and the auditor. Although music aesthetics deals with beauty and the import of that meaning, one cannot escape considering what music is or is not capable of doing to the whole-life of the performer and the listener.

## Developing a Christian Approach to Aesthetics

The fine arts are not the doorway to the Kingdom of God. A Christian must develop a biblical (Christ centered) approach to the arts rather than an artistic approach to religion. Neither the beauty of the music part of vocal music nor the words are the doorway to the Kingdom of God. Although artistic lyric poetry is a truly meaningful introduction to the Kingdom of God it is not the doorway to God's kingdom. The fact that beautiful rhetoric is artistic is not what matters. It is what they teach about who God is and what He does that makes them effective spiritual tools. However, their aesthetic or artistic form should not be worshiped.

Christian musicians are warned in the first chapter of the Book of Romans to not worship music which is a created thing. Romans 1:18, 19, 25, and 28 state, "The wrath of God is being revealed against all the godlessness and wickedness of men who suppress the truth by their wickedness since what may be known about God is plain to them... They exchanged the truth of God for a lie, and worshiped and served created things rather than the Creator – who is forever praised. Amen... Furthermore, since they did not think it worthwhile to retain the knowledge of God, he gave them over to a depraved mind; to do what ought not to be done." (NIV)

Although the Scripture lesson, which is not all quoted here, speaks primarily to the sexual sins it also speaks of worshiping created things. This includes art and art objects rather than the Creator. Therefore, worshiping aesthetics or any created art forms is nothing less than idolatry! The Scripture lesson above warns that those who worship created things rather than the Creator start by suppressing the truth that Christians must not worship any created thing.

The result of an aesthetic approach to religion is worshiping art for art's sake. Worshiping art for art's sake in music worship is the outcome of a faulty praxial view of the place of the arts in worship. Worship music must derive its greatest significance outside of itself. If it does not, it is autonomous. Therefore, a Christocentric Christian aesthetic must derive its significance outside of itself. A Christian aesthetic view will consequently not derive the same musical import as a secular aesthetic view does.

I want to make it very clear that aesthetic beauty in the art of music used in worship is not wrong. On the contrary, beauty in the arts is one of the proofs that an art form follows biblical principles. Beauty is a concomitant of God's orderly creation. When God created music as a part of His personal orderly creation He gave it the propensity to be very good or beautiful (see discussion in Chapter One on Genesis 1:31). Although misguided musicologists and some Christian musicians have purported that the music of the Bible was harsh and ugly, there is not a shred of biblical or extrabiblical proof of such an exotic hypothesis. On the contrary the *te'amim* (the musical notation of all Old Testament) have proven that the music of the Bible was very beautiful.[3]

## A Music Aesthetic Based on Beauty

The greatest commentary on a music *aesthetic based on aural beauty in the Bible is Amos 5:23: "Take thou away from me the noise

(1995) of thy songs; for I will not hear the melody of thy viols." The Hebrew word used in verse 23 for noise is *hamown* (1995) which means tumult, disquietude, or a multitude of noise. Ezekiel 26:13 likewise uses *hamown* in a negative sense: "And I will cause the noise (*hamown* 1995) of thy songs to cease; and the sound of thy harps shall be no more heard." The Bible never makes positive comments about noise, noisy songs, multitude of noise in music, or tumult in music. Musical noise (*qowl* 6963) is also condemned in Exodus 32:18.

At this point you may be wondering how a Christian musician is able to reconcile the references to "joyful noise" in Psalm 66:1, 81:1, 95:1, 95:2, 98:4, 98:6 and 100:1 in the King James Version to a music aesthetic based on aural beauty. In the original text the word *noise* never appears in any of the aforementioned Scriptures. The addition of the word *noise* in many English translations is most unfortunate. In all of these Scriptures, the phrase "make a joyful noise" is translated from the Hebrew word *ruwa* (7321). In all of these Scriptures, the actual meaning is "great acclamation" or with a "great shout of joy."

None of these Scriptures leave the example of a Christian aesthetic being connected to noise. It is only misguided understanding of what the Bible actually states in the original text that has caused Christian musicians to develop this completely false praxial aesthetic view. For a more thorough discussion of the meaning or the word *noise* in the AV, read the section "Beautiful Music Performed Beautifully" in chapter eight in *Music of the Bible in Christian Perspective*, pp. 246-350.

The NIV makes this point clear when it translates *hamown* (1995) and *shiyr* (7892) as noisy songs. If God demanded that music be free from noise then what makes a Christian musician believe that He will accept a musical offering of noisy songs today?

## Aesthetics and Embellishment

Below are portions of 1 Kings 6:1, 15-18, 20-22, 29:

> "... in the fourth year of Solomon's reign over Israel... he began to build the house of the LORD... And he built the walls of the house within with boards of cedar, both the floor of the house, and the walls of the ceiling: and he covered them on the inside

with wood, and covered the floor of the house with planks of fir. And he built...both the floor and the walls with boards of cedar... even for the oracle, even for the most holy place. And the house, that is, the temple... was carved with knops and open flowers: all was cedar; there was no stone seen...and he overlaid it [the oracle] with pure gold; and so covered the altar which was of cedar. So Solomon overlaid the house within with pure gold: and he made a partition by the chains of gold before the oracle; and he overlaid it with gold. And the whole house he overlaid with gold, until he had finished all the house: also the whole altar that was by the oracle he overlaid with gold... And he carved all the walls of the house round about with carved figures of cherubims and palm trees and open flowers, within and without."

The discussion above is introduced by several verses in 1 Kings that explain the elaborateness of the decoration of the First Temple. Parts of several of the verses were omitted in the interest of brevity. You are probably wondering why one would include an explanation of the aesthetic decoration of this ancient house of worship in a discussion of music aesthetics. Remember that aesthetics is the area of philosophy that deals with beauty rather than utility.

According to biblical scholars, the elaborate decorations that were added to the Temple were just that— aesthetic decorations. They made God's house look beautiful. They were beautiful additions that were of little or no necessity. They were added by King Solomon because he wanted the Temple, which was a house of worship, to honor God by being beautiful.

"And the house, that is, the temple... was carved with knops and open flowers: all was cedar; there was no stone seen...and he overlaid it [the oracle] with pure gold; and so covered the altar which was of cedar. So, Solomon overlaid the house within with pure gold..." (1 Kings chapter six, part). Some Bible scholars believe that there was a universal ban in ancient Israel on anything carved because of Scriptures like Leviticus 26:1. It states, "Ye shall make you no idols nor graven image, neither rear you up a standing image, neither shall ye set up any image of stone in your land, to bow down unto it: for I am the LORD your God." However, if one reads this verse carefully it says that one is not to make any images for the purpose of worshiping them.

There are two words used in 1 Kings 6:18 that should be mentioned here. The first is the Hebrew word *miqla'ath* (4734), carved, means something carved or engraved, possibly in bas relief or something made into a sculpture. The second word *knops* was translated from *peqa* (6497) which was an architectural name for an ornamental carving.

There are also three important words used in Leviticus 26:1 that deserve mention. The first is *pehsel* (6459) which was translated graven image in the AV. This word means graven, i.e., deeply carved. The second word is *maskiyth* (4906) translated image, which probably means an image carved on stone. The third word, *matstsebah*, (4676) is translated standing image. It is used with more latitude than the others and could be referring to a carved memorial stone, something carved on a standing column.

From the Scriptures studied above it is apparent that there was no universal ban on carved decorations or carved likenesses unless they were carved, graved, or molded into images for the purpose of worshiping them. So, a Christian musician should consider writings that claim a "no carving" policy in ancient Israel with reserve. Why all the fuss about carved decorations? It appears that there was a great respect in ancient Israel for carved decorations that were used to enhance the aesthetic effect and beauty of buildings like the First Temple.

Furthermore, this respect for aesthetic beauty was also apparent in the music recorded in the Old Testament. Suzanne Haïk-Vantoura's deciphering of the ancient *te'amim,* which were written below and above the entire text of the Old Testament, has revealed that there was a precise musical notation. The notation below the text was found to be precise notation of a musical scale. However, the *te'amim* above the text proved to be a close parallel to the ornamentation found in Western music. For a much more detailed discussion of the work of Suzanne Haïk-Vantoura read Chapter Eight of my book *Music of the Bible in Christian Perspective.*

The significance of the discussion of the *te'amim* above the Hebrew text of the Old Testament is that there is much biblical evidence that there was a respect for aesthetic embellishment in the music of ancient Israel, and that respect for embellishment was extended to sacred music. What does that evidence mean to a Christian musician who is developing a philosophy of music aesthetics in the twenty-first century? It means that there is a great amount of evidence found in the music of the Old Testament to support a music aesthetic based on beauty. Also, when it comes to aesthetic beauty in other fine arts like painting, photography, pottery, sculpture and other graven forms, historically there is no universal ban found in the Bible on such aesthetic beauty even when it is placed in a house of worship. However, these works should never be worshiped or they will become idols. If any of them are worshipped, they are universally banned in Scripture.

**Aesthetics and "Joyful Noise"**

We have been discussing the development of a Christian music aesthetic. We have also discussed a noise-based music aesthetic and translations that have mistakenly translated *ruwa* as joyful noise. As we mentioned earlier, the actual Hebrew word used in all of the texts mentioned that have been translated joyful noise is the word *ruwa* (7321) which meant to shout with joy. The NIV justly translates Psalm 66:1-2 as follows: "Shout with joy to God, all the earth! Sing the glory of his name; make his praise glorious!" It also translates 81:1 as "sing for joy"; 95:1, "come sing for joy"; 95:2, "extol him with music and song"; 98:4, "shout for joy"; 98:6, "shout for joy"; and 100:1, "shout for joy."

Some Christian musicians declare that these verses command Christian musicians to perform religious music with noise. There are no biblical imperatives for musicians to include noise in musical offerings to God. There is nothing in the Bible record that encourages Christians to include noise in musical worship to God. The use of beauty in the arts in worship serves the purpose of creating atmospheres and preparatory moods for the corporate worship experiences.

Beauty in music can cause the worshiper, who hears the created art object, to become more acutely aware of the Creator of the great art of music. I have personally gone away from worshiping through music with a heightened awareness of the Creator. (I have also left the concert hall, after hearing the Cincinnati Symphony Orchestra perform secular music, with an exalted view of the Creator who so marvelously created music.)

The beauty of music can cause a crowd to become calm and quiet before a worship service begins, or set a proper mood at the time of prayer. Although this function of music could be considered utilitarian it need not be only practical but also aesthetic. The musically aware perceive the beauty and import of the music (hopefully music worship should provide enriched, beautiful aural experiences for the musically aware).

Outside of the context of worship, i.e., the secular concert setting, a Christian music aesthetic can include music for music's sake. However, the Christian musician always brings to a secular performance an awareness of the God who created the great art of music. The musician who is musically aware will be able to listen to music at a much deeper level than the *neophyte who is enjoying his first listening experience in the concert hall. The musically educated will be much more aware of the beauty and import of the music being performed. Those who understand key structure, tonality, melody, harmonic practice and form will hear and perceive a multiplicity of aspects of a musical performance. This ability to perceive musically opens a whole realm of meanings and musical delights that completely escape the casual music lover. However, the Christian musician should always be cognizant of the marvels of the Creator who made aesthetic beauty and import available to the musically aware.

Claims that music is a closed system that reveals the true meaning of life to the musically aware without the possibility of any referential meaning have not been substantiated. Even though they have disagreed about whether music's meaning is referential or not, many music philosophers through the ages have believed that music does communicate something. What that something is has been a matter of much conjecture, argument, and disagreement.

## A Music Aesthetic must Retain God in its Basis

It stands to reason that the only immutable truth about aesthetics is found in God's perfect understanding, will, and knowledge. Outside of our knowledge of God's Word, everything Christian musicians postulate or perform in music comes from imperfect and partial knowledge. We know from 1 Corinthians 13:9-10 that "...we know in part and we prophesy in part, but when perfection comes, the imperfect disappears" (NIV). Paul went on to say in verse 12, "Now we see but a poor reflection in a mirror, then we shall see face to face. Now I know in part; then I shall know fully, even as I am fully known" (NIV).

Based on this truth, no one individual has the final answer when it comes to "knowing" or developing a philosophy of music aesthetics. With this in mind, the Christian musician, although aware of the inability to be all knowing, must not fall into the twenty-first century trap of believing that there is no objective true truth concerning music aesthetics. Those who believe that music has great power over the auditor and the performer are not the creators of some conservative farfetched notion that only relates to a fight against rock-based contemporary Christian music. On the contrary, this argument has existed for centuries. In Donald Grout's treatise *A History of Western Music* he quoted Aristotle as saying: "...when one listens to music that imitates a certain passion, one becomes imbued with the same passion, and if over a long time one habitually listens to the kind of music that rouses ignoble passions one's whole character will be shaped to an ignoble form."[4]

Aristotle was saying that the continued influence of *ignoble music would affect its message so thoroughly on the listener that it would influence the actual character of the auditor. Plato was famous for his classic philosophical statement, "Let me make the songs of a nation and I care not who makes its laws."[5]

Ancient Greek philosophers evidently believed that music could communicate not only beauty to the auditor, but also the message of the moral intent of the composer or performer, not merely by words, but also by the music part of the music. No one ever quotes Plato or Aristotle as believing that only words communicate. Both of these philosophers mention the effect of *modes on the auditor. They mention emotions like anger, gentleness, calmness, anxiety and personal restraint, and how the character of the various modes conveys these messages to the hearer.

## A Christocentric Music Aesthetic

If you have been reading this discussion from on an over-simplistic perspective, you are now ready for me to name the "seven songs which God approves," because He considers them to be beautiful, or the "one style of music that God approves," because He considers it to be beautiful. Sorry! No writer is qualified to give such a simplistic answer. If it was that easy there would be no disagreement or no battle for Christian music going on today. Many Christian musicians are aware that they have the responsibility to develop a Christocentric music aesthetic but do not know where to start. Proverbs 1:7 gives the answer. "The fear (*yirah* 3374) of the LORD is the beginning (7225) of knowledge (*daath* 1847): but fools despise wisdom (*ehokmah* 2451) and instruction."

The word *daath* (1847) means knowing or awareness, and *ehokmah* (2451) means to be wise or have a skillful wisdom. So the fear of God is the principal thing (*reshiyth* 7225) when it comes to knowing or having skillful wisdom concerning a God centered music aesthetic. Although the word *fear* sounds negative or restrictive, it is not! A reverence for God is the principally important aspect of acquiring the ability to spiritually discern God's way of knowing and His wisdom concerning "what is that good, acceptable, and perfect will of God" (Romans 12:2b, KJV).

The Christian musician is not left alone to struggle with the development of a music aesthetic. There are many references to music and beauty that are found in the Bible. These references are valid and valuable to the twenty-first century music philosopher. Also there is much written about aesthetics in music philosophy books. As a student of Christian music philosophy, one should be sure to only accept aesthetic philosophies that line up to the principles of musicing and beauty found in God's Word.

## Aesthetics and Bible Principles

There are several Bible principles that apply to sacred music. If the music has words, the Word of God is the most important element of that music. Sacred music should be characterized by an absence of excessive noise. Since the music should be melody oriented, rhythm must never obscure the melody (or melodies), the harmony or the words. Sacred music must be characterized by beauty rather than ugliness. All sacred music must be of a higher renovated character than the music of the world. All sacred music must be based on Spirit and truth. Sacred music must be non-carnal; it must not appeal primarily to the flesh. Sacred music must cause the worshipers to muse or think, as opposed to causing them to be amused (not to think) or merely entertained. Sacred music must represent the changed life principles expressed in Scripture. None of the above principles are a matter of taste or opinion. They are all requirements for the whole of sacred music.

A caution to conservative Christian musicians is necessary. We should be careful not to act as if we have all the answers or that there is no room for some variety in developing a Christian music aesthetic. No Christian musician has all wisdom or all knowledge concerning what God thinks about beauty in music.

Over a period of time the specifics of what is considered beautiful in music will undergo some changes. This does not mean that style and form in church music do not matter. They do matter since church music matters to God. Changes will come. Instrumentation, orchestration, choral arranging, small groups, and many other ways of accomplishing the Bible mandate of worshiping the Lord through music will change. Conservatives should not resist all change, but rather resist only destructive change. They must never lose sight of what will and will not fit the awesomeness and solemnity of worship of the Triune God. Also Christian musicians must remember that God's reputation, especially by the unchurched, will be judged in accordance with the music we sing and play in public worship. Developing a Christocentric music aesthetic in an atmosphere of change is not ever an easy task.

## A Distorted Music Aesthetic

The reason many Christian musicians have a distorted understanding of music's beauty is that they often do not have an understanding of great music. They only understand "consumer" music. Many times consumer music is shallow and sometimes inartistic. In some cases it is not well composed or arranged. It is produced by what is called a musical hack. Someone brings a poem, perhaps with a melody line, to an arranger. This arranger sets this music to a simple chord progression in the desired style with little thought of any intricate development of the formal properties of the music. The result is often a very predictable piece of music that will sell to the music consumer but is not very unique or great. Such music stays on the market for a while then virtually disappears. There is nothing intrinsically wrong with such music. It is simply not great music.

Since many Christian musicians only know, like, listen to, and perform consumer music, they have little or no understanding or appreciation of more profound styles of sacred or secular music. These musicians lack an understanding of music with well placed, organized and developed internal formal properties which make it truly great music.

Some banks teach new tellers to identify counterfeit currency by handling real bills. Similarly, the quickest way to enable the next generation of Christian musicians to understand quality worship music is to get them involved with quality musicing at an early age. Churches, Christian schools, and Christian colleges need to provide quality instrumental and choral organizations that provide enriched aesthetic performance experiences for children and youth.

Shinichi Suzuki, the great violinist and *pedagogue, believed that children should learn by listening and playing great music, i.e., the classics. A major tenet of his music praxis was having every child learn to music by what he called the "mother tongue" technique. He believed that music, like language, is best learned by hearing it from the child's mother and father. The same thing is true of church music. If our children hear and perform truly great music in church, home, and in the Christian school, they will very naturally learn to love to sing, play and perform the more profound styles of music.

## Aesthetic Meaning vs. Aesthetic Ends

All quality music performance will include valuable aesthetic meaning, but all quality musicing will not have only aesthetic ends. By the terminology *aesthetic ends* I mean that the sole purpose of the existence of the music is aesthetic beauty and hence the import of that meaning. The terminology *aesthetic meaning* is that which is concerned with beauty and emotion as opposed to that which is strictly intellectual. Robert Berglund explained the development of music from utilitarian purposes to aesthetic ends. "Art that exists for art's sake is art that has ends that are primarily aesthetic in nature. Historically, most vocal music created prior to the fifteenth century was of a utilitarian nature. Its purpose centered either in the experiences of the church or in social concerns... However, as instrumental music and the instruments themselves were developed, the performance of music for sheer pleasure increased. Parlor music led to concert hall music, the purpose of which was primarily enjoyment."[6]

Every Christian musician must have a clear understanding of the difference between aesthetically performed sacred music which has the primary purpose of being offered to God as a worship offering, and aesthetically performed religious music that has only the aesthetic end of enjoyment. This is not to say that an aesthetically performed musical offering to God should not be an enjoyable experience for the performer and the listener. There is a philosophical difference between a performance of a piece of sacred music which has aesthetic meaning and a performance that has only an aesthetic end.

What about a musical performance that is strictly art for art's sake? There is no Bible-based prohibition of a Christian musician performing a secular piece of music in a concert as art for art's sake. However, the matter is much more complicated when a musician's purpose is presenting a musical offering unto God. If God is to be the object of a Christian's sacred musicing, then one's musicing moves philosophically from mere artistic performance, i.e., art for art's sake, to the realm of utilitarian purposes. As one can deduce, any musical performance that is directly addressed to God cannot be strictly a performance of an art form for art's sake, although it may very well contain artistic meaning.

## Music and the Allied Arts

*Visual Art*

The visual arts are normally explained as the arts created primarily for people to view. They include etchings, drawings, paintings, sculptures, frescos, photography and various other decorative arts that most often exist in permanent form. The visual arts have been wonderful representations of spiritual things and things of God's creation in the heavens and on the earth. Multitudes of Bible scenes have been portrayed with the various visual arts. Stained glass windows in churches and cathedrals have depicted the stories told in the Bible to those who could and could not read its wonderful truths. The visual arts have for centuries been a wholesome way for civilizations to beautify their surroundings.

The visual arts have been a strong ally to music in more recent decades since advanced technology has made multimedia presentations possible. Music and the visual arts strengthen each other in the presentation of the scenes and message of the Bible. The visual arts, when coupled with music, have also been a source of wholesome entertainment, education and an aid to worship.

Like the other fine arts, the visual arts must be judged individually according to each work's content. Each visual representation must be in congruency with a Christian's beliefs. The eye gate is a direct path to the mind. Therefore, music should only be allied to visual arts that are compatible with the changed life principles of a Christian. Christians differ in opinion about violence, partial nudity, immodest attire, and subject matter of the various visual representations. There is also much argument about the inclusion of the famous well-known artifacts such as Michelangelo's sculpture of *David* and Gericault's painting of *The Raft of the Medusa*. Each music educator will have to make choices about which of the visual arts to ally with music in the worship service, classroom and concert hall in order to be congruent with biblical principles and to not offend students, parents, administrators, school board members, and the organization's constituency at large.

There is no overarching reason why a Christian musician should not consider the compatibility of visual art being allied to music. However, the psalmist David very carefully explained in Psalm 101:3, "I will set no wicked thing before mine eyes: I hate the work of them that turn aside; it shall not cleave to me." A Hebrew word study of this verse confirms that this verse is well translated in the AV. Simply put, a Christian should not view visual arts that are of a wicked nature and should not connect such images with the secular or sacred music that a Christian performs.

There is much debate about what makes art, such as paintings, sculptures, and frescos, an excellent piece of visual art. A fine representation of the human body naked or entwined with another person can be the result of an artist's excellent skill. However, although this visual representation may be an example of artistic skill, it is still pornographic art. If a particular painting, sculpture, etc. is sexually suggestive or pornographic it has the potential to harm the whole life of a Christian or a non-Christian who views it. So, allying pornographic visual art with music is incongruent and inconsistent with what a Christian is trying to accomplish.

*Photography and Videography*

Photography, like cinema, has the potential to bring a high degree of reality to the message of the Bible when allied with sacred music. To quote the age old *quip, "A picture is worth a thousand words." A photo or video placed on a large overhead screen of the rugged terrain over which Joseph and Mary traveled to reach Bethlehem has the unique power to cause the worshiper to instantly be mentally transported to that scene. Even more than words, instrumental accompaniment or vocal inflection, a photograph or a video of Mary on a donkey and Joseph trudging along beside her has much power to transport an audience from the padded pew to the bleakness of the long road to Bethlehem.

Christian musicians have not even begun to utilize the potential of multimedia involving photography and music. There is a sense in which a still photograph has the potential to imprint a visual message on an audience without the possible distractions that may be caused by a moving picture. If the tenor of a story is intended to be primarily presented through music, a photograph is most often a valuable and non-obtrusive ally and concomitant to the music being presented.

Can photography or videography be problematic when it is allied to sacred music? Yes, they most certainly can be more of a hindrance than a help if they are not used wisely. They, like the other allied arts, are a direct window through the eye gate to the mind of the viewer. It only stands to reason that extreme care should be used in choosing photographs and videos that are set before an audience to be a concomitant to the Gospel message.

*Drama*

Some Christian music educators have a strong aversion to dramatic productions. They often are opposed to not only secular drama but also religious dramatic productions. On the other side of the coin, there are those who use drama very effectively in worship and in education.

Stage settings, lights, props, and costumes are also a cause for much debate among church officials as well as among educational leadership in Christian schools, colleges, and universities. Questions over the appropriateness, necessity, and usefulness of dramatic productions are also the cause of much heated debate. The reason behind this disagreement and debate over drama and dramatic productions is that these Christian organizations have not established a basis for the inclusion of dramatic productions in their ministry and educational philosophies.

A source of further complication is a lack of understanding of the valuable connection between the nature and value of music and drama. After utilizing drama and music together for nearly forty years, I am convinced that drama and music are natural concomitants of public ministry and therefore should be a vital part of educating Christian musicians. Some people are primarily visual learners while others respond more readily to what they hear. Reinforcing the gospel message presented through music with sets, lights, costumes, spoken drama, sung drama, and instrumental music are all effective ways to increase the audience's mental intake.

The gospel message can be effectively presented through the suggested realism of a well-lighted stage setting while real people in authentic costumes are depicting the characters of the story being presented. For instance, Mary singing to the Baby Jesus, surrounded by the simplicity of His humble birthplace lighted with soft moonlight blue, mixed effectively with an amber, straw or no color pink can make the story of Jesus' birth a much more vivid realistic experience. So, rather than quibble over costs and necessity of the use of drama as an allied art to sacred music, Christian organizations should spend their energy on making sure that they are presenting depictions of the stories of the Bible that are accurate and efficacious. These Christian organizations should also make sure that the staging, lighting, costuming, and vocal and instrumental music are philosophically appropriate and God honoring.

*Decorative Arts*

This category includes art objects that are usually of a high quality as well as useful and beautiful. Although these art objects are often labeled as "useful art," this designation should not suggest that the other art forms are not useful. These art objects are often allied to music simply by fact that they beautify the place where we music. They decorate a sanctuary, rehearsal room, classroom, or concert hall.

There has been much debate during previous centuries over whether or not Christians should decorate God's houses of worship with these art objects. Because of this debate many churches that have been constructed in the past one hundred years are almost devoid of any artistic decoration. Where should the Christian stand on this issue? To help answer this question I have included a small portion from 2 Chronicles 3:6-10 and 14 of the description of how the Temple was decorated and embellished with art objects and expensive overlays.

"And he garnished the house with precious stones for beauty: and the gold was gold of Parvaim. He overlaid also the house, the beams, the posts, and the walls thereof, and the doors thereof, with gold; and graved cherubims on the walls. And the weight of the nails was fifty shekels of gold. And he overlaid the upper chambers with gold. And in the most holy house he made two cherubims of image work, and overlaid them with gold... And he made the vail of blue, and purple, and crimson, and fine linen, and wrought cherubims thereon."

As one can see, the Temple was very artistically decorated with fine linen and gold. Its furnishings included much statuary and other ornately decorated objects. So, there is absolutely no biblical prohibition on the decorative arts in a place of worship, or any other place for that matter. The art objects, most of them not mentioned in the short Bible excerpt above, were expensively decorated and many of them were not only beautiful but also useful. Some Bible historians claim that the Israelites never made any sculptures because of the fact that they were forbidden to do so by the statement in Exodus 20:4, "Thou shalt not make unto thee any graven image (*pecel* 6459)..." (Also see Lev. 26:1; Deut. 4:16; 4:23, 25; 5:8.) However, they often forget that Exodus 20:25 clears up the matter when it explains, "Thou shalt not bow down thyself to them, nor serve them: for I the LORD thy God am a jealous God..." So, God did not forbid ancient Israel to carve decorative art objects but rather *YHVH elohiym* only forbade them to worship these art objects. So, when 2 Chronicles uses the word *tsatsua* (6816), which means that the cherubims were carved or graven images, it is not a violation of the "no graven idols" commandment. Therefore, there is absolutely no prohibition in the Bible of anyone elaborately decorating a church.

How does all this discussion connect to music? As I said earlier, music is often allied to the decorative arts by the fact that these objects beautify the place where we music, such as sanctuaries, classrooms, and concert halls. It is the obligation of every music educator to beautify the physical surroundings of all the places we music or study about music. Also, making our music students aware of fine decorative art objects can be a source of educational inspiration to them. For instance, bringing a beautiful hand-painted glazed Rookwood vase or a Nileoak glazed pitcher to the rehearsal room can be a philosophical comparison of a fine pottery work to a fine musical performance.

*Dance*

An even more controversial area of our discussion of music and the allied arts is the discussion of dance as fine art. Although some Christians approve of secular and religious dance, there are many who have problems with this art form. Whether or not a Christian musician approves of dancing, he or she must admit that it is an art form. So, the issue is not whether or not dance is an art form but rather whether or not it belongs in the life of a Christian who is following the changed life principles taught in the Bible. Certainly the often misused quote from Ecclesiastes 3:4, "A time to weep, and a time to laugh; a time to mourn, and a time to dance..." does not solve the question of allying dance with worship.

Even classical ballet should trouble a careful Christian because of the problems with costuming and the actual dance movements of this art form. Since this book is a philosophical study, I will not thoroughly discuss the multitude of problems that come with the inclusion of this art form in the life of a Christian. I will also not discuss the "how to" of teaching about including or not including dance as an allied art. I will narrow this discussion to some thoughts on whether or not the Christian music educator should include dance in a discussion of music and the allied arts and some philosophical pitfalls to avoid.

To begin our discussion let me say that the Bible is not silent about dance. After many years of study of dance in the Bible, I have come to the strong conclusion that there are no Bible mandates for Christians to dance, and the inclusion of dance as a part of worship in the First or Second Temple is nowhere traceable. The reason I mention the First and Second Temple is because it is the only place in the Old Testament where we have examples of the use of music as a part of *codified public worship.

However, the Bible does mention dance. The worst mistake that a music educator could make would be to ignore the mention of dance in the Bible, because students should discuss dance in (and out of) the

Bible in the context of the Christian classroom. If a music educator ignores the mention of dance in the Bible and the history of dance in general, students will more than likely only have a secular view and/or a liberal Christian view of dance. Although it is outside the scope of this book to thoroughly study dance in the Bible, I suggest that the reader should refer to *Music of the Bible in Christian Perspective*, which has a very thorough word by word study of dance in the Bible.

The music educator should be cautioned not to make sweeping inaccurate statements concerning the mention of dance in the Bible. First, it is mentioned in both the Old and New Testaments. Second, there are serious difficulties with the way some of the Hebrew words for dance have been translated in many English versions of the Old Testament. Third, both religious and secular dancing is mentioned in the Bible. Fourth, although the Bible does not teach that Christians must dance, secular artistic dancing is mentioned in the Bible. Fifth, the Bible is an accurate record, and some of the dancing mentioned in the Bible was of a lewd, sensuous nature. Several times the dances mentioned in the Bible were used as a tool of harlotry, and at other times used by women to arouse sexual passions of the men who watched. Sixth, extra-biblical sources report that artistic solo dancing by men was allowed as public entertainment at feasts such as the Feast of Water Libation and the Feast of Tabernacles, but the Bible never mentions men and women dancing together.

The Christian musician must study dance in the Bible very thoroughly before mentioning it in the classroom. The fact that it is mentioned in the Bible does not codify its use in Christian education or in public worship. A host of articles that have been written in Christian periodicals that approved and recommended dancing often have made little or no attempt to give any scholarly proof from the original text of the Bible for their recommendation of religious and secular dancing. Before a Christian educator teaches that dance is an allied art of music in Christian education or in the worship service, he or she must understand that it was not mentioned in the Old or New Testament as a concomitant of organized public worship. In ancient Israel artistic solo dancing by men was permitted in public at some of the feasts, but on these occasions it was never use for sacred purposes.

As I have often said, "Direction determines destiny." So, when a music educator considers artistic secular dancing to be an allied art to musicing, or religious dancing as a part of organized public worship, it becomes almost impossible to philosophically control its use. The fact that a Christian musician makes the decision not to approve dance as allied to the secular or sacred music in his or her life does not mean that dance is not a fine art. It should be refused on similar grounds as the refusal to accept some visual art because it is not appropriate in the whole life of a Christian.

*Cinema*

At first thought it may seem that there would not be any connection between cinema and music. However, even the great classic religious motion pictures were greatly enhanced by their musical soundtracks. For instance, the classic film soundtracks of Miklos Rosa like *King of Kings*, *The Robe*, and *Ben-Hur*, and recent soundtracks such as *The Passion of Christ* (2004) by John Debney, are living proof that there has historically been a vital connection between music and religious cinema.

There are major philosophical problems with the mainstream of cinema in both the twentieth and early twenty-first centuries. A host of sensual and lewd films have included music soundtracks that were so effective that they made these films even worse. So what position should a music educator take about making the connection between music and cinema? First, be honest. Effectively composed music has the power to make a wholesome film a better artistic and spiritual medium, and it can make a lewd, sensual film even worse.

Ignoring the connection between cinema and music is a mistake, and ignoring the multiplicity of problems with this connection is short-sighted and also a problem. The philosophical problem extends to the visual content of each film and the power of music to arouse unhealthy passion in the mind of the listener. The problem is made even more complex by the fact that seeing and hearing at the same time results in enhanced emotional arousal. Every film must be judged on an individual basis and its use of music certainly must be a part of a Christian's evaluation. Summarily rejecting cinema and refusing to include it in classroom discussions of the allied arts is certainly not the answer.

#### Endnotes

1. Bowman, *Philosophical Perspectives on Music*, 194.
2. Stolba, *The Development of Western Music*, 775.
3. See *Music in the Bible in Christian Perspective*, chapter eight.
4. Grout and Palisca, *A History of Western Music*, 8.
5. Berglund, *A Philosophy of Church Music*, 18.

#### Chapter Twelve Word Meanings

**Aesthetic—** the guiding principles that shape the work of a particular musician.

**Aesthetic experience—** a listener's perception, interaction and response to a piece of music, including its expressive qualities. It is commonly believed to be a perceptive experience beyond the mere recognition of the elements of the music that reveals understanding of the import of the music.

**Anti-music—** any form or style of music intended to overthrow traditional conventions and expectations.

**Bellwether—** something that assumes the leadership or forefront, in this case, of Christianity.

**Codified—** something that has been arranged according to a plan or system. As used here it means a plan or system of public worship mentioned and approved in the Bible.

**Human Psyche—** the mental or psychological structure of a person.

**Ignoble—** not honorable in character or purpose.

**Metaphysical—** This term is concerned with abstract thought such as existence, causality, and truth, and is concerned with first principles and ultimate grounds, such as being, time, or substance.

**Modes—** The Greek modes were a series of seven-note diatonic scales, consisting of five whole tones and two semitones.

**Neophyte—** a person who is new to a subject, skill, or belief.

**Paradigm—** a philosophical framework containing the basic assumptions, ways of thinking, and methodology that is accepted by a musician.

**Quip—** a witty or clever remark.

***Tsatsua—*** (6816) is a hapax legomenon. So the two cherubims of image work, i.e., *tsagatzoogeem* were perhaps movable image work. For some reason the Chronicler desired to be more specific here than simply using the word *pecel*.

## 12: Aesthetics and the Christian Musician 267

### Chapter Twelve Questions for Discussion

1. Discuss the significance of the author's statement, "The Christian should not develop an aesthetic approach to religion, but rather a religious approach to aesthetics."

2. Explain some principles that are necessary in the process of a Christian musician developing a philosophy of music aesthetics.

3. Although beauty in music is not the doorway to the Kingdom of God, a Christian aesthetic should be built on the beautiful rather than that which is grotesque. Explain why.

4. Explain the significance of Pierre Schaeffer's *musique concrete*, which was an example of anti-music music composition. What philosophical trend did his compositional style help to develop and why was it harmful?

5. Outside of our knowledge of God's Word, everything Christian musicians postulate about a music aesthetic comes from imperfect and partial knowledge. We know from 1 Corinthians 13:9-10 that, "…we know in part and we prophesy in part, but when perfection comes, the imperfect disappears." Discuss the significance of these statements to the Christian musician who is in the process of developing a music aesthetic.

6. What did Schoenberg accomplish philosophically when he developed the concept of the destruction of musical absolutes?

7. Solomon declared in Proverbs 1:7, "The fear (*yirah* 3374) of the LORD is the beginning (7225) of knowledge (1847): but fools despise wisdom (2451) and instruction." Discuss how a Christian musician's fear or reverence of God can be a positive impetus in the development of a Christocentric music aesthetic.

8. Discuss the importance of understanding the Hebrew word *ruah* in the development of a music aesthetic.

9. Discuss the author's statement, "The reason many Christian musicians have a distorted understanding of music's beauty is that they often do not have an understanding of great music." Be sure to explain why it is important for a Christian who is developing a music aesthetic that includes an understanding of great music.

10. Discuss why you do or do not believe that the Christian should have an understanding of the allied fine arts and how this understanding will affect his or her music aesthetic.

# Part Four

# How We Should Music

# 13

# Sacred Music Should Be Worthwhile Music

### Finding what is Worthwhile in Music

RICHARD DEVINNEY ONCE SAID, "Try talking less about 'good' music and 'bad' music and talk more about profound, rich, powerful, dynamic, intense music and pale, trite, banal, obvious, weak, tired music. Talk about what music can offer that goes beyond a tickling of the eardrums or a tug at the memory."[1] There is merit in what he was saying about sacred music. However, in his book, he did not define just what each of the terms mean in terms of what is "good" and "bad" music. Christian musicians must develop a philosophical position on the value of all the secular and sacred music that they listen to and perform. This is partially accomplished by understanding what makes this music worthwhile or estimable because the issue is much deeper philosophically than mere choices of that which is "good" or "bad".

It is much more productive to first find out what is right about sacred music before identifying the elements of a particular music that are a hindrance to sacred musicing. Studying musical error first is much like studying comparative theology before one has studied the fundamental doctrines taught in the Bible. Without an understanding of the basic Bible principles of musicing unto a holy, infinite God, the Christian musician is not equipped to evaluate sacred music in terms of what is good, bad, appropriate or inappropriate. Along with a thorough study of what the Bible teaches about music, one also needs to study music history, music theory, and the history of church music (both ancient and modern) before attempting to evaluate the formal properties of church music. It is the responsibility of the minister of music to make wise choices all the time for all the music that he or she presents to God. These choices will include profound, rich, powerful and dynamic music.

## Profound Music Lends Itself to Being Worthwhile Music

Let us consider some of the aspects of well-written music that make it worthwhile music. First, there is the word *profound* that we will define as music that searches into the deep and subtle areas of truth and beauty. Truth and beauty are included in the definition of profound, although the study of aesthetics of music generally does not deal directly with truth. However, the Christian must include truth with beauty because aesthetic beauty often reveals truth to the viewer or auditor. Also, profound music composed without words will require deep thought and knowledge of its formal properties in order for the auditor to be able to thoroughly comprehend it.

If the observer believes that the trombonist he is watching is swallowing the slide as he plays, that person is not knowledgeable enough of instrumental music to make decisions about the profundity of the performer's playing. With the popularity of "dumbing down" church music, profundity in music is not often high on the priority list of many church musicians. Furthermore, evaluating the profoundness of a selection of sacred music is not the popular music praxis of many very knowledgeable Christian musicians who are worship leaders.

Regardless of the current trend to disvalue profundity, there also needs to be some evaluation of the music's text. Many ministers of music are not bothered by the fact that they are projecting song texts on the overhead screen that do not include the basic, necessary and proper punctuation marks for the coherent presentation of an English text. If they do not include punctuation, it is evident that they do not understand this lyric poetry as English rhetoric. Certainly they are not concerned about the cognitive presentation of the text. If they did, punctuation would be considered absolutely necessary to his or her music praxis. Projecting texts of religious music on an overhead screen without standard punctuation marks makes a statement that we do not have to give sacred lyric poetry the same respect that is given to non-sacred poetry.

### Formal Properties Should Support Profoundness

Next, we should consider the profoundness of the formal properties of the music. Secular musicians who are often strict formalists believe that music's meaning comes only through its formal properties. To them, the more profound the formal properties are the more information or meaning is to be found in the music. One of the problems with *formalists'* thought about music's meaning is that they believe that its meaning is not related to life but is encapsulated in music's own closed meaning. Although I am not a music *formalist*, I do believe that the profoundness of the formal properties of a piece of music makes a vital difference in that music's ability to express meaning. However, I part company quickly with strict formalists because music's meaning is not part of a closed system. If Christian musicians ignore the formal properties of the music they use to present the profound message of the gospel, they are *ipso facto* showing a lack of understanding of music's power and potential to express influential meaning.

This is not to say that the *prima facie* of sacred musicing is how difficult the formal properties of the music are, but simply that a profound sacred text deserves a music style whose formal properties support the depth of meaning of the lyrics. A deeply profound text should have as its concomitant a style of music whose formal properties explore the deepest levels of musical meaning that are congruent with the text. Again, not all quality sacred music needs to be difficult or needs to be in any way deeply esoteric. Simplicity may exude profoundness. A simple sacred text is often best presented with a simple musical expression. It is a philosophical fallacy to believe that the formal properties of a piece of music (the music parts of the music) do not matter because they are benign or neutral. It is also a philosophical fallacy to believe that they are incapable of expressing any meaning and *ipso facto* are incapable of supporting or hindering the message of the text.

## Formal Properties Should not be Banal

Now let us discuss the word *rich*. The dictionary defines one facet of the meaning of rich as being vivid, deep, and intense. *Banal religious music should be something that we as musicians should intensely dislike and avoid. Philosophically, sacred musicing should never be a commonplace act of worship. Church musicians must realize that there is nothing commonplace about worshiping the blessed Trinity with music. If we have had a fresh vision of our God as being "high and lifted up" (Isaiah 6:1-9) our musicing will demand vividness.

The Hebrew word *ruwa* (7321), mentioned several times in the Book of Psalms, expresses shouting joyfully unto Jehovah. This word connotes the necessity of great vividness when we music unto our God. Colossians 3:16 tells Christian musicians, "Let the word of Christ dwell in you richly; in all wisdom teaching and admonishing one another in psalms and hymns and spiritual songs, singing with grace in your hearts unto the Lord." The term *richly,* translated from *plousious* (4146) means abounding in richness or vividness of presentation. *Plousious* also connotes being crammed full, which in this verse means to be completely saturated with the Word of Christ. Again, the concept of vividness is included in this word's contextual meaning since being crammed full of God's Word will cause a Christian's musicing to be expressed more vividly. One thing made clear by this Bible discourse in the Epistle of Paul to the Christians at Colossae is that rich or vivid musicing is essential to efficacious musical worship. Those who tend to believe that sacred music should be performed without much (or any) emotion should be reminded of the many Bible references to singing to the Lord with a great emotional shout. How does one shout to the Lord without emotion?

## Sacred Music Should Be Powerful Music

Next, let us discuss the word *powerful*. Sacred music should be potent. Acts 1:8 states, "But ye shall receive power, after that the Holy Ghost is come upon you, and ye shall be witnesses unto me both in Jerusalem, and in all Judea, and in Samaria, and unto the uttermost part of the earth." The English word *power* is put for the word *dunamis*

(1411) which means miraculous power. So, Christian musicians who are filled with the Holy Spirit are promised the miraculous power necessary for efficacious musicing. Effective sacred musicing requires the powerful anointing made available by the Holy Spirit. It stands to reason that since the Holy Spirit provides power to the Christian, this *dunamis* should be utilized in a Christian's music to make it an effective witnessing tool. 1 Corinthians 1:18 explains that the preaching of Christ crucified is the power of God. The singing of Christ crucified can be an effective concomitant of the preaching of Christ crucified.

Music has a powerful influence over all who perform and hear it. However, it is not only sacred music but also secular music that has the potential to be very powerful. The music part of the music derives its power from the skillful arrangement of its formal properties. Therefore, form, style, and the way that the building blocks are arranged, all play a gigantic role in the effectiveness and power of every musical composition. Composers and arrangers attempt to communicate something specific through their music. Only those who are naïve believe that composers and arrangers have nothing that they wish to say and that, even if they do, their musical attempts are incapable of any effective communication. It is a mystery that so many Christian musicians believe that the music part of music does not exert power over both the performer and the auditor. Since Christian musicians exert great power over those who hear their musicing, they have an awesome responsibility to present music that will represent the moral nature of God in an intellectually honest manner.

### Sacred Music Should be Dynamic Music

Dynamic music connotes being forceful, energetic, and capable of transmitting power and energy as a moving and driving force. In a theological context it connotes music being endowed by divine power. As one can understand from Isaiah 55:11, "So shall my word be that goeth forth out of my mouth: it shall not return unto me void, but it shall accomplish that which I please, and it shall prosper in the thing whereto I sent it." If the music part of the music or the way the vocalist sings does not by its nature or enactment negate or hinder the

## 13: Sacred Music Should Be Worthwhile Music

Word of God being sung, God has promised that His Word will be efficacious. It is regrettable that sometimes God's Word is efficacious in spite of a Christian's musicing, instead of being more effective as a result of the musician's musicing. With all of this in mind one can understand that music which is of a religious nature is not automatically endowed with the power of the Holy Spirit merely because of its content. Music has power, whether it is sacred, secular or sinful. Music performances may be powerful whether they are given by those who know Christ or by those who are very wicked.

There is a vast difference between dynamic and anointed musical performances. It is sometimes difficult for Christians to discern the difference between performance energy and the anointed power for musicing that only is given to those who have a personal relationship with Christ. A performer's charisma and energetic presentation can easily be misunderstood for anointed singing or playing, but there is a difference that the discerning Christian can detect, since there is a distinct difference between musicing that is selfless and that which glorifies self.

To the casual observer there is not a distinct difference between religious "hype" and musicing that is done in the power and anointing of the blessed Holy Spirit. The important thing to note is that although they both have similarities on the surface, there is no substitute for the anointing of the Holy Spirit if the aim of one's religious musicing is music ministry. There is a world of difference between dynamic performance and the *dunamis* (1411) of the Holy Spirit. (See St. Luke 24:29.) Christian musicians must remember that Ephesians 5:18 stresses the necessity of musicians being continually filled with the Spirit in order to music in an efficacious manner.

### Sacred Music Should be Intense Music

Some Christian musicians may object to the philosophical concept of "intense" musicing unto God. The word *intense*, when connected to musicing, means very deeply concentrated or fervently earnest. There is a definite philosophical school of thought that, since sacred musicing is not about the performer, all sacred musicing must be reserved and detached or semi-detached from the Christian musician. It is true that the just shall live by faith rather than by sight, feeling, joy or any other emotion, since all of them are ephemeral. (See Romans 1:17, Galatians 3:11, and Hebrews 10:38.)

It seems almost impossible to have a real relationship with Jesus Christ that never produces any emotions or to music unto the blessed Trinity without some emotion. One of the major factors of effective musicing of sacred music is the believability of genuine heart-felt musical expressions that exude from a holy heart-life.

How can a Christian effectively express sincere love for God with vanilla-flavored musical expressions? John 7:38 explains, "He who believes in Me, as the Scripture has said, out of his heart will flow rivers of living water" (NKJV). Therefore, sincere sacred musicing must include an emotional outpouring of the Christian's heart-life which is expressed through music. These deep expressions of a living faith in Christ exude from a heart filled with love for God that pours out these feelings in genuine intense musicing unto God.

Some Christians believe that all sacred musicing must be subdued and without deep outward emotion. Sometimes those who have this belief fail to recognize that God endows musicians with charisma and an effervescence that attracts listeners. This attractiveness inspires devotion to God as the performer musics. Performance or musicing charisma is one of the gifts and graces that God gives to talented musicians. However, charisma is not synonymous with the anointing for musicing that God gives to musicians who are maintaining a deep spiritual life in the Holy Spirit.

Sometimes Christian musicians fail to recognize the difference between musical charisma and divine anointing that God gives to musicians who are living a deep life in the Holy Spirit. There is nothing inherently wrong with the listener being drawn emotionally into the musicer's performance. However, the Christian musician must understand that the ultimate goal of worship is not the audience being attracted to the performer's persona but rather to God. The performer who is a religious humanist will have a tendency to believe that music worship begins and ends with the performer. There is no philosophical problem with performances of sacred music that are intense, but performing sacred music in an intense manner should always be in order to bring the message of the music part of the music alive in such a way that the gospel message is made real or more clear to the listener. Performance intensity should never obscure the message of the music or draw undue attention to the musicer.

## Sacred Music Should be Interesting Music

Now let us consider some words that are used to express the other side of the musical coin. One word that is sometimes used to explain music is pale, which means, among other things, music that lacks intensity or music that lacks importance or quality. Some religious music is so lacking in intensity that it is dull, uninteresting, and totally predictable. When I studied composition at Pitt State University we were instructed to make sure that every musical phrase must have a forward directionality. That does not mean that phrases should have an incessant driving, propelling forward directionality. It simply means that every well-constructed musical phrase should have beginning, middle (climax), and an end which gives an element of finality and emotional release.

Without these three essential elements, music will either hammer on and on without emotional release or it will drone on and on and essentially go nowhere. Music that goes nowhere is "pale" music, lacking enough intensity to make it interesting to the performer or the listener. It is often overly predictable music lacking enough mystery, if I may use that word, to give the music a forward directionality, and thus keep the music going somewhere in order to keep it interesting. If the music part of the music is supporting lyric poetry, it needs to be the handmaiden of the text that is telling a story. Although we do not have time to discuss this concept here fully, the formal properties of the music should tell the same story as the text is expressing. In other words, the music part of the music should be a concomitant of the text instead of its rival or enemy.

If the music is "music alone", i.e., music without words, its formal properties must be arranged in such a way that it will tell its own story. If it is sacred music, its story must be congruent with the purposes of public or private worship, and this worship must be the worship of God and not the worship of music. This puts great responsibility upon the composer to organize the formal properties of the sound in such a way that it will suit the purposes of worship. This is easier said than done. Taking an art form and subduing it to the purposes of honoring God is an awesome responsibility. Furthermore, since music alone is not able to lean on a sacred text, its formal properties must be skillfully arranged so that the music will be compatible with the purposes of worshiping God. There is a vast difference between music that is pale and is not aesthetically worthwhile because it does not have a forward directionality, and music that hammers and incessantly drives with a forward propelling directionality without regular points of rest and finality. Surely a Christian musician can find a balance point somewhere between these two extremes.

## Sacred Music Should not be Obvious Music

Next let us consider "trite" music. A musical definition of *trite* is music that it has too frequent repetition which makes it boringly obvious. This type of music goes well with a religious text which is repeated over and over and over again. If the text is not going anywhere, then there is little or no need for the formal properties of the music to try to lead the text to a place that it is obviously not going! So, in all fairness to arrangers who are given a *seven-eleven text, there is little that a composer or arranger can do aesthetically with the formal properties of music that must be tied to an overly repetitive text. The result is a trite text accompanied by a trite musical setting. The ultimate end of such an endeavor is a stale musical composition that is often boringly obvious.

Another word that is used to categorize some religious music is the word *banal*. There are a number of words that may be used to identify banal music. They are *unoriginal, hackneyed, clichéd, trivial, trite, lackluster*, and *lacking originality*. This list is somewhat depressing when one considers that some of the religious music Christian musicians perform and listen to fits this definition quite well. Again, this is not referring to simple praise choruses and gospel songs *per se*. There is no doubt that the reason much of popular religious music disappears into obscurity rather quickly is that it fits the definition of trite or banal quite well.

# 13: Sacred Music Should Be Worthwhile Music

One of the reasons that some religious music fits the above definition is that the lyric poetry is also banal. Some religious music does not have anything theologically wrong with its text, but the text is shallow and the imagery is trite. Some religious lyric poetry is disappointing because of what it does not say. It seems that religious poets are afraid to tell the complete truth about a changed life, a life sold out to Christ, or a life controlled by the Holy Spirit.

Another definite problem with religious music texts is that many of the things that have been written in the twentieth and now in this century only talk about God's love. The dumbing down of religious music caused by the belief that the music part of music cannot be efficacious has also caused a gradual over-simplifying of the texts of much religious music.

## Sacred Music Should Expound the Message of the Bible

Psalm 85:10 states, "Mercy and truth are met together; righteousness and peace have kissed each other." God is worthy to be praised because of His great mercy to all of us when we were yet sinners. However, God is not only the Lord of mercy but also truth. To only sing praises about His love is shortsighted. Any musical ministry that only includes praise is an incomplete ministry. The complete truth of the gospel is that God is not only a God of love but also a God of justice. Praise music is not only appropriate for public and private worship, but also very necessary for true Christian worship. However, it is only part of what needs to take place in public musical worship.

Prayer songs, songs of supplication and confession, songs about God's claims upon the born-again Christian, and songs of admonition are vital and necessary to public music worship. So, religious music that omits the claims of the gospel and thereby avoids any content that might be convicting to those who attend church, but do not love and serve the Lord, has a tendency to be shallow or incomplete at best. It is not music about God being holy that confronts people, but rather songs that teach, "be ye holy for I am holy." (See Leviticus 20:7, I Peter 1:15, 16.)

It is necessary to have a balance and thoroughness in one's music ministry. Although many Christians are unaware of the fact, there is a battle going on over song texts. Those that speak of God's wrath, justice or judgment are far from popular as we have entered the twenty-first century. For instance, there has been a recent conflict over the Presbyterian Church (USA) refusing to include Keith Getty's and Stuart Townsend's hymn "In Christ Alone." The conflict came when the composers refused to let the hymn be published with an amended text that drastically changed its meaning. It is alleged that the hymnal committee wanted to amend the words, "the wrath of God was satisfied," to read, "the love of God was magnified."[83] Again, we see an attempt by modern church musicians to keep all worship music happy and without any confrontation that occurs when a congregation musics the truth of whole gospel. Many church musicians follow current trends in worship music without understanding that they are following a definite post-postmodern music philosophy and *ipso facto* its music praxis. If one had the opportunity to question these worship leaders privately one would learn that many of them believe in a "praise only" music praxis.

### Endnotes

1. Richard DeVinney, *There's More to Church Music than Meets the Ear*, (Philadelphia: Fortress Press, 1972), 53.
2. Bob Smietana, "Presbyterians' Decision to Drop Hymn Stirs Debate," Last modified August 5, 2013, accessed February 19, 2017, www.usatoday.com.

### Chapter Thirteen Word Meanings

**Banal**— music that is so lacking in originality as to be obvious and boring.

**Pedagogue**— an educator who teaches by a developed set of rules. In this instance, no negative connotations are intended.

**Seven-eleven text**— this terminology is a colloquialism for a text with only a few words that are repeated over and over again, as in, "seven words, sung eleven times."

### Chapter Thirteen Questions for Discussion

1. Discuss the philosophical significance of the author's statement, "It is much more productive to first find out what is right about sacred music before one

identifies the elements of a particular music that are a hindrance to sacred musicing."
2. Explain why you do or do not believe that profound music lends itself to being worthwhile music.
3. Discuss whether or not sacred music should be powerful music.
4. What happens to sacred music when the formal properties of a piece of music are arranged in a banal manner?
5. Explain whether or not a simple piece of music can support a profound sacred text.
6. Explain what you believe will happen if a church only sings religious music that omits the claims of the gospel and thereby avoids any content that might be convicting to those who attend church, but do not love and serve the Lord.
7. Explain why all sacred music, and secular music for that matter, should have a forward directionality.
8. Explain what is meant by the terminology, "dumbing down" of religious music.
9. Explain why you do or do not believe that prayer songs, songs of supplication and confession, songs about God's claims upon the born-again Christian, and songs of admonition are vital and necessary to public music worship.
10. Discuss your philosophical position on a "praise only" praxis.

# 14

# Styles in Conflict with Historical Church Music

### Styles that Came in by Default

MANY CHURCH MUSICIANS TODAY are not aware of the history of many styles of music that represent anti-biblical worldviews, nor do most people who attend church know the history of our more traditional forms of church music that have proven themselves to be congruent with the message and claims of the gospel. Sometime during the '60s and early '70s young people from various churches began forming religious rock groups and desired to sing and play this style of music in church youth services. Next, they asked if they could perform for Sunday evening services and then Sunday morning worship. Youth ministers were so happy to get some young people involved in worship that they allowed the worldly influence of rock music to become a part of public worship and thereby the influence of secular rock music style was accepted in public worship.

It was not a thought-out philosophical process but rather a desperate effort to involve young people in public worship. The thought that the church had allowed a style of music to be admitted to public worship that was basically antagonistic to Christianity was most often not considered. The fact that rock music was from its beginning a style of music that was antagonistic to the basic beliefs of Christianity was ignored. The church ignored the fact that it had opened its arms to a style of music that was never intended to be used in public worship and was not friendly to grace. The church had been squeezed into the world's mold without much of a fight. It all came about under the disguise of helping teenagers to get involved in public worship. Never before in church history had the church surrendered with hardly any fight to an influence that was almost totally at loggerheads with orthodox Christianity.

## Styles that did not Start like Historical Church Music

Many church musicians erroneously believe that nearly all church music was first secular music with sensuous words and intent. We often hear stories that church music was first earthy, profane, sexy or somewhat vulgar bar room music that was later "sanctified" by church musicians. It is a little-known fact among church musicians that until 1750, a great preponderance of all music composed was sacred music written specifically for the glory of God. As a matter of fact, much of the religious music was written specifically for public worship.

It is odd that so few church musicians are aware of the well-known fact that at least two species of music have existed since the time of ancient Israel. One is sacred music and the other is secular music. Furthermore, from the Middle Ages until 1900, a specific type of sacred music existed, and the bulk of this music was practical music to be used in regular church worship services. The remainder of the religious music was written in the same style, or nearly the same style, but was intended as religious concert music.

At least some of sacred and secular music of ancient times mentioned in the Bible was constructed very differently. As a matter of fact, writers like Robert Lachmann and Curt Sachs refer to different styles of music in ancient Israel as men's music and women's music.[1] Men's music was text and melody based with the rhythm of the words always being the rhythm of the text. Women's music was based on rhythm with only a few melodic turns repeated over and over again.

When it came to worship in the First or Second Temple, women's music was excluded from all public worship since it was rhythm based and was used for public mourning, dancing and even harlotry.[2] In ancient times the church had the right and responsibility to prescribe which styles of music were right and wrong, appropriate or inappropriate for music worship. It seems from the Jewish writers that the exclusion of music based on species or style was a common practice in ancient Israel.

Both sacred and secular music have existed since ancient times, and for centuries in the Occident there was often very little difference between the music part of sacred and secular music. Therefore, when composers like G.F. Handel used the same piece for secular and sacred settings there was often no contradistinction of style that would make this music inappropriate for use as sacred music. Generally speaking, there was little rhythmic, melodic or harmonic difference between Handel's sacred and secular music. So, he could use much of his music interchangeably without doing damage to the message of his sacred music. The same is generally true concerning the music composed by J.S. Bach.

At other times in the history of Western music there was admittedly a very distinct difference in the way composers organized the formal properties of sacred and secular music. In such cases secular music, especially dance music, did not interchange well with sacred music. When a *contradistinction of style did occur, the difference in the music centered around two aspects of the music. First, the purpose of composing secular and sacred music was sometimes quite different. Second, some secular music was created as dance music and was much more rhythm based than sacred music.

In modern times jazz, country rock, hard and acid rock, and several other related styles of *fusion music often have had substantial differences in the way that the formal properties are organized. These differences in style cause these forms of music to conflict with traditional sacred music. Therefore, there is legitimate cause for concern when these styles of music are juxtaposed with sacred texts.

## Keeping our Statements Accurate

One may wonder about the philosophical legitimacy of a church excluding styles of music based on their extreme use of the elements of music like extreme dynamics, *incessant rhythm, and driving beat. Christian musicians who do not approve of the use of all styles of secular and religious music in worshiping God have sometimes made statements concerning these styles of music that cannot be substantiated. Therefore, I am cautious of making these types of comments even though it is possible that many of them may be true or at least partially true. I will address some of the issues of the elements of these styles of music in the discussion that follows.

I am skeptical of results derived from playing music to milk cows or research projects involving playing music to plants. My reasoning is obvious – we are not plants and, although we are part of the animal kingdom, we are not cows. Furthermore, there is no empirical evidence to prove that humans respond to music in the same manner as cattle. Be it fact or fiction that cows give more milk to Bach's music than to other music, I do not place my philosophical basis on animal research. Although there may be truth in the concept of backward masking, there is no evidence to prove that humans hear rock music, or any music for that matter, in a backwards manner. The term *backward masking* means playing and listening to a tape played backward. I know of no empirical research that shows or tends to show that humans have a new hearing malady, which we might term *dyslexic hearing*. We should first concern ourselves with the many problems with listening to music in a forward direction. When we resolve the plethora of confusion about listening to destructive styles of music then perhaps we should analyze listening to them backwards.

One of the significant elements of many styles of music which were popular in the twentieth century and now in this century is that they are often meant to be played at extreme decibel levels. Noise pollution as a result of listening to some styles of music performance is a well-established fact. Music concerts and earphone listening to music is often experienced at extremely dangerous decibel levels. One of the important problems of popular styles of music performance is that they have controlling power over the mind at extreme decibel levels. This level of performance and listening is part of the culture of these styles of music. As a matter of fact, it is a good sign that the listener is deeply involved in the culture that surrounds these styles when they are played at a near deafening level or when the earphones are turned up so loudly that the entire household shares what was intended to be a private listening experience.

## Intentional Distortion

Along with extreme volume levels comes distortion. In the past one of the advantages of stereo hi fidelity listening was the ability to reproduce a performance without the annoyance of distortion. However, a most disconcerting element of some styles of music performance is the continuous use of intentional distortion of instruments and vocals. I know that to a point beauty in music is found in the mind of the auditor (listener). It is surprising that young people who will not listen to a classic LP because it was produced with "too much noise" will listen to continuous, intentional distortion on a modern recording for hours at a time. It is not too farfetched to recognize such behavior as the result of illogical thinking.

A standard part of Western music for centuries has been that a well-composed musical phrase always flows with a forward directionality from relaxation to tension to relaxation. Every good phrase has beginning, middle and end, or beginning, climax and then closing or relaxation. Even the *sound envelope of a single tone consists of the same concepts which are rise (attack time), sustain, and decay time of the sound until it releases.

Ravel's "Bolero" was a twentieth century example of the breaking down of this time honored principal of composition. Rock music picked up the baton with songs like *"In-A-Gadda-Da-Vida"* which was performed by the music group Iron Butterfly in the late 1960s. This selection went on for over seventeen minutes of tension with little or no release or relaxation. Now in the early twenty-first century it is not uncommon to produce a song that continues for a lengthy period of time with little or no resolution or relaxation. The result must have an unhealthy effect on the human psyche.

## All Music Represents Some Philosophical Presupposition

All art forms are the product of the artist's philosophical presuppositions that are instrumental in the development of worldview. Many composers who are not Christians believe that life exists in a purposeless universe with no absolutes, no order and no answers. In other words, to many twenty-first century musicians who are living outside of the grace of God, life is meaningless, and to them, there are no answers to life's questions.

These musicians often do not believe what Jesus said in St. John 14:6, "I am the way, the truth and the life: no man cometh unto the Father, but by me." Jesus didn't say, "I am the answer" but rather, "I am the way." This generation is searching for the answers without taking the way of Christ. Hebrews 10:20-23 states,

> "By a new and living way, which he [Christ] hath consecrated [made new] for us, through the veil, that is to say, his flesh; And having an high priest over the house of God; Let us draw near with a true heart sprinkled from an evil conscience, and our bodies washed with pure water. Let us hold fast the profession of our faith without wavering; (for he is faithful that promised)." (Words in brackets are mine.)

The word *hodos* (3598), translated way in both verses above, means figuratively the means or mode by which we can know—through Christ and His Lordship over our musical actions we can have assurance.

Many twenty-first century musicians still compose music that consists of incessant tension and distortion. These composers are faithless because they are looking for answers without coming under the "way" or Lordship of Christ. It is no wonder their music is so tense and grotesque since it is a mere reflection of their philosophy that man exists in a purposeless universe, trying to authenticate himself through an act of his will. When a musician's worldview dictates that humanity came from nowhere, has no purpose in life, and is ultimately going nowhere, that musician's artistic creativity will most likely represent chaos, tension, unrest, and confusion.

Composers and performers who have never passed from spiritual death unto life have never experienced the "new and living way." They are searching for truth within themselves. It is sad, but most often they will never come to the knowledge of truth because they will not accept Christ, who is "the way, the truth and the life."[2] Timothy 3:7 explains that they are "ever learning, and never able to come to the knowledge of the truth." This hopeless searching for truth often makes these musicians bitter, confused, and *nihilistic. Their distorted philosophical beliefs are often reflected by their distorted music. To accomplish this effect they use fuzz guitars and distorted sounds on keyboards and turn the volume up until the speakers distort while they literally scream out the vocal lyrics in an un-vocal manner. Music that largely consists of distortion, tension, and extreme dissonance is not a proper vehicle to represent the moral nature of God and should not be juxtaposed with sacred lyrics.

## Styles that Negate the Elements of Music

The major aspect of many styles of popular religious music is the rhythm and beat. From ancient times until the twentieth century the rhythm of most vocal church music was the natural rhythm of the words. Words were normally not set to music but rather music was set to words. Historically, church music was normally constructed so that melody, rhythm and harmony were servants of words rather than words as a servant of melody, harmony and rhythm. An ancient landmark of sacred music was music that conformed to the rhythm of the words rather than music which had a regular recurring beat without regard to the text. When regular occurring beat became a part of sacred music it was a servant of the words; it did not control or overpower melody and words.

In the music of the Bible, melody was a vehicle upon which the word of Jehovah rode into the hearts and minds of the worshiper. Biblical research has proven that the most important aspect of sacred music in ancient Bible times was the word of Jehovah. All the elements of music were servants or helpers of the Word of God. The rhythm of Bible music was always the natural rhythm of the words.[3] The word *music* originally came from "muse" which meant to think. So, music was not conceived as an artistic rhythmic experience, but rather an artistic intellectual experience. When one studies the *te'amim* it is evident that none of the melodies of the Old Testament covered up or distracted in any way from the word of Jehovah. If ancient Israel had some form of harmonic practice in either vocal or instrumental music, no Temple musician would have allowed it to cover up words.

## 14: Styles in Conflict with Historical Church Music

What does this all mean to us as we enter the twenty-first century? What is the philosophical biblical example given to us? When any style of religious music accompaniment is in competition with or covers up the words of a song this music does not follow the biblical example of how sacred music should be performed. Remember from the time of ancient Israel and for centuries after, words were most important in church music. Melody, being the handmaiden of God's Word, came second, and any harmony came next and rhythm followed the rhythm of the text. Many styles of modern music reverse this order. In these styles rhythm and beat are normally first, harmony is generally second, and words and melody are last. Since beat is first, it is the master of words and therefore more important. Through the use of extremely high amplification levels, beat becomes an even bigger giant. Instead of a flowing forward directionality, this music has a crushing, propelling forward directionality.

Until the twentieth century, rhythm was used to help build tension in music but always subsided in a final relaxation. As was said before, music flowed in a forward directionality from relaxation to tension to relaxation. All well-constructed musical compositions have a beginning, a climax and an ending. It is now common for styles of music to not relax anywhere, or at least not often, in the composition. Therefore, such music is not biblical in its enactment, because Jesus said in St. Matthew 11:28, "Come unto me, all ye that labor and are heavy laden, and I will give you rest." He did not say, "I will give you continuous tension," or "I will keep you heavy laden or burdened down." The heaviness and incessant tension created by the preponderant beat of some styles of music is not compatible with the good news of the gospel. Even our heartbeat is made of tension and release. The good news presented by sacred music should bring ultimate rest, not tension. Music that is compatible with the Gospel of Christ or the *Logos Christos* must come to regular points of rest.

## A Healthy Psyche Demands Release from Tension

We are psychological beings. A healthy psyche demands release from tension. Any music that does not give the listener regular reoccurring rest from tension becomes psychologically disturbing. No wonder that so many teenagers who listen to the various styles of pop music five or six hours a day are constantly depressed. Christian musicians should realize that adding religious words to a style of music does not solve the problems of that music. It only complicates matters to try to force sacred purposes on music that appeals to the flesh and was originally not created to worship God

It is amazing to me that when I lecture to church musicians who perform rock music, many of them do not see themselves as rock performers. They do not seem to realize that if they perform rock music at any level, they are rock performers. Somehow, they have developed a mindset that, although they perform music that exhibits all the elements of this type of music, somehow their music is not really the "bad stuff," since they only perform "good" music. Many of the "soft rock" musicians profess to be against rock music much in the same way that the country rock musicians who perform country music with a heavy rock beat deny being country rock performers. These church musicians have developed a worldly paradigm without recognizing that they have been squeezed into the world's mold of church music performance. It has been said, "There are none as blind as those who will not see." We all need to remember the admonishment found in 1 John 2:15 to "Love not the world, neither the things that are in the world. If any man love the world, the love of the Father is not in him."

## Connecting Righteousness with Unrighteousness

Some church fellowships are locking arms with the world in worshipping God. 2 Corinthians 6:14 states, "Be ye not unequally yoked together with unbelievers. For what fellowship hath righteousness with unrighteousness? And what communion hath light with darkness? And what concord hath Christ with Belial? or what part hath he that believeth with an infidel?" Never in the history of church music have there ever been so many genres of religious music that can directly yoke Christians to those who do not worship or believe in Jesus Christ. Some styles of music that can be identified with satanic worship are also being used in contemporary Christian worship. This yoking together has not come about because infidels and Christians both love the Lord, but rather because they both love the heavy pounding physical beat of their music. It is not possible that those who hate Christ are capitulating or that this present sinful age is turning to Christ.

Ever since Satan rebelled against God, there has been Christ vs. the Antichrist. There has always been right vs. wrong. We have not finally found styles of music that work equally well for appealing to man's sinful nature and worshiping God. The modern matrix has not finally found a unifying style of music that will unite the world of sin with the kingdom of Christ.

Post-postmodern philosophy has given up on a unified field of philosophical knowledge and no longer believes that there is thesis (truth) and antithesis (a lie). To post-postmodern man truth is relative and is always found in a combination of both good and bad, i.e., modern man believes that truth is always found in syntheses (combinations or blends of truth and error). Traditional philosophy has always believed in two contrasting worldviews:

| GOD | SATAN |
|---|---|
| Truth | Perversion |
| Right | Wrong |
| Good | Evil |

However, things have changed and now many philosophers purport that the answer is found in a mixture or amalgamation of truth and evil. The answer is neither good nor evil but something somewhere in between. Now post-postmodern man has styles of music that fit the synthesis paradigm. The church and the world now have something in common. Both believe in worship and both are deeply committed to the same styles of music. The pluralistic thinking church no longer believes 1 Corinthians 6:17, "Wherefore come out from among them, and be ye separate, saith the Lord, and touch not the unclean thing; and I will receive you." The philosophy of the pluralistic minded church no longer tolerates the "be ye separate" philosophy of the Bible. As a result of such thinking they no longer tolerate traditional church music performance but rather strongly believe in being yoked together with the world through the medium of music. It is believed by much of the "seeker sensitive" movement that any kind of separation from worldly music will dwarf the Church of Jesus Christ. They need to be reminded of 2 Thessalonians 2:1-3:

> "Now we beseech you, brethren, by the coming of our Lord Jesus Christ and by our gathering together unto him. That ye be not soon shaken in mind, or be troubled, neither by spirit, nor by word, not by letter as from us, as that the day of Christ is at hand. Let no man deceive you by any means: for that day shall not come, except there come a falling away first, and that man of sin be revealed, the son of perdition."

Verses eleven and twelve warn us, "for this cause God shall send them strong delusion, that they should believe a lie: that they all might be damned who believed not the truth, but had pleasure in unrighteousness." I am skeptical when the modern church purports that most of what is wrong with the church is time honored styles of music. The mainstream contemporary church has become unequally yoked together with unbelievers through the styles of music they perform in public worship.

## Religious Music is not the Bellwether of Christianity

Although church music matters, it should not be the *bellwether of Christian belief. When the emphasis of the Christian church is no longer theological belief and a relationship with Jesus Christ, but rather on music, the tail is wagging the dog. Historically, sacred music has always been a means to an end, not the end in itself. Church music has traditionally helped to bring the congregation into the presence of God so that the people's hearts might be prepared for the preaching of the Word of God. Anointed singing has always been a concomitant to anointed preaching but it has never been the main thing.[4] Singing is important in the worship of God. Psalm 100:2 states, "Serve the Lord with gladness: come before his presence with singing." The Hebrew words *rananah* (7445), translated singing, is used only four times in the Old Testament, meaning "with joyful voice." This Scripture is justly rendered, "Come before his presence with singing." However, 1 Corinthians 1:21-25 clearly establishes preaching as the method for winning the lost.

> "For after that in the wisdom of God the world by wisdom knew not God, it pleased God by the foolishness of preaching to save them that believe. For the Jews require a sign and the Greeks seek after wisdom: But we preach Christ crucified, unto the Jews a stumbling block, and unto the Greeks foolishness; But unto them which are called, both Jews and Greeks, Christ the power of God, and the wisdom of God. Because the foolishness of God is wiser than men, and the weakness of God is stronger than men."

On the authority of God's Word we know that it pleases Him to save those who will believe on Him through preaching, not singing. There is no place in the Bible where singing should be more important than preaching. When a church has a long, long, long, time of singing and a short, short, short sermon, the philosophical tail is wagging the dog. The fact that church music is a servant of preaching and is not the main thing does not mean that church music doesn't matter. Church music matters to God. Every part of the worship service matters to God. Sacred music has always been the handmaiden of God's Word. The fact that God mentions music over 600 times in His Word tells us that church music matters!

## The Influence of Music Style

Rock music has influenced church music more in the last twenty years than any other type of music. Alan Freed, a Cleveland, Ohio deejay, coined the term *rock 'n' roll*. Early rock 'n' roll musicians like Bill Haley, Chuck Berry, Little Richard, and Buddy Holly were influential in the early development of this style of music. One of the very early elements of rock music was sexual innuendo. The Jerry Lee Lewis songs "Whole Lotta' Shakin' Goin' On" and "Great Balls of Fire" were filled with sexual innuendoes— so much so that Lewis became a rock sex object. In 1956, Elvis Presley's "Heartbreak Hotel" started his career in rock 'n' roll music that made him eventually the "King of Rock 'n' Roll" and in the early '60s the Beatles stormed in from England with "She Loves You" and "I Want to Hold Your Hand." These early songs did not have shocking lyrics but by the time of their "Sgt. Pepper's Lonely Hearts Club Band" in 1967 it was well recognized that the Beatles were committed to drugs like LSD and Speed.[5]

The result was the beginning of drugs being considered "cool" by the teen generation in the USA. College students as well as high school students were soon involved in drug experimentation, and in many cases heavy drug use. Many of the rock musicians openly admitted writing music under the influence of drugs.

Drugs and gross nudity was a common occurrence during the 1969 Woodstock Music Festival. Next came the 1970s with pop rock giving way to heavy metal, with groups openly professing to worship Satan with their music. Groups like KISS (Kids/Knights in Satan's Service) were epitomized by men wearing makeup and singing witchcraft and devil worshiping songs. These dark, nasty, evil groups were followed by punk rock groups wearing all kinds of weird outfits and styles, including orange and purple hair. Concert antics included spitting, vomiting, violence, nudity and gross profanity.

The late 1970s brought on *disco, which gave way to shock rock and new wave rock in the 1980s. Performers like Madonna and Michael Jackson sang lyrics that openly mentioned sex as well and dressed with gross immodesty while exhibiting lewd actions on stage. Songs such as "Like a Virgin" and "Thriller" utilized twisted lyrics of rebellion and sexual revolution. Now we have death-funk, psycho pop, and grunge and a host of more recent rock idioms.

Rock music has grown into a multi-billion dollar industry. Teenagers spend more money on rock music each year than any other age group. Teenage drug use in the US has risen drastically in the last twenty-five years. The suicide rate in the US among teenagers has also taken a drastic upswing in the past twenty-five years.

In spite of the horrible facts surrounding rock music, pastors

## 14: Styles in Conflict with Historical Church Music   295

and ministers of music are more and more defending the use of rock music in worship services. How do pastors and music ministers conclude that music that was created to worship Satan should be used to worship God? It is not popular to say anything negative about rock music. It is even less popular to take a stand against religious rock music.

Is there anything good about rock music? As Steve Peters stated in his book, *Truth about Rock,* "Few want to touch rock 'n' roll because many listen to it and enjoy it on some level. Your favorite artist probably seems pretty tame compared to some of the material you've found.... so what's the big deal?"[6] The big deal is that when you place approval on rock music at any level you have just sanctioned rock music. Peters went on to say, "Rock is not all evil."[7] The problem is, where do you draw the line? If a Christian listens to religious rock music and condones its use in public worship, how can that musician say that rock music is bad? The way to shut church musicians' mouths forever about rock music is to get them to perform and condone it on some "mild" level. How can a pipe smoker condemn a cigar smoker? How can a wine drinker condemn a person who drinks a little vodka?

Some Christian musicians are afraid that if they do not perform popular styles of music in church they will become outdated and their musicing will not appeal to worldly people. I would be the first to say yes, it is very possible that church music may become stale and outdated and unattractive to the world. However, we should remember that the world's music is not a friend of grace and it never will be. At the same time it is very important that our church music appeal to the unsaved as well as to the saved members of our congregation. It is understandable that ministers of music and pastors are concerned that music as well as all parts of the worship service must relate to those who attend church services. Even though we need to be constantly looking for fresh new ways to present the gospel through our musicing, Christian musicians must not capitulate in the battle against destructive religious music.

## Is Rock a Better Vehicle?

Although rock music is by far not the only music genre that is of current concern, it is a very popular music genre, so let us consider some concerns that Christian musicians should consider. First, is religious rock a better vehicle for presenting the Word of God than all of the conventional forms of church music? Those who defend rock music would immediately say Yes! Why? Because it is the form of music that sinners like. To this argument I respond by asking the question, "Is it necessary to only do those things that sinners like to do in our worship services?" If the answer is yes, then we should not read Scripture because sinners do not read Scripture, they do not quote Scripture, and furthermore they do not like most of what it tells them to do and not to do. They do not understand Scripture because they are not familiar with it. Remember, the argument against the use of traditional church music is that sinners do not know it and do not understand it and therefore do not like it. Religious rock advocates act as if these seekers are simple, ignorant people who are not capable of deriving good from traditional forms of church music. I am not even slightly convinced that this generation of highly educated people is not capable of deriving spiritual truth from any kind of music except rock music.

If worshipers should only do the things that sinners do, they should not pray in church because sinners do not pray; furthermore they do not understand what prayer is or how we communicate with God in prayer. If one believes that worshipers should only do the things that sinners do, they should never partake of the Eucharist in church since it is near to impossible for a sinner to understand the spiritual benefit of taking the Lord's Supper. Also, we probably should not take an offering since sinners usually do not give to God and certainly do not understand the biblical concept of tithing. Of course this argument is ridiculous, but so is the idea that it is not "seeker sensitive" to expect the un-churched of this generation cannot understand any other styles of music except popular styles. It is not logical to believe philosophically that seekers are capable of understanding all aspects of public worship except traditional forms of church music.

## Is the Music Part of a Style Neutral?

Are all the elements of a style of music like rock music neutral except words? Exponents of religious rock music immediately say Yes without any qualification. If this is the case then the only thing that matters in sacred or secular music is words. Under this assumption a symphony or piano concerto can have no positive or negative effect on an audience. Rhythm, melody, harmony, tone color, and dynamics can have no effect on the listener; and no emotional effects, no psychological effects, no aesthetic experiences are possible.

An honest musician would have to admit that music without words does have an effect on the hearer. No one except contemporary Christian musicians would say that instrumental music does not have an effect on the listener. Instrumental music has a message. All serious musicians know that music affects us. If instrumental music is capable of having an effect on the hearer then it can have either a positive or a negative effect.

If instrumental music can affect the listener in either a positive or a negative way, then music without words is not neutral. Since all instrumental music sends a message to the hearer, some styles of instrumental music are more appropriate than others for use with sacred texts. If some styles of music are very well suited for use with sacred words, then there are styles of instrumental music that are very poorly suited to use with sacred words.

Furthermore, instrumental music used by itself in worship must pass the tests of suitability and appropriateness. Rock music has always been composed in such a manner as to appeal to the flesh. It has always been a style of music suited to arousing sexual passions. It has always been a style of music suited to tension, hate, mistrust, sex and passion. It has always been a style suited to the lust of the flesh. Only contemporary Christians deny this fact about rock music.

Rock music as a genre was not originally intended to be used in public worship of God the Father, God the Son and God the Holy Spirit. It was from the beginning the music of sex, drugs, and rebellion. Some rock music has been specifically composed for the explicit purpose of worshiping Satan. It is not primarily Christian musicians who have admitted that this music was composed to worship Satan, but the secular, godless rock musicians who have boldly and proudly promoted that this music was used to worship Satan. Admittedly not all rock music was composed for the worship of Satan, but sex, drugs and the lusts of the flesh have been the primary themes of rock music since the 1950s when it began. Rock music and a host of other styles are not appropriate vehicles of worship, prayer, and praise because they are too closely associated with antichrist culture, have many negative moral implications that are incongruent with the changed life of a Christian, and do not follow biblical principles of sacred musicing.

## Ancient Landmarks of Sacred Musicing

Proverbs 22:28 states, "Remove not the ancient landmark, which thy fathers have set." The Hebrew word translated "landmark" (*gabuwl* 1366) means a boundary or a border or a limit. Traditional church music styles are an *ancient landmark of Christian worship. Rock and pop genres are less than seventy years old. They are by no means ancient landmarks of Christian worship. Of course the "ancient landmark" in Proverbs 22:28 was a reference to a property boundary and in no way was referring to music. However, the principle referred to in this Proverb extends to many areas of Christian philosophy, including music. So, if you will indulge me, I am going to refer to ancient principles of musicing found in the Bible as "ancient landmarks."

Also there are time honored principles of musicing which have been observed by churches for centuries as ancient landmarks. What philosophical reasoning could bring pastors and church musicians to the conclusion that we should scrap all traditional styles of church music in favor of styles of music that were created to appeal to the lust of the flesh?

Romans 1:28 states, "And even as they did not like to retain God in their knowledge, God gave them over to a reprobate mind, to do those things which are not convenient." The Greek word *adokimos* (96) translated reprobate means unapproved, worthless or rejected. So we see musicians with an unapproved mindset. The Greek words *me katheko* (3361 2520) translated not convenient mean not becoming or not fit. So, we see musicians with an unapproved mindset that causes them to use styles of music that are not becoming or fit to be used with sacred words. Why have they come to this mindset? They have not retained God in their knowledge. They have been squeezed into the world's musical mold and have not developed a Christocentric music philosophy. Thus they propose that church music is without any absolutes, boundaries, or standards of suitability and appropriateness.

What about the lifestyle of religious as well as secular rock musicians? There is no doubt that there are Christian rock musicians who live a careful Christ-like life. There may be secular rock musicians, for that matter, who live a godly lifestyle. However the mainstream secular rock musicians live openly godless lifestyles. The same may be said about the mainstream of religious rock groups since some of them do not live Christ-centered lives. Admittedly the same may be said of many musicians who perform traditional styles of church music.

As Richard S. Taylor once said, "If we do not want the fruit, we had better not feed the root."[8] Adults may be able to listen to a style of music without changing their lifestyle, but teenagers most often get involved in the lifestyle of their favorite musical performers. They first purchase the music, then they go to their concerts, put their posters up in their rooms and wear their tee shirts. Eventually they dress like them, wear their hair like them, and act like them. Remember, "direction determines destiny." The root may appear to be harmless, but the fruit is often harmful to the auditor.

Those who develop a habit of listening to religious rock music will soon develop a taste for secular rock music as well. Pastors and church musicians often warn young people against secular rock music while at the same time they are responsible for developing habits of listening to rock music by giving teens and young adults a steady diet of religious rock music in the church.

No one can say that religious rock music cannot be used by the Lord or that no one has ever been saved when musicians sang or played rock music. Isaiah 55:11 states, "So shall my word be that goeth forth out of my mouth: it shall not return unto me void, but it shall accomplish that which I please, and it shall prosper in the thing whereto I sent it." So, whenever the Word of God is given out, God may use any means to make it prosper, because He is God and He is sovereign. The issue is not whether it is possible for rock to be used in worship but rather if it is a suitable vehicle for worship.

### Styles not Intended to be Worship Music

Why are Christian musicians so determined to use musical styles for public and private worship that were never intended to be used in Christian worship? Perhaps some Christian musicians are trying to be as much like the world as possible so that they can have "the best of both worlds." The Bible teaches in 1 John 2:15, "Love not the world, neither the things that are in the world. If any man love the world, the love of the Father is not in him." As mentioned earlier, one of the concerns about the use of rock music in public worship is that it is too closely associated with the world, sex, drugs, and ungodly lifestyles to be an appropriate vehicle for Christian worship. This association cannot be erased when a performer merely adds a religious text. Furthermore, the heavy forward propelling force of the incessant driving beat is not appropriate for the rest and comfort of the gospel since it upstages words and monopolizes the music.

Finally, the question may be asked; are rock-based music styles here to stay? They are. However, so are a lot of other influences that surround us. The list is long, including fornication, drugs, violence, immodesty, unfaithfulness, and a host of other influences that are ungodly. The fact that these styles of music are here to stay is not a good rationale for using them in Christian worship.

Romans 12:1, 2: "I beseech you therefore, brethren, by the mercies of God, that ye present your bodies a living sacrifice, holy, acceptable unto God, which is your reasonable service. And be not conformed to this world: but be ye transformed by the renewing of your mind, that ye may prove what is that good, and acceptable, and perfect will of God." As time continues until our Lord returns there will be more and more pressure placed on Christians to conform to the world's standards of conduct. Christians are already under pressure to join ranks with the "all styles are neutral" crowd.

It will never again be popular to be a traditional church musician who believes in a prescriptive approach to sacred music and musicing. Being a conservative church musician will never be popular until Jesus comes. However, being a careful Christian is not popular either. Christians who take a stand on any spiritual issue, including religious music, will not be popular. Remember Romans 12:2 warns Christians not to be conformed or squeezed into the world's mold. It further admonishes us to be transformed mentally and always remember to prove what is acceptable unto the Lord. We must search for the good, acceptable and perfect will of God in all areas of Christian living. This most certainly includes our choices of both sacred and secular music.

### Endnotes

1. Robert Lachmann, *Jewish Cantillation and Song in the Isle of Djerba* (Jerusalem: Archives of Oriental Music, The Hebrew University, 1940); Curt Sachs, *The Rise of Music in the Ancient World* (New York: W.W. Norton & Company, Inc, 1943), 91.
2. See *Music of the Bible in Christian Perspective*, Chapter 5.
3. See *Music of the Bible in Christian Perspective*, Chapter 8.
4. See *Church Music Matters,* Chapter 2.
5. Steve Peters and Mark R Littleton, *Truth About Rock* (Minneapolis, Minnesota: Bethany House Publishers,1998), 16-17.
6. Ibid, 82-83
7. Ibid, 82-83
8. Taylor, *A Return to Christian Culture*, 85.

### Chapter Fourteen Word Meanings

**Ancient landmark**— this term was used in the OT to refer to boundaries of property. In this context it is used to identify ancient Bible principles of musicing.

**Bellwether**— this term refers to the leading sheep in the flock which has a bell hung around his neck.

**Contradistinction**— as used here it is a distinction that is made because of the different quality of two musics.

**Disco**— pop music developed in the 1970s intended mainly for dancing.

**Fusion**— music that blends jazz elements and the heavy repetitive rhythms of rock but tends to be more electronic in nature. Fusion sets tend to include a variety of music styles, such as alternative tango, blues, soul, disco, jazz, pop, lyrical or rhythmic electronica, or any other style of music that has a definitive dance beat that can be felt.

**Incessant rhythm**— refers to an unceasing rhythm, to the point of becoming unpleasant.

**Nihilistic**— referring to those who reject all religious and moral principles, in the belief that life is meaningless.

**Sound Envelope**— consists of attack, which refers to sound changes occurring before a sound reaches its continuous intensity; sustain, which refers to the continuous intensity of a sound; and decay, which is the rate at which a sound fades to silence.

### Chapter Fourteen Questions for Discussion

1. Explain why you do or not believe that the use of music styles of music should be a well-thought-out process.
2. What do you believe about the church excluding styles of music on the basis of their extreme use of the elements of music, like extreme dynamics, incessant rhythm, and driving beat?
3. A standard part of Western music for centuries has been that a well-composed musical phrase always flows with a forward directionality from relaxation to tension to relaxation. What is the significance of this statement?
4. What is the value of knowing that all art forms are the product of the artist's philosophical presuppositions that are instrumental in the development of a worldview?
5. Historically how has church music normally been constructed and what is the significance of the way it has been composed and arranged?
6. Until the twentieth century, rhythm was used to help build tension in music but always subsided in a final relaxation to achieve finality. Explain the major changes in how rhythm began to be used during the twentieth century and the significance of those changes.
7. Explain why you do or do not believe that adding religious words to a style of music does not solve the problems of the music part of that music.
8. Explain why you do or do not believe that religious rock is a better vehicle for presenting the Word of God than all of the conventional forms of church music.
9. Many styles of popular music have successfully yoked unbelievers with Christians. Discuss why you do or do not agree with this statement.
10. Why are so many twenty-first century Christian musicians so determined to use a musical style for public and private worship that was never intended to be used in Christian worship?

# 15

# What Do We Do Now that Some Styles Are Here to Stay?

## From Rejection to Toleration

ROCK MUSIC, AND A HOST of other styles of music that are related to it by the way their formal properties have been arranged, have been around long enough that most Christian musicians have conceded to the fact that many of them are not going away. Many conservative Christian musicians have gone through the different stages of rejecting them, complaining about them, ignoring them and finally tolerating them as church music vehicles. Likewise, some conservative Christian musicians who earlier believed that they were not suited for sacred musicing now believe that they might be, in some situations, used of the Holy Spirit. Still others believe that, since they realize that most of these styles of music are not going away, we might as well get on with the program and use them regardless of their suitability or usefulness. Others of us have continuously refused to perform these styles of music based on their lack of suitability and appropriateness in public and private worship.

Richard S. Taylor once wrote,

> "Some readers will point to the conversions which apparently occur following the use of religious rock, with the dubious assumption that even one soul saved is a divine endorsement. The question is, 'What is true, appropriate, and inherently sound?' In some of our sincere but misguided evangelism, the Spirit reaches around our gimmicks and finds some conductor over which spiritual energy can flow to reach a hungry heart. If the Word is preached, if sincere testimonies are given, if there is an atmosphere of warm love, of course

there will be fruit. But let us not naïvely suppose the deafening rock music has been the instrument."[1]

Dr. Taylor's statements reach to the core of the matter. A host of Christian musicians have failed to understand that, in the long run, a discerning music leader will ultimately choose music that is "true, appropriate and inherently sound" in its enactment. Any other musical praxis leads a body of believers down a faulty musical and worship path. Those who believe that the musical vehicle does not matter as long as seekers enjoy it are Jesuit in their music philosophy and praxis. They should remember that the Bible never teaches that the end justifies the means.

## What Do We Do if Musical Tastes Change?

All of us who have worked with people over several decades know that times change and that musical tastes change and the way arrangers organize the formal properties of music changes from decade to decade. When I was a Bible college choral director, well-meaning church and Christian college officials would take me aside for counsel about the "fact" that church folks no longer like a legitimate collegiate approach to sacred choral music. However, I have lived long enough to know that people do want to hear a college choir or a church choir sing God-honoring hymns, anthems, and gospel music on pitch, with vibrato, with well-produced musical phrases, and with a correct approach to vocal production. A music director does not need to live in constant fear of not being trendy enough to be popular, relevant, and understood or liked by those who attend religious concerts or church services.

The same can be said of church music and sacred music in general. Panic will reign if a music leader or minister is not convinced that his or her music praxis is the right path to follow. I am made to think of the story of a military commander who allegedly once declared, "Follow me, I'm your leader." Then he hesitated and queried, "Now let me think, which way should this platoon go?" One of the greatest problems with Christian music leadership is that a great host of music worship leaders are like the military commander in that they are not sure which way to go with their musicing. They are not convinced of any definite music praxis. They become victims of leader-shift and change musical directions as often as the wind changes, simply because someone else has started a new trend.

I have watched them flip-flop philosophically from Bach to rock, or from hymn singing to head-banging hard rock music, never seeming to know philosophically why they are going with the latest trendy leader-shift. They often state that their reason for being a slave to current musical trends is that they believe that this new trend will bring to their church or organization their "market share" of people who happen to like a current musical fad.

The Bible never teaches the concept of "market share." On the contrary, it teaches that Christian servants are to be good and faithful servants of Jesus Christ regardless of whether they are liked or considered successful by the world. In the parable about how Christians should utilize their talents, the AV justly translated Matthew 25:21. In this verse Jesus taught that, "His lord said unto him, Well done, thou good (*agathos* 18) and faithful (*pistos* 4103) servant: thou hast been faithful over a few things, I will make thee ruler over many things: enter thou into the joy of thy lord." Christ's emphasis was not on quantity but rather on the faithfulness involved in good stewardship of what each servant was given by his lord.

So, to avoid such error and to remain a good and faithful musician, every Christian music leader must develop a music philosophy that is congruent with the Bible and its principles of musicing and Christian living. A strong personal music philosophy can and will do more than any other thing in a musician's life to stabilize one's music praxis and *ipso facto* establish a solid rational music ministry. The music ministry of a leader who operates without consistent, congruent music praxis is like a ship without a rudder.

Regardless of which music fad, fashion or current trend that Christian musicians are currently following, this maxim is true—direction determines destiny, because no musicing can be done without cause and effect. It is surprising that so many twentieth and twenty-first century Christian musicians have believed that they could follow a particular trendy musical path and then much later were unhappy with the end result, so they shifted to another trendy praxis and repeated their mistakes. It seems that they have failed to recognize that musical direction determines musical destiny.

## "Doing" Exercises One's Philosophy

Every time a music director musics, i.e., "does," that director is exercising a part of his or her music philosophy because all "doing" exudes from beliefs. There is often a difference between what a Christian musician purports to believe and what that musician's "doing" proves about his or her actual beliefs. Simply getting in someone's car, turning on the radio and punching each of the presets will reveal what that musician actually believes about music. Robert Berglund said, "One's *decisions* are actually based on one's *values*, that is, the actual values one has actually determine the kind of decisions one makes."[2]

So, we are back to our original question: "What do we do now since many styles of popular music will not go away?" The answer is quite simple. We will perform music that is in accordance with our actual philosophical beliefs about the nature and value of music. If a Christian musician follows a musical path that is questionable, it will be because that musician believes that is the right thing to do. No adult can hide behind the excuse that he or she was pressured into musicing in a certain manner. No Christian musician is forced by the norms and beliefs of other twenty-first century believers or non-believers to perform any style of music that is contrary to Bible principles of musicing or that which is not congruent with changed life principles. Musicians who perform various styles of music are acting on personal music philosophy and actual beliefs that those styles are the best way to music unto a holy, infinite God. That Christian musician is testifying that these types of music are more appropriate, proper and profound than the time-honored musical genres that have been used for multiplied centuries to honor and praise the triune God

A Christian musician may be convinced by another's arguments that a style of music is not philosophically the best music to use to worship God, and yet that musician may continue to perform that music. My father used to say, "If you convince a man against his will, he'll be of the same opinion still." So, regardless of what musicians say they believe philosophically, they are doing what they like to do. Again, Richard S. Taylor summed up the matter quite well when he wrote, "Free domestic philosophies, such as existentialism, exaggerate individualism. Freedom is the watchword, and personal autonomy is the aim."[3]

It is impossible to successfully discuss the necessity of having a Bible-based music philosophy and praxis with musicians who consider that musicing is an autonomous act. To them it is not discussable because freedom reigns in all areas of musicing unto God. Although there are without doubt convincing arguments for not using many styles of music to worship God, one should understand that probably only the Holy Spirit will effect change in the way an autonomous musician musics. As Christian musicians we have the power to make autonomous musical decisions, but when we all face Him whose eyes are as a flame of fire, we will have to give an account for how we have musiced unto God.

**Musical Meaning in Musical Sounds**

Although I have discussed musical meaning at length in this work, I would like to revisit it very briefly. One of the objectives of developing a Christocentric music philosophy is to incorporate the musical principles mentioned earlier into systematic beliefs about the nature and value of a musician's music praxis. Every Christian must recognize that if the words of the sacred songs we sing are truly biblical then they embody truth. These music texts represent truth because the message of the words is true. They represent what Francis Schaefer called "true truth."

If the texts of Christian music must be constant and reliable, then the music part of the music should be consistent with the message of the gospel of our Savior Jesus Christ. 1 Corinthians 14:7 teaches, "And even things without life giving (*didomi*, 1325) sound (*phone* 5456), whether pipe or harp, except they give a distinction (*diastole* 1293) in the sounds (*phthoggos* 5353), how shall it be known what is piped or harped?" The words that have been translated "giving sound" are referring to musical sounds, specifically the sounds of the *aulos* (836) which was a type of flute or pipe and the *kithara* (2788) which was a hand-held lyre. As Bible music historians know, both instruments were pitch producing instruments capable of playing accurate musical melodies. With this knowledge in mind one can understand the meaning of the Greek words *diastole* and *phthoggos*, translated "distinction in the sounds" in the AV. The word *diastole* means distinction or accurateness and the word *phthoggos* means the musical notes being played.

This Bible passage very clearly teaches that in ancient Israel, if the instruments played the intended notes accurately, their sound sent a distinctive message to the hearer. Note that nothing is written in this passage of Scripture about the singing of words. The distinction of the message came through the sounds produced by accurate production of the musical notes being played by the instrument. The message sent by the musician was the result of the message of the music rather than by words sung by a musician.

The common man in ancient Israel knew what the sounds meant merely by the selection of tones that the musician played. There is much more musical truth embedded in the meaning or this Bible reference than is commonly believed or understood by musicians today. We know that the way that the ancient musicians musiced sent either clear or "uncertain" messages to the hearer.

If at the time that St. Paul lived music had the capability and power to send clear or unclear messages to the people of Israel, surely it has no less power over audiences today. Therefore, all Christian musicians must take great care concerning the musical techniques they use in their musicing unto God. Ancient cultures and their philosophers believed that music had great power and expressed meaning. It has been only modern and postmodern philosophers, including many church musicians, who have believed that music was (and is) not capable of saying anything.

This mention of music is found in the midst of St. Paul's discussion of the controversy over known and unknown tongues. However, Paul made part of his point in his discussion of the sound produced by musical instruments (music alone). There is no logical reason to discount what this great linguist wrote here, under the inspiration of the

## 15: What Do We Do Now that Some Styles Are Here to Stay? 309

Holy Spirit, about the message of music having distinction if the notes are played accurately.

It is a mistake to try to write musical meaning into places in the Bible where music is not mentioned, but it is just as big a mistake to ignore musical sound when it is mentioned as succinctly as it is here in Paul's first letter to the Corinthians. Paul's discussion here as well as the musical discourse in 1 Samuel sixteen does not mention singing any words. The musical tones that David's *kinnor* produced when he played with his fingers was efficacious without the use of vocal music. The therapeutic effect was produced by the sounds, i.e., the notes produced on the *kinnor*.

1 Corinthians 14:8 is also a discussion of the significance of music alone. "For if the trumpet (*salpigx* 4536) give (*didomi* 1325) an uncertain (*adelos* 82) sound (*phone* 5456) who shall prepare himself to the battle?" Over many centuries this verse has become an esoteric reference to the blowing of the *shofar*, a ram's horn, to give meaning to all members of the ancient Jewish encampment. Again St. Paul referred to meaning that musical sound conveyed to the common man. As I said earlier the musical references to the *aulos* (836), which was a type of flute or pipe, and the *kithara* (2788), which was a hand-held lyre, were used because Paul no doubt knew that the people commonly understood that musical sound conveyed meaning. He also knew that if the musical notes played on the flute and the pipe were not produced accurately, the meaning of the sounds would be altered.

So, Paul considered the example of the blowing of the *shofar* (7782) to be a good reference to explain the importance of musical understanding simply because the blowing of the shofar and its musical meaning would help to prove his point. His audience knew that the shofar was chosen for sounding because of its ability to emit clear sounds. The Greek words *didomi, adelos* and *phone*, which were well translated here in the AV, connote that if the trumpet gave indistinct sounds the meaning of the sound would be uncertain. In this verse, admittedly, the meaning could have been that the association that the distinct sounding had was the issue rather than the message of the musical sounds themselves. It will suffice to say that Paul and his audience respected the meaning of accurately produced notes and that musical sound did have meaning. What is not absolutely clear is whether or not the formal properties of the music had meaning as music alone or how much of the music's meaning was associative.

## Performance Style Makes a Philosophical Statement

When a vocal soloist's performance style allows scooping up to pitches, breathy unvocal sounds, purposefully delayed vibrato (or purposefully no vibrato), the result is without doubt "uncertain" sound. As Dr. Frank Garlock has often taught in his *Symphony of Life Seminar*, breathing heavily into a microphone immediately places the musician in the listener's "intimate zone"— a place that the Christian vocalist does not belong![4] I have taught for years that scooping up to pitches is not a compatible vocal technique with the truth and constantness of the gospel. The way we music unto God sends associative messages to our audience.

When a vocalist initiates pitches that start without the use of vibrato, the sound produced creates two illusions. First, the sound will either be or seem to be under or above the pitch. The initial sound produced will leave the impression on the mind that the sound is not true, constant, or certain. Second, this initialized sound creates undue tension in the sound, because the listener does not have to have an earned doctorate in vocal pedagogy to hear that the sound produced is too tense and not exactly on pitch.

As a voice instructor of many years, I find it hard to concentrate on the spiritual message when I know that the vocalist has placed great tension on the arytenoid and cricoid cartilages that control the vocal folds. (This vocal technique is one of the chief reasons for the development of vocal nodes that often require laser surgery.) The comfort and rest of the message of the gospel should be certain, constant good news and should sound like "good news." Any musical technique that distracts from this message should be avoided by Christian musicians. Many Christian musicians avoid quality vocal performance techniques as if they are ungodly musical practices that will hinder the message of the Gospel.

15: What Do We Do Now that Some Styles Are Here to Stay?   311

## Style can say What the Musician did not Intend to Say

The musical performance style can actually *belie the truth presented by the text of the music. So, juxtaposing Biblical truth with overly tense vocal production above or below the pitch will actually hinder the message of the text. This is not to say that no truth will get past a faulty performance practice. However, it seems odd that Christian musicians encumber the gospel message with these vocal performance practices. It is like trying to remove the lug nuts that hold the tires on your car with a pair of pliers— pliers may help you get your flat tire removed, but they are definitely not the right tool for the job! Garlock and Woetzel have concluded the matter quite well, "Having discovered very early in this book that music is not merely a matter of preference and taste, we must now conclude from the evidence that the style is all-important, not in the world's philosophy of relativism. The style itself reflects and projects a philosophy."[5]

The history of the terminology "rock and roll", which was originally a *euphemism for the act of sexual intercourse, has been borrowed from jazz's (originally unwritten) etymological dictionary of pornographic words. It is of little wonder that this music with a driving incessant propelling directionality has been used as a concomitant to lyric texts that convey a sexual message. No rock musician, except Christian musicians, denies that rock music lends itself to being highly sexual. Secular rock musicians believe that this music sends a strong sexual message and they, of course, do not have any problem with rock's ability to do so.

Religious rock enthusiasts and performers categorically deny that rock has the power to say, represent, convey, transmit, or communicate anything at all. In order to justify the use of rock music alone or with a sacred text, they must subscribe to the "it is benign" theory. The benign theory purports that the music part of all rock music is nonthreatening, harmless and neutral in its effect. It is sort of a kinder, gentler, benevolent, no harm done musical philosophy that leads them to the faulty conclusion that all music is good because it all comes from God. For those Christian musicians who do not believe the "God made all music" theory, a religious humanistic approach works best.

If all religious musicing begins and ends with the musician then it can be considered a benign musical act (without cause and effect) of that autonomous Christian musician. Christian musicians who are trying to develop a congruent Christian music philosophy should understand that many Christians, who are conservative in many areas of their lives, consider the way that contemporary churches music to be an autonomous *adiaphorous form of worship. They really believe that the conflict over contemporary Christian music to be "much ado about nothing."

After I mentioned some performance styles and practices that I considered being offensive, one of my colleagues said to me, "I believe we've already lost that battle." The facts that the contemporary church musics a certain way and that many conservatives are so conditioned by repeatedly hearing these styles of religious music that they no longer oppose them, do not make these styles good choices for sacred musicing.

The "neither good nor bad" notion about religious music has become the slippery slope that has finally led to style and performance practice capitulation. Although his book was on a completely different topic, the title of Thomas Anthony Harris's *I'm OK, You're OK*, the New York Times best seller has been taken out of context in the development of a false notion by the postmodern church. This philosophical fallacy has allowed these musicians to believe a convenient falsehood rather than deal with an obvious truth. This "everything goes" philosophy fits well with the adiaphorous philosophy of contemporary Christian musicians. Many Christians, including a host of Christians who are conservative in many of their beliefs, seem to believe that all the possible ways that religious musicers can possibly music are okay. Simply put, although there are wonderful things happening in sacred music in this century, everything that is happening in church music is not okay!

## Christian Musicing Should Not Be an Autonomous Act

If religious music begins and ends with self, then Christian music is autonomous because, when it comes to music and musicing, all

## 15: What Do We Do Now that Some Styles Are Here to Stay?

music endeavors are acts of free will. Autonomous musicians own all their acts of worship, because autonomous actions are personal offerings that are brought to the worship altar as acts of free will. This philosophical mindset is somewhat complicated, but it is the basis for many church musicians' music praxis.

What is even more complicated is the fact that when a Christian musician owns musical offerings, they are not subject to any musical or worship standards, rules, regulations, or religious dogmas. Often the autonomous musician does not have to have any discussable justification for the inclusion of any type of worship music or religious music praxis.

Steve Peters wrote, "Few want to touch rock 'n' roll because many listen to it and enjoy it at some level."[6] He certainly touched a tender nerve even among conservative Christian musicians. I have traveled extensively in the past forty years, and I can verify that many Christian musicians, who are conservative in many areas of Christian living, are not so conservative when it comes to their personal music choices. Many Christian musicians that I have met in my travels like, listen to, and even perform rock music and its musical cousins at "some level."

If I were Satan, I would tempt conservative Christians to get involved with these styles of music at some mild level. I would first get them to develop a taste for the styles of music that amalgamated to become rock. The younger generation of Christian musicians seem to believe that rock music fell from the sky and that it does not have connections to very close "first cousins" that were very influential in the development of the multiplicity of rock styles that exist today.

David Cloud observed that "the average church member is inundated with rock music and has been inundated all or most of his or her life. Since the 1950's, rock has permeated Western society."[7] If I were Satan, I would develop a very large family of closely related musical style "cousins" and I would get them together somehow for a "family reunion" in the hope that they would stay together and develop a conglomerate of closely related styles. If I were Satan, the reason that I would desire to see this amalgamation or styles develop is that this plethora of styles, techniques, sounds, stereotyped rhythm patterns, clichéd melodic structures, and performance techniques would create an artistic musical conglomerate that would appeal to almost everyone.

## Squeezed into the World's Mold with our Musicing

At this point, if I were Satan, I would weary a great host of Christian musicians into caving in and getting involved, at least partially, with this very complicated musical development. If I were Satan, I would proceed very slowly and carefully with conservative Christian musicians. I would not be credulous enough to believe that I could change their musical tastes quickly. I would probably bypass a generation or two of Christian musicians who have studied music history, theory and literature very carefully. I would most definitely bypass those who had studied the history of church music and music in the Bible.

If I were Satan, I would get conservative Christian musicians so busy that they would not take time to catechize their children musically. I would tempt their children to weary their parents into allowing them to listen and perform these styles of music. Once I had their children hooked on this music, I would tempt the children to become much bolder in their demands to perform more extreme styles of music in Christian schools, Christian colleges and in church. I would know that once these permissive Christians' children were deeply involved with these styles of music that I would have, for all intents and purposes, silenced almost all objections to any form of religious rock-based music. If I were Satan I would not worry about these Christian parents' campaigns about the extremes of secular rock music because I would know that these vocal outbursts about "Satanic" rock music would keep these naïve permissive Christian parents from dealing with the real issue— religious rock-based music.

If I were Satan, while I was working with children of Christian parents I would also be very busy with the general population of Christians who were more unaware musically. I would work most with those who had never been catechized musically by the church or Christian school and had never developed a Christocentric Bible-based music philosophy. If I were Satan, my long-range master plan would be to get all Christians to become involved with rock music at "some level." As I said earlier, I would not start first with actual head-banging rock music, but I would try to get all Christians to involve themselves with rock music's "first cousins." If I was Satan, I would concentrate on Christians getting involved in mainstream country music (the sexy, highly rhythmically controlled type), jazz, techno pop music, reggae, ska, etc. The reason I would concentrate on the multitude of "first cousin styles" is that these styles of music are a major part of rock music's current amalgamation. As soon as they were hooked on these styles, I would have effectively silenced almost all the objections to these styles of religious music from Christians. By this time many Christians who were performing and listening to all the styles of music mentioned above would pride themselves in the fact they were not performing and listening to anything that was spiritually offensive.

**An Irresistible Connection to Rock Music**

If I were Satan, I would know that after I had beguiled Christians into getting deeply involved in these *fusion styles, they would develop an irresistible connection to rock music (and its closely related musical cousins). I would also be aware that this connection would be evidenced by personal taste since this complicated mixture music contains sounds and rhythmic patterns, etc. that Christians have previously learned to like. Now, I would know that they were hooked on these sounds so thoroughly that they would be at a point of no return. If I were Satan, I would know that with this accomplishment I had basically won the battle for rock and fusion music addiction.

At this point in our discussion one may be somewhat upset and angry. One of two things may have caused this anger. First, this anger may have been caused because the Holy Spirit has located a musician's musical addiction. Second, it is upsetting to realize how effective Satan's musical stratagems have been during the late twentieth century and now at the beginning or the twenty-first century.

Although young people have been affected by the music part of music, most writers of the past thirty or forty years have concerned themselves with the lyrics of rock and fusion, and the involved and complicated plethora of opinions about the secular vs.

religious music dichotomy. These discussions of the secular vs. religious music dichotomy have been necessary because there are some subtle differences between religious and secular rock music. However, only a few writers and Christian music philosophers have had the courage to tackle the profound influence of the music part of rock and fusion music.

Lowell Hart's statement about young people who only understand rock music caught my attention: "The Christian young person who is caught in this trap and refuses to listen to other music because he doesn't like it or it makes him 'nervous' is very much like the alcoholic who is addicted to the bottle. The teenager is actually addicted to the enticing sounds of rock and does not wish to change."[8] Hart was astute and bold enough to recognize that it is the fascinating, intriguing, and enticing qualities of rock's sounds and rhythms that are the most addictive parts of rock music. One may draw the same conclusion about several styles of fusion music.

**Addicted to the Elements and Themes of Rock**

Those who had the greatest understanding of rock music from its inception were in many instances those who were a part of the lifestyle of illicit sex, violence, drugs, and lawlessness. It is equally unfortunate that many rock enthusiasts enjoyed and still enjoy lyrics that degrade and treat women as sex objects. However, it is the incessant forward propelling directionality of the music part of the music that is perhaps the most addictive element of this incredibly powerful art form. Hart made an insightful analogy of the addicted alcoholic and the addicted listener. One may reject the analogous comparison of musical style addiction to the power of alcohol addiction, but it is real. The alcoholic is almost always unable to quit by his or her own power. The same is true of the rock enthusiast. This incredible fascination and addiction most often renders the rock enthusiast incapable of breaking this sound and rhythmic and lifestyle addiction.

Rock music's ability to cause sound and rhythmic addiction blocks many rock enthusiasts' ability to explore and appreciate other musics. This condition is, however, not without exception because some rock enthusiasts enjoy a multiplicity of the fine arts. That exception being noted, sound addiction to rock music can and will often block one's "other arts" exploration and enjoyment. Although the removal of rock music from a new Christian's life may and will, in many instances, create a vacuum, it is necessary if a new Christian is going to, as Ephesians 4:23 teaches, be renewed by the renewing of the mind. This vacuum may be filled with many other styles of music that are not harmful to the whole life of this new Christian.

Some new Christians find that they have brought from their past a state of physiological and psychological dependence on rock music and are unable to break from its power. However, the born-again Christian becomes a "new man" in Christ Jesus and is given the power to break musical addiction. 2 Corinthians 5:17 teaches, "Therefore if any man be in Christ, he is a new creature: old things are passed away; behold, all things are become new." The sixth chapter of Romans identifies the born-again Christian as one who has put off the "old man." Furthermore, Colossians 3:10 states, "And have put on the new man, which is renewed in knowledge after the image of him that created him." Psalm 40:2 also teaches that those who have been brought out of the pit of sin (which the Cambridge AV margin calls "a pit of noise") will sing a "new song", i.e., a song of renovated and higher character. So, the Bible supports the philosophical concept that born-again Christians make changes in the way that they live and the way they music by renewing their mind with "new song."

## What Do We Do Now that Rock Won't Go Away?

Much has been written in the past twenty-five years about the fact that conservative Christian musicians stubbornly resist change in religious music. It should be emphasized that rock music enthusiasts are also very adamant about not accepting any changes in the music that they like and understand, and that rock— and perhaps rock's musical "cousins" — are often the only music styles they understand and enjoy. So, it is of little wonder that they are at loggerheads with each other about religious music. It has been said that during the last half of the twentieth century music has split and splintered more churches than theological beliefs. Worship music, which is supposed to draw the congregation together in Christian love in order that they might corporately worship our wonderful triune God, has instead become the war department.

Early in this discussion of music styles I mentioned that rock-based music is not going to go away. Churches that have split and splintered into inner-church musical sub-cultures are not going to wake up some Sunday morning and all meet in the sanctuary and sing out of the hymnbook. There will be no supposed future worship utopia in which a formerly bitterly divided congregation will suddenly see eye to eye philosophically about music. As a result of unreconciled music philosophies this divided church will probably continue to have part of the congregation in the gymnasium banging out ear-splitting sounds that are supposed to represent true worship renewal, while a second part of the congregation is in the cafetorium swinging and swaying with Sammy Kaye, and finally the separate but equal third part of the trilogy of worshipers is in the sanctuary singing hymns and praise choruses.

## What is the Answer to the Worship Music Dilemma?

What is the answer to this worship dilemma? There is no easy solution to such a plethora of worship confusion. Once a church fellowship is led into such a mess by "leadershift" philosophy that erroneously supposes that the church must *pander to everyone's musical tastes, that fellowship of believers is permanently divided by music styles. Unless the church is financially able to keep building little sanctuaries to accommodate each new musical clique that can exert enough power to demand its own style of worship experience, this diversity praxis is a dead end street. What will most often happen is that those who yell the loudest will win the argument and traditional worshipers will slink into the shadows.

It has never been easy for a church's pastor and board of stewards to make the leadership direction decisions that are absolutely necessary to prevent constant leadershift confusion that would keep the church's purposes from being fulfilled. I am not credulous enough to believe that all fellowships of believers are going to draw the musical lines in the same place. However, as I have often stated in my writings, it isn't the fact that all Christian churches do not draw all the musical lines in exactly the same places that is most bothersome, but it is the fact that so many churches are no longer drawing any musical lines in the proverbial sands of time. Philosophically speaking, all Christian musicians must remember that direction determines destiny. If we continually go in the wrong direction musically we can, without doubt, be responsible for debouching public music worship.

Christian musicians should remember that it was the advent of attaching religious words to rock music that brought on the music division that has separated the church's unity of worship. It was also rock music's first cousins that contained the same common musical dependence on rhythm, repetition and extreme decibels that helped to bring the irreconcilable differences that have permanently divided many fellowships of believers. The current generation of church musicians who will oversee the direction that church music is going to take in the future need to remember that it was the advent of rock that brought on the multiplicity of church music worship wars. Many church musicians are too young to remember what church music was like before the advent of rock music and *ipso facto* how the worship wars ensued. Although young people were blamed for the drastic music changes that formed the basis for the worship wars in church music that began in the 1970s and 1980s, it was blind leadershift among pastors, church boards, and worship leaders that actually encouraged the worship wars.

### What do We do About the Worship Wars?

At this point in time, there is little that one can do to try to undo all the trouble and hard feelings that have arisen from the music styles worship wars. There is nothing productive that can come about as a result of laying blame to those who have been involved in the worship wars over the recent decades. What I am trying to do with this philosophical discussion is to admonish all those involved who are ministers of music in traditional churches to proceed with much caution. It is much easier to divide a congregation philosophically than it is to try to pull them back together after the damage has been done.

Before you treat everything that has been traditionally included in churches for the past 100 years with complete contempt, please study the history of church music very thoroughly and also study music in the Bible very carefully. This intense study will reveal to you what has historically fueled the fires of public music worship and music evangelism. It will also reveal what the Bible says about worshiping God with music.

Young musicians should recognize that it is just as nearsighted to make a wholesale condemnation of all gospel songs and hymns as it is for a traditionalist to make the same condemnation of all new worship music. The solution involves two things— utilizing the best of the old and the new, and rejecting the use of the trite, shallow, and banal music of both new and old church music. Blended music worship goes far beyond being politically correct. It is the result of the utilization of good music and worship common sense. To ignore the quality and depth of musical works like those of Getty is just as nearsighted as omitting the hymns of Watts and Wesley or the gospel songs of Fanny Crosby.

### Is it Possible to Keep Worshipers United?

If you want to know how hard it will be to ever reunite your congregation after you separate them over music, take a feather pillow up on the roof of the church and scatter the feathers over the church yard and then go pick them up again. The best way to keep styles of music such as rock, reggae, and rap music out of the sanctuary is to remove the need for them. Many churches have let worship music become routine (rutual) and in doing so it has become stagnant and very uninteresting. If a worship leader loses passion for traditional church music, the spiritual fervor dies and worship musicing is performed mechanically. There is a myriad of reasons why a music director's musicing may become routine and passionless. I would love to discuss spiritual and musical burnout at some future date, but this is a philosophical discussion rather than a "how to" discussion.

It is not the slightest bit surprising that so many Christian fellowships have become disillusioned with traditional church music. When the minister of music's demeanor shows that there is little or no understanding of the worship music being led, the people in the sanctuary will lose interest in it very quickly. The only way for a worship leader to draw others into spiritual music worship is to lead with "Spirit and understanding" (see 1 Corinthians 14:15).

Church musicians who are trying to music unto God and are devoid of the aforementioned two essential elements (the fullness of the Spirit and understanding) are bound to fail in their attempts to have an efficacious ministry. It has been said that we cannot effectively teach what we do not know and understand. The same is true concerning worship music.

Sometimes ministers of music have forgotten that there is an Ephesians 5:18 before the famous Ephesians 5:19. No amount of education, talent, energy or charisma can replace the *dunamis* (1411—Romans 15:19) of the blessed Holy Spirit. There is a vast difference between a musician who leads music sequences about Christ and an anointed musician who has a personal relationship with Christ and is living a life in the Spirit (see Ephesians 5:19). I have often told my conducting classes that enthusiasm is no substitute for the anointing of the blessed Holy Spirit. Also, trying to lead the great historic hymns, gospel hymns, and gospel songs without any research knowledge will almost always insure that performing them will result in failure.

### Understanding Imagery and Art Forms

I also want to add that studying the imagery of any lyric poem is absolutely necessary before public performance is attempted. It does not matter if the song or chorus is ancient, old, fairly old, or if it was written this year. Music leadership without understanding of the mental imagery is an almost sure formula for failure. When I observe worship leaders trying to lead a contemporary worship chorus sequence, I often notice the same evidences of a lack of understanding of the mental images in the music that I notice when they try to lead a hymn.

Some conservative Christian musicians have rejected a style of music based on one or more of the following presuppositions: it is not really music, it is not an art form, or it is not a quality art form. In order for a Christian musician to make such judgments, careful musical analysis of the formal properties of the music must be made.

Although many styles of popular music have been composed and performed by musical groups who were not very skilled or musical, this observation certainly does not encompass the whole of every popular music genre. The same could be said of a host of traditional church musicians that have composed traditional church music. So, the justification for the inclusion or exclusion of a style of music as religious music cannot be logically based on whether or not it is a high-quality art form.

Although I have always rejected all forms of rock music as sacred music, I have never made the mistake of believing or purporting that it was or now is an inferior art form. Since the advent of rock 'n' roll in the 1950s, there has been both well written and poorly composed music among the plethora of styles of music that later *amalgamated to become rock music as we now know it. Since that time rock has had more than a half century to "grow up" as a musical art form.

Although it is very difficult to even develop an accurate definition of this huge conglomeration we understand to be rock music, it is a truism that rock is serious art form. Furthermore, it is a serious philosophical and musical mistake for conservative Christian musicians to lump all of rock music under a "musical junk" classification and reject it as sacred music on such an unfounded basis.

Art, and particularly music as an art form, is not the doorway to the Kingdom of God. The Christian musician must always be *cognizant of the fact that Christian worship is never about art. In other words, in our worship of the triune God we utilize art forms, but Christians never worship art (the created thing). The New Testament in Romans 1:25 warns us not to worship the creature (*ktisis*- 2937-the created thing) but rather the Creator (*ktizo*-2932-the Creator). Therefore, it is a philosophical fallacy to accept or reject a musical art form for use in Christian musical worship solely on the basis of its being a high or low quality musical art form.

Christian musicians who only use traditional forms of Western music should be cautioned that rejecting musical styles music be-

## 15: What Do We Do Now that Some Styles Are Here to Stay?

cause one believes that they are not a quality art forms opens that musician up to legitimate musical and philosophical criticisms. This is a faulty premise, because much of traditional church music is certainly not high quality musical art. Many time-honored traditional musical compositions are very simply composed with only a few chord progressions repeated over and over again. These compositions are often very predictable and do not provide many musical surprises or intricate musical nuances for the performer and auditor. So, the philosophical and musical basis for rejecting any music must be predicated on other criteria than quality musical art forms.

### Understanding the Music Genres We Perform

Remember that a worship music philosophy should be a series of systematic statements (beliefs) concerning the *nature* and *value* of the whole of the music. These systematic beliefs must include a thorough understanding of the music's essential nature, i.e., what makes the music part of the music what it is. This underlying set of beliefs must also include an understanding of the formal properties of the music and how they influence the meaning and message of the music, i.e., what it actually does or says or how it influences the performer and auditor.

A worship music philosophy must also very clearly provide a systematic understanding of the value of this music to the worship experience and what it can do to the whole-life of the performer and worshiper. To deny that religious music does something to the worshiper is naïve and short-sighted. Any style of music should be carefully scrutinized for its ability to affect the whole-life of the performer and auditor in a positive or negative spiritual manner. All musics have the ability to affect change in the whole-life of the worshiper. The amount and quality of the positive influence of the music part of the music will determine whether it is a poor, mediocre or quality vehicle and concomitant of a sacred text.

Now back to what rock music is. It is an art form and it is a very effective art form, but it is not an effective vehicle or concomitant to the gospel of our Lord and Savior Jesus Christ. Its driving incessant beat is not a proper vehicle to represent the essential moral nature of

God because rock's essential nature appeals to the flesh rather than to the spirit. Frank Zappa said as far back as 1968 that "Rock music is sex. The big beat matches the body's rhythms."[9] Gene Simmons once explained while on the *Entertainment Tonight Show* in December of 1987, "That's what rock is all about— sex with a 100 megaton bomb, the beat!" I could quote a multitude of famous rock musicians who have concurred with Zappa and Simmons, but I will not do so in the interest of time and space in the context of this book on music philosophy. Rock music is a very powerful and effective art form. It has accomplished what it was intended to accomplish over the decades since the 1960s. It appears that it is only Christian musicians who incessantly deny that rock is synonymous with a culture of lawlessness.

### Endnotes

1. Richard S. Taylor, *A Return to Christian Culture*, 90.
2. Robert Berglund, *A Philosophy of Church Music* , 8.
3. Richard S. Taylor, *A Return to Christian Culture,* 66.
4. I attended this seminar at Merriam Christian School, Merriam Kansas.
5. Frank Garlock & Kurt Woetzel, *Music in the Balance*, (Greenville, SC: Majesty Music, Inc., 1992), 99-100.
6. Steve Peters, *Truth about Rock*, 82.
7. David W. Cloud, *Contemporary Christian Music in the Spotlight,* (Port Huron, MI: Way of Life Literature, 1998),11.
8. Lowell Hart, *Satan's Music Exposed,* (Huntingdon Valley, PA: Salem Kirban, Inc., 1991),144-145.
9. Frank Zappa, "The Oracle Has It All Psyched Out," *Life Magazine* 64 no. 26 (June 28, 1968): 82-86, 88, 91.

### Chapter Fifteen Word Meanings

**Adiaphorous**— indifferent or neutral, i.e., neither right nor wrong or beneficial or harmful.

**Amalgamated**— as used here it refers to music styles that have been blended or combined to form a fusion or recognizable structure (genre).

**Belie— fail to give a true notion or impression of something so as to disguise or contradict it.**

## 15: What Do We Do Now that Some Styles Are Here to Stay? 325

**Cognizant**— having knowledge or being aware of something.

**Euphemism**— a mild or indirect word or expression substituted for one considered to be too harsh or blunt when referring to something embarrassing.

**Fusion**— the combination of two or more styles of music that produces a music that tends to be a synthetic or electronic combination of dance styles. This alternative music is easy to dance to and includes styles like, but not limited to, tango, blues, soul, disco, jazz, pop, lyrical or rhythmic electronica.

### Chapter Fifteen Questions for Discussion

1. Discuss the problems involved with selecting styles of music to be used in worship based on the concept of "market share."
2. Why do you believe St. Paul used a musical example in his discussion in 1 Corinthians 14:7?
3. Discuss why a Christian musician may be convinced by another's arguments that a style of music is not philosophically the best music to use to worship God, and yet that musician may continue to perform that music.
4. Why is it impossible to successfully discuss the necessity of having a Bible-based music philosophy and praxis with a musician who considers that musicing is an autonomous procedure?
5. Discuss why a musical performance style can actually belie the truth presented by the text of the music.
6. Discuss why it is that if religious music begins and ends with self then this musicing is an autonomous act, and why musicing as an autonomous act does not follow biblical principles of musicing unto God.
7. Discuss why so many religious rock enthusiasts and performers categorically deny that the music part of rock music has the power to say, represent, convey, transmit, or communicate anything at all.
8. Discuss why it is just as nearsighted for one to make a wholesale condemnation all gospel songs and hymns as it is for a traditionalist to make the same condemnation of all new worship music.
9. Discuss why you do or do not believe that rock music is an art form and how this affects your position on its use or disuse as worship music.
10. Why must a worship music philosophy very clearly provide a systematic understanding of the value of this music to the worship experience and what it does to the whole-life of the performer and worshiper?

# 16

# How Should We Then Music?

## What Should the Music Leader Do?

A PERSON WHO STANDS IN FRONT of a congregation (or a musical organization) of people who wish to worship God by musicing unto Him should determine a specific purpose and plan of action (praxis). Many worship leaders I have observed over the years that I have traveled have had only a vague understanding of what they were supposed to do (both in and out of the worship experience) in order that their musicing and the musicing of those under their leadership could be effectual.

There are a variety of names for this person who is standing in front of the people. Is this person a minister of music, a worship leader, a music director, a conductor, a chief musician, a song leader, a musician, not a musician at all, or most of the above? Those who were responsible for placing this person in front should first decide what they expect that person to do. Giving this person a specific or not-so-specific name is part of the philosophical process but it is by far not all of it.

I understand this music person (Homo sapiens) to be a bipedal primate that has two arms and hands (quite useful for conducting functions); language skills (for communicating with the worshiping congregation or music organization); the ability to use complex tools (like a baton); and also having at least a reasonable amount of brain power (quite useful in the process of music leadership). So, this musician has sight, all these moving appendages, and brain power that are all capable of functioning in tandem to effectively enhance musicing, and should be able to figure out how to effectively go about doing what the job of music leadership requires.

I fail to understand why church leaders, educational administrators and the musicians involved often seem to have so much trouble understanding that regardless of which name you give this person, there is much more involved in doing this job effectively than standing on a platform looking upward (with the eyes closed) while singing and pointing at things that no one else can see, or standing in the background mouthing words while watching a praise team perform his or her music leadership responsibilities. There is no objection to leadership calling this person a worship leader or music director if everyone involved in leadership, the musician included, understands that the term "worship leader" or "music director" only philosophically touches the tip of the proverbial iceberg. Personally, I prefer the title of Minister of Music or the Bible name Chief Musician, since they both more accurately connote the philosophical responsibility of this person.

There is absolutely no philosophical problem with the use of a praise team as long as they function as music worship leaders, are dressed modestly, and do not usurp the role of the chief musician. This is not to intimate that leading music worship or a musical organization is not extremely important to public worship because it most certainly is. At the same time, the use of music in public worship, although vitally important to the work and responsibility of every public ministry, is only part of the work of that organization's music ministry. Because of the time and space it would take, I will not discuss thoroughly the other very important aspects of public worship philosophy at this point in our discussion. For a more thorough discussion of this topic, I suggest that you read chapter two (pp. 28-37) of the book *Church Music Matters*.

Church leaders, educational administrations, and the musicians involved must realize that the music educator and the minister of music have many more philosophical responsibilities than those involved in worship service leadership. Many Christian organizations are trying to travel first class but are only paying coach fare. Many Christian elementary and secondary schools as well as Christian colleges are not preparing their students to enter adulthood with the necessary musical literacy, i.e., being able to read, write, perform, and evaluate music. Churches have also abdicated their historic and biblical responsibility to musically and philosophically educate their own (read 1 Chronicles chapter twenty-five). In ancient Israel the church trained its own musicians. So, public music worship leadership is vitally important, but it is only the part of the music iceberg that one can readily see. However, it is the part beneath the surface which one cannot readily see that gives the music ministry its real substance.

## Philosophical Justifications for "Doing"

A Christian musician often musics in a certain manner simply because of personal musical and spiritual instincts or because of musical traditions established by others. However, musicing by accident can be a risky policy. A worship leader and a music educator must be able to articulate reasons for performance and teaching choices. It is better for one not to teach others than to teach them in a willy-nilly manner because the *onus probandi falls on the one who attempts to teach (Matthew 18:6, Mark 9:42, Luke 17:2).

Although the Bible gives us principles of musicing unto God, it does not cover every aspect of music that concerns the twenty-first century Christian musician. So, every performer, music director, and music educator must, in the fear of God, interpret and apply principles taught in Scripture. Furthermore, performers, directors, worship leaders, and music educators must also come to philosophical conclusions about aspects of music that do not appear to be covered by Scripture. With this in mind, I have covered several aspects of music which are vital to a Christian's musicing in the twenty-first century. The NIV translates Isaiah 28:10 as, "For it is: Do and do, do and do, rule on rule, a little here, a little there." The translation above makes sense in the context of understanding how we music. We "do" over and over again until we are conditioned to do what we do musically. As a result, we develop musical tastes—likes and dislikes— from what we listen to and perform.

## Why Should we Use a Song Book with Written Musical Notation?

Many church music worship leaders can think of several reasons to *jettison the "Song Book." They include: it costs too much money; the new families (with children whom some people think should be in children's church) let their kids write in it; it weighs a proverbial ton; it has too many selections in it; it has outdated gospel songs in it; the congregation will want to "shop" for new stuff (we only use about two dozen of the hymns and, of course, all of the praise choruses and three of the gospel songs— we sing those for Grandma Jones); the newest praise choruses are not in it; it also has a type of song in it called a "gospel hymn" that no one but people over sixty-five can understand.

Contemporary praise leaders also do not seem to understand songs about the "shed blood of Jesus" and gospel songs like, "Are You Living Where God Answers Prayer?" These music leaders believe that the types of songs mentioned above make seekers uncomfortable. They also do not seem to understand why a twenty-first century church would benefit from singing the hymns that are translated from Latin since everyone knows that Latin is a dead language. Unfortunately, these worship leaders read in worship renewal books that seekers cannot understand most of the hymns and gospel songs in published hymn books. They also have been made to believe the notion that no one likes or connects with hymns and gospel songs anymore. They also believe most of the songs in hymn books have too many words in them.

Now, let us discuss the rest of the story about hymn books. I have traveled some in Europe and have noticed that many of their congregational song books do not have printed music in them. I have also noticed that although the people usually participate wholeheartedly in congregational singing, most of them sing only the melody. When I am in Europe I miss hearing a worshiping congregation singing parts because my logical German mind desires to experience the congregation singing the harmonies that the musical instruments are playing when we sing.

Not all people who hear a part are capable of reading music. One reason they can hear a part, i.e., audiate it without having music reading skills is simply that they grew up hearing others, who could read the parts in the hymn book, sing parts during the worship service. If hymn books do not contain written music, congregations are not encouraged to sing parts. When congregations do not sing parts, the next generation of worshipers probably will probably not sing parts. So within a generation or two a fellowship of believers will doubtlessly have lost most of their propensity to sing parts. It is not necessary for a congregation of believers to sing parts during musical worship, but losing the ability to do so will certainly impoverish public musical worship.

Over many centuries, the church has been responsible to train its own to sing parts. Is it necessary for the congregation to sing parts? No, it is not a matter of necessity. It is a matter of giving a more beautiful and excellent response to the God who created harmony. Psalm 33:1 and 147:1 both say that praise is comely. In both verses the AV translated the word comely from the Hebrew word *naveh* (5000) which means, among other things, suitable or beautiful.

If the church does not provide written music for the congregation, there will be less and less part singing when the congregation sings together. Unless children are involved in an excellent choral music reading program in school or they grow up singing parts in church, it will be difficult for them to learn a part when singing in a small group or in a choir. There is more truth in the sayings "doing requires knowing" and "use it or lose it." Such a decline in the quality of musical offerings in churches and schools will contribute to the dumbing down of sacred musicing.

### Why Should we Sing Praise Choruses?

The Old Testament is full of references to singing praise unto God. There are so many references (at least thirty-one) that command us to sing praises unto the Lord that I will not list all of them here. Many of these Scriptures refer specifically to singing praises unto God. However, these verses do not specifically command believers to sing praise choruses. The words *sing praises* have been translated from the Hebrew word *zamar* (2167) which primarily means to touch the parts of a stringed instrument. However, many translations have used the word *praises* in their exegetical rendering of this word. This word most properly refers not only to playing an instrument but also to praising God as one sings psalms.

## 16: How Should We Then Music? 331

Many of us who worship by musicing unto God week after week appreciate a new worship chorus that has meaningful words set to a new artistically composed melody. The two operative words here are *meaningful* and *artistic*. Either of these without the other will produces a less than desirable result in worship. There have been many articles written about the value or lack of value of modern praise choruses for public worship. These writings have stirred up some controversy, but they have caused Christian musicians to give much needed thought about the selection and utilization of praise choruses in public worship. It is most certainly the responsibility of the music worship leader to use quality praise choruses that are both theologically accurate and musically meaningful.

Nick Page recounted an occasion of having new people in the worship service that did not understand the religious imagery of the worship songs the church was singing. He remembered that "...as we sang songs about two-edged swords and anointing oil and lots and lots of sheep, we also showed them that, when it comes to song lyrics, Christians speak an entirely different language."[1] One of the reasons we sing praise choruses is that there is general belief that they are understandable to new people. If they are not, then we need to find worship choruses that use understandable imagery.

The minister of music should be aware of those who will be singing the music. If the congregation is familiar with the meaning of the song texts, there is no reason to change all the worship choruses just because they do not use twenty-first century urban imagery. Also, the song leader can explain the meaning of unfamiliar words in the praise choruses to the congregation. This explanation does not have to include a developed *homily of dignity and length. On second thought, we can deal with the dignity part; it is the length part that tends to interrupt the flow of meaning of the sequence of songs in public worship.

We should sing praise choruses because, although the Bible does not command us to sing choruses, it does command us to sing praises because they are a valid way for Christians to respond to God when they sing. New worship music can provide the church with fresh new expressions of worship. They can bring spiritual understanding to both saint and sinner. Thinking biblically, we should sing praise choruses because "Praise is comely (*naveh* 5000, i.e., pleasant and suitable) for the upright" (Psalm 33:1).

## Why Should we Sing Hymns?

God's people do not sing time-honored hymns because they are old but rather because they are a great source of spiritual truth. They bring to the worship service a depth of understanding that other forms of worship music do not always bring. Worship music with only a few words sung over and over to remind us of some attribute of one or all of the persons of the Trinity may be proper for worship, but they sometimes leave the worshiper dangling because of their lack of completeness of content. By the very fact that hymns are versified, they often are much more thorough in their ability to explain one or more attributes of God.

The great hymns are deeply cerebral. They follow a line of theology or spiritual concepts that causes us to truly "muse" as we sing unto God. The fact that we say they are cerebral is not an indictment of any other genre of worship music. It is simply the truth that when this amount of well-organized text is exposed, the spiritual and doctrinal concepts expressed in hymns are easier to effectively communicate to the worshipers. The great hymns of the church bring to musicing what expository preaching brings to sermonizing.

Another important reason for singing hymns is that Jesus considered hymn singing to be important! Matthew 26:30 and Mark 14:26 both state, "And when they had sung an hymn (*humneo* 5214) they went out into the Mount of Olives." Hebrews 2:12 quotes Jesus as saying, "...I will declare thy name unto my brethren, in the midst of the church will I sing praise (*humneo*) unto thee." We can see from these verses that Jesus considered it important to hymn (*humneo*) with His disciples and in the church (*ekklesia*- 1577). Bible exegetes may argue all day and night about what genre of music Jesus sang, but the fact remains that Jesus considered hymning to be important enough to perform this act of worship himself. In Acts 16:25 the two great patriarchs also chose to sing praises, i.e., hymns unto God: "And at midnight, Paul and

## 16: How Should We Then Music? 333

Silas prayed, and sang praises (*humneo* 5214) unto God: and the prisoners heard them."

There are those Bible expositors who would quote scholarly writings and even the works of the early Church Fathers that Jesus and His disciples sang a psalm from the *Hallel rather than a hymn. On that point, even the Church Fathers do not quote anyone who was there with Jesus on that occasion as saying that they sang a psalm before they went out to the Mount of Olives. Two of the disciples who were there said that they sang a hymn. St. Matthew recorded in 26:30, "And when they had sung an hymn (*humneo* 5214), they went out into the mount of Olives." St. Mark stated in 14:26, "And when they had sung an hymn (*humneo* 5214), they went out into the mount of Olives." It is commonly understood that *humneo* means to hymn or sing a religious ode. Also, it is certain that both Matthew and Mark knew about the three categories of sacred music called *psalmos* (5568), *humnos* (5215), and *pneumatikos oide* (4152, 5603).

Therefore, if they did sing a psalm from the Hallel (Psalms 113-118) or sang the Great Hallel (Psalm 136), why didn't either of them identify the psalm or at least use the word *psalmos* in their respective Gospels? So, no one who was there clearly ruled out the possibility that the disciples hymned together with Jesus. On the contrary, both Matthew and Mark used the Greek word *humneo* which is now seemingly an esoteric term. Furthermore, since no one ancient or modern who was not there has written from the authority of quoting those who were there, we should not definitely rule out the possibility that they actually sang a classification of religious ode together called *humnos* that was distinctly different from *psalmos*. Although no one knows exactly what the terms *humnos* and *humneo* mean, it is very probable that they represent songs of laudation to God that are separate from the psalms of the Bible.

So, the hymn singing church should take heart because it is performing an act of worship that is an ancient landmark of the Christian faith. If Jesus considered it important to sing hymns with His disciples, then it is still a valid way to sing praises unto Him today. Many modern day Christians consider hymning unto God to be an outdated expression of worship. However, cheer up when you sing hymns; you are historically and philosophically in good company. You are worshiping with music the way that Jesus worshiped.

## Why Should we Sing Gospel Songs?

The message of the gospel of Jesus Christ is "good news." All Christians desire to share this good news through their musicing. The gospel of our triune God is much broader in scope than what we are able to express in our praise music. Gospel songs allow a fellowship of believers to share many diverse aspects of full salvation by faith. These songs are very positive songs that tell not only who God is but what He has done for sinful men and women in the past, and what He will do for them now, and what He can do for the seeker now and in the future.

Praise is the Christian's response to God, i.e., thanks, adoration, and love for the Trinity— it is what a worshiper does in response to what God has done for him. Gospel songs explain very vividly what God has done and what He is doing. My soul is blessed when I think about the difference between Christianity and the other world religions. Christianity's God is alive and is doing because He is not merely a god who was, but on the authority of His word, He declares, "I AM THAT I AM." It is no wonder that Christians want to brag on this God who is alive and well and is doing by singing gospel songs about Him. Psalm 34:2 states, "My soul shall make her boast (*halal*-1984) in the LORD: the humble (*anav* 6035), i.e., the depressed in mind) shall hear *thereof,* and be glad."

When Christians brag on the Savior it is not only good news to Christians but it is also good news to those who do not know the Lord. One of the most positive things that a congregation of believers can do musically is to tell the good news of what God has done for them individually. Although worship is not about us but rather our Savior, salvation is about what God has done for us individually. This salvation is a personal "know so" salvation, because as Romans 8:16 teaches, "The Spirit itself beareth witness with our spirit, that we are the children of God." Salvation does not mean very much to us until we as individuals have become partakers of the divine nature, as explained in 2 Peter 1:4, "Whereby are given unto us exceeding great and precious promises: that by these ye might be partakers of the divine nature, having escaped the corruption that is in the world through lust."

One of the wonderful things about musicing unto God through personal testimony presented in gospel songs is that our being excited about singing the good news through gospel songs is in no way a put-down of praise music, hymn singing or Psalm singing. Our God is so awesome that the diversity of musics mentioned above helps us to fully express the awesomeness, solemnity, wonder, and majesty to the Triune God.

If you will remember, Ephesians 5:19 mentions, "Speaking to yourselves in psalms (*psalmos*-5568) and hymns (*humnos*-5215) and spiritual (*pneumatikos*-4152) songs *(ode* -5603), singing and making melody in your hearts to the Lord:" Although we do not know with certainty what the *pneumatikos oide* were like, they may have been somewhat like our gospel songs. Also, note that verse nineteen also reminds those who make melody that our musicing unto the Lord should be done in the presence of others.

Therefore, the Christian's musicing takes on a multi-directional communication that includes musicing unto God and musicing to others at the same time. For this reason the gospel song enables the singer to praise God and tell others about His goodness and saving power at the same time. Colossians 3:16 also reminds Christian musicians to "Let the word of Christ dwell in you richly in all wisdom; teaching and admonishing one another in psalms and hymns and spiritual songs, singing with grace in your hearts to the Lord." Those who believe that all public "worship", "worship events" (or whatever it is now politically correct to call the gatherings of Christians and seekers on Sunday morning) are for the exclusive purpose of singing praise sequences, need to take a serious look at what the Bible teaches in Ephesians 5:19 and Colossians 3:16 about the public musicing of Christians who gather to gather to sing unto God and seekers who attend these services.

Those who believe that the scripturally accurate gospel songs cannot relate to moderns, postmoderns, post-postmodern, young people and seekers are testifying that they do not believe that the good news of the gospel of our Lord and Savior Jesus Christ is still relevant and "quick and powerful" (Hebrews 4:12). Nor do they believe, as Psalm 100:5 declares, "For the LORD is good; his mercy is everlasting; and his truth endureth to all generations." Also, those who believe that the demands of Scripture that are accurately taught in gospel songs are too offensive and too confrontational for the un-churched seeker are confessing that they are ashamed of the many truths taught in the Bible that are so succinctly presented in gospel music.

One of the reasons that the New Testament church thrived spiritually was that, like St. Paul (Romans 1:16), they were not ashamed of the gospel of Jesus Christ. The twenty-first century church should think long and hard about following a music praxis that denies the use of the gospel presented through well-written, scripturally accurate gospel songs.

## Why Should we Sing Psalms?

Without doubt the most important reason that we should sing psalms is that the Bible very clearly instructs us to sing psalms. It is amazing that many Christian musicians completely disregard this Bible command. The Bible does not leave psalm singing completely up to those who feel like it, but rather it commands us to sing psalms unto God. 1 Chronicles 16:9 states, "Sing unto him, sing psalms unto him, talk ye of all his wondrous works." Psalm 105:2 repeats the command, "Sing unto him, sing psalms unto him, talk ye of all his wondrous works."

James 5:13 also teaches very clearly, "Is any among you afflicted? Let him pray. Is any merry? Let him sing psalms." I suppose those who completely ignore psalm singing may only legitimately do so if they are afflicted and are not happy in the Lord. So, the Old and New Testaments both mandate very clearly that we are to sing the psalms unto God.

Ephesians 5:19 continues the mandate to sing the psalms as well as other genres:. "Speaking to yourselves in psalms and hymns and spiritual songs, singing and making melody in your heart to the Lord." Colossians 3:16 continues this teaching: "Let the word of Christ dwell in you richly in all wisdom; teaching and admonishing one another in psalms and hymns and spiritual songs, singing with grace in your hearts to the Lord."

Another reason that we are instructed in Scripture to sing the psalms is that they give Christian musicians the wonderful opportunity to teach (*didasko* 1321) and to admonish (*noutheteo* 3560). The Bible puts a premium on sacred musicing being a vehicle for teaching and learning by gentle admonition and warning. Psalm singing is not the only type of musicing that gives the aforementioned opportunities, but it is definitely one of the ways of teaching the doctrines taught in the Bible.

### Why Should we Sing Songs that "Sting"?

You are probably wondering from the title what the word "sting" has to do with singing sacred music. Probably the best way to explain what I mean is to quote a song from the Bible which we know was written under the inspiration of the Holy Spirit. In Deuteronomy 31:19 God instructed Moses, "Now write ye this song for you, and teach it [to] the children of Israel: put it in their mouths, that this song may be a witness for me against the Children of Israel." Verse 22 records, "Moses therefore wrote this song the same day, and taught it [to] the children of Israel." Verse 30 states, "And Moses spake in the ears of all the congregation of Israel the words of this song, until they were ended." Various portions of the text of this song are as follows:

> Give ear, O ye heavens, and I will speak;
> And hear, O earth, the words of my mouth.
> My doctrine shall drop as the rain,
> My speech shall distill as the dew,
> As the as the small rain upon the tender herb,
> And as the showers upon the grass...
> But Jeshrum waxed fat, and kicked:
> Thou art waxen fat, thou art grown thick,
> Thou art covered *with fatness*;
> Then he forsook God *which* made him,
> and lightly esteemed the Rock of his salvation.
> ...For the LORD will judge his people,
> And repent himself for his servants;
> When he seeth that *their* power is gone...

For the complete lyric text read Deuteronomy 32:1-44. You will note that it is not a happy "I'm OK, You're OK" religious song. It is very important to note that the meaning of *shiyr* (7892), which has been translated song in this scripture passage, definitely means a song, or abstractly, singing a song. Although some exegetes suppose that it means saying, which it does not, it is without doubt referring to singing this text.

Although it is not popular among modern, postmodern and post-postmodern worship leaders to sing any religious text that might confront a seeker or worshiper, it is exactly what God commanded Moses to do in this situation. There is no place in the New Testament where our Lord commanded musicians to quit confronting the seeker and the worshiper or any person who is in God's house with the claims of Scripture.

Jesus certainly confronted people with the truth of what God required. He did not say to the money changers in the Second Temple, "God loves you and has a wonderful plan for your life." I want to make it very clear that I am not contending for worship music to be highly confrontational or negative. The Gospel of Jesus Christ is good news –not bad, negative, depressing news. The tenor of public worship should be a joyful and reverential adoration of the Trinity. However, to ignore the entire truth taught in the Bible is shortsighted and less than honest.

The seeker must be aware that Jesus demanded in St. John 14:15, "If ye love me, keep my commandments." Again, it is the responsibility of music ministers to select music that teaches the great love of God toward all men. But, a well-balanced music ministry must include not only songs that speak of His kindness, longsuffering, love and mercy, but also "songs that sting". The Bible speaks of the justice and judgment of God when it states in Hebrews 9:27, "…it is appointed unto men once to die, but after this the judgment."

## Utilizing Great Music in Worship

There is no doubt about the fact that one can make it to heaven without ever singing any of the sacred classics. As a matter of fact, it is not imperative that a Christian sing any great music. Worship is about God. It is not about great art music. However, although it is possible to sing unto the Lord with only trite, shallow, inferior, *mundane musical offerings, well-composed melodies and harmonies often are a much more effective concomitant to the marvelous message of the good news of the gospel than poorly written music. This is not to intimate that only the sacred classics are composed and arranged well, because there are many praise choruses, hymns and gospel songs that are well composed. But the sacred classics are classics because they are great music—the music part of the music and the way that the words are set to the music are both masterfully accomplished.

More and more Christian musicians seem to not make much distinction between inappropriate, poorly written, mediocre music and great sacred music. Although a Christian does not worship the greatness in music, most of the time great music is a better vehicle to represent the message and divine character of our great and wonderful God. However, philosophically speaking, the earnest Christian musician values the use of an excellent musical vehicle with the excellent message of the gospel. It is one thing to give lip service to the appropriateness of the sacred classics but it is another to actually utilize them in public worship. The Christian musician who never includes the sacred classics is making a philosophical statement about the awesomeness and solemnity of worshiping the high and lifted up triune God.

As I have often said, the music part of music does not always have to be complicated or esoteric in order to be a proper vehicle to use in our musicing unto God. However, there are auspicious religious occasions when great sacred music is without doubt a better choice than some trite, predictable and mundane musical composition that is obviously the work of a *musical hack.

There is a reason why some sacred music is great and other music is either mediocre or so poorly constructed that it is not a good vehicle for musical worship. The best sacred music throughout the centuries has been produced by composers and arrangers who skillfully organized melody, harmony and rhythm into compositions that would properly represent the awesomeness and solemnity of worshiping the Triune God. This has been accomplished by utilizing a number of appropriate musical styles that were and are better vehicles to represent the moral nature of God. The condition of an accomplished musician's musicing and the quality of the music in his or her repertoire makes a philosophical statement about his or her passion for presenting God the best possible musical offering.

One can survive on a diet of bologna sandwiches and white bread with all the quality ingredients removed, but that diet can be greatly improved by eating foods which contain quality ingredients. The same is true of our musical diet. Poorly written music does not support the awesomeness and solemnity of our worship of the Triune God as well as well-written compositions. Certainly the sacred classics are excellent vehicles for the presentation of the biblical message.

A total diet of the more simple forms of music sends the message that excellent quality musicing does not matter. In other words, it testifies to those who attend our church services that the kind and quality of musical offerings we present to God do not matter. It subtly testifies to the fact that these musicians believe that God does not need to be worshiped with the best musical offerings we are able to present. When we present all of our musical offerings with inferior musical genres, we are testifying to the fact that we believe that it is acceptable to present our Heavenly Father a musical three-legged lamb. Remember that, in the sacrificial system, God required a lamb of the matrix which was without defect or blemish of any kind (Leviticus 1:3, Numbers 28:19 etc.).

I am well aware that there are many people who do not have an appreciation for the sacred classics. Appreciating the great sacred music works is an acquired skill. If a local congregation does not understand or enjoy great works of music, then they will not be ministered to by hearing and performing these compositions. It is unfortunate that many people are impoverished musically by not having an understanding of great sacred music. Great music enables one to have a greater understanding of the deep profoundness of the lessons to be learned in the Bible.

There is another reason that we should include the sacred classics as a part of our balanced musical ministry. There are many people who attend public worship who are musically aware. Accomplished musicians are often offended or at least disappointed by the shallow and shoddy nature of trite and mundane religious music. A church full of educated people who understand and appreciate great sacred music deserves to hear quality musical offerings at least part of the time.

Many church musicians wonder why astute accomplished musicians are often not involved in church music programs. The main reason is that so many church music ministries do not include any high quality artistic musical offerings. A worshiper who has sung a part in a quality choir in junior high, high school, and college is offended when a church choir sings only overly-simple two part, or worse yet, unison choral music. Ministers of music need to understand the importance of having some musical "meat" on the worship table as well as the diet of musical "frosting" that is so prevalent in many fundamental Christian churches at present.

The fine arts are not the door to the Kingdom of God, but they are wonderful concomitants of quality musical worship. As Romans 1:25 explains, we should never worship created things (*ktisis* 2937 which includes music) but always the creator of music *(ktizo* 2936, i.e., God). A steady diet of sacred classics should not be forced upon a congregation with little understanding of music, but it will not harm them to be introduced to some great sacred classics occasionally. It will also give those of us that have spent a lifetime studying and performing great music an opportunity to worship with music at a much deeper level of import.

## Why Should we Sing with Musical Instruments?

The Bible repeatedly refers to singing with the use of musical instruments. In fact, they are so numerous and well known that it is not necessary to enumerate them in this discussion. Musical instruments were used in pre-Temple worship and in both the First and Second Temples. This we know with a surety from the biblical record and from extra-biblical writings.

Some writers who object to the use of musical instruments with singing refer to Amos 6:5 for reasons no one can successfully explain or defend. They also sometimes refer to Amos 5:23. "Take thou away from me the noise of thy songs; for I will not hear the melody of thy viols." They contend that the use of musical instruments caused their songs to be "noisy" and that God refused to hear their songs because of the use of musical instruments with their singing. The words *hamown* (1995) *shiyr* (7892) translated noise and songs in Amos 5:23 mean the noise or tumult of songs or singing. A portion of Ephesians 5:19, that mentions "making music in your hearts," is also used by those who do not believe in using instruments in the church.

Looking at the context of the fifth chapter of Amos, the nation of Israel had fallen into manifold transgressions and mighty sins (see vs.12). At the same time they were offering burnt offerings and presenting musical offerings unto the LORD while they were in deep sin. For these reasons God said that He would not accept their musical offerings. This refusal was not because they were accompanying their vocal music with viols (*nebel* 5035), but rather because of their refusal to obey Jehovah. Therefore, God referred to their musicing as "noise."

A portion of Ephesians 5:19 is also used by those who do not believe in using instruments in the church. They use the words *psallo, en, humon,* and *kardia* (5567, 1722, 5216, 2588) which have been translated "making melody in your heart" in the AV, to connote that a Christian is prohibited from using musical instruments because it is only permissible to make melody in the worshiper's heart. The objection to the use of musical instruments stems from this misunderstanding of Ephesians 5:19. However, the Greek word *psallo* (5567) which has been translated "making melody" in the AV, means to touch the parts of a stringed instrument. It means literally the twitching and twanging sound which is produced when a musician plays a stringed instrument.

The writer of the epistle to the Ephesian Christians knew what this Greek word meant, so since he knew its meaning he would never have used the word *psallo* if he was teaching that Christians should not use musical instruments to accompany vocal music. So, there is absolutely no logical or biblically based argument for refusing any Christian assembly of believers to accompany their vocal music with instruments.

Those who have chosen to exclude the use of musical instru-

## 16: How Should We Then Music? 343

ments in public and/or private musical worship should do so as a matter of preference rather than biblical mandate. Any fellowship of believers has the right to worship without using instruments, but they should not condemn those who do use musical instruments. The use of musical instruments in public worship is never condemned in the Old or New Testament. Acapella singing can be a very beautiful and reverent way to music unto God. Therefore, there is no philosophical problem in making the choice to music in this manner.

### The Song of Fools

Ecclesiastes 7:5 states, "It is better to hear the rebuke of the wise, than for a man to hear the song of fools." Church musicians sometimes get a little worried that their musicing unto God is too serious, because all of us want people to like our music ministry. What did the writer of the Book of Ecclesiastes mean by "the song of fools"? Was he suggesting that the content of the song is foolish, or that those who are singing the songs are fools? He probably meant all of the above.

Never be afraid of the seriousness of the musical message of Christ crucified. The awesome depth and true truth of this message is the very thing that makes it worthwhile. The message of Christ being obedient to the will of His Father, which included being reviled, rebuked, rejected, misunderstood, abused, and tortured physically and mentally, is a very solemn and worthwhile message. Never be ashamed of the awesome and solemn truth about Christ's suffering and death which we sing about in God's house. The Christian musician should never water it down or fail to sing about the precious blood that Christ shed for the sins of the whole world.

Although the message of His suffering and death is a very solemn message, there is another side to this musical coin. Turn it over and you will see victory through our Lord and Savior Jesus Christ. You will see the joy of the debt of sin being paid by His suffering and death and resurrection. You will also see that we can have a clean and pure heart through the efficacy of His precious blood that was shed on Calvary. (See Acts 29:28, Hebrews 9:12, 13:12 and Revelation 1:5.) You will see freedom from the guilt of sin, and the joy of having an eternal relationship with our Lord and Savior Jesus Christ. Sing and play and tell through your musicing not only the suffering and death of our Savior, but also of His victory over sin, death, hell and the grave.

The message of the "song of fools" is very different because it is mostly an empty social gospel. The gospel message of Christ crucified is far better than the foolish, light, chaffy, religious music that contains little eternal value. Church musicians that are still musicing the whole gospel should not allow themselves to be intimidated. The true truth of the deep message of Christ crucified, buried, and risen again and seated on the right of the Father praying for us all is exactly what this post-postmodern world needs to hear.

### *Soli Deo Gloria*

Johann Sabastian Bach once said, "The aim and final end of all music should be none other than the glory of God and the refreshment of the soul." There is much said in the Bible, especially in the Old Testament and also in the New Testament, about our responsibility to music unto God for His glory and honor and praise. It is less understood whether or not we should music in order to refresh the soul.

First, we should give some explanation of what J.S. Bach could have meant by making the statement that one of the final ends of our musicing should be for "the refreshment of the soul." A general definition of soul is "the spiritual part of a human being" or the "the seat of affections of mankind." The Greek word *psuche (5590)* appears in ninety-five verses in the New Testament and is translated life, lives, soul, souls, and minds. It is not clear what Bach meant but it is safe to conjecture that he meant that one of music's purposes was the refreshment of the inner man.

Bach was correct in believing that music was created by God for His glory and for the refreshment and edification of man. Christian musicians have the awesome responsibility and privilege to use this wonderful art form to honor God and to edify and refresh the psyche of mankind. We also know that Bach put God first in much of his compositional efforts because he often inscribed S.D.G. (*soli Deo gloria*) at the end of his compositions. This Latin phrase was used in all (or nearly all) of his sacred compositions and in some or his secular compositions. It was also used by G.F. Handel in his *Te Deum*. The term *soli Deo gloria*, which was abbreviated by Bach S.D.G., means glory to God alone or to the only God.

It is concerning that Christians are moving away philosophically from this important concept. In the twenty-first century, many times God has to share the glory of music with Christian musicians. Isaiah 48:11 records God's words, "For mine own sake, even for mine own sake, will I do it: for how should my name be polluted? and I will not give my glory unto another." Isaiah 42:8 warns against giving glory and praise to anything or anyone but God, "I am the Lord: that is my name: and my glory will I not give to another, neither my praise to graven images."

Isaiah 42:10-12 very carefully explains that we are to give God the praise when we sing sacred music. "Sing unto the Lord a new song, and his praise from the end of the earth, ye that go down to the sea, and all that is therein; the isles, and the inhabitants thereof. Let the wilderness and the cities thereof lift up their voice, the villages that Kedar doth inhabit: let the inhabitants of the rock sing, let them shout from the top of the mountains. Let them give glory unto the Lord, and declare his praise in the islands."

The intent of the musician whose heart is sold out to Christ should be, "Not unto us, O Lord, not unto us, but unto thy name give glory, for thy mercy, and for thy truth's sake" (Psalm 115:1). God deserves all the glory and all the praise every time we bring Him a musical offering. Philosophically it is *repugnant to supposedly bring the great God who spoke worlds into existence a musical offering and then receive all the honor and praise while an audience bestows lavish honor on the performer.

### Endnote

1. Nick Page, *And Now Let's Enter Into a Time of Nonsense*, (Waynesboro, GA: Authentic Media, 2004, 1.

## Chapter Sixteen Word Meanings

**Hallel**— the general term used for Psalms 113-118 as a unit. The "Great Hallel" refers to Psalm 136 and is called *Hallel ha-Gadol*.

**Homily**— a short sermon that is intended primarily for spiritual edification rather than doctrinal instruction.

**Jettison**— as used here it means to drop or throw something worthless from the "musical ship."

***Onus probandi***— the philosophic burden of proof.

**Musical hack**— a composer or arranger who works solely for mercenary reasons.

**Mundane**— refers to music that is common, ordinary, banal, or unimaginative.

**Pander**— as used here, to cater to the lower musical tastes and desires of others.

**Repugnant**— extremely distasteful or unacceptable.

## Chapter Sixteen Questions for Discussion

1. Why is it a faulty praxis to music in a certain manner simply because of a musician's instincts or because one follows musical traditions established by others?
2. Discuss why you do or do not believe that a congregation should sing from written notation.
3. Give scriptural basis for singing praise music in public worship. Quote Scripture to support your belief.
4. Discuss several reasons for singing hymns in public worship.
5. Discuss the author's statement, "Gospel songs allow a fellowship of believers to share many diverse aspects of the salvation."
6. Discuss why so few churches utilize psalm singing and why you do or do not believe that psalm singing should be revived in public worship.
7. Defend your position on singing some of the sacred classics in worship services.
8. Since the Old Testament is full of references and admonitions to sing with the use of musical instruments, do you believe that there is scriptural justification for using them in the twenty-first century?
9. Discuss the importance, or lack of importance, of a minister of music including great music in the church's musical repertoire.
10. Discuss the importance of the concept of *soli Deo gloria* in developing a church music.

# 17

# To the Chief Musician

THIS CHAPTER IS DESIGNED to help Christian musicians to do the right thing and to put their trust in our loving Heavenly Father. Christian musicians are often impulsive and are prone to go through times of depression. It is one thing to know what God has said in His Word, but it is entirely another thing to know He will do what He has declared in His Word. St. Paul said in Galatians 2:20, "I am crucified with Christ: nevertheless I live; yet not I, but Christ liveth in me: and the life which I now live in the flesh I live by the faith of the Son of God, who loved me, and gave himself for me." It is my prayer that these short discussions will be helpful to Christians as they live by faith.

### How Should the Chief Musician use his Tongue?

Psalm 30:12, "To the end that my glory may sing to thee, and not be silent. O LORD my God, I will give thanks unto thee for ever." The authorities do not agree as to what the words "my glory" mean. The Hebrew word *kabod* (3519) generally means copious or glorious. Many Bible exegetes believe that this word is referring to the tongue. I have known several musicians whose tongue was not used in a very glorious manner. However, the use of the Hebrew word *kabod* connotes that the sweet Psalmist of Israel was pledging to sing praise unto *Jehovah Elohim* (3068 430) for as long as he was alive.

The psalmist not only promised to give praise unto *Jehovah* the self-existent, eternal God who is *Elohim*, the most high lofty supreme God, but he also promised to give thanks (*yadah* 3034). The word *yadah* means to use or hold out one's hands in worship reverence. Since thanksgiving requires remembrance, it is a good thing for all of us to remember what we were like before we became Christians. Often some of the memories are not very enjoyable. Most of us were not very nice before the cleansing power of Christ changed us. No wonder we sing, "He changed me completely"!

Passing from death unto life spiritually is certainly not a joke— it is a reality. With all our praise singing we remember what God has done for us. We praise and glorify *Jehovah Elohim* for who He is and for what He has done in our lives. We raise our hands in *avowal and worship because He is truly a wonderful Savior.

David promised to keep his tongue singing praise and thanks to God for as long as he lived. He pledged to use his tongue in a positive way. For many of us, the tongue is seldom silent during the time we are awake. Why not practice praising God? If we use our tongue to sing the high praises of God, we will be sure that we are using it in a positive way.

## Will God Protect His Chief Musicians?

1 Samuel chapter twenty-four records how God protected David when Saul sought to do him harm while David was in the Wilderness of Engedi. In 1 Samuel 27:1 "...David said in his heart, I will now perish one day by the hand of Saul..." In a time of trouble David became convinced that Saul was going to succeed in his quest to kill him. So, what did David do? He went to live in Gath in the Land of the Philistines.

David made friends with King Lachish and lived in Ziklag because he did not trust God to take care of him. The result was that Ziklag was burned to the ground and David's wives and the wives and children of David's six hundred men were kidnapped while David and his faithful men were out fighting for King Lachish.

If we are not careful we, as God's ministers of music, will decide that someone is going to get us. Like David, we will decide to give up and go live with the "Philistines." We will forget that God was able to protect David and He is also able to take care of us at our place of ministry. God is able to even protect us from a wicked church boss or an obstinate school administrator or anyone else that plans to do us harm.

God is abundantly able to keep and protect His musicians wherever they are. Hebrews 13:5b reminds us that God said, "I will never leave thee nor forsake thee." He can and will take care of His musicians that He has placed out there in "Smirgly Junction" where it seems like there is no source of help.

David went to Ziklag; Jonah ran from God's call to Nineveh and got swallowed by a big fish. David and Jonah thought and it got them both in trouble. Quit thinking negatively and start trusting. If you must think, think about God's might, power, great love, and ability to keep and protect you.

### Nothing Matters to the Chief Musician as Much as God

On Sundays Christian musicians need to take a break from all music efforts that are not necessary. Church musicians certainly are not going to get the day off, but there are some things that can be put off until Monday. Christian musicians need to recognize that this day is the Lord's Day, but as Mark 2:27 explains, "And he [Jesus] said unto them, The sabbath was made for man, and not man for the sabbath."

I have lived long enough for my flesh and my heart to fail. A few years ago I was placed in a Heart Cath Lab and actually watched the doctor work on my heart. After experiencing that procedure I have no trouble saying "…there is none upon the earth that I desire beside thee. My flesh and my heart faileth: but God is the strength of my heart, and my portion forever" (Psalm 73:25b-26). God has truly become the strength of my heart. I will tell you that as I lay there in Christ Hospital in Cincinnati that day, nothing mattered but God. Nothing that I owned or thought I owned mattered! Christian musicians must learn to lean hard on the Savior in the time of trouble. Your health may have already failed or it may be near to failure. Christian musicians should take courage because God promised in verse 26 to be your portion (*cheleq* 2506, i.e., inheritance). It is God and God alone that you must have in this world and in the world to come.

As the psalmist said in verse 28, "It is good for me to draw near to God." Be sure that you can say, "I have put my trust in the Lord God." As George Duffield stated in his gospel hymn "Stand Up, Stand Up for Jesus", "the arm of flesh will fail you, ye dare not trust your own." Also, God has promised in this psalm that He would be your portion forever. You may not have much of this world's wealth, but if you know Him in a personal way, you have God as your portion. The wealth of this world will fade away, but the heavenly inheritance will last forever. You can take your heavenly treasure with you to the glory world.

### Chief Musicians with Broken *Cisterns

God sent His prophet Jeremiah to plead with the nation of Israel, who had begun to worship false gods. "For my people have committed two evils; they have forsaken me the fountain of living water, and have hewed them out cisterns, broken cisterns, that can hold no water" (Jeremiah 2:13). After all that God had done for Israel, they still addressed their worship to false gods. Notice that they had forsaken the fountain of living water. They had gone after their own source of spiritual strength (broken cisterns). Their worship had left them dry spiritually because these cisterns would not hold spiritual water.

The ministering musician is constantly giving to others. As I have told my ministering music groups for years, "You cannot feed others unless you eat." If you have some kind of broken cistern that has failed to sustain you spiritually, get out your ladder, broom and mop and clean out the inside of your cistern. If your cistern is not clean on the inside the plaster will not adhere to your spiritual cistern's walls. All the junk in your life must be removed! If you are going to store up the pure living water, you may have to clean house or the means of grace will not be efficacious.

Remember, the Children of Israel were incurable worshipers. When they quit drinking the living water they started worshiping false gods. Satan does not care which thing we worship as long as it is something other than our loving Heavenly Father. He does not care if we worship religious music.

The Bible lesson to be remembered is that we should make sure we are taking advantage of the Fountain of Living Water. Isaiah 12:3 states, "Therefore with joy shall ye draw water out of the wells of salvation." God has enough of this water to sustain every ministering musician. We also must be sure that we have not started worshiping music fads, trends or any genre of music, old or new, but rather we only worship GOD with music that appropriately represents and honors Him. Anything less is a broken cistern.

## Weary Chief Musicians

Galatians 6:9 gives this admonishment to the chief musicians: "And let us not be weary in well doing: for in due season we shall reap if we faint not." How can a musician keep going when it seems that the great task has not been accomplished? This verse is not teaching that the Christian musician will never get tired. I have seen some high-energy musicians that appear to never get tired, but surely they have to get weary emotionally and physically at times. This Scripture is an encouragement to Christian musicians to not quit when they are tired and face burnout. Isaiah 40:29 confirms, "He giveth power to the faint; and to them that have no might he increaseth strength." God never gets tired but He knows that His chief musicians do, so He bestows power and strength upon weary Christian musicians.

I remember being so emotionally weary that one morning on our way to work I announced to my wife Sheila, "This is it— I quit." I remember her saying to me very calmly, "If you leave I will not go with you because you know that the Lord wants you to stay here." I thought that perhaps she was joking, but I did not test her to see if she really meant it. I ministered thirty-eight years full time as a Bible college music director. If I had quit after only a few years, I would have missed a multitude of God's richest blessings.

Galatians 6:9 includes a little word with a big meaning. This word is *if*. The promise of spiritual harvest comes to those who refuse to quit. None of us know when the "due season" will come. So, as ministering musicians we must be sure to keep our souls fed because we cannot keep going without spiritual strength. The answer is to keep up the everyday "well doing." A musical ministry does not have to be large in order to please God. It is not large successes in the eyes of people that matters. Rather, it is your faithfulness and well doing that matters to God. Matthew 25:23 records one of Jesus' parables. "His lord said unto him, Well done, good and faithful servant; thou has been faithful over a few things, I will make thee ruler over many things: enter thou into the joy of thy lord."

One of Satan's tricks is to get musicians so busy that they fail to wait upon God and to be bound unto Him. The closer that a Christian musician is to God, the harder it becomes for Satan to tempt and to overcome that musician. Many times a Christian will need a "change in strength." Sometimes musicians need what I call a "spiritual oil change." In other words they need to be freshly bound together with God. One of the things that auto mechanics stress is that the moving parts of an engine need to have fresh oil that will stick to the pistons, cylinder walls and bearings, etc. Without the freshness of clean oil, dirt and sludge will tend to gum up the chief musician's spiritual engine. The fact that a Christian had a fresh anointing from the blessed Holy Spirit a few months ago does not preclude the need for the fresh oil of the Spirit today. Again, auto mechanics tell us that you do not have to do anything wrong for your engine to be in need of an oil change. As a matter of fact, all you have to do is use that engine and it will routinely be in need of fresh oil.

Isaiah 40:31 explains, "But they that wait upon the LORD shall renew their strength; they shall mount up with wings as eagles; they shall run, and not be weary; and they shall walk, and not faint." So, Christians who "wait upon the LORD" will have the fresh oil of the Spirit which is absolutely necessary for the Christian to renew spiritual strength in order to have the power to get above the troubles and temptations of Satan in this life. It is only by having the fresh oil (anointing) of the Holy Spirit that a Christian musician will be able to walk and run with spiritual power. Without this *dunamis* of the Spirit, the musician will become weak and in danger of failing. However, the great shepherd's psalm (Psalm 23:5) says, "Thou preparest a table before me in the presence of mine enemies: thou anointest my head with oil; my cup runneth over."

The formula for receiving spiritual strength is simple. First, receive strength from God by believing that He is the creator of all things (including music). Second, believe that He created you personally (therefore you belong to him). Third, believe that He cares for all His creation (that includes you). Fourth, take time to be holy. Make sure that you spend time bringing yourself together with God. Fifth, lift up your heart and mind as though they were the wings of an eagle, and let God take you above and beyond your troubles. Sixth, receive strength from God to walk and run the spiritual race that has been set before you.

## God Never gets Tired

Isaiah 40:28 states, "Hast thou not heard the LORD, the creator of the ends of the earth, fainteth not, neither is weary? There is no searching of his understanding." The passage of Scripture in which this verse is found reminds the Christian musician that the LORD who is the creator of everything above, below, in, on, and around the earth gives strength and power to the weary. God meant what He said in the book of Genesis. He really did create everything. (Doubting the authenticity of God's literal creation in the Genesis record dumbs down the power of God.) If Jehovah did not create everything as the Genesis record declares then perhaps He does not have the power and the ability to give strength to weary Christian musicians.

However, YHVH had the power to take nothing and make something out of that nothingness.Furthermore, God now has the power to give strength to weary Christian musicians. He exercises this power on the behalf of weary Christian musicians. I have experienced that power and strength many, many times since I confessed my sins with godly sorrow and received His forgiveness and, by faith, accepted Him as my Lord and Savior.

How can a weary Christian musician receive help and strength? The answer is very simple. It is so simple that that many Christian musicians fail to receive this help and assistance from the self-existent, independent, eternal "God who is." First and foremost, Christian musicians must remember that He is, and that He is the rewarder of them that seek Him. (See Hebrews 11:6.)

The passage of Scripture in Isaiah chapter forty that we quoted earlier in this discussion also says in verse 31, "But they that wait upon the LORD shall renew their strength; they shall mount up with wings as eagles; they shall run, and not be weary; they shall walk and not faint." The Hebrew word which has been translated renew in verse thirty-one is *caliph* (2498) which means literally a change in strength. So, if we as Christian musicians need to have a change in the amount of strength that we have, either physically, spiritually or emotionally, we need to "wait" (*qavah* 6960) or be "bound together" with the self-existent, independent, eternal God who is alive and seated at the right hand of the Father, making intercession for Christian musicians right now! (See Romans 8: 26-27.) So, the secret of your renewed strength is getting close to the Lord and telling Him how much you need Him.

## Some Chief Musicians Feed on Ashes

Isaiah 44:20 uses an unusual statement, "He feedeth on ashes: a deceived heart hath turned him aside, that he cannot deliver his soul, nor say, Is there not a lie in my right hand?"

This verse is an exhortation about the folly of idol makers. Have you made an idol lately? Do you have any idols that you have made or purchased in the past? Do you have any idols that were given to you? I ask these questions because I know several musicians who are now worshiping their "idols."

Some Christian musicians get side-tracked by things they love more than God. They have not quit worshiping God but they have other trinkets that are before Him (Exodus 20:3). As a matter of fact, they are very good at acts of worship. They seem to worship very well in church because they have developed their worship skills to the point of near perfection. They know all the words to the latest worship choruses and they are able to put clever worship sequences together. However, they worship trinkets and toys and a host of things more than they worship God. Anything that obscures the face of God in our lives is "before" (*paniym* 6440) God.

A Christian musician must be careful to keep the main thing the main thing! Everyone needs a hobby, but the Christian musician must not let a hobby become a *hobble. Be sure that you use your time of recreation to "re-create" your body and mind. Be sure that you do not simply live for your trinkets or your life foundation will become "wood, hay, and stubble" (see 1 Corinthians 3:12). If you do not keep the main thing the main thing, it will not be very long until you will be "feeding on ashes." It is sad to see a talented Christian musician who has been turned aside by his or her deceived heart. Be sure you are not carrying around a lie in your right hand. (For that matter, do not carry around a lie in your left hand either.)

## The Chief Musician's Inheritance

Numbers 18:20 tells us, "And the LORD spake unto Aaron, thou shalt have no inheritance in their land, neither shalt thou have any part among them: I am thy part and thine inheritance among the children of Israel." It must have disturbed the priests and the Levites that they were not given any land as an inheritance. They were supposed to receive a tithe for their inheritance. Many Christian musicians have a tendency to question the fact that they have so little in this life. These musicians often work part-time in a church, Christian school, or Christian college and "mend tents" as a means to pay the bills. The striking import of this Scripture is that YHVH promised the priests and Levites that, "I am thy part and thine inheritance." There is no place in the Old Testament where God made this promise to any of the Israelites who were not from the Tribe of Levi.

The self-existent eternal God who is has promised to be the portion and inheritance of the musician who ministers for Him. Praise God! He has promised to be our portion if we will be faithful at our place of music ministry. We may not be able to claim very much of the *terra firma* but God himself claims us as His heirs. Wow! God claims us as His own heirs. It is far better to inherit a portion of God's eternal riches than to have this world's ephemeral riches. Looking at the Levites' situation philosophically, they had ultimate wealth at their disposal because God was their portion and their inheritance. Likewise, Christian musicians who have God as their portion are rich.

## Deliverance for Chief Musicians

In Jeremiah 20:13 those who love God are told, "Sing unto the LORD, praise ye the LORD: for he hath delivered the soul of the poor from the hand of evildoers." The enemy of the Christian musician's soul desires to take his revenge out on the Christian musician. He waits for an opportunity to entice Christian musicians into sin. Satan is smart and he is subtle. Jeremiah 20:11 says, "But the LORD is with me as a mighty terrible one: therefore my persecutors shall stumble, and they shall not prevail." Although Satan is crafty by using other people to persecute the chief musician, our God is a "mighty terrible one" (*gibbowr ariyts* 1368 6184). Satan is no match for our Lord. God is big enough and mighty enough to not only fight Satan but to also to win the battle for the Christian musician's soul, because He is *gibbowr ariyts*, i.e., the mighty, fearfully, powerful God.

Jeremiah was a lot like Christian musicians. He was prone to depression (Jeremiah 20:14-18), and so was Elijah (1 Kings 19:4). One moment their faith reached out to YHVH and in the next they were deep into despair. We as musicians should learn from these men's mistakes. When Satan begins to accuse you, you must look to Jesus for deliverance. In the time of depression move in closer to the great heart of God and trust Him and believe His Word. You will find strength in reading Scripture, praying, and singing His praises. You should count your God-given blessings and resist Satan in the name of the Lord as we are instructed to do in James 4:7. "Submit yourselves therefore to God. Resist the devil, and he will flee from you." On the authority of God's Word, if we resist, Satan will have to withdraw because of the power of our God that surrounds us.

Note that Scripture admonishes us to sing unto the Lord. When you are oppressed and become depressed, praise the Lord with singing. If you praise God with singing, God will "inhabit your praise" (Psalm 22:3). Our Heavenly Father will abide with you, i.e., He will dwell with you because Jesus is a friend that will stick closer than a brother (Proverbs 18:24).

## Why God Created Music

As was mentioned in chapter ten, Psalm 49:4 states, "I will incline my ear to a parable: I will open my dark saying upon the harp." God has promised to open hidden and hard to understand mysteries of the Bible through music. Matthew 13:35b also declares that, "I will open my mouth in parables; I will utter things which have been kept secret from the foundation of the world." As we know, Jesus spoke many parables to His disciples and to the multitudes that He taught. God could have said that He would only open His difficult mysteries with parables or written communication alone, but He included the music part of music as one of His ways to reveal His deep mysteries to mankind.

Music has historically been a vehicle upon which the word of Jehovah could ride into the hearts of the common man. Sacred music has historically been a means to an end— not an end in itself. All of the Old Testament has been notated precisely by the *te'amim* (the musical signs below and above the Sacred Text).

Why was the entire Old Testament notated and intended to be sung? It has been faithfully transmitted to us in sweet tune over thousands of years in order that it could be understood and remembered by the common man. Everyone knows that music is a wonderful aid to memory. So, it is no mystery that our loving Heavenly Father made special provision for us all to understand and remember His Word by making provision for Christians to sing and play music in and out of God's House. Is music strictly a performance art to you? Do you perform and lead others in musical performance only for your and their personal pleasure?

Christian musicians should sing and play to one another and unto God (Ephesians 5:19) in order that the Body of Christ may be drawn closer to the blessed Trinity through a greater understanding of biblical principles of holy living. Sacred music should reflect the nature and holiness of God as well as His love and directions for His church. Our musicing should lift up God and tell us more about who He is and what He does. As we lift up the Trinity through our musicing, sinners should be reminded of their low estate, their spiritual condition as well as being made aware of God's justice, judgment, love and forgiveness. All of our sacred musicing should ultimately lead us to the Throne of Grace.

## If Chief Musicians Save, They Lose

St. Mark 8:35-37, "For whosoever will save his life shall lose it; but whosoever shall lose his life for my sake and the gospel's, the same shall save it. For what shall it profit a man, if he shall gain the whole world, and lose his own soul? Or what shall a man give in exchange for his soul?"

As mentioned earlier, most Christian musicians are not well-to-do financially. Much of their time is often spent on a second or even third part-time job just to make ends meet. You may be in a place in your life where you are afraid that you are going to come up on the short end of the stick financially. So maybe I should label this little pep talk the "profit-loss ledger."

As one takes a careful look at verse thirty-five above, one can deduce that if you save you lose, and if you lose you save. So, what does your profit-loss ledger look like? Jesus said in verse thirty-four, "Whosoever will come after me, let him deny himself and take up his cross, and follow me." You will often need to remember why you are working as a ministering musician and for whom you are working.

The ideal for life is to come to the end of your career with a good-looking profit-loss statement. You have chosen to forfeit accruing this world's goods so that you can lay up treasures in heaven. Matthew 16:26 reminds us that, "For what is a man profited, if he shall gain the whole world, and lose his own soul? or what shall a man give in exchange for his soul?" So, be sure that you are laying up treasure in the right place. Never forget that you have made the right choice, even though it may not look like you have when the going gets rough.

Remember that market timing does not matter as much as time in the market. What that means is that as you stay in God's work you are laying up quality investments (treasures) in heaven. Even though you are not able to see God's ledger, believe me, your eternal investments are recorded there. When you get to heaven you will see clearly that "It pays to serve Jesus, It pays every day".[1] This song means that your eternal interest is compounded daily.

## Good and Faithful Chief Musicians

In Matthew 25:21 Jesus said, "His lord said unto him, Well done, thou good and faithful servant: thou hast been faithful over a few things, I will make thee ruler over many things: enter thou into the joy of thy lord." A musician can be a good servant morally and not be passionately faithful to the responsibilities of the music ministry where God has placed that musician. Christian character is what makes a musician a good (*agathos* 18) person. *Agathos* means good in any sense but its meaning is different than *pistos* (4103) which means objectively "trustworthy", i.e., in the case of a Christian musician, one who experiences the actual reality of being a completely trustworthy servant musician of Christ. It stands to reason that moral goodness is a necessary requirement of the ministering musician who is a bond servant (*doulos* 1401) of our Lord and Savior Jesus Christ. Ralph Earle stated that "these are the only two things God requires of everyone— that he be good in character and faithful in service."[2] Although God requires both, being a morally good person does not automatically make one a quality musician or does it make one a faithful trustworthy music leader.

A part of being a faithful musical servant is learning how to use music as a worship vehicle. Love for music and passion for performance do not necessarily make a musician a faithful musical servant. There is a vast difference between loving music so much that one worships it and loving God so much that one has a great passion to use music to worship the God who created music. As was mentioned in this work several times, the Bible condemns worshiping created things (see Romans 1:25). The faithful musical servant uses the music as a vehicle to worship God and lead others in worship.

The faithful musical servant is not only a leader and a worshiper but also a faithful teacher. Faithful musical leadership includes teaching others to worship God by musicing unto Him. The faithful musical servant utilizes teaching skills in their most profound form— teaching by example. The faithful musical servant is not only a technical leader but also a touched leader. The touched servant is an anointed servant. Starting late in the twentieth century Christian writers and music philosophers began to make acrid comments about those who sought the anointing of the Holy Spirit as though such philosophical belief was egotistical or somewhat fanatical. Although it may not be a popular concept among Christians in this century, the visitation of God upon human servants is certainly a biblical concept. (For examples see Leviticus 7:35, 8:12, 1 Samuel 15:1, and Isaiah 10:27, James 5:14, and 1 John 2:27.)

The good and faithful musical leader should and must be moved deeply by the message of the music that is being used as a worship vehicle. It is one thing to be moved intellectually by the meaning of the music but it is another to have the *dunamis* (1411) of the Spirit, which comes only to good and faithful Spirit-filled musical servants. As I have often stated in my philosophical writings, many Christian musicians seem to forget the great musical discourse in Ephesians chapter five not only includes verse nineteen but also verse eighteen: "And be not drunk with wine, wherein is excess; but be filled with the Spirit." What is taught in verse nineteen can only happen to those who are living a life in the Spirit. Verse eighteen teaches a continual life in the Spirit after the Christian is once filled. The good and faithful musical servant that is spoken of in the fifth chapter of Ephesians is also admonished to let the Holy Spirit have control of every aspect of life and music ministry.

The influence of the Divine upon the human can and should be a reality in the twenty-first century. The musician who is touched and moved by the Holy Spirit has the right to be passionate about worship music. All of the Christian musicians that I have had the privilege to know who were accomplished musicians have been very passionate about their secular musicing. However, some of them believe that their sacred musicing should be very *sedate and *staid and should be executed in a manner that is seemingly almost detached from any passion or emotion. There is no place in Scripture where Christian musicians are instructed to perform sacred music in a manner that is devoid or outward emotion, outward evidence of meaning (understanding), or outward physical expression of being passionate about the music being performed. Therefore, although sacred musicing is very serious business, we may and should perform it with great joy.

Nehemiah 8:10 states, "Then he said unto them, Go your way, eat the fat, and drink the sweet, and send portions unto them for whom nothing is prepared: for this day is holy unto our Lord: neither be ye sorry; for the joy of the LORD is your strength." Psalm 89:15 states, "Blessed is the people that know the joyful sound [*teruah* 8643—great acclamation of joy]: they shall walk, O LORD, in the light of thy countenance." Psalm 149:1-2, "Praise ye the LORD. Sing unto the LORD a new song, and his praise in the congregation of saints. Let Israel rejoice in him that made him: let the children of Zion be joyful [*giyl*, 1523] in their King." The word *giyl* is used in a great variety of applications in the OT but it most often connotes gladness and rejoicing. These Scriptures are only a few of the multitude of Scriptures that teach worshiping with much joy. Certainly the fact that the Bible repeatedly mentions singing with joy should encourage us to music with outward joy and emotion. 1 Chronicles 15:16 states, "And David spake to the chief of the Levites to appoint their brethren to be the singers with instruments of musick, psalteries and harps and cymbals, sounding, by lifting up the voice with joy [*simchah*, 8057-exceeding gladness and pleasure]." Isaiah 12:2-3 states, "Behold, God is my salvation; I will trust, and not be afraid: for the LORD JEHOVAH is my strength and my song; he also is become my salvation. Therefore with joy [*sasown*, 8342—cheerfulness, gladness and mirth] shall ye draw water out of the wells of salvation." Zephaniah 3:17 states, "The LORD thy God in the midst of thee is mighty; he will save, he will rejoice over thee with joy; he will rest in his love, he will joy [*giyl*, see above] over thee with singing [*rinnah*, 7440— singing with gladness and joy]."

Sacred musical performance that is devoid of the aforementioned characteristics is one of the reasons that so many Christian musicians have become disillusioned with traditional sacred music. One of the other reasons has been that some busy musicians have failed to seek the aid and anointing of the Holy Spirit upon their sacred musicing. Therefore, a part of being a faithful servant (*pistos doulos* 4103, 1401) is being completely submissive to the leadership of the Holy Spirit. Furthermore, a part of faithful musical servanthood involves being passionate, and being even more passionate about sacred musicing than about secular musicing.

### Endnotes

1. Frank C. Huston, "It Pays to Serve Jesus", 1909.
2. Ralph Earle, *Matthew*. Vol. 6 of *Beacon Bible Commentary,* (Kansas City: Beacon Hill Press), 237.

### Chapter Seventeen Word Meanings

**Avowal**— an action or statement asserting the existence, worth or the truth of something or someone.

**Cistern—** an underground reservoir for rainwater.

**Hobble—** to tie or strap together the legs of a horse or other animal to prevent it from straying.

**Sedate—** quiet and undisturbed by any passion, excitement or emotion.

**Staid—** proper, serious, decorous, solemn.

## Chapter Seventeen Questions for Discussion

1. Discuss ways that a Christian musician can avoid using the tongue in a negative way. Also discuss ways for a Christian musician to use the tongue in a positive manner.
2. Discuss ways to avoid negative thoughts about what others might do to us and ways to avoid our own negative thoughts about others.
3. Since ministers of music work on Sunday, how should they go about observing a Sabbath day of rest?
4. Psalm 73:26 states, "My flesh and my heart faileth: but God is the strength of my heart, and my portion forever." Discuss the significance of this statement in the Bible.
5. Jeremiah 2:13 states, "For my people have committed two evils; they have forsaken me the fountain of living water, and have hewed them out cisterns, broken cisterns, that can hold no water." Discuss what it means for a Christian musician to have a broken cistern.
6. Galatians 6:9 is an admonishment to the Chief musician when it states, "And let us not be weary in well doing: for in due season we shall reap if we faint not." Consider this scripture and discuss ways for a Christian musician to fight physical and mental burnout.
7. Isaiah 40:28 states, "Hast thou not heard the LORD, the creator of the ends of the earth, fainteth not, neither is weary? There is no searching of his understanding." Discuss the significance of what Isaiah had to say about God and apply what he said to the life of a Christian musician.
8. The enemy of the Christian musician's soul desires to take his revenge out on the Christian musician. He waits for us to be enticed into sin. Satan is smart and he is subtle. Discuss the statements above and how the Christian musician should withstand the "wiles of the devil."
9. "A musician can be a good servant morally and not be passionately faithful to the responsibilities of the music ministry where God has placed that musician." With the statements above in mind, discuss ways for a Christian musician to become a passionate music leader.
10. St. Mark 8:35-37 states, "For whosoever will save his life shall lose it; but whosoever shall lose his life for my sake and the gospel's, the same shall save it. For what shall it profit a man, if he shall gain the whole world, and lose his own soul? Or what shall a man give in exchange for his soul?" Discuss a philosophical perspective that follows the Bible principles mentioned in this verse.

# Appendix A

## Annotated List of Some Well Known Philosophers
## (Including Several with Flawed Philosophies)

**Thomas Aquinas** (1225-1274) One of the Church Fathers who believed that man had fallen in matters of grace but not in matters of nature. Therefore man's intellect became autonomous.

**Francis Bacon** (1561-1626) A philosopher and essayist that believed philosophically that science was not autonomous. (Do not confuse him with the Irish painter Francis Bacon.)

**Karl Barth** (1886-1968) He held the higher critical theory that the Bible contains mistakes, but we are to believe it anyway. He also thought that religious truth is separated from the historical truth of the Scripture. Thus there is no place for reason and there is no point of verification. This constitutes the leap in religious terms. Barth is the man who opened the door of philosophical despair in theology.

**Albert Camus** (1913-1960) He was a French secular existentialist writer who wrote of man's lonely and absurd condition in an irrational universe. He wrote two novels and a play, "Caligula." He received a Nobel Prize in 1957, chiefly for such philosophical tracts as "the Rebel."

**Cenno di Pepe Cimabue** (1240-1303) He was a Florentine painter who began to paint the things of nature as nature. He, therefore, painted the lesser things naturalistically but painted spiritual things as a symbol.

**Alighieri Dante** (1265-1321) He was a writer who has caught up in life duality. Natural things became important to him. He fell in love with one woman and married another to have his children and keep his house.

**Donatian Alphonse François de Sade** (known as Marquis de Sade, 1740-1814) He was the French writer after whom sadism was named. His works contain descriptions of sexual perversions. Sadism is deriving pleasure from inflicting pain on another, especially as a form of sexual perversion.

**Jan Van Eyck** (1380-1441) He was the first known artist to paint real nature. In 1410 he produced a tiny miniature that contained the first real landscape. He was also one of the founders of the Flemish school of painting. He marks a moment in Northern Europe when medieval art gives way to "modern" modeling perspective and lighting based on close observation.

**Sigmund Freud** (1856-1939) He was an Austrian psychiatrist who was the founder of psychoanalysis. He outlined the two dominant principles of the mind as the pleasure-pain complex and the repression-compulsion complex. He believed that the ego and the super-ego were in constant tension with each other.

**Nicholas Fouquet** (c1416-1480) He was a French painter who painted the king's mistress, Agnes Sorel, as Mary. Furthermore he painted her partially naked.

**Martin Heidegger** (1889-1976) He was a German philosopher who believed in an angst which was a vague feeling of dread— a kind of basic anxiety. He is generally regarded as the founder of existentialism.

**George Wilhelm Friedrich Hegel** (1770-1831) He argued that attempts had been made for thousands of years to find an answer on the basis of thesis and antithesis and they had not come to anything. He thought in terms of thesis-antithesis with the answer always being synthesis.

**Aldous Huxley** (1894-1963) He is famous for his "first order experience." In order to have such an experience he advocated the use of drugs. You take a drug in order to try to have a direct mystical experience that has no relation to the world of the rational. He believed that men function better if they think that there is a God. There is no god, according to Huxley, but we will say there is a god.

**Karl Japers** (1883-1969) A psychologist who believed in a "final experience", i.e., an experience so big that it gives you a certainty that you are there and have hope of meaning— although rationally you could not have such hope. He believed that you could not prepare for this experience.

**Immanuel Kant** (1724-1804) He believed that we are justified in applying the concepts of the understanding to the world as we know it by making *a priori* determinations of the nature of possible experiences. He developed transcendental categories as pure concepts of the understanding that were applicable *a priori* to these experiences.

**Soren Aaby Kierkegaard** (1813-1855) He put away all hope of a unified field of philosophical knowledge. He believed that man has no meaning and no purpose or significance. He believed that on the basis of a non-rational, non-reasonable leap, there is a non-reasonable faith which gives optimism.

**Martin Luther** (1483-1546) He believed in a Biblical total fall of man. This belief included that man's will and his intellect were fallen. He believed that final and sufficient knowledge rested in the Bible. He disbelieved the Roman Catholic position that there was a divided work of salvation, i.e., that Christ died for our salvation, but man had to merit the merit of Christ. Luther believed that man is saved by faith alone. He believed that God had spoken to man in the Scriptures and that we know truly about God, because God revealed truth to man in the Bible.

**Friedrich Wilhelm Nietzsche** (1844-1900) He radically questioned the objectivity of truth. His influence has been substantial in existentialism and postmodernism. His philosophy included the Apollonian/Dionysian dichotomy, perspectivism, the will to power, and the death of God.

**Jean-Jacques Rousseau** (1712-1778) By the time of Rousseau there was no longer an idea of grace, but rather rationalism was entrenched in the concept of "nature and freedom." He considered reason to be the root of all problems, and that it was precisely through reason that people are led to be compared with each other. He developed a system of numbered music notation that was rejected by musicians.

**Jean-Paul Sartre** (1905-1980) Sartre believed that the great philosophic question is that something exists rather than that nothing exists. Man is a tragic joke in a context of total cosmic absurdity. He is also famous for "existential experience." He believed that we live in a universe which is rationally absurd and that each person must try to authenticate him or herself by an act of free will.

**Francis Schaeffer** (1912-1984) He was an American evangelical Christian theologian and philosopher. His works include *The God Who Is There, Escape from Reason, He Is There and He Is Not Silent, Death in the City,* and *How Should We Then Live?* He was able to simplify the philosophical beliefs of the major philosophers, artists, etc. *Escape from Reason* is especially valuable since it is a short work that explains the basic beliefs of many of the world's historic philosophers.

**Leonardo da Vinci** (1452-1519) He was an Italian painter, sculptor, architect, military engineer, and an accomplished musician. His art works include the Mona Lisa and the Last Supper. He was a true genius in many areas.

# Appendix B

## Selected List of Terms Often Used by Music Philosophers

**Absolutists**— believe that music's meaning is contained completely within the context of the music itself. It is the theory that music is not about anything.

**Absolute formalism**—is the belief that instrumental music without words (absolute music) is autonomous and is not a form of language or meta-language that is capable of having semantic content, tell stories, refer outside of itself. However, *enhanced* formalists do believe that it can be expressive of emotions.

**Aesthetics** (esthetics)— the theory of beauty in music as opposed to music's utility.

**Arousal Theory**— the belief that music arouses in us feelings of emotion.

**Autonomous freedom** –a freedom that is without restraint.

**Autonomous Philosophy** —philosophy that is separated from the revelation of Scripture.

**Byzantine Philosophical Thought** – These philosophers and theologians believed that heavenly things were "all important" to the exclusion of the natural world.

**Designated meaning**— meaning given to music which comes from outside of the music itself.

**Determinism** —the theory that human actions are controlled by antecedent (preceding) causes and not by the exercise of free will.

**Embodied meaning**— is meaning that lies completely within the formal properties of the music itself.

**Emotive cognitivism**— involves various theories that characterize emotions primarily in terms of their associated cognitions. However, there are several different ways of understanding the cognitions involved. This theory is sometimes applied to enhanced formalism music philosophy.

**Enhanced Formalism**— is the theory that emotions are moved from the hearer to the music itself. These emotions are not felt but cognized. This view is sometimes referred to as emotive cognitivism. This view purports that we are not emotionally moved by music.

**Emotive Properties of Music**— those properties of music that are believed to excite or arouse emotion or recall the memory of emotion.

**Epistemology**— the theory of knowledge and limits of knowing.

**Expressionists**— believe that music's relationships are in some sense capable of exciting feelings and emotions in the performer and auditor. This belief is sometimes referred to as "arousal theory." They contend that music's meaning "belongs to music and music alone." They seem to believe primarily music's meaning is intellectual.

**Formalists**— are non-referentialists who are sometimes called absolutists. They believe that the music is autonomous and only has meaning within itself (bubble theory).

**Garden variety of emotions**— is a phrase often used by the music philosopher Peter Kivy to refer to emotions such as melancholy, anger, fear, joy, etc. These are emotions that some philosophers (not Kivy) believe are aroused in us.

**Intrinsic noumenon**— is believed by some philosophers to be pure thought not connected with sense perception.

**Isolated disciplines** –refers to the study of knowledge in unrelated parallel lines. It is the study of philosophy without recognizing the necessary associations between all disciplines.

**Metaphysics**— is a general speculative worldview which is a systematic account of all reality and experience.

**Natural theology**—is a theology that is pursued independently of what the Bible teaches.

**Nature**— is the nature of music and the essence or quality or qualities that make music what it is.

**Nature/grace theory**— a philosophical belief that natural phenomena, including things such as music, belong to the category called nature, and that things such as man's spiritual condition belong to the category called grace.

**Neo-Platonism**—is a revival of Plato's philosophy in a transformed manner. Its central doctrines are emanation (the belief that the human spirit can participate in the divine) and the belief in the transcendent one who is beyond all knowledge and all being.

**Ontology**— is the area of metaphysics that deals with the essence of being.

**Persona theory**— is the belief that we hear all music performance as though it is a human utterance.

**Phenomenal**—refers to something that is recognized by or experienced by the senses rather than through thought or intuition.

**Pluralism**— is the notion that reality is composed of two or more kinds, conditions or systems in which two or more groups, principles, and sources of authority coexist.

**Postmodernism**— is the era after modernism that holds the belief that denies the existence of any universal philosophical or religious truth. It would be in direct opposition, for instance, with Francis Schaeffer's belief that the Bible contains "true truth".

**Praxis**— is a Greek term meaning practice, which in this book, represents an action-based philosophy of music education that stresses deliberate thinking and deliberate "doing".

**Rationalism**—is the belief that all knowledge and truth consist in what is ascertainable by rational processes of thought, and that there is no supernatural revelation. It is the doctrine that true and absolute knowledge is found only in reason.

**Rationality**— is a belief that is of or is related to reason and is based on and in accordance with reason or reasoning.

**Referentialists**— are music philosophers who believe that music can and does refer to meanings outside itself. They are sometimes referred to as heteronomists.

**Symbolists**— believe that music has symbols that represent abstract insight into the understanding of the nature of human feeling.

**Value**—the usefulness or worth of music. It refers to the inherent qualities (existing as permanent characteristics) that make the music intrinsically what it is.

# Bibliography

Abeles, Harold, and Lori Custodero. *Critical Issues in Music Education.* New York: Oxford University Press, 2010.

Abeles, Harold, Charles R Hoffer, and Robert H. Klotman. *Foundations of Music Education.* London: Collier Macmillan Publishers, 1984.

Addis, Laird. *Of Mind and Music.* Ithaca, New York: Cornell University Press, 2004.

Aldama, Frederick Luis. *Why the Humanities Matter: A Commonsense Approach.* Austin: University of Texas Press, 2008.

Almén, Byron and Edward Pearsall. *Approaches to Meaning in Music.* Bloomington: Indiana University Press, 2006.

Alperson, Philip. *What is Music? An Introduction to the Philosophy of Music.* University Park, Pa: Pennsylvania State University Press, 1994.

Barclay, William. *The Daily Study Bible.* 17 vols. Edinburgh, Scotland: The Saint Andrew Press, 1954.

Barnes, Albert. *Barnes' Notes on the New Testament.* Grand Rapids: Kregel Publications, 1962.

Beck, Guy L. *Sacred Sound: Experiencing Music in World Religions.* Waterloo, Ontario: Wilfrid Laurier University Press, 2006.

Berglund, Robert. *A Philosophy of Church Music.* Chicago: Moody Press, 1985.

Best, Harold M. *Music Through the Eyes of Faith.* San Francisco: Harper, 1993.

Bill, J. Brent. *Rock and Roll Proceed with Caution.* Old Tappan, NJ: Fleming H. Revell Company, 1984.

Bonds, Mark Evan. *A History of Music in Western Culture.* Upper Saddle River, NJ: Prentice Hall, 2003.

Bloom, Allan. *The Closing of the American Mind: How Higher Education Has Failed Democracy and Impoverished the Souls of Today's Students.* New York: Simon and Schuster, 1987.

Bloom, Allan, ed. *The Republic of Plato.* Chicago: Basic Books, 1968.

Boonshaft, Peter. *Teaching Music with Passion.* Galesville, MD: Meredith Music Publications, 2002.

Borroff, Edith. *Music in Europe and the United States.* Englewood Cliffs, N.J: Prentice Hall, Inc., 1971.

Bowman, Wayne. *Philosophical Perspectives on Music.* New York: Oxford University Press, 1998.

Braun, Joachim. *Music in Ancient Israel/Palestine.* Grand Rapids: William B. Eerdmans Publishing Company, 2002.

Brown, Francis, S. R. Driver, and Charles A. Briggs. *The New Brown-Driver-Briggs Gesenius Hebrew-English Lexicon*. 2 Vols. Peabody, Massachusetts: Hendrickson Publishers, 1979.

Brown, Raymond. *1 Corinthians*. Vol. 10 of *The Broadman Bible Commentary*, J. Allen, ed. Nashville: Broadman Press, 1970.

Bruner, Jerome. *The Process of Education*. Cambridge: Harvard University Press, 1960.

Budd, Malcolm. *Music and the Emotions: The Philosophical Theories*. London: Routledge & K. Paul, 1985.

Buttrick, George Arthur ed., *The Interpreter's Dictionary of the New Bible*. 4 Vols. New York: Abingdon Press, 1962.

Carter, Charles W. *The Wesleyan Bible Commentary*. Grand Rapids: Wm. B. Eerdmans Publishing Company, 1967.

Clarke, Adam. *Clarke's Commentary*. 6 Vols. Nashville: Abingdon Press, n.d.

Cloud, David W. *Contemporary Christian Music under the Spotlight*. Port Huron, MI: Way of Life Literature, 1998.

Coblentz, John. *Music in Biblical Perspective*. Kalona, Iowa: Calvary Publications, 1986.

Copland, Aaron. *What to Listen for in Music*. New York: McGraw-Hill Book Company, Inc., 1957.

Dahlhaus, Carl. *The Idea of Absolute Music*. Chicago: University of Chicago Press, 1989.

Davies, Steven. *Musical Meaning and Expression*. Ithaca, New York: Cornell University Press, 1994.

Davies, Steven. *Themes in the Philosophy of Music*. New York: Oxford University Press, 2003.

Davidson, Benjamin. *Analytical Hebrew and Chaldee Lexicon of the Old Testament*. MacDill AFB, Florida: MacDonald Publishing Company, n.d.

Dean, Talmage. *A Survey of Twentieth Century Protestant Church Music in America*. Nashville, TN: Broadman Press, 1988.

Deutsch, Dianna. *The Psychology of Music*. Orlando: Harcourt, Brace, Jovanovich Publishers, 1982.

DeViny, Richard. *There's More to Church Music than Meets the Ear*. Philadelphia: Fortress Press, 1972.

Elliott, David James. *Music Matters: A New Philosophy of Music Education*. New York: Oxford University Press, 1995.

Elliott, David James. *Praxial Music Education: Reflections and Dialogues*. New York: Oxford University Press, 2005.

Engel, Carl. *The Music of the Most Ancient Nations*. New York: Books for Libraries Press, 1970.

Ernest, James D., trans. *Theological Lexicon of the New Testament*. 3 Vols. Peabody, MA: Hendrickson Publishers, 1994.

Exell, Joseph S. *The Biblical Illustrator*. 23 Vols. Grand Rapids: Baker Book House, nd.

Ferguson, Donald N. *A History of Musical Thought*. Second Ed. New York: Appleton-Century-Crofts, Inc., 1935.

Fisher, Tim. *The Battle for Christian Music*. Greenville, SC: Sacred Music Services, 1992.

Friedmann, Jonathan L. *Music in the Hebrew Bible: Understanding References in the Torah, Nevi'im and Ketuvim*. Jefferson, NC: McFarland & Company, Inc., 2013.

Foster, Henry J. *The Preacher's Homiletic Commentary*. 38 Vols. Grand Rapids: Baker Book House, n.d.

Garlock, Frank and Kurt Woetzel. *Music in the Balance*. Greenville, SC: Majesty Music, Inc., 1992.

Geisler, Norman and Paul Feinberg. *Introduction to Philosophy: A Christian Perspective*. Grand Rapids: Baker Books, 1980.

Girdlestone, Robert B. *Synonyms of the Old Testament*. Grand Rapids: Wm. B. Eerdmans Publishing Company, 1974.

Glenn, Neal E., William B. McBride, and George H. Wilson. *Secondary School Music; Philosophy, Theory, and Practice*. Englewood Cliffs, NJ: Prentice-Hall, 1970.

Gloag, Kenneth. *Postmodernism in Music*. Cambridge: Cambridge University Press, 2012.

Gradenwitz, Peter. *The Music of Israel: From the Biblical Era to Modern Times*. Portland, OR: Amadeus Press, 1996.

Green, J., ed. *The New Englishman's Greek-English Concordance*. Wilmington, DE: Associated Publishers and Authors, 1976.

———. *The New Englishman's Hebrew and Chaldee Concordance*. Wilmington, DE: Associated Publishers and Authors, 1976.

———. *The Interlinear Hebrew-Greek English Bible*. Wilmington, DE: Associated Publishers and Authors, 1976.

Grout, Donald and Claude Palisca. *History of Western Music*. New York: W.W. Norton & Company, Inc., 1988.

Hamilton, Andy. *Aesthetics and Music*. New York: Continuum International Pub. Group, 2007.

Harris, R. Laird, ed. *Theological Wordbook of the Old Testament*. Chicago: Moody Press, 1980.

Harrison, Thomas J. *1910, The Emancipation of Dissonance*. Berkeley: University of California Press, 1996.

Harper, A.F., ed. *Beacon Bible Commentary*. 10 Vols. Kansas City, MO: Beacon Hill Press, 1969.

Haïk-Vantoura, Suzanne. *The Music of the Bible Revealed*. Berkley: Bibal Press, 1991.

Harris, R. Laird, Gleason L. Archer, and Bruce Waltke, eds. *Theological Wordbook of the Old Testament*. 2 Vols. Chicago: Moody Press, 2007.

Hart, Lowell. *Satan's Music Exposed*. Huntingdon Valley, PA: Salem Kirban, Inc., 1991.

Henry, Matthew. *Matthew Henry's Commentary*. McLean, VA: MacDonald Publishing Company, n.d.

Henry, Matthew. *Matthew Henry's Commentary on the Whole Bible*. 6 Vols. Mclean, VA: Macdonald Publishing Company, n. d.

Houlgate, Stephen. *Hegel and the Arts*. Evanston, IL: Northwestern University Press, 2007.

Howell, Peter. *Musical Structure and Cognition*. Orlando: Harcourt, Barce, Jovanovich Publishers, 1985.

Huckvale, David. *The Occult Arts of Music: An Esoteric Survey from Pythagoras to Pop Culture*. Jefferson, NC: McFarland & Company, Inc. Publishers, 2013.

Hustad, Donald. *Jubilate II Church Music in Worship and Renewal*. Carol Stream, IL: Hope Publishing Co., 1993.

Idelsohn, A.Z. *Jewish Liturgy*. New York: Schocken Books, 1932.

———. *Jewish Music in its Historical Development*. New York: Schocken Books, 1967.

Iverson - Norman Associates. *The Six Version Parallel New Testament*. Wheaton, IL: Christian Life Publications, 1974.

Jamieson, Robert. *A Commentary of the Old and New Testaments*. Grand Rapids: Wm. B. Eerdmans Publishing Company, 1978.

Jeffries, Doug. *Musical Concordance of the Bible*. Lillenas Publishing Company, 1987.

Jenni, Ernst and Claus Wersterman. *Theological Lexicon of the Old Testament*, 3 Vols. Peabody, MA: Hendrickson Books, 1997.

Katz, Ruth, and Carl Dahlhaus. *Contemplating Music: Source Readings in the Aesthetics of Music*. Stuyvesant: Pendragon Press, 1987.

Keil, C.F. and Franz Delitzsch. *Commentary on the Old Testament*. 10 Vols. Grand Rapids: Wm. B. Eerdmans Publishing Company, reprinted 1976.

Kittel, Gerhard. Ed. *Theological Dictionary of the New Testament*. 10 Vols. Grand Rapids: Wm.B. Eerdmans Publishing Company, 1976.

Kivy, Peter. *Introduction to a Philosophy of Music*. Oxford: Clarendon Press, 2002.

———. *New Essays on Musical Understanding*. Oxford: Clarendon Press, 2001.

Larson, Bob. *Rock*. Wheaton, IL: Tyndale House Publications, 1980.

———. *The Day Music Died*. Carol Stream, IL: Creation House, 1972.

———. *Rock and the Church.* New Testament Carol Stream, IL: Creation House, 1971.

Lenski, R.C.H. *The Interpretation of St. Paul's First and Second Epistles to the Corinthians.* Volume 7 of *Commentary on the New Testament*, Minneapolis, MN: Augsburg Publishing House, 1937.

Lightfoot, John. *A Commentary on the New Testament from the Talmud and Hebraica.* 4 vols. Peabody, MA: Hendrickson Publishers, Inc., 1979.

Lippman, Edward A. *The Philosophy & Aesthetics of Music.* Lincoln: University of Nebraska Press, 1999.

Lockyer, Herbert, Jr. *All the Music of the Bible.* Peabody, MA: Hendrickson Publishers, Inc., 2004.

Lucarni, Dan. *Why I Left the Contemporary Christian Music Movement.* Webster, NY: Evangelical Press. 2002.

Lunde, Alfred. *Christian Education Through Music.* Wheaton, IL: Evangelical Teacher Training Association, 1978.

MacLaren, Alexander. *Expositions of Holy Scripture.* Grand Rapids: Baker Book House, 1984.

Madell, Geoffrey. *Philosophy, Music, and Emotion.* Edinburgh: Edinburgh University Press, 2002.

Makujina, John. *Measuring the Music.* Salem, OH: Schmul Publishing Co., 2000.

Marcel, Gabriel, J. Stephen Maddux, and Robert E. Wood. *Music and Philosophy.* Milwaukee: Marquette University Press, 2005.

Marcuse, Sybxl. *A Survey of Musical Instruments.* New York: Harper and Row, Publishers, 1975.

Meyer, Leonard B. *Emotion and Meaning in Music.* Chicago: University of Chicago Press, 1956.

Miller, Stephen. *Worship Leaders We Are Not Rock Stars.* Chicago: Moody Publishers, 2013.

McLaughlin, Terence. *Music and Communications.* London: Faber & Faber, 1970.

Montagu, Jeremy. *Musical Instruments of the Bible.* Lanham, MD: Scarecrow Press, 2002.

Norris, Christopher. *What's Wrong with Postmodernism: Critical Theory and the Ends of Philosophy.* Baltimore: Johns Hopkins University Press, 1990.

Nulman, Macy. *Concise Encyclopedia of Jewish Music.* New York: McGraw-Hill Book Company, 1975.

Page, Nick. *And Now Let's Move Into a Time of Nonsense.* Waynesboro, GA: Authentic Media, 2004.

Peters, Steve and Mark R Littleton. *Truth About Rock.* Minneapolis, MN: Bethany House Publishers, 1998.

Pierce, Timothy M. *Enthroned on Our Praise*. Nashville, TN: B & H Publishing Group, 2008.

*Practical Word Studies in the New Testament*. 2 Vols. Chattanooga: Leadership Ministries Worldwide, 1998.

Rothmuller, Aaron. *The Music of the Jews*, New and Revised Edition. New York: A.S. Barnes and Company, Inc., 1967.

Rahn, John. *Perspectives on Musical Aesthetics*. New York: W.W. Norton, 1994.

Reimer, Bennett. *A Philosophy of Music Education*. Englewood Cliffs, NJ: Prentice Hall, 1989.

Ridley, Aaron. *The Philosophy of Music: Theme and Variations*. Edinburgh: Edinburgh University Press, 2004.

Robertson, Archibald T. *Word Pictures in the New Testament*. 6 Vols. Nashville: Broadman Press, 1931.

Robinson, Jenefer. *Music & Meaning*. Ithaca, NY: Cornell University Press, 1997.

Roth, Cecil, ed. *Encyclopedia Judaica*. 16 Vols. NY: The Macmillan Company, 1972.

Ryken, Leland. *Culture in Christian Perspective*. Portland, OR: Multnomah Press, 1986.

Sachs, Curt. *The History of Music Instruments*. New York: W.W. Norton & Company, Inc., 1943.

———. *The Rise of Music in the Ancient World*. New York: W. W. Norton & Company, Inc., 1943.

———. *World History of the Dance*. New York: W.W. Norton & Company, Inc., 1965.

Schaeffer, Francis. *Art and the Bible*. Downers Grove, IL: InterVarsity Press, 2007.

———. *Death in the City*. Downers Gro—ve, IL: InterVarsity Press, 1976.

———. *Escape From Reason*. Downers Grove, IL: InterVarsity Press, 1968.

———. *The God Who Is There*. Downers Grove, IL: InterVarsity Press, 1968.

———. *How Should We Then Live?* Fleming H. Revell Company, 1976.

Scheer, Greg. *The Art of Worship A Musicians Guide to Leading Modern Worship*. Grand Rapids: Baker Books, 2006.

Scruton, Roger. *The Aesthetics of Music*. Oxford: Oxford University Press, 1999.

———. *Understanding Music: Philosophy and Interpretation*. New York: Continuum US, 2009.

Seidel, Leonard. *Face the Music: Contemporary Church Music on Trial*. Springfield, VA: Grace Unlimited Publications, 1988.

Sendrey, Alfred. *Music in the Social and Religious Life of Antiquity*. Cranbury, NJ: Associated Presses, Inc., 1974.

Shanks, Hershel and Ann Kilmer. "World's Oldest Musical Notation Deciphered on

Cuneiform Tablet." *Biblical Archaeological Review* 6, no. 5 (Sept-Oct 1980):14-25.

Sharpe, R.A. *Philosophy of Music: An Introduction*. Ithaca: McGill-Queen's University Press, 2004.

Smietana, Bob. "Presbyterians' Decision to Drop Hymn Stirs Debate," Last modified August 5, 2013. Accessed February 19, 2017, www.usatoday.com.

Spence, H.D.M. and Joseph S. Exell, ed. *The Pulpit Commentary*. New York: Funk and Wagnall's Company, n.d.

Spencer, Jon Michael. *Theological Music: Introduction to Theomusicology*. New York: Greenwood Press, 1991.

Spicq, Ceslas. *Theological Lexicon of the New Testament.* 3 Vols. Peabody, MA.: Hendrickson Publishers Marketing, LLC, 1994.

Stainer, John. *The Music of the Bible*. Revised Edition. New York: Da Capo Press, 1970.

Stern, Max. *Bible & Music: Influences of the Old Testament on Western Music*. Jersey City, NJ: KTAV Pub. House, 2011.

Stock, Kathleen. *Philosophers on Music: Experience, Meaning, and Work*. Oxford: Oxford University Press, 2007.

Stolba, K. Marie. *The Development of Western Music, A History*. Dubuque, IA: Wm. C. Brown Publishers, 1990.

Strong, James. *The Exhaustive Concordance of the Bible*. Peabody, MA: Hendrickson Publishers. n.d.

Taylor, Richard S. *A Return to Christian Culture*. Minneapolis: Dimension Books, 1975.

Topp, Dale. *Music in the Christian Community.* Grand Rapids: Wm. Eerdmans Publishing Co., 1976.

Thayer, Joseph. *The New Thayer's Greek-English Lexicon of the New Testament*. Peabody, MA: Hendrickson Publishers, 1981.

Thiessen, Don. *A Compilation of Scripture Passages on Music*. Otterburne, Manitoba: The Christian Book Nook, 1983.

Tregelles, Samuel, trans. *Gesenius' Hebrew and Chaldee Lexicon of the Old Testament*. Grand Rapids: Wm. B. Eerdmans Publishing Company, 1949.

Vaughan, Curtis, ed. *The New Testament from 26 Translations*. Grand Rapids: Zondervan Book Publishers, 1978.

Vincent, Marvin R. *Vincent's Word Studies in the New Testament.* 4 Vols. Peabody, MA: Hendrickson Publishers, *n.d.*

Vine, William Edwy. *The Expanded Vine's Expository Dictionary of New Testament Words*. Edited by John R. Kohlenberger. Minneapolis: Bethany House Publishers, 1984.

———. *An Expository Dictionary of Old Testament Words*. Old Tappan, NJ: Fleming H. Revell Company, 1978.

Washburne, Christopher, and Maiken Derno. *Bad Music: The Music We Love to Hate*. New York: Routledge, 2004.

Weiss, Piero and Richard Taruskin. *Music in the Western World: A History in Documents*. New York: Schirmer Books, 1984.

Wellesz, Egon. *The New Oxford History of Music*. Vol. I. London: Oxford University Press, 1957.

Whedon, D.D., ed. *Commentary on the Old and New Testaments*. Cincinnati: Walden & Stowe, 1882.

Whiston, William trans. *The Works of Josephus Complete and Unabridged*. Peabody, MA: Hendrickson Publishers, 1987.

Wigram, George. *Analytical Greek Lexicon of the New Testament*. Wilmington, DE: Associated Publisher and Authors, Inc., n.d.

———. *The New Englishman's Greek-English Concordance of the New Testament*. Wilmington, DE: Associated Publishers and Authors, 1976.

———. *The New Englishman's Hebrew and Chaldee Concordance*. Wilmington, DE: Associated Publishers and Authors, 1975.

Wigram, George and Ralph D. Winter. *The Word Study Concordance*. Wheaton, IL: Tyndale House Publishers, Inc., 1978.

Wilson, William. *New Wilson's Old Testament Word Studies*. Grand Rapids: Kregel Publications, 1987.

Winter, Ralph D. and Roberta H. Winter. *The Word Study New Testament*. Wheaton, IL: Tyndale House Publishers, Inc., 1978.

Wolf, Garen. *Music of the Bible in Christian Perspective*. Salem, OH: Schmul Publishing Company, 1996.

———. *Church Music Matters*. Salem, OH: Schmul Publishing Company, 2004.

Young, Robert. *Analytical Concordance to the Bible*. Grand Rapids: Wm. B. Eerdmans Publishing Company, 1970.

Zodhiates, Spiros, ed. *The Hebrew-Greek Key Study Bible*. Grand Rapids: Baker Book House, 1984.

Zuckerkandl, Victor. *Sound and Symbol; Music and the External World*. Princeton, NJ: Princeton University Press, 1969.

# Index

## A

absolute 27, 32, 40, 75, 93, 191, 193, 195, 201, 203, 209, 210, 389
absolute expressionists 210
absolutes 49, 54, 67, 75, 78, 81, 92, 93, 100, 175, 245, 248, 249, 274, 305, 317
absolutists 189, 190, 192, 205, 367, 368
academic 99, 100, 101, 123, 137, 141, 149, 154, 170, 207, 241
accomplished 107, 112, 113, 339, 358, 369, 381, 389
actualization 74, 75, 76, 208
adiaphorous 312, 324
aesthetic 21, 37, 93, 100, 101, 106, 107, 108, 123, 124, 135, 145, 146, 165, 207, 211, 220, 229, 242, 243, 244, 245, 246, 247, 248, 249, 251, 252, 253, 254, 255, 256, 257, 258, 259, 260, 261, 262, 263, 274
aesthetic beauty 248, 253, 256, 257, 258, 263, 277
aesthetic decorations 255
aesthetic embellishment 257
aesthetic end, ends, 263
aesthetic experience 100, 146, 147, 242, 243, 274
aesthetic experiences 99, 100, 107, 123, 126, 145, 146, 147, 242, 303
aesthetic meaning 243, 263
aesthetic music experiences 146
aesthetic musical experiences 146
aesthetic qualities 99, 145, 148, 149, 242
aesthetic quality 243
aesthetically beautiful 248
aesthetician 123, 132
aesthetics 36, 221, 236, 242, 243, 244, 245, 246, 247, 249, 250, 251, 252, 253, 257, 259, 261, 277, 389
aesthetics and embellishment 255
affective 99, 132
aggrandizement 74, 75, 164, 215, 217
Akkad 98
Akkadians 38
amalgamate 164, 313, 322, 324
amalgamation 31, 39, 49, 159, 211, 291, 313, 315
Ambrose 142
amenable 42, 64, 66, 225
Amphion 379
ancient landmark 142, 169, 172, 177, 178, 205, 288, 298, 301, 333
ancient landmarks 29
anoint 352
anointed 34, 175, 275, 292, 321, 359
anointing 213, 214, 232, 236, 274, 275, 276, 321, 331, 352, 359, 361
anti-Christ 64, 121, 124, 221
anti-music 238, 239, 240, 241, 242, 266
antithesis 46, 47, 48, 49, 66, 67, 85, 86, 241, 291, 364
appropriate 33, 36, 37, 41, 65, 66, 117, 122, 128, 130, 164, 169, 170, 174, 175, 179, 183, 184, 185, 187, 192, 199, 232, 244, 261, 265, 270, 279, 283, 297, 298, 300, 303, 304, 306, 340
appropriately 144, 351

appropriateness 31, 49, 51, 59, 65, 97, 155, 169, 199, 201, 260, 297, 299, 303, 339
Aquinas, Thomas 83, 363
Aristotle 128, 129, 132, 135, 163, 197, 253
arousal theory 100, 190, 192, 193, 202, 367, 368
Arp, Jean 243
art for art's sake 247, 257
art forms 35, 247, 261, 286, 321, 322, 323
Asaph 98, 102, 103, 115, 116, 131
assessment 101
audiating 195
auditor 37, 149, 163, 186, 189, 190, 191, 192, 194, 195, 196, 201, 206, 209, 212, 217, 218, 219, 224, 246, 253, 254, 271, 274, 286, 299, 323, 368
autonomous 49, 53, 73, 74, 80, 82, 89, 91, 92, 133, 147, 192, 193, 219, 245, 246, 247, 307, 312, 313, 325, 363, 367, 368

## B

Bach, J. S. 32, 198, 241, 242, 284, 285, 305, 344, 345
Bach, Johann Sebastian 344
banal 37, 270, 273, 278, 279, 280, 320, 346
band 114, 139, 140, 144, 147, 192, 294
Baronnett, Jean 240
Basil 142, 143
belief system 47, 59, 66, 86, 87, 88, 89, 193, 246
Berglund, Robert 50, 165, 200, 201, 257, 306
Bible college 83, 98, 102, 304, 351

Bible principles of musicing 88, 97, 124, 129, 155, 156, 169, 172, 174, 187, 209, 270, 301, 306, 379
biblical accents 153
Bingham, Hiram 142, 143
bitonality 244
Book of Psalms 273
Borroff, Edith 70
Bruner, Jerome 132, 138
bubble theory 368

## C

Cage, John 240, 241, 242
Calvin, John 173
cantillating 204, 216
carnal music 188, 202
catechize 98, 314
catechizing 99
cause and effect 246, 305, 312
CCM 176, 177, 193
cerebral 189, 332
Cézanne, Paul 243
changed life 37, 54, 97, 109, 117, 119, 121, 130, 160, 161, 177, 200, 255, 258, 263, 279, 298, 306
character 17, 66, 76, 81, 98, 106, 119, 130, 137, 151, 189, 197, 199, 200, 232, 253, 254, 255, 261, 266, 317, 339, 358, 359
charisma 75, 275, 276, 321
cheironomy 103, 115
Chenaniah 116
Chicago jazz 201
chief musician 98, 115, 116, 326, 327, 347, 348, 349, 350, 351, 352, 354, 355, 356, 357, 358, 362
choir 114, 147, 171, 214, 233, 304, 330, 341
Christian Music Education 100, 101
Christian Music Education Philosophy 99

Christian school 16, 60, 65, 98, 99, 101, 102, 104, 105, 110, 112, 118, 119, 120, 124, 134, 138, 167, 179, 256, 260, 314, 355
Christian worship 34, 36, 147, 232, 279, 291, 298, 300, 302, 322
Christocentric 26, 42, 46, 47, 52, 55, 61, 66, 74, 75, 78, 79, 84, 85, 86, 88, 102, 105, 109, 123, 124, 238, 239, 247, 254, 255, 299, 307, 314
Chrysostom 142
Church Fathers 142, 143, 333, 363
church music 26, 39, 46, 49, 51, 55, 60, 72, 73, 79, 87, 129, 161, 162, 163, 170, 171, 174, 182, 183, 198, 199, 200, 201, 216, 225, 233, 255, 256, 270, 271, 282, 283, 288, 289, 290, 291, 292, 293, 295, 296, 298, 299, 303, 304 312, 314, 319, 320, 322, 323, 328, 341
cinema 259, 265, 265, 266
Clement of Alexandria 142
closed system 189, 190, 192, 193, 198, 202, 205, 207, 208, 209, 219, 220, 221, 224, 246, 252, 272
CME 21, 100, 101, 102, 103, 104, 105, 107, 112, 113, 121, 123, 125, 128, 136, 137, 142, 145, 183
CMEP 21, 99, 104, 109, 111, 112, 123, 124, 125, 127, 128, 136, 138, 142
Coblentz, John 92
cognitive 99, 100, 101, 132, 139, 214, 271
communicate 48, 51, 92, 148, 149, 162, 163, 182, 183, 186, 188, 194, 195, 196, 197, 198, 201, 206, 209, 212, 218, 219, 220, 222, 223, 224, 225, 236, 252, 253, 274, 296, 311, 332
communicated 148, 149, 194, 197, 201, 212, 214, 221

communicates 50, 92, 106, 146, 147, 163, 182, 183, 186, 190, 194, 196, 218, 221, 222, 223, 225, 237
communicating 92, 162, 188, 195, 196, 198, 201, 202, 220, 222, 223, 226, 326
communication 50, 51, 122, 146, 152, 182, 194, 197, 199, 201, 207, 220, 222, 223, 237, 274, 335, 356
community 22, 43, 65, 66, 101, 119, 129, 135, 141, 145, 147, 148, 149, 191, 206, 207
composer 30, 31, 36, 92, 117, 158, 163, 164, 186, 201, 224, 229, 230, 231, 237, 245, 253, 278, 346
composers 25, 34, 36, 69, 159, 196, 200, 208, 228, 230, 232, 239, 241, 242, 243, 245, 274, 280, 284, 286, 287, 339
congregational singing 144, 172, 213, 329
consonance 244
contemporary Christian musicians 48, 221, 245, 297, 312
contradistinction 176, 178, 284, 301
conviction 60, 79, 88, 93, 101, 102, 104, 111, 127, 141, 151, 163
Copland, Aaron 224
correctness 65, 68, 73, 97, 244
Coryville jazz 201
cosmopolitan 32, 39
country 223, 284, 290, 315
Cowell, Henry 240
Cowen, C. E. 16
created 24, 25, 26, 27, 28, 29, 32, 34, 35, 36, 38, 40, 48, 64, 68, 69, 70, 72, 73, 74, 79, 80, 81, 90, 130, 147, 160, 164, 182, 190, 193, 195, 196, 208, 209, 211, 228, 229, 234, 235, 239, 244, 246, 247, 251, 252, 257, 258, 284, 289, 290, 295, 298, 317, 322, 330, 344, 352, 356 359

created things 146, 247, 341, 359
creation 24, 25, 26, 27, 28, 29, 31, 36, 38, 44, 48, 53, 68, 69, 70, 71, 72, 73, 80, 122, 146, 193, 196, 228, 229, 230, 234, 239, 247, 258, 352, 353, 354
creative ownership 221
creator 28, 36, 40, 161, 229, 253, 341, 352, 353, 362
Creator 90, 147, 160, 211, 247, 251, 252, 322
critical thinking 108, 109, 110
culture 69, 71, 98, 102, 124, 125, 153, 206, 208, 285, 298, 308, 324
cunning 98, 102, 112, 113, 116, 131
curriculum 99, 100, 101, 104, 108, 110, 112, 121, 126, 132, 138, 139, 140
curriculum spiral sequence 118, 139

# D

Dadaism 243
Dali, Salvador 243
dance 140, 263, 264, 265, 284, 301, 325
Davies, Richard 191
Debussy, Claude 242, 244
decibel 144, 285
decibels 319
decorative arts 258, 261, 262
Degas, Edgar 243
designated meaning 205, 206, 367
despair 241, 242, 244, 245, 356, 363
destructive change 169, 255
Dewey, John 75
dissonance 239, 244, 245, 288
distortion 240, 241, 286, 287, 288
diversity 318, 335
dodecaphonic 244, 245
drama 260, 261
drum 28, 29, 49, 144, 171

Duffield, George 349

# E

Earle, Ralph 359
eclectic 176, 178
education 15, 21, 43, 46, 49, 51, 55, 60, 68, 75, 77, 79, 87, 89, 93, 97, 98, 99, 100, 101, 102, 103, 104, 105, 106, 107, 108, 109, 110, 111, 112, 113, 114, 116, 117, 118, 119, 120, 121, 122, 123, 124, 126, 127, 128, 129, 130, 131, 132, 133, 134, 135, 136, 137, 138, 139, 140, 141, 142, 144, 145, 146, 151, 154, 156, 177, 183, 208, 222, 233, 258, 260, 264, 321, 369
educational conviction 102
educational preference 102
educator 34, 57, 79, 98, 100, 103, 105, 106, 107, 108, 109, 110, 111, 112, 114, 115, 116, 117, 119, 120, 121, 122, 123, 124, 125, 129, 133, 137, 139, 150, 151, 153, 154, 158, 258, 262, 263, 264, 265, 280, 327, 328
educators 17, 19, 46, 49, 54, 98, 101, 103, 104, 105, 106, 107, 108, 109, 110, 111, 114, 117, 118, 119, 120, 121, 122, 123, 124, 125, 126, 128, 129, 130, 133, 138, 139, 140, 141, 145, 146, 150, 151, 153, 154, 155, 233, 241, 260, 328
effectual 175, 326
efficacious 29, 38, 90, 92, 162, 213, 216, 222, 224, 242, 261, 273, 274, 275, 279, 309, 321, 350
Egypt 38, 72, 98
elementary 99, 100, 106, 108, 110, 114, 116, 117, 118, 136, 139, 140, 155, 233, 327
Elliott, David 39, 127, 135, 141

emancipating dissonance 244
embodied meaning 37, 149, 208, 368
embodies absolute truth 27
emotional meaning 190, 212, 214
enactment 63, 274, 289, 304
epistemology 48, 49, 52, 84, 168, 244, 368
esoteric meaning 42, 183, 205, 208
esoteric reference 172, 204, 309, 226
ethical 140, 221
evolution 44, 228
excellence 79, 104, 130, 199
existentialism 243, 307, 364, 365
expressionists 188, 205, 368
extra-curricular 101
extrinsic 145, 208, 231, 235
Ezekiel 214, 248

**F**

faulty view 27, 73
flesh 30, 63, 121, 176, 192, 199, 200, 211, 225, 255, 287, 290, 297, 298, 324, 347, 349, 362
folk 163, 171, 304
formal properties 27, 36, 37, 73, 117, 139, 145, 148, 154, 159, 162, 186, 187, 188, 189, 190, 191, 201, 205, 206, 207, 208, 209, 210, 217, 218, 220, 222, 224, 225, 237, 256, 270, 271, 272, 273, 274, 277, 278, 284, 303, 304, 310, 322, 323
formalism 190, 192, 198, 367, 368
formalist 148, 198, 206, 221, 272
formalists 188, 190, 198, 205, 207, 218, 272, 367, 368
forward directionality 238, 277, 278, 286, 289, 302
forward propelling directionality 197, 278, 316
foundations 66, 87, 169, 244
Foundry 176, 177

free will 49, 243, 245, 313, 366, 367
fusion 301, 315, 316, 324

**G**

Garlock, Frank 16, 17, 206, 310, 311
Geisler, Norman 146
Getty, Keith 280, 320
God created music 24, 26, 27, 29, 40, 68, 69, 70, 72, 74, 79, 90, 211, 239, 247, 356
gospel music 182, 304, 336
gospel songs 233, 278, 320, 321, 325, 329, 334, 335, 336, 339, 346
grace 62, 81, 82, 83, 105, 133, 141, 149, 150, 157, 175, 211, 273, 276, 282, 287, 295, 335, 337, 350, 357, 363, 365, 369
Greek fragments 38
Greek philosophers 183, 253
Gregory of Nyssa 142, 143
Grout, Donald 70, 253
guidelines 121, 124, 184

**H**

Haggadah 205, 216
Haik-Vantoura, Suzanne 56, 72, 250
Halakhah 205, 216
hand 28, 111, 113, 115, 132, 199, 229, 236, 240, 348, 354, 355
handmaiden 147, 172, 205, 277, 289, 293
hands 98, 102, 103, 111, 115, 116, 131, 326, 347, 348
harmonic practice 210, 244, 245, 252, 288
harmony 39, 134, 150, 153, 195, 229, 255, 288, 289, 297, 330, 339
harp 28, 29, 70, 98, 102, 103, 112, 113, 115, 116, 130, 131, 142, 156, 164, 194, 223, 239, 248, 307, 356, 361

heart-life 276
Hegel, Georg Wilhelm Friedrich 48, 67, 364
Heman 98, 102, 103, 115, 116, 131
Hendrix, Jimi 224
heptatonic 56, 66, 71, 72, 76, 153
human psyche 238, 239, 266, 286
humanism 74, 76, 77, 141, 175
humanist 75, 83, 85, 235, 276
humanistic 46, 74, 75, 80, 85, 86, 98, 140, 141, 175, 205, 214, 311
hymns 62, 130, 160, 164, 170, 182, 187, 199, 233, 273, 304, 318, 320, 321, 325, 329, 332, 333, 335, 336, 337, 339, 346
hypocrisy 161

# I

idioms 294
import 37, 42, 53, 72, 84, 100, 122, 148, 149, 186, 194, 210, 246, 247, 252, 257, 266, 355
impressionism 243
impressionistic 243
inappropriate 65, 106, 117, 144, 164, 165, 177, 183, 231, 235, 270, 283, 284, 339
incorrectness 65, 68
indeterminacy 241
infallible 27, 28, 53, 63, 83, 184
inspired 17, 18, 27, 28, 39, 47, 53, 58, 59, 63, 67, 85, 86, 137, 157, 184, 195
instrumental music 29, 35, 142, 143, 144, 145, 165, 208, 225, 238, 257, 260, 261, 271, 288, 297, 367
instruments 28, 29, 108, 124, 128, 131, 139, 140, 142, 143, 144, 145, 153, 165, 171, 233, 257, 286, 308, 329, 341, 342, 343, 346, 361
intentionality 210, 211, 216, 217, 218

intimate zone 310
intoning 172, 173, 204, 216
intrinsic 106, 145, 208, 231, 235, 368

# J

jazz 201, 223, 225, 284, 301, 311, 315, 325
Jeduthun 98, 102, 103, 115, 116, 131
Jehovah 22, 38, 185, 187, 273, 288, 342, 347, 348, 353, 357, 361
joyful noise 248, 251
joyful sound 184, 185, 186, 187, 190, 192, 198, 203, 360
Jubal 28, 70

# K

Kansas City jazz 201
Karaites 168, 169
Kierkegaard, Sören Aaby 84, 243, 365
Kilmer, Ann 71
Kinder-Music 220
Kivy, Peter 198, 206, 368
"knowing" 28, 48, 49, 50, 52, 84, 196, 219, 220, 226, 227, 244, 245, 246, 253
Kodaly, Zoltan 140

# L

Lachmann, Robert 283
Langer, Susan K. 75
leadershift 52, 66, 69, 173, 318, 319
Levite 98, 102, 103, 115, 131, 170, 179, 204, 215, 355, 361
Levite musicians 102, 103, 115, 131, 170, 179, 204, 215
listening based 99, 113, 123, 127
Lordship of Christ 63, 64, 79, 83, 122, 133, 161, 170, 219, 221, 225, 246, 287

lust of the flesh 121, 176, 200, 211, 225, 297, 298

# M

Manet, Édouard 243
Maslow, Abraham B. 75
mathematical ratios 26, 27, 28, 193, 207, 211
matrix 47, 48, 59, 86, 88, 92, 149, 150, 291, 340
matstsebah 250
MEAE 21, 99, 123, 124, 126, 127, 128, 145, 146, 148
menial worshiper 215
meta-language 121, 194, 195, 218, 202, 221, 222, 227, 367
methodology 48, 49, 51, 84, 168, 244, 266
Metz, Donald 55
Meyer, Leonard B. 75, 189, 205, 206
Midrash 205, 217
minister of music 34, 165, 169, 270, 320, 326, 327, 331
mirror of life 197
mode 39, 163, 183, 223, 287
Monet, Claude 243
moral influence 212
moral nature of God 155, 211, 221, 225, 231, 232, 234, 274, 288, 323, 340
multi-cultural 124
muse 109, 130, 164, 208, 209, 255, 288, 332
music aesthetic 124, 211, 220, 236, 237, 238, 240, 241, 242, 245, 247, 246, 248, 249, 251, 252, 253, 254, 255, 256, 267
music alone 145, 165, 195, 202, 225, 231, 235, 238, 277, 278, 308, 309, 310, 311, 368
music appreciation 107, 114

music education 15, 21, 46, 49, 51, 55, 60, 75, 77, 79, 87, 89, 93, 97, 98, 99, 100, 101, 102, 103, 104, 105, 106, 107, 108, 109, 110, 111, 112, 113, 114, 116, 117, 118, 119, 120, 121, 122, 123, 124, 126, 127, 128, 129, 130, 131, 132, 133, 134, 135, 136, 137, 138, 139, 140, 141, 142, 144 145, 146, 151, 154, 156, 183, 222, 233, 369
music educator, educators 17, 19, 34, 46, 49, 54, 57, 79, 98, 100, 101, 103, 104, 105, 106, 107, 108, 109, 110, 111, 112, 114, 115, 116, 117, 118, 119, 120, 121, 122, 123, 124, 125, 126, 128, 129, 130, 133, 137, 138, 139, 140, 141, 145, 146, 150, 151, 153, 154, 155, 158, 241, 258, 260, 262, 263, 264, 265, 327, 328
Music Educators National Conference 122
music genres 199, 323
music in a vacuum 209, 220
music lover 107, 113, 252
music ministry 26, 39, 49, 59, 60, 61, 63, 89, 98, 112, 131, 155, 170, 174, 182, 215, 222, 275, 280, 305, 327, 328, 338, 343, 355, 358, 360
music notation 39, 70, 71, 72, 124, 173, 366
music paradigm 236
music part of music 26, 38, 92, 148, 162, 182, 183, 189, 190, 191, 194, 196, 200, 202, 206, 218, 220, 221, 222, 223, 241, 242, 245, 246, 274, 279, 315, 339, 357
music psychologists 220
music therapy 113
music without words 198, 203, 225, 277, 297, 367
musical change 118, 155, 170

musical communication 182, 194
musical instruments 29, 142, 143,
    144, 145, 153, 165, 171, 308, 329,
    341, 342, 343, 346
musical meaning 188, 189, 191, 192,
    196, 202, 272, 307, 309
musical message 194, 343
musical offering, offerings 26, 33,
    34, 35, 36, 169, 174, 175, 214,
    215, 231, 232, 235, 248, 251, 257,
    313, 330, 339, 340, 341, 342, 345
musical paradigm 236
musical preparation 114
musical score 195, 210, 230, 231, 235
musical skill 24, 112, 133
musical sound 182, 184, 186, 187,
    188, 192, 194, 195, 196, 197, 198,
    240, 265, 307, 309, 310
musical tastes 73, 107, 119, 168, 174,
    304, 314, 318, 328, 346
musically literate 107, 113, 117, 127,
    128, 138
musicer 54, 66, 68, 77, 83, 89, 90, 93,
    127, 159, 206, 208, 215, 219, 226,
    236, 237, 276, 277, 312
musics 32, 54, 68, 77, 87, 109, 118,
    124, 125, 158, 159, 161, 163, 164,
    206, 210, 211, 230, 231, 276, 280,
    301, 306, 307, 312, 316, 323, 328,
    335
musing 241
Musique concrète 240

## N

National Association for Music
    Educators 122
national standards 108, 122, 123,
    124, 139
nature and grace 211
Neo-Platonism 369

neutral 183, 195, 225, 272, 297, 300,
    311, 324
new man 317
New Orleans jazz 201
new song 197, 200, 234, 317, 345,
    360
noise 35, 178, 185, 187, 198, 238,
    240, 247, 248, 251, 255, 285, 286,
    317, 341, 342
non-carnal 153, 188, 199, 255
non-rational 52, 53, 365
notation 38, 39, 70, 71, 72, 77, 170,
    173, 179, 204, 247, 250, 328, 346,
    366
nuts and bolts 27, 100, 107, 108,
    123, 127, 133, 139, 210

## O

objective truth 84, 85, 90, 109, 167
Occident 56, 124, 125, 133, 166, 284
orchestra 114, 140, 144, 147, 229,
    252, 255
Orff instruments 139, 140
Orff-Schulwerk 140
overt response 237
ownership 26, 79, 80, 83, 91, 221
Oxyrhynchus 72

## P

Page, John I. 16
painting 243, 251, 258, 259, 364
Pandora's Box 146, 166
paradigm 42, 65, 236, 266, 290, 291
pastors 122, 157, 294, 295, 298, 299,
    319
Peretti, Frank 47
performance based 99
performance practice 87, 93, 104,
    108, 110, 154, 311, 312
persona 75, 276, 369
Peters, Steve 295, 313

Index  387

photography 251, 258, 259, 260
Plato 70, 71, 130, 163, 164, 197, 253, 369
Platonic 130
pluralistic 32, 51, 159, 291
postmodern 52, 83, 91, 312, 365
Postmodernism 369
post-postmodern 49, 52, 54, 58, 59, 83, 91, 147, 167, 170, 225, 242, 280, 291, 335, 338, 344
post-secondary 100, 118, 136
pottery 251, 263
praise choruses 278, 318, 329, 330, 331, 332, 339
praxial 52, 66, 73, 74, 77, 93, 99, 123, 135, 247, 248
praxialist 123, 124, 126, 128, 133
praxis 26, 39, 49, 51, 63, 65, 86, 87, 88, 93, 97, 100, 106, 107, 108, 109, 110, 111, 113, 119, 123, 124, 126, 127, 128, 129, 131, 135, 136, 140, 141, 174, 175, 176, 184, 190, 191, 192, 222, 223, 226, 233, 245, 256, 271, 280, 281, 304, 305, 307, 313, 318, 325, 326, 336, 346, 369
preeminence 46, 74, 80, 85, 93, 160, 175, 212
preference 79, 83, 101, 102, 104, 141, 144, 311, 343
premise 43, 80, 93, 150, 200, 323
prescriptive 32, 33, 34, 97, 301
Presley, Elvis 201, 202, 294
presupposition 24, 44, 53, 59, 66, 68, 70, 77, 118, 286, 321
profane 30, 59, 173, 174, 177, 178, 183, 187, 198, 283
profundity 34, 59, 97, 122, 241, 245, 271
prophesy 82, 98, 103, 116, 131, 157, 253, 267
psychomotor 99, 100, 101, 133

## Q

quadrivium 98

## R

Rabbinic Judaism 168, 178
rap 320
readiness theory 138
referential 37, 109, 189, 190, 191, 192, 198, 205, 206, 218, 219, 220, 221, 223, 224, 231, 245, 246, 252, 368, 370
reggae 315, 320
Reimer, Bennett 75, 110, 126
religious humanist 83, 276, 311
Renoir, Pierre Auguste 243
renovated character 98, 130, 197, 200, 255
reprobate 62, 81, 84, 88, 298
retasking music 176
rock-based 51, 253, 300, 314, 318
rutual 232, 234, 235, 320

## S

Sachs, Curt 283
sacred classics
sacred music 30, 32, 33, 36, 37, 51, 64, 72, 98, 122, 155, 158, 159, 160, 162, 164, 174, 175, 186, 188, 200, 205, 212, 213, 214, 216, 221, 225, 226, 231, 232, 235, 238, 240, 245, 251, 255, 257, 259, 260, 261, 265, 270, 271, 272, 273, 274, 275, 276, 277, 283, 284, 288, 289, 292, 298, 301, 303, 304, 312, 322, 330, 333, 337, 338, 339, 340, 341 345, 357, 360, 361
sacred music 64, 160, 179, 255, 270, 273, 274, 275, 277, 278, 279, 293, 298 357, 361
sacred trust 133, 134, 156, 157, 158

Sartre, Jean-Paul 366
Satan 29, 30, 40, 47, 48, 72, 73, 86,
    90, 149, 150, 152, 163, 192, 193,
    194, 291, 294, 295, 297, 298, 313,
    314, 315, 350, 352, 355, 356
Schaeffer, Francis 50, 53, 54, 84, 93,
    152, 211, 366, 369
Schaeffer, Pierre 240
Scheer, Greg 32
Schoenberg, Arnold 244, 245
Scruton, Roger 196, 197, 210, 211
sculpture 250, 251, 258, 259, 262
secondary 99, 100, 106, 108, 110,
    117, 118, 136, 327
seeker sensitive 162, 171, 175, 292,
    296
seer 115
self-actualization 75, 76, 208
Septuagint 25, 142, 143
Serugin 170, 179
sexual arousal 193
sexual innuendos 193
sexual meaning 193, 201
ska 315
skillful 113, 131, 201, 224, 254, 274,
    278, 339
SME 21, 105
songs of the Lord 97, 98, 102, 103,
    104, 116, 131
songs that sting 338
sound addictions 197
sound envelope 286, 302
sounds 22, 38, 135, 146, 156, 184,
    185, 186, 187, 188, 189, 190, 192,
    193, 194, 195, 196, 197, 198, 199,
    220, 237, 238, 240, 241, 254, 288,
    307, 308, 309, 310, 313, 315, 316,
    318
St. John 26, 42, 61, 62, 74, 80, 82, 89,
    105, 122, 127, 137, 147, 178, 193,
    214, 287, 338
standardless art 65, 73

Stolba, K. Marie 70, 71, 72, 242
stratagems 315
Stravinsky, Igor 241, 242, 244
strict formalists 190, 198, 203, 207,
    272
style implications 201
suitable 66, 159, 164, 199, 300, 330,
    332
Sumer 76, 98
Sumerians 38
surrealism 240, 243
suschematizo 42, 150
Suzuki, Shinichi 256
symbolists 188, 219, 224, 370

T

Taylor, Richard S. 173, 199, 299, 303,
    304, 307
techno pop 315
temple 131, 145, 153, 179, 249, 250,
    261, 262, 263, 283, 288, 338, 341
theistic 228
theological 19, 58, 159, 174, 179,
    274, 279, 292, 317, 331
thesis 48, 49, 50, 52, 53, 58, 59, 66,
    67, 148, 190, 197, 207, 222, 225,
    291, 364
thesis thinker 49, 50, 52, 53
Tillich, Paul 75
Townend, Stuart 280
traditional 48, 49, 50, 51, 108, 158,
    162, 163, 168, 171, 177, 178, 182,
    183, 216, 225, 237, 239, 242, 243,
    244, 245, 266, 282, 284, 292, 296,
    298, 299, 300, 318, 319, 320, 322,
    323, 325, 361
Traditional 99, 183, 199, 291, 298
transmittable musical meaning 192
trendy 155, 171, 172, 179, 304, 305

true truth 50, 53, 55, 58, 59, 66, 67, 83, 84, 93, 152, 168, 219, 253, 307, 343, 344, 369
truth basis 50, 55, 67, 84, 112, 127, 133
twelve-tone 244
Tzara, Tristan 243

**U**

*ugab* 28
Ugarit 71, 72, 76, 77
Ugaritic notation 71, 77
understandable meaning 195, 196, 203
unified field of knowledge 48, 84
urban imagery 182, 183, 203, 331

**V**

videography 259, 260
Vincent, Marvin 142
visual art 243, 258, 259, 265

**W**

Wesley, Charles 177, 320
Wesley, John 173, 176
Western music 56, 70, 71, 72, 124, 133, 250, 253, 284, 286, 302, 322
whole life philosophy 60

whole of music 27, 41, 42, 43, 45, 46, 54, 60, 64, 84, 85, 86, 87, 88, 109, 117, 120, 121, 122, 134, 139, 159, 167, 168
whole-life 88, 102, 109, 112, 129, 133, 146, 149, 186, 189, 197, 219, 222, 246, 323
wise choices 64, 67, 100, 117, 121, 122, 125, 164, 186, 212, 226, 271, 384
Woodstock 294
world music 38, 72, 125, 133, 159
world system 97, 106, 146, 150, 384
worldview 41, 42, 43, 54, 67, 153, 282, 286, 287, 291, 302, 369
worship wars 319
worshiping 34, 36, 99, 145, 146, 159, 160, 164, 165, 169, 170, 172, 176, 178, 187, 247, 250, 252, 255, 273, 278, 284, 291, 294, 297, 320, 326, 329, 334, 339, 350, 354, 359, 361

**Y**

YHVH 22, 34, 72, 103, 131, 208, 262, 353, 355, 356
YHWH 22
Yung, Carl G. 75

**Z**

Zappa, Frank 324

# Index of Hebrew, Aramaic, and Greek Words

## A

*abodah* 103
*adamah* 31
*adelos* 309
*ado* 188
*adokimos* 62, 298
*aer* 149
*aesthesis* 136, 137
*agathos* 82, 305, 358
*ainigmati* 55
*aion* 86, 105, 146, 149, 150, 161, 166
*aletheia* 43
*ametameletos* 158
*amoral* 44, 104, 154, 193, 198, 221, 245
*anachusis* 155
*anakainosis* 42, 141
*anav* 334
*anepaischuntos* 58
*aoratos* 38, 195
*apate* 46, 85
*aproskopos* 130, 138
*ariyts* 356
*asotia* 155
*aulos* 308, 309
*auratos* 38

## B

*badal* 103
*bara* 25, 28, 228, 230
*biyn* 173, 204, 217

## C

*caliph* 353
*cheleq* 349
*chiydah* 223
*Christos* 38, 39, 62, 289

## D

*daath* 254
*diaphero* 130, 137
*diastole* 194, 307, 308
*didasko* 158, 337
*didomi* 194, 307, 309
*dokimazo* 42, 89, 91, 130, 137
*dorema* 82
*dosis* 82
*doulos* 359, 361
*dunamis* 230, 273, 274, 275, 321, 352, 360

## E

*echo* 62, 81
*ehokmah* 254
*ekklesia* 332
*Elohiym* 25, 115, 228, 262
*en* 158
*epignosis* 136, 137
*erets* 31
*esher* 185
*eth* 25, 228, 230
*exertizo* 85
*exousia* 196

391

## F

## G

*gabuwl* 298
*gibbowr* 356
*ginosko* 55, 195
*giyl* 360, 361

## H

*halak* 185
*halal* 116, 334
*Hallel* 333, 346
*hamown* 248, 342
*hayah asher hayah* 25
*heilikrines* 138
*hodos* 287
*horatos* 38, 195
*humneo* 332, 333
*humnos* 188, 333, 335
*humon* 342

## I

## J

## K

*kabod* 347
*kainos* 200
*kardia* 342
*kenos* 46, 85, 91
*kinnor* 28, 29, 113, 240, 309
*kinnore* 240
*kinowre* 240
*kithara* 308, 309
*kosmos* 21, 47, 86, 105, 146, 149
*ktisis* 90, 322, 341

## L

*lamad* 98, 103, 119, 120, 131
*Logos Christos* 38, 39, 62, 289

## M

*ma'od* 29, 40, 193
*male* 31
*maschil* 184
*maskiyth* 250
*massa* 116
*matstsebah* 250
*me katheko* 298
*me suschematizo* 42
*metamorphoo* 42, 141, 151
*miqla'ath* 250
*miqra* 204, 217

## N

*naba* 116
*nabiy* 116
*naiym* 240
*nebel* 342
*noutheteo* 337

## O

*oide* 153, 187, 188, 200, 333, 335
*orthotomeo* 58
*owr* 185

## P

*paniym* 354
*parash* 172, 204, 205, 217
*pas aletheia* 43
*pehsel* 250
*perissos* 122, 193, 209
*philos* 45
*philosophia* 44, 45, 46, 85
*philosophos* 45
*phone* 194, 307, 309

*phthoggos* 194, 307, 308
*pistos* 305, 358, 361
*pneumatikos oide* 152, 153, 188, 333, 335
*poimen* 157
*pokus* 157
*poneros* 105, 230
*prasso* 135
*proteuo* 175
*psallo* 143, 188, 207, 208, 342
*psalmos* 143, 188, 333, 335
*pseudodidaskalos* 157
*psuche* 344

## Q

*qara* 204, 217
*qavah* 354

## R

*radah* 31
*reshiyth* 228, 254
*rinnah* 361
*ruwa* 184, 248, 251, 273

## S

*salpigx* 309
*sasown* 361
*sekel* 204, 217
*sharath* 215
*shiyr* 28, 98, 103, 115, 131, 248, 338, 342
*simchah* 361
*sophia* 44, 85
*sophos* 45, 85
*stoicheioin* 47, 85
*sulagoges* 47

## T

*taphas* 28
*te'amim* 38, 39, 56, 71, 72, 77, 125, 153, 170, 172, 173, 179, 204, 205, 247, 250, 288, 357
*teleios* 82
*telios* 82
*teruah* 184, 185, 360
*toph* 28
*Torah* 169, 172, 179, 204, 205, 216
*towb* 29, 90, 193
*tsatsua* 262, 266
*tsav* 139
*tselem* 229

## U

## V

## W

## X

## Y

*yad* 98, 103, 113, 115
*yad ab shiyr* 98, 103
*yada* 112, 113, 185
*yadah* 347
*yirah* 254

## Z

*zamar* 330

Members of Schmul's Wesleyan Book Club buy these outstanding books at 40% off the retail price.

Join Schmul's Wesleyan Book Club by calling toll-free:
**800-S$_7$P$_7$B$_2$O$_6$O$_6$K$_5$S$_7$**
*Put a discount Christian bookstore in your own mailbox.*

Visit us on the Internet at
www.wesleyanbooks.com

*You may also order direct from the publisher by writing:*
**Schmul Publishing Company**
PO Box 776
Nicholasville, KY 40340

www.ingramcontent.com/pod-product-compliance
Lightning Source LLC
Chambersburg PA
CBHW071949220426
43662CB00009B/1060